FREE PRESS PAPERBACKS
Published by Simon & Schuster

New York   London   Toronto   Sydney   Singapore

The

CONCISE
CONSERVATIVE
ENCYCLOPEDIA

200 of the Most Important Ideas, Individuals,

Incitements, and Institutions That

Have Shaped the Movement

A Personal View

by

BRAD MINER

FREE PRESS PAPERBACKS
A Division of Simon & Schuster Inc.
1230 Avenue of the Americas
New York, NY 10020

Copyright © 1996 by Brad Miner

THE FREE PRESS and colophon are trademarks
of Simon & Schuster Inc.

Designed by Carla Bolte

Manufactured in the United States of America

10 9 8 7 6 5 4 3 2 1

Library of Congress Cataloging-in-Publication Data

Miner, Brad.
    The concise conservative encyclopedia: 200 of the most important
ideas, individuals, incitements, and institutions that have shaped
the movement: a personal view / by Brad Miner.
        p.   cm. — (Free Press paperbacks)
    Includes bibliographical references.
    ISBN 0–684–80043–8
    1. Conservatism—Encyclopedias.   I. Title.
JC573.M56   1996   96–5788
320.5′2′03—dc20   CIP

ISBN 0–684–80043–8

For

ROBERT BRADFORD MINER, II

and

JONATHAN FREDERICK MINER

When all night long a chap remains
On sentry-go, to chase monotony
He exercises of his brains,
That is, assuming that he's got any.
Though never nurtured in the lap
Of luxury, yet I admonish you,
I am an intellectual chap,
And think of things that would astonish you.
I often think it's comical
    How Nature always does contrive
That every boy and every gal
    That's born into the world alive
Is either a little Liberal,
    Or else a little Conservative!

        —W. S. Gilbert, *Iolanthe* (1882)

In the United States at this time liberalism is not only the dominant but even the sole intellectual tradition. . . .[T]he conservative impulse and the reactionary impulse do not, with some isolated and some ecclesiastical exceptions, express themselves in ideas but only in action or in irritable mental gestures which seem to resemble ideas.

        —Lionel Trilling, *The Liberal Imagination* (1950)

Conservatives suffer a very different political problem from liberals these days. Avowed liberals have a difficult time winning power in this country; avowed conservatives do not.

        —David Frum, *Dead Right* (1994)

Contents

Preface

A Small Circle of Instruction

I am no Diderot, and this little encyclopedia is neither, by reason of its intent, revolutionary nor, by reason of its brevity, definitive. My goal has been initially to identify appropriate topics, then *briefly* to delineate them, and finally to direct the reader to further study of the many sources of **conservative** thought, past and present.

THE SCOPE OF THE BOOK

A book such as this one—written, as the publishing-industry terminology puts it, for the "general reader"—is meant to be an easily accessible reference tool, and cannot possess the depth of fact found in, say, the *Encyclopaedia Britannica* (not that *Britannica* is always deep), or one of the multi-volume specialty encyclopedias that comprehensively cover religion, philosophy, politics, economics, and any and all of the other categories of knowledge that concern contemporary conservatives. And because this book had to be concise, I needed to establish some pretty strict—although not absolute—rules about the range of its topics and the scope of its entries. Rule 1: For the purposes of this book **conservatism**, per se, does not exist much before 1800. (Exceptions to this rule are the five sidebar essays under the heading "The Origins of Conservative Thought," about which more in a moment.) Rule 2: To be listed herein, an idea must be alive . . . and a person really ought to be dead. (As it turns out, though, this latter condition has been honored more in the breach than in the observance.) This book is neither an intellectual history of the West— or of conservatism for that matter—nor a *Who's Who on the*

Contemporary Right. (It is also not a public-policy manual. Only a handful of "hot-button" issues, e.g., **abortion**, are dealt with here.)

That Plato or especially Aristotle may be read with profit by conservatives (or anyone else) is indisputable; whether either of them was a *conservative* (at least as we understand the term today) is far from certain. Ever since Thomas Aquinas "baptized" Aristotle, modern men have looked to the ancients for confirmation of contemporary ideas, and there is much to be said for this practice, especially among traditionalists. But *The Concise Conservative Encyclopedia* takes the view that the conservative mind—and the principles that lead to and derive from it—did not (indeed could not) exist until the West found itself squinting into the bright promises and glaring illusions of the **Enlightenment**. Of course it may be true, as one commentator has declared, that it is impossible to discern conservatism in politics before the Reformation, "not because there was none, but because there was nothing else." But that former political reality—largely the philosophical justification of feudalism—has little in common with what we call conservatism today.

Conservatism begins quite specifically with **Burke**'s *Reflections on the Revolution in France* (1790). However, neither Burke nor the Enlightenment sprang *ex nihilo* from history, and indeed Burke's version of Enlightenment thought put great emphasis upon **tradition**. Accordingly, I have asked five of America's leading scholars to contribute short abstracts on "The Origins of Conservative Thought," ranging from antiquity through the modern era. My hope is that the reader will gain from these contributions what it will be difficult to obtain from the alphabetical listings, namely a coherent, historical view of the intellectual development of conservatism. Let me here offer my gratitude to Professors Carnes Lord, Jacob Neusner, James V. Schall, S.J., Peter J. Stanlis, and Charles R. Kesler. The reader needs to know that their commissions were limited to the essays that bear their names, and that the rest of *The Concise Conservative Encyclopedia* was written by me. Therefore, any errors, oversights, or plain idiocies that appear in the rest of the book are my fault and mine alone.

As to *living* ideas and *dead* men . . . Well, although I've allowed a number of exceptions to the latter, the general rule is justified, I believe, by two facts: first by the book's conceptual ambit, and second by the imperatives of historical prudence.

It would not be wrong to say that monarchism has been an enduring conservative ideal (certainly it loomed large in Burke's view of English constitutionalism), and only a neo-Jacobin view of history would deny it a place in the *larger* annals of conservatism. Nonetheless, I do not consider *monarchism* to be a term of any relevance whatsoever to the condition or content of modern American conservatism. Accordingly, it is not an entry in this book. Another, perhaps more germane, example: the **Adams** family. *The Concise Conservative Encyclopedia* contains entries on **John**, **Henry**, and **Brooks**, but not on John Quincy. Why? Because in my view, John Quincy Adams, remarkable as his career was, did not play an *influential* role in America's developing conservative ethos, whereas his father and grandsons did. Those few living men and women who are profiled in this book are here because it would simply be jarring if they were missing. I am not unaware of how odd it would seem to flip through such a book and not find an entry for **Buckley**.

But I take this "judgment-of-history" business seriously enough to consider prudence—never less than a sound principle—to be especially required in an assessment of one's contemporaries. And it seems to me that most of us need a reference to our intellectual antecedents more than we need a guide to contemporary thinkers. After all, the work of Buckley, **Will**, **Sowell**, **Kristol**, and others regularly appears in the print and electronic media. Because of this—and, again, because you can't properly summarize work that is "in progress"—entries about them tend to be less interpretive (and often briefer), and profiles of many of those "others" will not be found here at all.

The constraint of a 200-topic limit has meant, among other things, that I've had to piggyback certain topics. I wince to note, for instance, that data on Midge Decter and *Commentary* magazine have been presented in the entry for **Podhoretz**. It rings hollow to claim that brevity dictated the conflation, but it did.

These comments notwithstanding, the reader may wonder a bit more about the author's criteria for the inclusion of the specific "Ideas, Individuals, Incitements, and Institutions" profiled in this book. The author has also wondered about this. This is a "personal view," and as nearly as I can tell from the end result, there were three premises behind my decisions about what (and what not) to include. First, there is *consensus*. (One must have Burke.) Second, there is *preference*. (*I* had to have **Chesterton**. And I always wanted to write an article about **anti-disestablishmentarianism**.) Third, there is *literature*. (There are good books to read.) A number of prominent conservatives, past and present, have been excluded because, although their public careers and private lives may have exemplified conservative principle, they left no written record of their lives or ideas. It's a narrow focus to be sure: nearly every individual profiled in this little encyclopedia is a writer. But, for most of us, there is no legacy without books.

Above all, I have tried to present a "case" for the conservative worldview, while at the same demonstrating its complexities, not to say its incoherencies. I'm not sure if I have succeeded—in the sense of demonstrating that conservatism is, in **Weaver**'s famous aphorism, that "paradigm of essences towards which the phenomenology of the world is in continuing approximation." I have tried to tip the balance between fact and opinion to the fact side of the scale, but this is not a textbook in mathematics. Some conservatives despise **capitalism** and **democracy** and admire **McCarthyism** and the **John Birch Society**, but it should be clear that I'm not one of them.

I am personally uncomfortable with any label but the basic one: I'm conservative, plain and simple, neither neo- or paleo-, New or Old. The roots of my conservatism are in a view of **human nature** that took shape after I studied *The War Against the Jews: 1933–1945* by Lucy S. Dawidowicz. I read the book shortly after it was published in 1975—and just after I had become a convert to Roman Catholicism—and I realized I now knew something about Man that must utterly destroy the brash optimism of my youth. The first consequence of this sea change was my decision to vote for Gerald Ford—hardly a definitively conservative afflatus, I know, but for a former McGovernite it was an *almost* mystic moment. Since then I have been engaged (like everybody else, I suppose) in the process of understanding the implications of first principles. In this regard—and to close this discussion of the "personal view"—it is fitting that the first entry in this encyclopedia is abortion; fitting since few other controversies so clearly reveal the importance of premises. So-called "pro-choice" advocates may be struck by what they consider the "subjective voice" in the entry, although I doubt that so-called "pro-life" partisans will praise its orthodoxy: I'm not pro-life, I'm anti-abortion; I believe in killing the guilty but not the innocent. One is not really in agreement with a position if one's premises conflict with it. And it is better to be wrong about policy than about principle.

THE PLAN OF THE BOOK

The plan of the book is very simple. After this preface, the entries are listed alphabetically, from "abortion" to **Wilson**. In every case, suggested readings and a quote by or about the subject of the entry are included. When you see **Read**: this means the books that follow are either about the topic or *by the person profiled*. In the biographical entries there are also books listed after **About**:, which in many cases are biographies (or autobiographies), but which may also be inquiries into the profiled individual's work and thought. (These suggested readings are always books. I thought it unwise to refer the reader to his local library's collection of microfilmed periodicals.) Each entry then ends with a quote set off from the rest of the entry by being entirely in bold type. Interspersed throughout are the five sidebar essays I mentioned above, on "The Origins of Conservative Thought." Following the main section there is an afterword, an essay by me called "On Reformation," which is an attempt to place conservatism in the context of everyday life, not just "elevated" thinking. Next is "A Conservative Reading List," in which I suggest some good books for a basic, dozen-volume library. (Many of the books recommended at the end of each entry are no longer in print, but all those discussed in "A Conservative Reading List" are widely available—more or less.) *The Concise Conservative Encyclopedia* concludes with a Bibliography and an Index. Why an index in a succinct, alphabetical encyclopedia? Because the reader may be interested to know where and how many times the names of **Strauss** or **Hayek** come up, and because, as suggested above, certain expected topics or individuals may be discussed only within other entries; e.g., *Chronicles* magazine is discussed under **Rockford Institute**. The index lists all of the key topics.

By now the attentive reader will have begun to get a feel for the method I have chosen to indicate cross-referenced topics. The scheme is quite simple: words and names discussed elsewhere in the book appear in underlined, bold-face type, resembling the "hot spots" in a CD-ROM text. Only last names of persons are used; exceptions are the few cases in which there are more than one individual of the same last name, as in the before-mentioned Adams family. Each cross-referenced topic appears in underlined bold only once, the first time it is used, in each entry. I hope the reader will indulge the few articles that seem about to collapse under the weight of their bold (type) words, and, yes, I'm sure I could have bypassed *conservatism* and *conservative*, since this is a "conservative" encyclopedia, but I opted for consistency. (By the way, there is no cross-referencing within quotations, since my view of a meaning may differ from another author's.)

Just two other matters of usage: I have used "Man" to stand for common humanity, and I have placed the word "federal" in quotation marks where the entity described is the national government. (See **federalism**.)

The purpose of a "reader's encyclopedia" such as this one is not to provide the last word on the topics and people it covers, but to offer the inquiring reader just enough information about the subject in question to enable him *to go on reading* in some other book with a modicum of improved perspective. Over the years I have found William Rose Benét's *The Reader's Encyclopedia* to be an indispensable companion on my own literary journeys. That book is not without its weaknesses of course (an entry for Helen Hayes, but none for Hayek), but it manages to satisfy most of the time, and I hope *The Concise Conservative Encyclopedia*, its weakness only too apparent, will in its way offer some of the same tour guidance as Benét's fine work. *Deo favente.*

List of Entries

[Note: Please also consult the Index. Although this book's scheme limits it to 200 entries, many more ideas, individuals, incitements, and institutions are actually referred to in the text, and the Index lists most of them. *Ideas*, however, are listed only in cases where the citation involves a definition.]

The
CONCISE
CONSERVATIVE
ENCYCLOPEDIA

abortion: The termination of a pregnancy, whether voluntary or involuntary. The history of abortion in the United States follows a peculiar course of alternating cycles of rejection and acceptance. Legal opposition did not emerge actively nationwide until the middle of the 19th century, and then the question—raised by the American Medical Association—was not moral but *functional*: who shall be allowed to perform medical procedures? Since many abortions were performed by non-physicians, the AMA was opposed. The rising influence of the Catholic Church in America in the first half of this century helped to affect the debate, taking the issue beyond questions of professional or personal sovereignty to concerns of morality and theology. There is no moral issue involved in an involuntary abortion, and the moral issue in deliberate termination hinges upon the view of what is being aborted. In the (so-called) extremes: the "products of conception" (pro-abortion, a.k.a. pro-choice) versus a "human being" (anti-abortion, a.k.a. pro-life). Opposing a priori judgments make agreement impossible; the disputants become "moral strangers." However, **conservative** prudence tends to the view that, given the logical—even scientific—impossibility of knowing *exactly* when human life does begin (and assuming that, at some point, all sides would agree that human life deserves legal protection), life ought to be assumed to begin at the beginning, i.e., at conception. *Roe v. Wade* (1973), the case through which the Supreme Court legalized abortion, was a fateful decision for any number of reasons, not least for its seething statism. **Read:** R. C. Sproul, *Abortion: A Rational Look at an Emotional Issue* (1990). **"Women have a right to reproductive freedom, I hear it argued, and I agree: all women, even little girls yet unborn who have the right to be free to grow to the age when they in their turn can make love and have babies. Women should have control over their own bodies, it is said, and I agree; but not life-and-death control over the bodies of their children (and in the case of male children, whoever heard of a male part of a female body?) Make abortions illegal, we hear it said, and they will still go on, but in the back streets, and I agree. Yet rape goes on despite our laws; should it no longer be a crime? And if the day came when the nation was no longer willing to go on record that rape was criminal, would there**

be no more of it? Can anyone who knows that we record 1,500,000 abortions a year in America imagine that most of these would have occurred without the legal protections of 1973? ... But back to the point, the chief point, the much-avoided point, the only point at issue: to abort is to destroy one's son or daughter." James T. Burtchaell, *Rachel Weeping* (1982)

[*Human Life Review*, Room 840, 150 East 35th St., New York, NY 10016; J. P. McFadden, editor. Subscriptions (quarterly): $20/year.]

absolutism: In politics, unlimited government, either whole or in part (the U.S.S.R. or the I.R.S.); the dream equally of hot-blooded optimists and cold-hearted pessimists. Totalitarianism (principally **communism** and fascism) has been the 20th-century successor of feudal despotism, and, although deadlier by far, has proved no more durable. But the impulse may reappear in bureaucratic fiat, and when it does—no matter whose good intentions are being promoted—it is the antithesis of **conservatism**. [Note: an absolutist regime may not necessarily be totalitarian; unlike modern dictators, medieval despots rarely saw their power as sovereign over *every* aspect of a citizen's life.] In matters philosophical, the absolute is the opposite of the relative. So it is that religious conservatives, who decry **relativism**, are sometimes assumed to favor absolutist values and government, and a few may actually be guilty as charged. But the number of these Christian Caesars and their followers is small; they are no multitude justifying and sparking an American theocratic state. But whereas conservatism rejects absolutism in government (and thereby spurns a theocratic state), it does not reject absolute standards in morality and religion. It is logically absurd to assert the existence of God while also asserting the relativity of truth. (See also **republicanism**, **democracy**, **natural law**, and, finally, **antidisestablishmentarianism**.) **Read:** J. Locke, *Second Treatise on Government* (1690); J.-F. Revel, *The Totalitarian Temptation* (1977). **"Power tends to corrupt and absolute power corrupts absolutely. Great men are almost always bad men, even when they exercise influence and not authority; still more when you superadd the tendency or the certainty of corruption by authority."** Lord Acton, letter (1887) in *Essays in Religion, Politics, and Morality* (1988)

academic freedom: Traditionally, the **liberty** of scholars to teach the truth (and to do research and to write) without official interference. It is a claim of special privilege by college professors; a demand to be protected—in a way other citizens are not—from the consequences of their utterances. Tenure is often declared an indispensable protector of academic freedom. What the claim entails—at least in its most expansive conception—is the teacher's right to live without contractual obligations to either his employer or the **community**. What cannot be overlooked in assertions about the *right to* academic freedom (and what was emphasized first in 1925 and then in the 1940 revision of the "Statement of Principles on Academic Freedom and Tenure" of the American Association of University Professors) is the parallel *responsibility of* academic ethics, first among which is to teach the truth. (See **relativism**.) This is what Robert Maynard Hutchins meant (1956) by the "standard of competence," which he considered sufficient to protect students from propagandizers, since a professor who "sought to indoctrinate his pupils, which is the only circumstance under which he could be dangerous as a teacher, . . . would be incompetent, and should be removed as such." What Hutchins, the former University of Chicago president who died in 1977 (and who was a liberal's liberal), would make of the recent political-correctness controversy is anybody's guess. **Hook**, who may or may not have been a "liberal," boldly asserted that heterodox opinions should be welcome in the classroom, unless their effect is to politicize curricula or their intention is conspiratorial. "Accused of reading their own political bias . . . [in order to] further the indoctrination of their students," Hook wrote (*National Review*, October 13, 1989), "the New Left respond that . . . 'objectivity' exists in the eye of the beholder." This, Hook concludes, is "tantamount to denying the distinction between fiction and history, guilt and innocence, in relation to the admitted evidence." Those 1940 "Principles" of the AAUP clearly state that teachers "should be careful not to introduce into their teaching controversial matter which has no relation to their subject . . ." (See also **liberal arts**.) **Read:** D. D'Souza, *Illiberal Education* (1991), R. Kimball, *Tenured Radicals* (1990); S. Hook, *Heresy Yes, Conspiracy No* (1952); R. Kirk, *Academic Freedom* (1955). **"The logical positivist went too far when he said that theological utterances were devoid of**

meaning: in order to reach that conclusion, he needed to re-define 'meaning' in absurdly narrow terms which made his own utterances meaningless as well. But the skeptic or agnostic is on much stronger ground when he says that while theological utterances can have their sufficiently clear meanings, they cannot be made by an academically respectable thinker because we have no way of knowing whether they are true or not, on this side of the grave at least. We are all entitled to cherish our personal hunches and opinions and guesses, and to put these forward as such. But the university deals— we hope—in more objective and verifiable things . . . The campus is no place for hunches and opinions and guesses." Christopher Derrick, *Church Authority and Intellectual Freedom* (1981)

Acton, Lord (John Edward Emerich Dalberg, 1st Baron, 1834–1902): Anglo-Catholic historian, editor (of the *Cambridge Modern History* and—succeeding **Newman**—of the *Rambler*), and enthusiast for **liberty**. Educated primarily on the Continent by teachers steeped in both **ultramontanism** and **liberalism**—in the latter case especially by the German historian-theologian Johan Ignaz von Döllinger (1799–1890)—Acton attended the First Vatican Council, where he opposed the doctrine of papal infallibility, just as he had earlier disputed the Syllabus of Errors. But he accepted both rather than risk the excommunication that Döllinger did suffer. Acton believed that the Church would better promote its ends by encouraging scientific inquiry and political liberty. He was—in the best European sense—an apostle of **classical liberalism**, although, as befitting an orthodox Catholic, with a somewhat greater emphasis upon **authority** and **tradition**. Acton's justly famous aphorism that power corrupts is best understood as an expression of the value of checks and balances: no "branch" (in his thinking, more like the French notion of *estates*) should impinge upon the sovereignty of any other. Thus the integrity of each is preserved; likewise their unity. (See also **subsidiarity**.) In addition to Döllinger, Acton himself counted **Burke** (from whose **empiricism** he seemed to separate himself with time) and **Tocqueville** as the greatest influences on his political thinking. In his later years he began writing a massive *History of Liberty*, which was too immense even for this great scholar to complete, and which has been called "the greatest book that was never written." Upon his death his personal library (now at Cambridge University) contained 60,000 volumes. **Read:** *Essays in Religion, Politics, and Morality* (Fears, ed., 1988). **About:** G. Himmelfarb, *Lord Acton: A Study in Conscience and Politics* (1952). "The great question is to discover, not what governments prescribe, but what they ought to prescribe; for no prescription is valid against the conscience of mankind. Before God, there is neither Greek nor Barbarian, neither rich nor poor, and the slave is as good as his master, for by birth all men are free; they are citizens of that universal commonwealth which embraces all the world, brethren of one family, and children of God. The true guide of our conduct is no outward authority, but the voice of God, who comes down to dwell in our souls, who knows all our thoughts, to whom are owing all the truth we know, and all the good we do; for vice is voluntary, and virtue comes from the grace of the heavenly spirit within." "Freedom in Antiquity" in *The History of Freedom and Other Essays* (1907)

Adams, Brooks (1848–1927): American historian, the brother of Henry and great-grandson of John, and a first-rate—if eccentric—social scientist in his own right. He developed a view of American cultural ascendancy based upon economic vitality that saw progress as both desirable *and* illusory: growth leads to centralization which leads to decline. Adams was openly hostile to **capitalism**, because he saw it sweeping away **tradition** and **order** in its flood of innovations. Famously predicted (c. 1900) that in the 20th century the dominant powers would be the United States and Russia. **Read:** *The Law of Civilization and Decay* (1895); *The Theory of Social Revolutions* (1913); **About:** see Adams, Henry. "If expansion and concentration are necessary . . . then America must expand and concentrate until the limit of the possible is attained; for Governments are simply huge corporations in competition, in which the most economical, in proportion to its energy, survives, and in which the wasteful and slow are undersold and eliminated." *The Law of Civilization and Decay* (1895)

Adams, Henry (1838–1918): American writer with a claim to be the nation's premier exponent of **tradition**; of both its beauty and its burden. As the grandson and great-grandson of presidents he had a subjective sense of an American legacy with a very personal claim to the deepest possible roots, but being a Harvard professor of medieval history—and an indefatigable world traveler—his more objective sense of the roots of Western tradition went deeper still. His sophisticated disenchantment clashed with the brash optimism of his own era, and—although surely influenced by the suicide (1885) of his wife (Marian Hooper Adams)—his pessimism was principally a reaction to the tension between, in his phrase, the Virgin and the Dynamo. ("I am a dilution," he wrote to his brother Brooks, "of Lord Kelvin and St. Thomas Aquinas.") He saw, as clearly and as early as anyone, how **modernism**'s passion for innovation wars with humanity's need for order. ("Chaos was the law of nature; Order was the dream of man.") It may be said of Adams that he gave cynicism a good name. Of all his many sage observations, none cuts more to the heart of things than the first clause of the first sentence of the twelfth chapter of his great memoir, *The Education of Henry Adams* (1918): "Knowledge of human nature is the beginning and end of political education . . ." **Read:** *Mont Saint-Michel and Chartres* (1913) and its sequel *The Education of Henry Adams* (1918); **About:** J. T. Adams, *The Adams Family* (1930). **"To educate—oneself to begin with— had been the effort of one's life for sixty years; and the difficulties of education had gone on doubling with the coal output, until the prospect of waiting another ten years, in order to face a seventh doubling of complexities, allured one's imagination but slightly. The law of acceleration was definite, and did not require ten years more study except to show whether it held good. No scheme could be suggested to the new American, and no fault needed to be found, or complaint made; but the style of education promised to be violently coercive. The movement from unity into multiplicity, between 1200 and 1900, was unbroken in sequence, and rapid in acceleration. Prolonged one generation longer, it would require a new social mind. As though thought were common salt in indefinite solution it must enter a new phase subject to new laws. Thus far, since five or ten thousand years, the mind had successfully reacted, and nothing yet proved that it would fail to react,—but it would need to jump."** *The Education of Henry Adams* (1918)

Adams, John (1735–1826): American political philosopher, first vice president, and second president (1797–1801) of the United States. A Founder whose career was defined in part by conflict with (for different reasons) **Hamilton** and **Jefferson**, which, in the case of the latter, began with the drafting of the **Declaration of Independence**. But his clashes with Jefferson, who called him a "colossus," were more often a matter of personality than of substance, since they shared similar views of American life: a republic of small property owners, of businessmen and farmers. The **constitution** of Massachusetts, of which Adams was the main author, remains in force today and is a model of its kind. Above all, Adams was a **conservative** in his view of **human nature** and in his conviction that Man must be taken as he is, not as what he might become. Against the almost innate Yankee optimism, he warned: "There is no special providence for Americans." In this he differed greatly from Jefferson. Thus his *Defense of the Constitutions of Government of the United States of America* (1787) anticipated by several years **Burke**'s famous attack on French democratic **absolutism**. He and Jefferson died hours apart on the fiftieth anniversary of American independence. "Here was no lover of government by plutocracy, no dreamer of an America filled with factories and hard-packed cities. Here was a man who loved America as it was and had been, one whose life was a doughty testament to the trials and glories of ordered liberty. Here . . . was the model of the American conservative" (**Rossiter**, 1955). **Read:** *Thoughts on Government* (1776); **About:** P. Shaw, *The Character of John Adams* (1977); L. J. Cappon, *The Adams-Jefferson Letters* (1959). **"A constitution founded on these [i.e., republican] principles introduces knowledge among the people, and inspires them with a conscious dignity becoming freemen; a general emulation takes place, which causes good humor, sociability, good manners, and good morals to be general. That elevation of sentiment inspired by such a government, makes the common people brave and enterprising. That ambition which is inspired by it makes them sober, industrious, and frugal. You will find among them some elegance, perhaps, but more solidity; a little pleasure, but a great deal of business; some politeness, but more civility. If you compare such a country with the regions of domination, whether monarchical or aristocratical, you will fancy yourself in Arcadia or Elysium."** *Thoughts on Government* (1776)

affirmative action: A philosophy of **egalitarianism** (racial and sexual) that justifies preferential treatment (in hiring for jobs, public or private, or in admission to higher education) of those who, it is asserted, are victims of *past* discrimination. Such programs and policies are usually aimed at "minorities," but may be applied to "majorities" as well, as in the case of women. Begun in the 1960s as a series of government programs aimed at encouraging blacks and women to participate in the competitive hiring process, affirmative action soon became a template for determining the *results* of that process. The shift was thus made from individual rights to group rights; from opportunity based upon individual merit to quotas and set-asides based upon color or gender. Whereas the first wave of laws (especially the 1964 Civil Rights Act—in which the government urged itself to take "affirmative action" to hire those previously excluded) were designed to outlaw discrimination and to offer redress to victims of specific acts of discrimination, affirmative action policies quickly generalized both the problem and the solution. For instance, the Equal Opportunity Act of 1972 mandated governments and their contractors to increase minority employment levels until said levels equal the distribution of said minorities (and women) in the population at large; thus applying "democratic principles to races and cultures rather than to citizens, despite the fact that there is nothing to indicate that real diversity is the same thing as proportional representation" (Steele, 1990). One consequence of affirmative action has been *reverse discrimination*—white males being excluded from hiring or admission because of their color and gender—a dispute played out before the Supreme Court in such notable cases as *Regents of the University of California v. Bakke* (1978), in which quotas in graduate school admissions were struck down, and *United Steel Workers of America v. Weber* (1979), in which similar quotas were upheld in private businesses and unions. In the November 6, 1995 issue of **National Review**, Paul Craig Roberts and Lawrence M. Stratton offered this summary: "Originally, affirmative action meant that [when] the scores of a black candidate and a white candidate were equal, the black candidate would be chosen. Then, with race-norming, blacks with lower scores would be chosen. The latest stage was demonstrated in February 1994, when the Los Angeles Fire Department refused thousands of white applicants permission to take its job test." **Read**: W. Bennett and T. Eastland, *Counting by Race* (1979); N. Glazer, *Affirmative Discrimination* (1978); F. R. Lynch, *Invisible Victims* (1991); T. Sowell, *Preferential Policies* (1990). "A society that puts equality—in the sense of equality of outcome—ahead of freedom will end up with neither equality nor freedom. The use of force to achieve equality will destroy freedom, and the force, introduced for good purposes, will end up in the hands of people who will use it to promote their own interests. . . . On the other hand, a society that puts freedom first will, as a happy by product, end up with both greater freedom and greater equality. Though a by-product of freedom, greater equality is not an accident. A free society releases the energies and abilities of people to pursue their own objectives. It prevents some people from arbitrarily suppressing others. It does not prevent some people from achieving positions of privilege, but so long as freedom is maintained, it prevents those positions of privilege from becoming institutionalized; they are subject to continued attack by other able, ambitious people. Freedom means diversity but also mobility. It preserves the opportunity for today's disadvantaged to become tomorrow's privileged and, in the process, enables almost everyone, from top to bottom, to enjoy a fuller and richer life." Milton and Rose Friedman, *Free to Choose* (1979)

agrarianism: See **Southern conservatism**

alienation: A term that originally meant the removal of rights or property (thus the "unalienable rights" of the **Declaration of Independence**), but which has come to mean the estrangement of citizens from society. Either way, good examples of alienated individuals are Adam and Eve; **sin** being *the* primary condition of alienation. But the contemporary sense of disaffection owes more to *Das Kapital* than to the Book of Genesis. Karl Marx (1818–1883) expanded the notion of G. F. W. Hegel (1770–1831) concerning successive personal-psychological and impersonal-historical alienations and applied it to the conflict of the proletariat with the owners of capital. As a reality of estrangement—as opposed to a fantasy of oppression—alienation may clearly exist in three aspects of Man's life: in relation to himself, to others, and to God. Curiously, the Judeo-Christian *and* existentialist views of alienation converge, and they differ markedly from the secularist/liberal view: both of the former see the disunity as both pre-social and inevitable; the latter sees it as arising from society and as reformable. For existentialists of course there is, per se, no solution to Man's alienation; there is only resignation. For secularists (including Marxists) or liberals there is either revolution (led by an *un*alienated vanguard) or reform designed to return Man to a putative natural balance. For **conservative** skeptics of resignation, revolution, and radical reform there are the mediating structures of traditional life: **faith**, **family**, and **community**—embraced without illusions. (See also **ideology**.) **Read**: K. Minogue, *Alien Powers* (1985). **"The subjective aspect of 'increasing misery' among the working class revolves around the concept of 'alienation'—essentially thwarted human development. But this very concept implies that third-party observers can tell untold millions of their fellow human beings how they should 'really' evolve, feel, and act. If they could, it would be a mandate for totalitarianism. Humane and intelligent people excuse lies, repression, slave labor, and mass extermination when they are done in the name of 'ultimately' promoting the 'real' interest and development of the working class—as conceived by others. Marx and Engels . . . postulat[ed] that what ordinary people actually preferred reflected only . . . their 'alienation.' For example, the kind of freedom sought by the common man was . . . 'the perfection of his slavery and his inhumanity.' A hundred years later, it has become all too painfully clear that it was Marx and Engels whose ideas led to the perfection of slavery and inhumanity . . ."** Thomas Sowell, *Marxism* (1985)

America First: See **isolationism**

American Enterprise Institute (AEI): Washington, D.C.-based organization founded in 1943 (as the American Enterprise Association) to promote understanding "of the social and economic advantages accruing to the American people through the maintenance of the system of free, competitive enterprise." Its first chairman was Lewis H. Brown, and under his leadership the organization concentrated on pamphleteering—issuing reports on the minutiae of congressional legislation and public policy. In the mid-1950s, William J. Baroody, a "political conservative who insisted on calling himself a liberal," began to lead AEI (then still AEA; the name change coming in 1962) into its present high visibility as a home for leading **conservative** and libertarian scholars and a conduit for the dissemination—through op-ed pieces in major newspapers, policy monographs, and books and magazines—of their views. AEI board members, advisors, and scholars have included **Hazlitt**, Roscoe Pound, **Friedman**, **Wilson**, Gottfried Haberler, **Banfield**, James M. Buchanan, Gerhart Niemeyer, **Kristol**, Robert Bork, **Novak**, and **Nisbet**. Read: *The American Enterprise* [magazine]. "The free enterprise system, which Adam Smith called 'the system of natural liberty,' is not natural: it is not foreordained and it cannot be taken for granted, even in America. It is rather a social and political artifact, requiring for its survival . . . understanding and consent . . . At the same time, the social advantages of free enterprise are demonstrable—they are matters of fact more than of ideology or factional interest." AEI policy statement (1995).

[American Enterprise Institute, 1150 17th Street, N.W., Washington, DC 20036; telephone (202) 862-5800; Christopher C. DeMuth, president. *The American Enterprise* (magazine), subscriptions (bimonthly): $29/year from P.O. Box 3000, Denville, NJ 07834; (800) 562-1973 or fax (201) 627-5872. AEI Press (books): (800) 269-6267.]

The American Spectator: Magazine founded in 1967 by R. Emmett Tyrrell, Jr. (1944-) as *The Alternative*. Editorially, the original magazine reflected Bob Tyrrell's age (23) and his mood (anger), but with the years and a name change (1977), *The American Spectator* [*TAS*] became more intellectually subtle—and successful. Midway through the **Reagan** years, several dozen of the magazine's contributors held posts in the Executive Branch. Nonetheless, *TAS* has never lost its brashness, and has lately taken to the kind of investigative journalism that brings headlines, as in David Brock's reporting on the Anita Hill-Clarence Thomas hearings (which led to Brock's book, *The Real Anita Hill*, 1993). What made Bob Tyrrell perceive the need for an "alternative" in the 1960s was the "historic inflammation [that] was beginning to afflict America's latest Old Order" (Tyrrell, 1987), namely liberalism. Originally *The Alternative* was basically an off-campus journal at Indiana University that Tyrrell managed to enrich with reports from "a network of anti-radical students" from a number of the nation's elite schools. Despite its animus toward "welfare" liberalism (for which the magazine has had a generous inventory of colorful synonyms), *TAS* managed to be a bridge between liberalism and conservatism, and was the first magazine to regularly publish both traditionalists and neoconservatives. Sometimes pilloried as too sophomoric, *TAS* is rarely accused of being soporific. From P. J. O'Rourke's "New Enemies List" to Ben Stein's chronicles of life in Hollywood to Tyrrell's own Mencken-like editorial sarcasm ("The Continuing Crisis"), *The American Spectator* never fails to demonstrate that conservative skepticism is as rich a source of hilarity as it is of sagacity. Since changing from a tabloid to a glossy format, *TAS* has undergone rapid growth. Its list of contributors includes many of the best young writers on the Right, including Brock, David Frum, James Ring Adams, and Francis X. Rocca. **Read:** R. E. Tyrrell, *The Conservative Crack-Up* (1992); **About:** R. E. Tyrrell, ed., *Orthodoxy* (1987). Tyrrell writes in his introduction: **"Those scholars who have assayed great lives probably recognize boredom's place in history, but who would respect these scholars if they were to lay the great deeds of a Napoleon, a Niels Bohr, a T. Boone Pickens, to mere boredom? Nonetheless, the cognoscenti must recognize that there is plenty of evidence confirming that Alexander the Great left Macedonia because the place was getting on his nerves, that Chaucer wrote *The Canterbury Tales* to fill his vacant days, and that had Richard Nixon starred on the golf team at Whittier College he would not have given politics a moment's thought, so delighted would he have been with the capacities of a #1 wood. . . . Having established this much about the motives of history's great men, surely you will not mistake me for a humble man if I tell you in the well of our friendship that I founded *The American Spectator* . . . out of boredom."**

[*The American Spectator*, 2020 North 14th Street, Suite 750, Arlington, VA 22201. Subscriptions (monthly): $35/year; (800) 524-3469.]

Ames, Fisher (1758–1808): American political thinker and leader of the Federalists, closely allied with **Hamilton** and vehemently opposed to **Jefferson**, who was an anti-egalitarian advocate of public **order** and **private property**. One of the founding generation's most brilliant men (he entered Harvard at twelve and was graduated at sixteen), Ames was noted as a superb orator and was instrumental—against great opposition—in winning approval of Jay's Treaty (1796), which may have averted renewed war with Britain. Like **Madison**, Ames' experience led him to modify his espousal of strong central power, but nothing dissuaded him from a distrust of "public opinion," a term he largely coined (but for which **Tocqueville** generally gets credit). As he put it, "A monarchy is a merchantman, which sails well, but will sometimes strike on a rock and go to the bottom; while a republic is a raft, which would never sink, but then your feet are always in the water." (*House of Representatives*, 1795.) He defeated Sam Adams to become Boston's first representative in Congress. **Read:** *The Dangers of American Liberty* (1805) in Hyneman and Lutz, *American Political Writing during the Founding Era*, vol. II (1983); **About:** W. Bernard, *Fisher Ames: Federalist and Statesman* (1965). "Before the French Revolution, it was the prevailing opinion of our countrymen, that other nations were not free, because their despotic governments were too strong for the people. Of course, we were admonished to detest all existing governments, as so many lions in liberty's path; and to expect by their downfall the happy opportunity, that every emancipated people would embrace, to secure their own equal rights for ever. France is supposed to have had this opportunity, and to have lost it. Ought we not then to be convinced, that something more is necessary to preserve liberty than to love it? Ought we not to see that when the people have destroyed all power but their own, they are the nearest possible to a despotism, the more uncontrolled for being new, and tenfold the more cruel for its hypocrisy?" *The Dangers of American Liberty* (1805)

ancient constitution: The idea—popular at the beginning of the modern era—that the legal structure of society is based upon an age-old (and lost) document/**tradition**. As developed in England by Edward Coke (1552–1634, "Old ways [are] the safest and surest ways"), the ancient constitution was both the basis of common law and a limitation upon absolute power; also, significantly for **conservatism**, it formed for **Burke** the sense that British institutions and liberties were not derived from reason but evolved through tradition. **Read:** J. G. A. Pocock, *The Ancient Constitution and the Feudal Law* (1967). Pocock writes: **"If the constitutionalists could show that the laws were as old as, or older than, the kings, they might go on to assert a contractual or elective basis for kingship; but if the laws had come into being at a time when there was already a king, then nothing but the king's authority could have sanctioned them or made them law, and the king might assert a sovereign right to revoke what his predecessor had granted. The constitutionalists were therefore always being driven to argue that the laws were of a practically infinite antiquity, immemorial in the sense of earlier than the earliest king known."**

anticommunism: That view of the communist threat, from the 1920s through the 1980s, which was both a central tenet and a divisive aspect of American **conservatism** throughout the period. Writing today (1996), one might say that the most striking thing about it is—quite naturally, given the fate of **communism** itself—that anticommunism has all but disappeared. The most visible single aspect of American **conservative** thought in the 20th century is now invisible, and the change came in less than half a decade. Predictions that conservatism would founder without communists to kick around have proved utterly false. (See **Gingrich**.) All conservatives were united in opposition to communism, because communism was fundamentally destructive of economic and political **liberty**, religious **faith**, and **individualism**, and yet anticommunism divided at least as much as it united the **Right**. The **Old Right** saw the communist threat as evidence of the virtue of **isolationism**, whereas the **New Right** saw the same threat as an imperative for an aggressive foreign policy. As communism spread in the three decades after World War II, conservative leadership increasingly fell to either former communists or refugees from communist states, i.e., to the New Right or **neoconservatism**, and the **authority** of the Old Right or **paleoconservatism** retreated until the rise of the **Christian Right**, which happened to coincide with the fall of communism. What must not be forgotten is the extreme courage of so many American anticommunists; of people such as **Eastman** and **Hook**; **Burnham** and **Buckley**; **Kristol** and **Podhoretz**. They broke ranks; they exposed themselves to ridicule; and they never wavered. (See also **cold-war liberal**.) Believing that **socialism**—if properly implemented—offered the only hope for the future of mankind, many liberals became advocates of *anti-anticommunism*: So it was that some proclaimed, "Better Red than dead." In this regard, **Read**: Sidney Hook, *Out of Step* (1987). Hook writes: "**It is better to be a live jackal than a dead lion—for jackals, not men. Men who have the moral courage to fight intelligently for freedom have the best prospects of avoiding the fate of both live jackals and dead lions. Survival is not the be-all and end-all of a life worthy of man. Sometimes the worst thing we can know about a man is that he survived. Those who say that life is worth living at any cost have already written for themselves an epitaph of infamy, for there is no cause and no person they will not betray to stay alive. Man's vocation should be the use of the arts of intelligence in behalf of human freedom.**"

antidisestablishmentarianism: A factitious word (purporting to be the longest in English) meaning *opposition* to the (largely 18th-century) European movement to eliminate or prohibit state religions, which was one of the central tenets of **classical liberalism**. Thus the first clause in the First Amendment to the United States **Constitution** ("Congress shall make no law respecting an establishment of religion," a.k.a. the "establishment clause") was a kind of preemptive *disestablishmentarian* (or, more precisely, *antiestablishmentarian*) rule. At the time of its adoption, several states had established churches, and the Framers knew well enough that the prospect of a *national* church would doom ratification. Conservative utopians, oxymorons all, have sometimes wished to unify church and state (see **absolutism**), but such an antidisestablishmentarian (or, again in the case of America, *establishmentarian*) sensibility flies in the face of a proper conservative commitment to **individualism** and **liberty**. And while the scope of **Locke**'s influence on the Framers is controversial, there can be no doubt that **Madison** totally accepted Locke's view that, since Man is free and **faith** cannot be coerced, religious liberty is a **natural right**. Just the same, the "separation of church and state" does not build a "wall of separation," and religious liberty is not meant to be a purge of religion from public life. (See **Neuhaus**.) Rather it is a protection of religious conscience, which must lie outside the reach of the state, and which has a greater claim upon the individual than does the state or could *any established religion*. However, it needs to be remembered that the greatest of all antidisestablishmentarians was none other than **Burke**. A substantial portion of his *Reflections on the Revolution in France* (1790) is devoted to the refutation both of the French revolutionary disestablishment and to the proposal that England follow suit. Notwithstanding those views, Burke never believed that establishment should be accompanied by intolerance. **Read**: M. S. Evans, *The Theme is Freedom* (1994); Russell Kirk, *The Conservative Constitution* (1990). Kirk writes: "**The general understanding of the Framers of the Constitution and of the Congress that approved the First Amendment, was this: Christian teaching, like Jewish teaching, is intended to govern the soul, not to govern the state. But also the leading Americans of 1787–1791 believed that religious convictions form the basis of any good society. They were aware that both Christianity and Judaism have co-existed with imperial structures, feudalism, national monarchies, aristocracies, republics, democracies. Religion, they assumed, is not a system of politics or of economic management: it is an attempt, instead, to relate the human soul to divine power and love.**"

Aron, Raymond (1905–1983): French sociologist (*Main Currents in Sociological Thought*, 1965), teacher (the Sorbonne), and political commentator (*Le Figaro*). Aron studied in France and in Germany, where he watched the birth of Nazism and began his study of Max Weber (1864–1920) and Karl Marx. During World War II, Aron was an adjutant to Charles de Gaulle and editor-in-chief of the Resistance journal, *La France Libre*. His war experiences and his historical scholarship led to a profound appreciation of the American experience, and to **anticommunism**. He was not, however, an admirer of **McCarthyism**, as he made clear during his visits to the U.S. at the time. After thirty years of writing commentary for *Le Figaro*, Aron switched to *L'Express* in 1977. His *Main Currents in Sociological Thought* (in two volumes) is the best survey and summary of that embattled discipline that has ever been written. In it Aron develops one of his lifelong themes, the clash between **liberty** and determinism in the contrast between the works of **Tocqueville** (and to a lesser extent **Montesquieu**) and Marx. Although he analyzed many similarities between the governing entities of **socialism** and **capitalism**, Aron came down squarely on the side of **classical liberalism**. "Western societies today," he wrote (1978), "have a triple ideal, bourgeois citizenship, technological efficiency, and the right of every individual to choose the path of his salvation. Of these three ideals, none should be sacrificed." He carried forward Tocqueville's distinction between **democracy** as a form of governance, and democracy as a spirit of the age, and he was pessimistic about both; thus his version of classical liberalism. **Read:** *Main Currents in Sociological Thought* (1965); **About:** A. de Crespigny and K. Minogue, *Contemporary Political Philosophers* (1975). **"Marx's sociology, at least in its messianic and prophetic form, presupposes the reduction of the political order to the economic order. But the political order is essentially irreducible to the economic order. Whatever the economic and social regime may be, the political problem will remain, because it consists in determining who governs, how the leaders are chosen, how power is exercised, and what the relationship of consent or dissent is between the government and the governed. The political order is as essential and autonomous as the economic order. . . . The myth of the state's disappearance is the myth that the state exists only to produce and distribute resources and that, once this problem of production and distribution of resources is solved, there is no longer any need for a state, i.e., for leadership."** "Karl Marx" in *Main Currents in Sociological Thought* (1965)

Austrian School: The group of neo-classical economists whose anti-statist approach was "founded" by Karl Menger (1840–1921) (*Principles of Economics*, 1871), expanded by Eugen von Böhm-Bawerk (1851–1914, author of *Capital and Interest*, 1884) but which became most visible (in America at least) through the later work of **Mises** and **Hayek**, and—to a lesser extent—Israel Kirzner and **Rothbard**. The

Austrian view is often called individualist and subjectivist, because it emphasizes the complexity of human action (*only* individuals act) and the spontaneous order that "creates" the institutions of economic, political, and social life through "discovery." Because there are so many human decisions involved in economic activity, attempts by central planners to account for—or *discover*—them are doomed. Unlike entrepreneurs, whom the Austrians admire, governments are not "alert" to the myriad and contradictory interests of consumers. Although the Austrians are proponents of the free market, they are not necessarily opposed to monopolies per se—except of the governmental variety—since in a free market monopolies must still "compete" for consumers through discovery. Although properly termed neo-classical, the Austrian view does differ from the classical in some significant ways, most especially in its theory of value, which rejects Smith's view that price (value) is determined by labor and production factors, and instead sees consumer markets (millions of individuals making decisions) as the sole determinant of a product's worth. Compare with classical liberalism; contrast with Chicago School. Read: L. von Mises, *Human Action* (1949); F. A. Hayek, *Individualism and Economic Order* (1948); E. Dolan, ed., *The Foundations of Modern Austrian Economics* (1976); A. Shand, *Free Market Morality* (1990). "The competitive search for adaptation to an uncertain future induces us to try to use as fully as possible the dispersed knowledge of continually changing detailed information. This process necessarily becomes a sort of game in which individual success usually depends on a combination of skill and luck which can never be clearly distinguished. The right thing for the individual to do at a given moment—what is both in his own and the general interest—must depend on the accidental position into which history has placed him. We have learned to play this game of discovery, which we call 'competition,' because the communities that experimented with it and gradually improved its rules have flourished above others. Consequently they have been imitated. But the outcome of the game, the rules of which require people to take the fullest advantage of the opportunities that come their way to serve both themselves and others, can be no more 'just' than that of any game of chance." Friedrich A. Hayek, *Economic Freedom* (1991)

[*Austrian Economics Newsletter*, Ludwig von Mises Institute, Auburn University, Auburn, AL 36849; (334) 844-2500; Mark Brandly, editor. "Published periodically."]

authority: The right to act, the rightness of the action, or, perhaps most importantly, the basis for the action. From **Burke** on, **conservatism** has equated authority with **tradition**, has understood it to be that force in life which restrains the potentially destructive power of **liberty**, and has insisted that authority be grounded in "laws not men." Thus has the need for authority (and **order**) in everyday life led some conservatives to a healthy skepticism of **democracy**, and an energetic affinity for religion. **Bonald** presented a view of authority rooted in three institutions—**family**, church, and state—each in its way derived from Divine authority; each sovereign in its own realm. (See **subsidiarity**.) Obedience (or obligation) to authority is—socially, politically, and theologically—a "perfection inferior to liberty" (Aquinas), and ought never to be conceded or compelled without just cause. However, authority is essential if liberty is to function as anything other than anarchy, a distinction sometimes lost in **libertarianism**. The question of authority is inextricably bound to the question of sovereignty. Sovereignty defines and limits the scope of authority, and, indeed, authority is often denominated as "legitimate power," and the power exercised by any authority is legitimate only insofar as it remains limited to its sphere of sovereignty. **Read:** T. Molnar, *Authority and Its Enemies* (1976); R. A. Nisbet, *Twilight of Authority* (1975). **"Authority formulates, and when there is a need for it, modifies the objectives, articulates and keeps alive tradition, and reminds the members of the loyalty they owe to the social group. . . . [W]e may distinguish between two types of authority: *charismatic* and *institutional*. The first is an unplanned exception, and in spite of its rareness, it strengthens the human material over which it is exercised; the second is the rule, the normal, the routine. . . . Yet those who crave charismatic authority and scorn or would disobey institutional authority make a grievous mistake: an institution might be defined as the place where all members benefit by the authority that the best among them would have naturally."** Thomas Molnar, *Authority and Its Enemies* (1976)

autonomy: Literally, "self-rule" (from the Greek, "a law to oneself"), and usually applying to the political rights of nations (as in *self-government*), but beyond that an important concept in libertarian philosophy. The autonomy of <u>libertarianism</u> is derived in part from Immanuel Kant (1724–1804): Man alone stands at the source of *moral* action. Although libertarians may believe in God as that source, their <u>individualism</u> places each Man in an autonomous role concerning his decisions and actions in this world. This may lead to the kind of individualism to which many conservatives take exception, and to which few traditionally religious people may offer assent, because it suggests an atomistic individuality of the sort that animates Marxist and other avant-gardes—the reservation of authentic freedom of action to an elite that stands outside history and so may judge it without reference to <u>tradition</u>. And autonomy tends, in the extreme libertarian view, to amount to "self ownership," a concept anathema to any religion that "understands man as a being whose free, sinful acts are not his 'private affair' which he himself can absolve by his own power and strength" (Rahner, 1978). At its best, autonomy stands as a bold assertion of individual <u>liberty</u> against the power of the state. But when individual autonomy becomes the embodiment of <u>natural rights</u> theory (taken in its positivistic sense—see <u>positivism</u>), there is a tendency to ignore the claims of <u>faith</u>, <u>family</u>, <u>community</u>, and other claimants upon individual responsibility. <u>Oakeshott</u> used the example of language to suggest the corporate character of individual moral autonomy. Like language, he wrote (1975), moral autonomy is a consequence of the needs of human beings "to be upheld by something more substantial than the emanations of their own contingent imaginations." **Read**: Michael Oakeshott, *On Human Conduct* (1975). Oakeshott writes: **"What is called 'moral autonomy' does not require moral choice to be a gratuitous, criterionless exercise of so-called 'will'** . . . **in which a lonely agent simultaneously recognizes or even creates a 'value' for which he is wholly responsible and places himself under its command, thus miraculously releasing himself from organic impulse, rational contingency, and authoritative rules of conduct. Nor is it conditional upon an agent's critical consent or approval of a rule of conduct in terms of a recognition of purported**

reasons for considering it to be desirable. Nor, again, does it require some other release from having to recognize a rule of conduct merely in terms of its being a rule; that is, in terms of its authority. . . . Human conduct is not first having unconditional wants (individual or communal) and then allowing prudential reason and moral sensibility to indicate or to determine the choice of actions in which their satisfaction is sought; it is wanting intelligently (that is, recognition of prudential and moral considerations) and doing this successfully or unsuccessfully."

Babbitt, Irving (1865–1933): American scholar-critic and a founder with **More** of the New Humanism (sometimes *neo-humanism*), which was a **conservative** reaction to 19th-century romanticism—seeking literary restraint and celebrating classicism—and which was later subsumed by the New Criticism (see **Ransom**). After a difficult and itinerant childhood (spent in, among other places, Ohio, Wyoming, and New York City), Babbitt went to Harvard, which he found uninspiring, but where he learned half a dozen languages and graduated (1889) magna cum laude in classics. Among his languages (learned at Harvard and later in Paris) was Sanskrit, and Babbitt developed a profound interest in and admiration for Eastern religion, especially Buddhism. From 1894 until his death, he taught French at Harvard. Admired by **Eliot** (who was his student), Babbitt's traditionalism was no mere endorsement of representational or realistic art, but an attack on romanticism's dangerous didacticism, its evasion of moral responsibility, and its abandonment of the idea of sin. In particular, he criticized Jean-Jacques Rousseau (1712–1778) for his "sentimental humanitarianism." **Read:** *Rousseau and Romanticism* (1919); *Democracy and Leadership* (1924). **About:** J. D. Hoeveler, *The New Humanism* (1977). "We are assured . . . that the highly heterogeneous elements that enter in to our [i.e., America's] population will, like various instruments in an orchestra, merely result in a richer harmony; they will, one may reply, provided that, like an orchestra, they are properly led. Otherwise the outcome may be an unexampled cacophony. This question of leadership is not primarily biological, but moral. Leaders may vary in quality from the man who is so loyal to sound standards that he inspires right conduct in others by the sheer rightness of his example, to the man who stands for nothing higher than the law of cunning and the law of force, and so is . . . imperialistic. If democracy means simply the attempt to eliminate the qualitative and selective principle in favor of some general will, based in turn on a theory of natural rights, it may prove to be only a form of the vertigo of the abyss." *Democracy and Leadership* (1924)

Bagehot, Walter (1826–1877): British classical-liberal (a.k.a. **conservative**) social scientist, and editor of *The Economist* from 1861 until his death. The grandson and son of bankers, Bagehot trained for the law, tried his hand at journalism, and then decided to enter the family bank at age twenty-five. However, he continued to write, even founding a magazine, *The National Review*. Bagehot married the daughter of the founder of *The Economist*, and in 1859 he became director of that magazine. After his father-in-law's death, Bagehot became editor as well. Woodrow Wilson called *The Economist* under Bagehot's leadership "a kind of supplemental Chancellor of the Exchequer." Bagehot was a superb writer; his *Physics and Politics* (1872) was a powerful neo-Burkean defense of "social evolution," in which he extolled the "cake of custom" that is the treasure of culture, but also championed **capitalism**, which is the source of its renewal. In his earlier *The English Constitution* (1867), Bagehot came down on the side of a mixed **democracy**, along the way suggesting that real power in the British government is divided between Commons and the executive (the prime minister and his cabinet) and that the House of Lords and the monarchy had been reduced to "theatrical parts." He was not a fan of American democracy, however, because he believed it too rigidly fixed the procedures of governance. (His view, of course, was based in part upon the apparent breakdown of the American system in the Civil War.) What was needed for democracy to work properly (conservatively) was the more fluid structure of the English **Constitution**. He was especially disdainful of the procedures for choosing the American president, which he saw as so based upon compromises that the choice of a true (opinionated, fearless) statesman would be rare. Of **Lincoln**'s qualities (which he came to appreciate only after the president was killed), Bagehot simply observed that "success in a lottery is no argument for lotteries." Accordingly, he was no great supporter of the "conservative" Disraeli, whom he considered a political opportunist. His best single epigram: "The essence of Toryism is enjoyment." **Read**: *Bagehot's Historical Essays* (1965); *The English Constitution* (1867); **About**: A. Buchan, *The Spare Chancellor* (1959); N. St. John-Stevas, *Walter Bagehot* (1959). "It has been Mr. Disraeli's misfortune throughout his main political career to lead a party of very strong prejudices and principles, without feeling himself any cordial sympathy with either the one or the other. No doubt that is precisely the fact which has enabled him on most great emergencies to be of use to his party. His completely external intelligence has been to them what the elephant driver's— the mahout's—is to the elephant, comparatively insignificant as a force, but so familiar with all the habits of the creature which his sagacity has to guide, and so entirely, if it only knew, at its mercy, that all his acuteness is displayed in contriving to turn the creature's habits and instincts to his own end, profit, and advantage—which, however, cannot be done without also preserving the creature itself from great dangers, and guarding it against the violence of its own passions. In this way Mr. Disraeli has necessarily been of great use to the Tory party. But something more than this is needed . . . [e.g., 'professional counsel,' 'power to inspire enthusiasm,' 'sense of common interest,' and 'sentiment . . . of mutual dependence']. . . . But . . . [h]e could only calculate the chances of success[ful policy] without reference to . . . [the] aims and wishes [of Tory principle] . . . It seemed a policy in the air, calculated to succeed, not calculated for any special object higher and better than success." "Mr. Disraeli's Administration" in *The Economist*, September 7, 1867, from *Bagehot's Historical Essays* (1965)

Bartley, Robert L. (1937–): See *Wall Street Journal*

Banfield, Edward C. (1916–): American political scientist and author of *The Unheavenly City: The Nature and Future of Our Urban Crisis* (1968, updated in 1974), which was the first book to identify the existence of a seemingly permanent "underclass" in America's cities, and which criticized government programs designed to renew ghettos as hopelessly flawed and ineffective—as being, in fact, a part of the problem. His own controversial proposals included eliminating the minimum wage and providing sex education, although he had few illusions about the probability of *enforced* success. Banfield has always been more concerned with the "is" than the "ought." Banfield early realized that so long as social policy is based upon notions of what ought to be, there can never be an end to social policy, since relative differences in wealth and achievement must always exist; this despite the fact that actual progress has been substantial. Although among the most thoughtfully conservative of social scientists, Banfield has not lacked a taste for the provocative, as in the title of the most famous chapter of *The Unheavenly City*: "Rioting Mainly for Fun and Profit." **Read:** *Here the People Rule* (1991); *The Unheavenly City Revisited* (1974); **About:** R. Fryer, *Recent Conservative Political Thought* (1979); G. Nash, *The Conservative Intellectual Movement in America* (1976); M. Rozell and J. Pontuso, eds., *American Conservative Opinion Leaders* (1990). **"A political system is an accident. It is an accumulation of habits, customs, prejudices, and principles that have survived a long process of trial and error and of ceaseless response to changing circumstance. If the system works well on the whole, it is a lucky accident—the luckiest, indeed, that can befall a society, for all of the institutions of the society, and thus its entire character and that of the human types formed within it, depend ultimately upon the government and the political order. . . . To meddle with the structure and operation of a successful political system is therefore the greatest foolishness that men are capable of. Because the system is intricate beyond comprehension, the chance of improving it in the ways intended is slight, whereas the danger of disturbing its working and of setting off a succession of unwanted effects that will extend throughout the whole society is great. . . . Democracy must always meddle, however. An immanent logic impels it to self-reform, and if other forces do not prevent it, it must sooner or later reform itself out of existence."** "In Defense of the American Party System" in *Here the People Rule* (1991)

Bastiat, Frédéric (1801–1850): French anti-statist economist who championed **private property**, **laissez-faire**, and **free trade**. He was a disciple of sorts of Jean-Baptiste Say and **Smith**, and, due in part to his having learned English at an early age, an Anglophile. Thus he became interested in Richard Cobden's struggle to repeal Britain's protective tariffs. In 1846 he founded *Les Associations pour la Liberté des Échanges* (free-trade associations), which led to his election to the national assembly and a short but fruitful public life. Bastiat was a satirist worthy of Swift, as in his fictitious appeal by candlemakers against the "ruinous competition" of the sun. ("Please pass a law ordering the covering of all windows and skylights . . .") His **empiricism** was summed up thus: "What makes the great division between the two schools is the difference in their methods. **Socialism**, like astrology and alchemy, proceeds by way of the imagination; political economy, like astronomy and chemistry, proceeds by way of observation" (*Economic Harmonies*, 1850). In *The Law* (1850), Bastiat made a bold plea for **limited government** based upon the restraints of **natural law**. As he eloquently explained, a transcendent standard in law is necessary, lest Man imagine all right is of his own devising. That a majority believes slavery is licit cannot make it right. Government exists to provide for common needs only: defense in war; policing against crime; construction of roads, sewers, and other public works; and the keeping of records. What Bastiat called the "seen and the unseen" of economic reality is what formed the basis of his attack on government intervention. As **Hazlitt** (1946) put it, planners see "only what is immediately visible to the eye," and miss the complex interactions always present in (leading to and following from) human action. **Read:** *The Law* (1850); **About:** G. Roche, *Free Markets, Free Men* (1993); D. Russell, *Frédéric Bastiat* (1969). **"The socialist says, 'But there are persons who have no money,' and he turns to the law. . . . But nothing can enter the public treasury for the benefit of one citizen or one class unless other citizens and other classes have been forced to send it in. If every person draws from the treasury the amount he has contributed, it is true that the law then plunders nobody. But that procedure would do nothing for the persons who have no money. It would not promote equality of income. The law can be an instrument of equalization only as it takes money from some persons and gives it to other persons. When the law does that, it is an instrument of plunder. . . . With that in mind, examine the protective tariffs,** subsidies, guaranteed jobs, relief and welfare schemes, government education, progressive taxation, free credit, and such. You will find that they are always based on legal plunder, organized in justice." *The Law* (1850)

Bell, Daniel (1919–): American sociologist, sometime critic of **conservatism**, and leading proponent, with reservations, of **neoconservatism**. He is a graduate of Columbia University and a long-time professor at Harvard. As a co-editor with **Kristol** of *The Public Interest*, Bell would seem to have impeccable neocon credentials, but—unlike Kristol—he is notably uncomfortable with the term. Indeed, he describes himself as "a socialist in economics, a liberal in politics, and a conservative in culture." In this he resembles **Hook**. But the **socialism** Bell believes in is apparently little more than the **welfare** "safety net," and his version of a politics of **classical liberalism** emphasizes **individualism** and thus opposes **affirmative action**. Bell has been prophetic about the impact of the American economy's shift from heavy industry to high technology upon the cultural cohesiveness of traditional life. Bell's *The End of Ideology* (1960) proclaimed a new era in which "social reform would be accompanied by calculating, pragmatic steps; in which a thick membrane of skepticism would stand between utopian vision and practical politics" (in Steinfels, 1979). As Bell's thought has evolved, he has come to oppose the idea of "holistic culture" so popular in his field. Instead, he sees contemporary culture as "radically disjunctive," meaning that the three main realms of modern life are often in conflict. Those realms are the "techno-economic" (governed by bureaucracies of rationality and efficiency), the political (which seeks equality through participation), and the cultural (the "cultivation of taste and judgment" dominated by the search for self-realization). "It is the tensions between the norms of these three realms—efficiency and bureaucracy, equality and rights, self-fulfillment and the desire for novelty—that form the contradictions of the modern world . . ." (1980). Thus what is most **conservative** about Bell's work is his embrace of complexity and his rejection of any reductionist **ideology**. As he says at the end of *The Winding Passage*, ". . . I am bound by the faith of my fathers, to the thread, for the cord of culture—and religion—is memory. As Louis MacNeice once wrote: '. . . I cannot deny my past to which my self is wed/The woven figure cannot undo its thread.'" **Read:** *The Cultural Contradictions of Capitalism* (1975); *The Winding Passage* (1980); **About:** H. Brick, *Daniel Bell and the Decline of Intellectual Radicalism* (1986); R. Fryer, *Recent Conservative Political Thought* (1979); P. Steinfels, *The Neoconservatives* (1979). **"If science is the search for unity of nature, religion is the search for unity of culture. Culture is a different realm from nature. If one is reductionist, the other is emergent, through consciousness. It is more concerned with the knower than with the known. Culture seeks meaning on the basis of purpose. It cannot be indifferent to the imperatives of nature (for example, the death of the individual for the necessary continuation of the strength of the species), for it is the conscious response of men to the existential predicaments that arise out of the interaction of men with nature, and with one another. The very search for meanings that transcend one's own life drives a culture to find common meanings regarding the human condition in other cultures, and to seek some unity, not in any ecumenical or theological sense, but in the oneness of the human predicament. The road of culture always leads one to a beyond, a beyond that modern culture has trivialized."** "The Return to the Sacred" in *The Winding Passage* (1980)

Berns, Walter (1919–   ): American legal scholar—Cornell University (from which he resigned when administrators kowtowed to 1960s radicals, see also **Sowell** and **Bloom**), Harvard, Georgetown and the **American Enterprise Institute**—who is often accused of being a big-government **conservative**. A student of **Strauss**, Berns has been a constant critic equally of the permissive views of civil libertarians and of the doctrine of judicial restraint as advocated by some conservatives. Both views, he believes, tend to demean the proper, albeit limited, role of government. In *Freedom, Virtue, and the First Amendment* (1957), Berns argued that "the formation of character" (*good* character, obviously) is government's first responsibility. He is, therefore, a nationalist, and has always been uncomfortable with a conservatism that emphasizes **states' rights**. Specific to his stance against **libertarianism** is Berns' view of pornography, regarding which—against absolutist interpretations of the First Amendment—he favors a sophisticated version of "community standards."

Read: *The First Amendment and the Future of American Democracy* (1976); *In Defense of Liberal Democracy* (1984); *Taking the Constitution Seriously* (1987); **About:** G. Nash, *The Conservative Intellectual Movement in America* (1976). "The typical student today . . . is not ready to believe that what stands between him and despotism is something on the order of good table manners. . . . Of course, the student is right about this, but the suggestion is not quite so ridiculous as it might at first appear. Forms and good manners, even good table manners, have something more in common than the fact that Tocqueville sees reason to discuss them both in a book about modern democracy. The formal way and the well-mannered way are the less efficient ways and, almost for that reason alone, are understood to be the proper ways. . . . Criminals can be lynched rather than indicted and then tried according to the cumbersome processes of law, but by indicting and trying them we mark the difference between civilized and barbarous practice . . . Good manners and forms are barriers between ourselves and the objects of our desires, and there is much to be said for barriers of that sort; at a minimum, they restrain us or force us to act indirectly. Constitutionalism has much in common with acting indirectly. . . . [Note:] The day before this was written a group calling itself Direct Action accepted responsibility (or as they would say, claimed credit) for the bombing of a Paris police station. Direct action is the opposite of formal action and, not accidentally, is the way of terrorists." *Taking the Constitution Seriously* (1987)

big government: See **limited government**

I

The Greco-Roman Influence

by
Carnes Lord

The legacy of classical Greece and Rome, an important point of reference for European and American conservatism until a century ago if not beyond, is not easy to locate along today's political spectrum. Nevertheless, it remains a rich source of moral and political wisdom.

Virtually all of the most important writers of Greece in its greatest age (roughly 450–330 B.C.) were conservative in a recognizable sense of the term: all were critical of the politics and culture of Athenian radical democracy, and all hoped for the restoration in some form of the more aristocratic "ancestral constitution" that the city had once enjoyed. Like most Greek aristocrats of the time, they looked to Sparta, rival of Athens, as a model of social discipline, cultural simplicity, and political sobriety. At the same time, these writers—especially Thucydides, Plato, and Aristotle, and to a lesser extent Aristophanes, Xenophon, and Isocrates—were less opposed to democracy than is sometimes assumed, and they were far from blind to the defects of the Spartan alternative. Indeed, they were more concerned with the culture of Athens than with its politics. The cultural decay reflected in the decline of traditional religious belief and the

31

growing role in education of professional sophists and rhetoricians had undermined the traditional public-spiritedness of the political class, a development which encouraged demagogy and hence fed the worst tendencies of popular rule.

The most powerful and influential response to this situation (in some ways strikingly familiar to our own) was that formulated by Socrates and his followers, especially Plato and Aristotle. The Socratic movement attempted for the first time to bring rigorous philosophical analysis to bear on the practical problems of human life. It did so not merely with a view to achieving intellectual clarity but out of a concern to improve the moral and political health of contemporary society. The Socrates of Plato's *Apology* acts as a "gadfly" to the city of Athens, and not merely in the sense that he challenges conventional thinking (the popular interpretation today); Socrates makes himself a nuisance above all as a relentless advocate of education, virtue, and the care of one's soul. This stress on virtue or excellence (*arete*) and how it is to be fostered is perhaps the leading theme of Socratic-Platonic political philosophy as a whole, and its most unambiguously conservative feature. In particular, it is the theme of what are widely considered the two greatest works of this tradition, Plato's *Republic* and Aristotle's *Ethics*.

The *Republic*, perhaps the most famous surviving work of antiquity, is at first sight not conservative at all. It argues that no existing political order is truly just, and that justice can only be achieved by creating a society based on a scheme of radical communism (not only property but women and children are to be held in common) and rule by an elite of "philosopher-kings." The question is how seriously one is supposed to take this Platonic alternative. There are many reasons for believing that Plato himself views his "best" regime finally as both undesirable and impossible, or contrary to human nature, and that his ultimate intention in the *Republic* is less to sketch a blueprint of Utopia than it is to underline the limits of all political action. [For the classic statement of this interpretation, see Leo Strauss, *City and Man* (1964).] In a later work, the *Laws*, Plato offers quite a different account of political life, one focusing on moral education, the rule of law, and traditional piety rather than on exotic political institutions as the core requirements of the good society. This work, unfortunately little read today, may be said to be the most deeply conservative product of the Socratic tradition.

The moral and political writings of Aristotle build directly on the teaching of the *Laws*. In his *Ethics*, Aristotle discovered and articulated the phenomenon of moral virtue (as distinct from both vulgar or utilitarian and philosophic virtue), thereby founding the discipline of moral philosophy. Although retaining the aristocratic accents of its cultural context, the *Ethics* offers an account of moral experience that has proved persuasive across historical and cultural divides. (Winston Churchill once remarked that it was "pretty much as I have always understood these things.") The *Ethics* offers the classic account of "prudence" as a virtue of private as well as political life; and its remarkable discussion of the moral dimensions of friendship is without parallel in later literature. In very recent years, there has been a potent revival of Aristotelianism within contemporary moral philosophy, in reaction to the manifest poverty of modern utilitarianism, intuitionism, and other competing approaches. [See, notably, Alasdair MacIntyre, *After Virtue* (1981).]

Also of continuing interest today is Aristotle's great treatise on politics. The famous analysis of the natural character of the *polis* or political community at the beginning of this work remains of fundamental importance as *the* alternative to the contractarian individualism of modern political theory. Aristotle's notion of man as the "political animal" is often misconstrued—whether as incipiently totalitarian or as supporting the participatory politics of contemporary democratic communitarianism. In fact, the *Politics* provides a nuanced and supple account of the relationship between the political community and its various component parts, one that acknowledges the need to accommodate differences among individuals and social classes and that accepts an important role for the family and private property.

Classical conservatism is not a conservatism of the free market. Aristotle's brief but seminal treatment of economic questions in the *Politics* stresses the unnatural character of unlimited acquisition. Yet it would be a mistake to conflate his view with the traditional prejudices of a landed aristocracy. It is striking that Aristotle holds up the commercial republic of Carthage as well as agrarian Sparta as a political model to be emulated. His analysis of Carthaginian institutions is the place to begin attempting to understand what Aristotle might have thought about America.

In turning last and briefly to Rome, one enters a very different cultural world, one more profoundly and self-consciously traditional in outlook than that of the Greeks. It is not accidental that Roman authors have had a disproportionate influence on traditional aristocratic education in the West. The moralizing historians and poets of the late Republic and early Empire—especially Livy, Sallust, Vergil, Horace, Tacitus, and Juvenal—not only celebrate Rome's greatness but provide powerful commentary on a timeless spectacle of political folly and moral collapse. One other author merits special mention. Marcus Tullius Cicero, Rome's greatest philosopher and one of its most accomplished orators and politicians, surely deserves recognition as a fundamental source of conservative thought in the West, both as an exponent of the natural law teaching of the Stoics and through his direct influence on Edmund Burke.

Carnes Lord is the author of *Education and Culture in the Political Thought of Aristotle*. His translation of Aristotle's *The Politics* is widely acclaimed.

Blackstone, William (1723–1780): English jurist whose *Commentaries on the Laws of England* (4 volumes, 1765–69)—an unprecedented systemization of the labyrinth of Britain's common law—influenced the views of America's founding generation. (In the two decades following the American Revolution, Blackstone was the most frequently cited writer in American political literature.) The "judicious Blackstone" (**Hamilton**) was the first legal professor (Oxford) to teach other than Roman jurisprudence. He was an advocate of **natural law** (with qualifications), which he saw as creating three **natural rights**: personal security, individual **liberty**, and **private property**. And he believed that common law was the embodiment, albeit imperfect, of natural law. (The *Commentaries* are inconsistent: sometimes Blackstone seems to believe that laws are right because they are in accord with Nature, and at other times he seems to say they are right simply because Man has enacted them.) His views have been summarized as (proto-) "Burkean **conservatism**," and they share Burke's **empiricism**, although Blackstone was decidedly not a philosopher, and the *Commentaries* are far from offering a coherent theory of the law. He was very much an Old Whig (although nominally a Tory), meaning he was a classical liberal. He was by no means a legal **reactionary**, and was in favor of prison reform and opposed to Poor Laws. He returned to private practice in 1766, at about the same time as the publication of the *Commentaries*, which were essentially his collected lectures from Oxford. Blackstone's influence may have been greater in America than in England, where James Kent and Joseph Story made his example the standard in American legal education. (See also **Maine**.) **Read**: and **About**: D. Boorstin, *The Mysterious Science of the Law* (1941). "**This law of nature, being co-eval with mankind and dictated by God himself, is of course superior in obligation to any other. It is binding over all the globe, and all countries, and at all times; no human laws are of any validity if contrary to this; and such of them as are valid derive all their force, and all their authority, mediately or immediately from this original.**" *The Commentaries* (1769)

Bloom, Allan (1930–1992): American philosopher, social critic, professor of politics at Yale (1962), Cornell (1963–1970), the University of Toronto (1972–1979), and (from 1979 until his death) a member of the University of Chicago's Committee on Social Thought. (Bloom was also a graduate of Chicago, having matriculated there at the age of sixteen, and having studied the Great Books under the tutelage of Robert Maynard Hutchins [1899–1977]. He kept his enthusiasm for the **liberal arts** throughout his life.) Bloom was a legendary teacher and a noted classicist (a translator of Plato and Rousseau), but hardly a household name until the publication of his *The Closing of the American Mind: How Higher Education Has Failed Democracy and Impoverished the Souls of Today's Students* (1987). The book was an epoch-changing attack on the politicization of American universities in particular and of American society in general. As a graduate student in Chicago's Committee, Bloom studied with **Strauss** and, like his teacher, believed in an enduring, "transforming," and "transcultural" truth. The impetus behind *The Closing of the American Mind* was partly the experience of three decades of teaching (especially the increasing spectacle of his students' **relativism**), and partly the haunting memory of the infamous black-student rebellion at Cornell in 1969, during which university officials capitulated to the demands of an armed group of militants. (See also **Berns** and **Sowell**.) Bloom gave his ideas about America's educational quagmire a test run in *National Review* (December 10, 1982), where his condemnation of liberal relativism received a stunning response, which encouraged him to expand the article into the book that became *The Closing of the American Mind*. By abandoning the liberal arts, Bloom argued, the university was abandoning what is both most beautiful and most essential in its mission. By pandering to every new ism and educational fad, the university—like the public-relations-crazy culture at large—was losing track of the moral unity established in Western history and codified in the **Constitution**. **Read:** *The Closing of the American Mind* (1987); *Giants and Dwarfs* (1990); **About:** Bloom's own *Love & Friendship* (1993). **"It is important to emphasize that the lesson ... students are [currently] drawing from their studies is simply untrue. History and the study of cultures do not teach or prove that values or cultures are relative. All to the contrary, that is a philosophical premise that we now bring to our study of them. This premise is unproven and dogmatically asserted for what are largely political reasons. History and culture are** interpreted in the light of it, and then are said to prove the premise. Yet the fact that there have been different opinions about good and bad in different times and places in no way proves that none is true or superior to others. To say that it does so prove is as absurd as to say that the diversity of points of view expressed in a college bull session proves there is no truth. On the face of it, the difference of opinion would seem to raise the question as to which is true or right rather than to banish it. The natural reaction is to try to resolve the difference, to examine the claims and reasons for each opinion." *The Closing of the American Mind* (1987)

Bonald, Louis Gabriel de (1754–1840): French political philosopher, proto-sociologist, and critic of the Enlightenment, whose *Theory of Power* (1796) was indebted to Burke and Thomas Aquinas. He stands in a line between Maistre and Tocqueville as a primary expositor of the religiously conservative tradition in European thought, although he went further than they in his reaction against the movement of modern life—especially in economics (i.e., capitalism), which he roundly condemned for leading to centralization and urbanization. His version of agrarianism influenced the work of novelists Honoré de Balzac and Gustave Flaubert. Bonald was a precursor of the view later called subsidiarity, but with a rural, aristocratic twist. **Read:** and **About:** M. Quinlan, *The Historical Thought of the Vicomte de Bonald* (1953). "Since the key words in the philosophes' fashion-creating discourse were science and virtue . . . ordinary, imperfect government, 'irrational' institutions, belief in God, and the idea of social hierarchy became objects of contempt and ridicule. No wonder that just before the end, nobility, Church, King and Court were literally embarrassed by their rank, privileges, piety— or simply by their position of authority and its exercise. The philosophies, . . . Bonald wrote, preached atheism to the higher classes and a republican ideology to the people at large. The result . . . was that the governing class, persuaded to despise religion, began to have doubts concerning the legitimacy of the power with which they governed; the people learning to hate . . . political authority began to have doubts of a religion that prescribed obedience to government." Thomas Molnar, *The Counter-Revolution* (1969)

Brownson, Orestes A. (1803–1876): American author and theologian. Early a utopian transcendentalist who later became a Catholic convert, Brownson's career came to symbolize the American **conservative**'s need to reconcile **liberty** and **authority**. In *The American Republic* (1866), Brownson insisted that America awaken to the distinction between the **democracy** of **republicanism** and the pure democracy of the **Enlightenment**. Above all this meant opposition to **socialism** and **liberalism**. Brownson's former **faith** in "the people" was shattered by the "Hard Cider" campaign of 1840, in which incumbent Martin Van Buren lost to William Henry Harrison. (Brownson was easily overwrought.) It confirmed for him the dangerous possibilities of a philosophy of majority rule (in his mind more like Rousseau's "general will"), and the necessity of a legal structure that recognizes right and wrong in transcendent standards: "Laws that emanate from the people, or that are binding only by virtue of the assent of the governed, or that emanate from any human source alone, have none of the characteristics of law, for they bind no conscience, and restrain, except by force, no will." **Read:** and **About:** R. Kirk, ed., *Orestes Brownson: Selected Political Essays* (1990): **"[C]ommunism, which demands equality in material goods, is not only an impossibility, but an absurdity. Equality of wealth is equivalent to equality of poverty. Wealth consists in its power to purchase labor, and no matter how great it is, it can purchase no labor, if there is none in the market; and, if all were equally rich, there would be none in the market, for no one would sell his labor to another."** "The Democratic Principle," in *Quarterly Review* (1873)

Buckley, William F., Jr. (1925–   ): American journalist, founder of *National Review*, host of the television series *Firing Line*, and author of more than thirty books, both fiction and non-fiction. His magazine, his books, his widely syndicated newspaper column, his high visibility through television, and his agile intellect and sharp wit have made him the most admired and influential **conservative** of the last fifty years. In one of the most public and event-filled careers in recent times, Buckley has written best-sellers (*God and Man at Yale*, 1951, was the first, a blistering indictment of his alma mater's scorn for both Christianity and **capitalism**), founded or helped to found organizations (**ISI** and Young Americans for Freedom), run for political office (for mayor of New York, 1965), and generally managed to exemplify **conservatism**'s dispositions and principles. (Those principles have been consistent but fluid. Buckley was early an admirer of **Nock** and **isolationism**, but his opposition to **communism** and embrace of **capitalism** led to a more aggressive conservatism.) Above all it was *National Review*—and his leadership of it—that molded the postwar conservative movement into the ascendant political and cultural force in American life. His career—though far from over—may be said to be bracketed between two quotations, each in *National Review*, but separated by thirty-six years: "[National Review] stands athwart history, yelling Stop, at a time when no one is inclined to do so, or to have much patience with those who do." (November 19, 1955, the magazine's premiere issue); and "We won." (September 23, 1991, the issue celebrating the fall of communism). In his flawed biography of Buckley, Judis (1988) was surely right that Buckley's career brought to "American conservatism a philosophy of radical dissent rather than accommodation with the status quo." Radical, we should say, as in "to the roots." Buckley's colleague at *National Review*, William Rusher, put it this way in 1984: ". . . [W]ho, or what, could bring the prickly components of the conservative movement together and induce it to speak with a single journalistic voice? Who could proclaim and refine conservatism's fundamental principles, resolve or compromise disputes on internal issues, promote . . . lead . . . raise the necessary money . . . referee the inevitable quarrels, and bring the whole enterprise into being? Who (we now know History's answer) but William F. Buckley, Jr.?" **Read:** *God and Man at Yale* (1951); *Up From Liberalism* (1959); **About:** J. Judis, *William F. Buckley, Jr.: Patron Saint of the Conservatives* (1988). "**I do not understand liberalism as a historical continuum. I refuse to submit to the facile expositions of liberal historians who do not shrink from coopting for the liberal position any popular hero out of the past. Thomas Jefferson, a liberal when he lived, would be a 'liberal' were he alive today because, so their argument goes, the principles he then propounded,** *mutatis mutandis*, **have evol[ved] . . . into the principles of the contemporary liberal. Thomas Jefferson, the humane, as-**

cetic, orderly patrician, countenance the mobocratic approach to belly-government of Harry Truman and the Americans for Democratic Action? But why? What has befallen us, that liberalism should be, ineluctably, the only approach to democratic government, mid-20th century? And if what has befallen us is a historical imperative with which we must necessarily come to terms, must we do so joyfully, even to the sacrilegious point of arrogating for it the enthusiasm of Thomas Jefferson? It may be that as James Stephens wrote, 'the waters are out and no human force can turn them back'; but is it necessary, he wondered, that 'as we go with the stream, we . . . sing Hallelujah to the river god'?" *Up From Liberalism* (1959)

bureaucracy: Administration, especially in government, undertaken through different departments and by, as a common dictionary entry appropriately puts it, "petty officials." <u>Nisbet</u> (1982) has called it "the new despotism" and a fourth branch of government, whereas <u>Wilson</u> has characterized it as officious but necessary and, in America at least, open. The growth of the national bureaucracy has been indisputably explosive: at the turn of the century "federal" employees (see <u>federalism</u>), including the armed forces and the post office, numbered about 100,000. Today their numbers exceed 5,000,000. (Similar increases have generally affected the administrations of universities and of some private industries. As Max Weber pointed out, it does not matter whether a bureaucracy is "private" or "public," except that private bureaucracies are not isolated from necessary refinements of competitiveness and profit.) Costly and inefficient bureaucracy has led to increased interest in privatization, and an appreciation of the distinction (as detailed by Donahue, 1989): "The profit-seeker, in exchange for a *price*, agrees to *deliver a product*. The civil servant, in exchange for a *wage*, agrees to *accept instructions*." **Read:** J. D. Donahue, *The Privatization Decision* (1989); L. von Mises, *Bureaucracy* (1944); James Q. Wilson, *Bureaucracy* (1989). Wilson writes: "To do better we have to deregulate the government. If deregulation of a market makes sense because it liberates the entrepreneurial energies of its members, then it is possible that deregulating the public sector also may help energize it. The difference, of course, is that both the price system and the profit motive provide a discipline in markets that is absent in non-markets. Whether any useful substitutes for this discipline can be found for public-sector workers is not clear ... But even if we cannot expect the same results from deregulation in the two sectors we can agree at a minimum that detailed regulation, even of public employees, rarely is compatible with energy, pride in workmanship, and the exercise of initiative. The best evidence for this proposition, if any is needed, is that most people do not like working in an environment in which every action is second-guessed, every initiative is viewed with suspicion, and every controversial decision denounced as malfeasance."

Burke, Edmund (1729–1797): Irish-born English statesman, orator, and author; generally agreed to be the founder of modern **conservatism**. Burke's preeminence comes from the astonishing complexity—and timing—of his criticism of **Enlightenment** thought (see also **Locke, Montesquieu**). The son of a Catholic mother and a (nominally) Protestant father, Burke was educated at Trinity College, Dublin. His vision of what he called "ordered liberty" was already well formed in his twenties when he published *A Vindication of Natural Society* and *Philosophical Inquiry into the Origin of Our Ideas on the Sublime and the Beautiful* (both 1756). He worked in government and served for nearly thirty years in Parliament, where his application of general principles to specific problems reflected what has been termed his "Christian pessimism," which is to say that his policy recommendations reflected a belief in original **sin**, not in human perfectibility. Burke was in favor of the movements for (Irish) Catholic emancipation and native autonomy in India, and he believed the American rebellion was justified on constitutional grounds, although he lamented the British misrule which made it necessary. But it was the revolution in France that provoked his most vehement opposition, because—whereas the American revolt was basically a **conservative** affirmation of the traditional rights and liberties of Englishmen—the French Revolution was a radical break with civilization itself, a leap into the abyss. "You are now to live in a new order of things," Burke wrote to the putative Frenchman to whom his monumental *Reflections on the Revolution in France* (1790) is addressed, "under a plan of Government of which no Man can speak from experience." (A lifelong Whig, Burke led a coalition of conservative Whigs that joined forces with Pitt's Tories in the aftermath of the controversy that followed publication of the *Reflections*.) It was not theory he disdained so much as ideological speculation and abstraction, especially when its intention was to impose itself upon the evolved **order** in society. Individuals are foolish, Burke believed, but corporate societies are not. (He opposed **individualism**, believing that the basic unit of society is not the person but the **family**.) He accepted the necessity of reform ("A state without the means of some change is without the means of its conservation"), but he abhorred the destruction of **tradition** in the name of abstract rights. (Thomas Paine's *The Rights of Man* [1792] was written as an answer to Burke's *Reflections*.) Burke was a member of the circle of friends (the Literary Club) clustered about Dr. Samuel Johnson that included the painter Joshua Reynolds, the actor David Garrick, playwrights Oliver Goldsmith and Richard Brinsley Sheridan, the lawyer-author James Boswell, and upon occasion Boswell's countryman **Smith**. Of Burke, **Acton** wrote: "Why not an entire Liberal? How thoroughly he wished for liberty—of conscience, property, trade, in slavery, etc. What stood against it? His notion of history, the claims of the past, the **authority** of time, the will of the dead, continuity. Others held this before, but with other parts of conservatism. Burke was conservative by that alone. And that alone devolved all the rest of his principles, and made the first of liberals, the first of conservatives." **Read:** *Reflections of the Revolution in France* (1790); **About:** F. Canavan, *The Political Economy of Edmund Burke* (1995); R. Kirk, *The Conservative Mind: From Burke to Eliot* (1953); P. Stanlis, *Edmund Burke and the Natural Law* (1986). **"The science of constructing a commonwealth, or renovating it, or reforming it, is, like every other experimental science, not to be taught a priori. Nor is it a short experience that can instruct us in that practical science; because the real effects of moral causes are not always immediate, but that which in the first instance is prejudicial may be excellent in its remoter operation, and its excellence may arise even from the ill effects it produces in the beginning. The reverse also happens; and very plausible schemes, with very pleasing commencements, have** often shameful and lamentable conclusions. . . . The science of government . . . therefore . . . requires . . . more experience than any person can gain in his whole life—however sagacious and observing he may be—[and] it is with infinite caution that any man ought to venture upon pulling down an edifice which has answered in any tolerable degree for ages the common purposes of society . . ." *Reflections on the Revolution in France* (1790)

Burnham, James (1905–1987): American intellectual who was early a Marxist, later a **conservative**, and became one of the founding editors of *National Review*. Burnham was perhaps the most noted Trotskyist in America in the 1930s, although by the end of the decade he was at odds with Trotsky himself. Burnham had learned empirically that **communism** and despotism were synonymous. His movement from communism to the **Right** was accomplished in less than half a decade, and he almost immediately became a leading conservative spokesman. "I suspect," **Hook** (1987) wrote rather acidly of his old friend, "that Burnham's wife, family, and friends were rather relieved when, in the course of his evolution towards **anticommunism**, then anti-**Marxism**, and finally anti-**socialism**, his social life suffered no embarrassing lapses." Burnham's *The Web of Subversion* (1954) was a detailed account of communist activities in the U.S., and was one of the most important books ever to champion anticommunism. Burnham's version of anticommunism was assertive: he believed that the Communist Party should be outlawed in the U.S., and that communist expansion abroad should be forcibly stopped. His most famous book, *Suicide of the West*, was a meticulous analysis of **liberalism**, which he called the "ideology of Western suicide." The book's seventh chapter presents an ingenious table in which the assertions of the liberal **ideology** are contrasted with "corresponding contrary beliefs," i.e., **conservatism**. Burnham received the Medal of Freedom in 1983. **Read:** *The Managerial Revolution* (1941); *The Machiavellians* (1943); *Suicide of the West* (1964); **About:** K. Smant, *How Great the Triumph* (1992); S. Francis, *Power and History: The Political Thought of James Burnham* (1984). **"The guilt of the liberal causes him to feel obligated to try to do *something* about any and every social problem, to cure every social evil. . . even if he has no knowledge of**

the suitable medicine or, for that matter, of the nature of the disease; he must *do something* about the social problem even when there is no objective reason to believe that what he does can solve the problem—when, in fact, it may well aggravate the problem instead of solving it. 'We cannot stand idly by while the world rushes to destruction . . . or women and children are starving . . . or able men walk the streets without jobs . . .' or whatever. The harassed liberal is relentlessly driven by his Eumenidean guilt. It does not permit him to 'let well enough alone' or . . . decide that the trouble is 'none of his business'; or to reflect that, though the evil is undoubtedly there and he sincerely sorry for its victims, he doesn't understand damn-all about it and even if he did he hasn't got the brains and resources to fix it up." *Suicide of the West* (1964)

Calhoun, John C. (1782–1850): American statesman (Secretary of War under Monroe, Vice President under J. Q. Adams and Jackson, South Carolina senator, Secretary of State under Tyler) and political philosopher, whose view of states' rights led to the South Carolina ordinance (or "exposition") of nullification (1832) that voided a "federal" protective tariff affecting Charleston. Calhoun—with Henry Clay—also negotiated the compromise that led to repeal of the nullification, thereby temporarily cooling the heated question of state sovereignty until it exploded—ironically in Charleston harbor—in 1861. (Note: Calhoun was by no means the first Southerner to assert nullification; a generation earlier two Virginians had been the doctrine's champions, namely Jefferson and Madison. However, another Virginian, Calhoun's contemporary and sometime mentor Randolph, said: "Nullification is nonsense.") An early nationalist and "war hawk," Calhoun came finally to believe in the "league-of-states" theory of the Union, and in what he called *concurrent majorities*. By this latter view the majority opinion *within* a minority group, e.g., 51 percent of the South, would have a veto power over proposed actions by the majority of the majority, in this case the North, voting as the legislature of the national government. Only in this way might the rights of minorities truly be protected. That his concern for minorities did not extend to the rights of African-American slaves reflects the simmering tragedy of his day, but does not diminish the significance of his warning about national (i.e., majority) incursions against its component communities; incursions undertaken in the name of **democracy**. Above all Calhoun feared majority tyranny: ". . . Government of the uncontrolled numerical majority, is but the absolute and despotic form of popular governments; just as that of the uncontrolled will of one man, or a few, is of monarchy or aristocracy; and it has . . . as strong tendency to oppression, and the abuse of its powers, as either of the others" (*Disquisition on Government*, 1850). Calhoun may have been the first American to speak of "conservative principles" (1832). His plantation is now the Clemson University campus. (See also **Southern conservatism.**) **Read:** and **About:** *Union and Liberty: The Political Philosophy of John C. Calhoun* (R. M. Lence, ed., 1992); **About:** A. Spain, *The Political Theory of John C. Calhoun* (1951). ". . . [I]t is . . . clear that man cannot exist in . . . a state [of nature; apart and separated from all others]; that he is by nature social, and that society is necessary . . . [T]o call it a state of nature was a great misnomer, and has led to dangerous errors; for that cannot justly be called a state of nature which is so opposed to the constitution of man as to be inconsistent with the existence of his race and the development of the high faculties, mental and moral, with which he is endowed by his Creator. . . . Nor is the social state of itself his natural state; for society can no more exist without government, in one form or another, than man without society. It is the political, then, which includes the social, that is his natural state. It is the one for which his Creator formed him, into which he is impelled irresistibly, and in which only his race can exist and all its faculties be fully developed." "Speech on the Oregon Trail" (1848) in *Union and Liberty* (1992)

capitalism: In its simplest conception, the ownership of the means of production by private individuals, whose transactions are conducted in a free market. Arguments in favor of capitalism may be either economic or philosophic; may emphasize the system's efficiency, which is by now beyond question, or assert its morality, which is largely irrelevant. Leftist opposition to capitalism usually condemns its inability to achieve "economic or social justice" (in that it creates inequities and does not always reward merit), whereas conservative wariness about it stems from its inherent instability (in that profit seeking has no respect for **tradition**). But in a free society all that any "just" system can do is agree about the rules of procedure; it cannot agree about the future results of human activity, because, by definition, those results cannot be known. As **Hayek** (1976–1982, vol. II) wrote: "In a free society in which the position of the different individuals and groups is not the result of anybody's design—or could, within society, be altered with a generally applicable principle—the differences in reward simply cannot meaningfully be described as just or unjust." A distinction is often made between **laissez-faire** capitalism and corporate (or monopoly) capitalism, the point being that the latter may actually diminish the free market and depress entrepreneurship. But—except in the case of state-run monopolies—this is unlikely, since a private monopoly (operating legally) is never really safe from competition. **Read**: M. Friedman, *Capitalism and Freedom* (1962); F. A. Hayek, ed., *Capitalism and the Historians* (1967). Hayek writes: **"There is . . . one supreme myth which more than any other has served to discredit the economic system to which we owe our present-day civilization . . . It is the legend of the deterioration of the position of the working classes in consequence of the rise of 'capitalism' . . . That this was the case was at one time indeed wisely taught by economic historians. A more careful examination of the facts has, however, led to a thorough refutation of this belief. . . . The true fact of the slow and irregular progress of the working class . . . is of course rather unsensational and uninteresting to the layman. It is no more than he has learned to expect as the normal state of affairs; and it hardly occurs to him that this is by no means an inevitable progress, that it was preceded by centuries of virtual stagnation of the position of the poorest, and that we have come to expect continuous improvement only as a result of the experience of several generations with the system which he still thinks to be the cause of the misery of the poor."**

Cato Institute: See **Rothbard, Murray**

The Cato Journal: See **public choice theory**

Chambers, Whittaker (1901–1961): American journalist whose transit from communist spy to conservative patriot was one of the century's most stunning stories. His testimony before the House Un-American Activities Committee revealed that he had, on behalf of the Soviets, "run" a State Department official, Alger Hiss (1904–   ), who was subsequently convicted of perjury. "I know," he told the Committee, "that I am leaving the winning side for the losing side, but it is better to die on the losing side than to live under Communism." Before, during, and after, Chambers wrote for respectively *The New Masses, Time*, and **National Review**. When the HUAC call came (August 1, 1948), he told *Time* founder Henry Luce, ". . . you will not want me around here any longer," and he was right. But Chambers' forced retirement resulted in a book, *Witness* (1952), which **Hook** called "one of the most significant autobiographies of the 20th century." For Chambers the challenge faced by the contemporary West was only partly the threat of the communist "religion"; it was also—and more especially—the West's own loss of **faith**. History, he wrote, "is cluttered with the wreckage of nations that became indifferent to God, and died." Of Chambers, Arthur Koestler (1905–1983) said he "committed moral suicide to atone for the guilt of our generation." Upon reading *Witness*, André Malraux (1901–1976) wrote to Chambers, "You have not come back from hell with empty hands." **Reagan** made Chambers a posthumous recipient of the Medal of Freedom in 1984. (See also **anticommunism**.) **Read**: T. Teachout, ed., *Ghosts on the Roof: Selected Journalism of Whittaker Chambers, 1931–1959* (1989); **About**: his own *Witness* (1952); H. Klehr, et al., *The Secret World of American Communism* (1995); A. Weinstein, *Perjury: The Hiss-Chambers Case* (1979). "I do not know how far back it began. Avalanches gather force and crash, unheard, in men as in the mountains. But I date my break [with communism] from a very casual happening. I was sitting in our apartment on St. Paul Street in Baltimore. It was shortly before we moved to Alger Hiss's apartment in Washington. My daughter was in her high chair. I was watching her eat. She was the most miraculous thing that ever happened in my life. I liked to watch her even when she smeared porridge on her face or dropped it meditatively on the floor. My eye came to rest on the delicate convolutions of her ear—those intricate, perfect ears. The thought crossed my mind: "No, those ears were not created by any chance coming together of atoms in nature (the Communist view).

They could have been created only by immense design." The thought was involuntary and unwanted. I had to crowd it out of my mind. But I never wholly forgot the occasion. If I had completed it, I should have had to say: Design presupposes God. I did not then know that, at that moment, the finger of God was first laid upon my forehead." *Witness* (1952)

change: "A state without the means of some change," Burke wrote in his *Reflections on the Revolution in France* (1790), "is without the means of its conservation." And yet conservatism has long been associated with a defense of the status quo; is assumed to be inherently *resistant* to change. To what degree is this true? Only to the extent that changes proposed or implemented are focused upon short-term goals and/or ignore long-term consequences. Change is providential when it is an incremental, even evolutionary process of renewal. This a distinction noted by Oakeshott as between a politics of "repair" on the one hand and of "destruction and creation" on the other. On both a personal and a political level, change has always been understood as the deeper movement between being and becoming—as organic growth, which may be defined as change that maintains order. Change will actually be attractive to conservatism if it arises in continuity with what has gone before, and a basic difference between liberalism and conservatism is the liberal's assumption, in the words of Strauss (1968), "that on the whole change is change for the better, or progress." (And thus, he points out, *progressivism* is "a better term than liberalism for the opposite to conservatism.") However, change is inextricably wedded to that system of economic order most favored by conservatives, namely capitalism, and in economics at least change is the probable, if not the inevitable, partner of liberty. Read: R. Bendix, ed., *Embattled Reason* (1970); P. Marris, *Loss and Change* (1974); A. Toffler, *Future Shock* (1971). "The conservative is bewildered by the comprehensive dissatisfaction of people who are always headlong about 'reform' (as they conceive it) or are even eager to 'build a new society.' What, exactly, is wrong with society as it is already? We don't have the power to change everything, and it may not be such a bright idea to try; there are plenty of things that deserve the effort (and it *is* an effort) of preserving, and the undistinguishing mania for 'change' doesn't do them justice—isn't even *concerned* with doing them justice. What we really ought to ask the liberal, before we even begin addressing his agenda, is this: In what kind of society would he be a conservative?" Joseph Sobran, *Pensées* (1985)

Chesterton, G. K. (1874–1936): English man of letters, whose sense of life's complexity and contradictions led him to be known in his time as a "master of the paradox." He was a literary critic of the first order (and a radio personality of renown), and wrote books of lasting importance about Dickens, Shaw, and Browning, and a noteworthy treatment of the period, *The Victorian Age in Literature* (1913). His *Orthodoxy* (1908)—written more than a decade before his conversion to Catholicism—is a comprehensive view of the <u>conservative</u> approach to religious and social life. In it Chesterton argues that in life it is sensible to change anything, except our goals—what he termed "fixed ideals." His point being: so long as we hold to a single end, our failures to achieve it still move us closer to success; but if the goal keeps changing, all our failures are pointless. Chesterton also wrote a series of celebrated detective stories about the priest-sleuth Father Brown. He has the well-deserved reputation for being one of the wittiest men who ever lived, and he was rarely bested in riposte. One case in which he was bested happened when the gargantuan Chesterton ran into his cadaverous friend George Bernard Shaw (1856–1950) at a London restaurant: Chesterton: "To look at you, people would think there is a famine in England." Shaw: "And to look at you, they would think you were the cause of it." **Read:** *Orthodoxy* (1908); *The Everlasting Man* (1925); *The Man Who Was Thursday* (fiction, 1908); **About:** M. Coren, *Gilbert: The Man Who Was G. K. Chesterton* (1990); A. S. Dale, *The Outline of Sanity: A Life of G. K. Chesterton* (1982). **"Certain new theologians dispute original sin, which is the only part of Christian theology which can really be proved. . . . The strongest saints and the strongest skeptics alike took positive evil as the starting point of their argument. If it be true (as it certainly is) that a man can feel exquisite happiness in skinning a cat, then the religious philosopher can only draw one of two deductions. He must either deny the existence of God, as all atheists do; or he must deny the present union between God and**

man, as all Christians do. The new theologians seem to think it a highly rationalistic solution to deny the cat." *Orthodoxy* (1908)

Chicago School: The free-market economic theories (from about 1950 forward), sometimes (not quite properly) called **monetarism**, associated with Frank Knight (1885–1972), James Buchanan, **Friedman**, George Stigler and others who taught—and teach—at the University of Chicago. Like the founders of the **Austrian School**, Knight stressed the importance of human (behavioral), as opposed to "scientific," factors. The Chicago School concerns itself with empirical microeconomics. Through economic **liberty** we recognize the limits of human knowledge; in state planning we ignore those limits. Unlike the Austrians, Knight's view was not thoroughly **laissez-faire**; thus he was opposed to monopolies. Of the thirteen Americans who have won the Nobel Prize in economics, ten either taught at and/or were educated at Chicago. **Read:** F. Knight, *The Ethics of Competition* (1935); M. and R. Friedman, *Free to Choose* (1980); G. Stigler, *Memoirs of an Unregulated Economist* (1988), where Stigler writes: **"The emerging Chicago tradition [in industrial organization] . . . had three main facets. The first was that the goal of efficiency is pervasive in economic life, where efficiency means producing and selling goods at the lowest possible cost (and therefore at the largest possible profit). This goal is sought as vigorously by monopolists as by competitors, and monopoly power is of no value in explaining many phenomena which have efficiency explanations. . . . A second main theme . . . is that it is virtually impossible to eliminate competition from economic life . . . The combination of the shift in attention to efficiency, and the restoration of the powerful role of competition, has done much to weaken the arguments for an antitrust policy that seeks to deal with minor or transitory or (as in the case of vertical integration) erroneously identified monopolistic practices. . . . A third facet of the Chicago school's work was on the theory of public regulation . . . [which found] that no matter how disinterested the goal of public policy, the policy is bent to help politically influential groups at the cost of the less influential."**

Chodorov, Frank (1887–1966): American libertarian journalist and philosopher, and a disciple of **Nock**. Chodorov's early views were shaped in part by reading Henry George (founder of the single-tax-on-land movement in the 1870s), and he became director of the Henry George School of Social Science in New York City in 1937, and editor of its journal, the original *The Freeman* (see FEE). In 1944, he founded the journal *analysis*, and in 1953—to combat 1950s-style political correctness—the Intercollegiate Society of Individualists (of which twenty-eight-year-old William F. Buckley, Jr. was first president). ISI survives to this day as the Intercollegiate Studies Institute. Chodorov emphasized one aspect of libertarianism above all: individualism, which was both America's defining heritage and its best weapon against collectivism. However, Chodorov was uninterested in the communist threat abroad that weighed so heavily upon the minds of many conservatives, and remained staunchly isolationist throughout his life. His response to the specter of communists infiltrating the "federal" bureaucracy: "abolish the bureaucracy." **Read:** *Fugitive Essays* (1980); *One Is a Crowd* (1952); **About:** his own *Out of Step* (1962). **"The present disposition is to liquidate any distinction between the state and society, conceptually or institutionally. The state *is* society . . . In the operation of human affairs, despite the fact that lip service is rendered to the concept of inherent personal rights, the tendency to call upon the state for a solution to all the problems of life shows how far we have abandoned the doctrine of rights, with its correlative of self-reliance, and have accepted the state as the reality of society. It is this actual integration, rather than the theory, that marks the 20th century off from its predecessors."** "The Dogma of Our Times" in *Fugitive Essays* (1980)

Christian Right: The great sleeping giant of American politics, now awake. Although America is largely made up of Christians of various denominations, and although throughout American history there have been numerous instances of Christian political mobilization (the Abolition and Prohibition movements to name just two), it was not until the 1980s that a unified, nationwide, and conservative apparatus emerged as a (possibly) permanent force in American political life. This new movement, encompassing countless entities but nationally focused from 1989 forward in the Christian Coalition (see also **Robertson**), emerged as a result of realities both ancient and current: it was the traditional ministry of the Word wedded to modern satellite and computer technology. The Christian Coalition has largely supplanted the Moral Majority (founded by Jerry Falwell) of a decade earlier. Although largely Protestant, the Coalition has made common cause with Roman Catholics, and although its grass-roots character has led the media to portray it as a latter-day Know-Nothing movement, intellectuals such as **Neuhaus**, Avery Dulles, and William J. Bennett have supported and participated in its activities. The Coalition's ecumenism has also embraced Jews, and conservative Jewish writers such as Don Feder, Dennis Prager, and Michael Medved figure prominently in the literature of the Christian Right. When in 1993 the Coalition began an informational campaign concerning school-board elections in New York City, the American Civil Liberties Union called it the "the greatest civil liberties crisis" in the city's history. Such hyperbole clouds the Christian Right's reform agenda, which includes proposals for safe streets, strong families, effective schools, and **limited government**. Whether or not religious conservatives can find common cause with **libertarianism** (of the sort **Mencken** espoused) remains to be seen. **Read**: N. J. Cohen, ed., *The Fundamentalist Phenomenon* (1990); M. Cromartie, *No Longer Exiles* (1993); R. J. Neuhaus, *The Naked Public Square* (1984); R. Reed, *Politically Incorrect* (1994), where Reed writes: **"Religious conservatives want to move forward, not backward. They do not want to turn back the clock. They believe that many of the social advances of the past thirty years can and must be acknowledged and preserved. For example, the movement of women to a position of equality in the workplace where they can advance as far as their talents can carry them is clearly progress. The civil rights movement has brought minorities closer to full equality than at any time since the Civil War. Those who suggest that people of faith look nostalgically back to the 1950s and Ozzie and Harriet are mistaken."**

Churchill, Winston S. (1874–1965): British statesman and author, occasional **conservative**, and courageous leader of the free world in mid-century. Churchill's life, one of the most extraordinary ever, is a study in the necessary (anyway, *inevitable*) contradictions of public life. As **Nisbet** (1986) puts it: "To try to derive the ideology from the decisions and acts of even the greatest of politicians more often than not leads to confusion." Although he was a member of Britain's Conservative Party for most of his career, his views were often not congenial with theirs. He saw himself as the successor of **Disraeli**, and like him, Churchill was a believer in "Tory democracy," nationalism, and **free trade**. Early in the century he advocated the evolution of the Conservatives into a British version of the Republican Party in the U.S., as he put it, "rich, materialist, and secular," and, although he was often accused of radicalism early in his political career, it seems clear his reformist impulses were largely a reflection of his intense **anticommunism** and his desire to improve the conditions that he thought fostered it, and to thus maintain **order** in society and steal the socialist thunder. As Nisbet concludes, the authentic Churchill was "the Burkean Churchill, the Churchill of boundless devotion to landed property, to aristocracy, to monarchy, and empire." He is doubtless best described as an advocate of **classical liberalism**. A first-class writer (he received the Nobel Prize in 1953—partly for his histories of the English-speaking peoples and World War II, and partly for his stirring oratory), he was also a fine painter (in the Impressionist style), and a prodigious drinker. **Read:** *The Second World War* (1995); **About:** J. Charmley, *Churchill: The End of Glory* (1993); H. Jaffa, ed., *Statesmanship* (1981). **"The other day, President Roosevelt gave his opponent in the last Presidential Election a letter of introduction to me, and in it he wrote out a verse, in his own handwriting, from Longfellow, which he said, 'applies to you people as it does to us.' Here is the verse:**

. . . Sail on, O Ship of State!
Sail on, O Union, strong and great!
Humanity with all its fears,
With all the hopes of future years,
Is hanging breathless on thy fate!

What is the answer that I shall give, in your name, to this great man, the thrice-chosen head of a nation of a hundred and thirty millions? Here is the answer which I will give to President Roosevelt: Put your confidence in us. Give us your faith and your blessing, and, under Providence, all will be well. . . . We shall not fail or falter; we shall not weaken or tire. Neither the sudden shock of battle, nor the long-drawn trials of vigilance and exertion will wear us down. Give us the tools, and we will finish the job." Radio address of February 9, 1941, from *Blood, Sweat, and Tears* (1941)

classical liberalism: The (primarily) European view of a decentralized society that coalesced in the 19th century. It emphasized limited government and laissez-faire economics. It is not synonymous with the nascent liberality of certain classical thinkers, e.g., Plato, Aristotle, or Lucretius, and it bears little resemblance to modern-American "welfare" liberalism. On the Continent, this earlier liberalism was partly a response to Church authority, whereas in Britain it was chiefly concerned with secular jurisdictions, but wherever it appeared, it was simultaneously a view of religion, commerce, and politics more or less as follows: in religion, a separation of church and state (see antidisestablishmentarianism); in economics, free trade; in politics, democracy. Then as now, much of the rancor surrounding liberalism has to do with the degree to which it is accepted *in each sphere* by a given individual. Classical liberalism found incipient expression in Thomas Hobbes (1588–1679), who was no liberal. "The liberties of subjects," he wrote in *Leviathan* (1651), "depend on the silence of the law." He was, at best, a believer in the primacy of the individual. But it was his later contemporary, Locke, who is to liberalism what Burke is to conservatism, especially in his assertion that the contract between citizens and the state is based upon the consent of the governed. (Jefferson's "life, liberty, and the pursuit of happiness," is said to paraphrase Locke's "life, liberty, and estate.") But it fell to Mill to wed Lockean politics to classical economics (see also Smith). Mill made a distinction between individual liberty and republican participation—both aspects of liberalism—and clearly preferred the former. Thus Mill (with Tocqueville and Acton) asserted a liberalism quite distinct from its rationalist, Enlightenment cousin. The instrumentalism of Rousseau's version of Enlightenment liberalism evolved to become the "welfare" liberalism of today, and classical liberalism abides primarily as one version of conservatism, especially in America. Indeed, were it not for their attachment to faith and tradition, many contemporary conservatives might more accurately be described as classical liberals; some, like Hayek, steadfastly did so represent themselves. However, liberalism has long been precariously associated with the related idea of *liberation*. Beginning with L. T. Hobhouse and his 1911 book *Liberalism*, the movement has fought "free from the shackles of an individualist conception of liberty," and devoted much of its passion to collectivism and egalitarianism. Read: J. Gray, *Liberalism* (1986); H. Mansfield, *The Spirit of Liberalism* (1978); L. Strauss, *Liberalism: Ancient and Modern* (1968). "Liberalism is not averse to evolution and change; and where spontaneous change has been smothered by government control, it wants a great deal of change of policy. So far as much of current governmental action is concerned, there is in the present world very little reason for the liberal to wish to preserve things as they are. It would seem to the liberal, indeed, that what is most urgently needed in most parts of the world is a thorough sweeping-away of the obstacles to free growth. . . . The difference between liberalism and conservatism must not be obscured by the fact that in the United States it is still possible to defend individual liberty by defending long-established institutions. To the liberal they are valuable not mainly because they are long established or because they are American but because they correspond to the ideals which he cherishes." Friedrich A. Hayek, "Why I Am Not a Conservative" in *The Constitution of Liberty* (1960)

cold-war liberal: A term emerging in the 1950s and describing that group of individuals who espoused both liberalism (or classical liberalism) *and* anticommunism. Hook was the quintessential cold-war liberal, who—arguably—remained a liberal through the 1980s, but men such as Kristol and Podhoretz made a transit through cold-war liberalism before abandoning liberalism (as understood in its contemporary American sense) altogether. Read: S. Hook, *Out of Step* (1987), where he writes: "Most [leftist] critics of the pragmatic or Cold War liberals were . . . knowledgeable and intelligent . . . Their most persuasive arguments were directed against the existing evils within the United States—the disparities, in many areas from civil rights to urban housing, between the ideals of American democracy and its practices. To which we made a threefold response. First, it was possible to combine a vigorous activity to remedy existing evils within the United States by the politics of coalition and at the same time defend the institutional practices of the open society wherever it existed against Communist aggression. Second, our critics themselves, during the Second World War, found not the slightest incompatibility in supporting the conflict against fascism in all its varieties and in engaging in active reform movements. This was at a time when, relatively speaking, domestic conditions were far worse than in the period of the Cold War, at a time when materially and politically the status of labor and the ethnic minorities was much more deplorable. Third, we argued that the evidence was compelling that great gains had been achieved all along the line in the domestic life of the American people, despite the Cold War, and that the temporary setback resulting from McCarthy's demagogy had been overcome."

Coleridge, Samuel Taylor (1772–1834): English poet-philosopher of the romantic movement. Early a utopian—he and the poet Robert Southey (1774–1843) planned an ideal community in America (which they called a *pantisocracy*, and which they hoped would "make virtue inevitable")—Coleridge became friendly with William Wordsworth while the latter was still in the thrall of the French Revolution, and in 1798–1799, under Wordsworth's watchful eye, lived his "wonderful year," writing *The Rime of the Ancient Mariner*, part of *Christabel*, and *Kubla Khan*. Not so wonderful was his growing addiction to opium. With maturity, however, Coleridge became an opponent of radical democratic notions, and a proponent of religious authority in social and political life. He was a strong influence on Mill's movement away from the rationalism of Jeremy Bentham (1748–1832). But Coleridge lacked the "liberal" commercial spirit of Mill or Smith, and thought capitalists should be barred from voting, since theirs was a "pocketbook politics" that ignored both national and transcendent interests. **Read:** *The Constitution of Church and State* (1830); **About:** M. Perkins, *Coleridge's Philosophy* (1994). "The luminous faith and penetrating intelligence of Coleridge . . . became a chief force in the reinvigoration of British religious conviction . . . after its drubbing at the hands of 18th-century rationalism. . . . And he went farther: better even than Burke, he demonstrated that religion and politics are inseparable, that the decay of one must produce the decay of the other." Russell Kirk, *The Conservative Mind* (1953)

collectivism: See **communism, Marxism,** and **socialism**

Commentary: See **Podhoretz, Norman**

communism: The social philosophy that sought the revolutionary overthrow of **capitalism** through a dictatorship ("of the proletariat," which is akin to saying "by the people") with the end of creating a society in which everything would be owned in common. Although communism is sometimes said to have had its origins in Platonic thought, in "primitive Christianity," in Medieval monasticism, or in the **Enlightenment** writings of Rousseau, Babeuf, and Saint-Simon, it was Marx who deserves credit for defining the concept and being the inspiration for its propagation in the 20th century. *The Communist Manifesto* (1848), which Marx wrote with Friedrich Engels (1820–1895), promised class war to achieve a classless society. (For the **conservative** critique of Marx, see also **Marxism** and **socialism.**) It was V. I. Lenin (1870–1924), his successor Joseph Stalin (1879–1953), and the subsequent leaders of the USSR—until Mikhail Gorbachev (1931–   )—not to mention Mao Zedong (1893–1976) in China, who extended communism's hegemony throughout Eastern Europe, Asia, and Latin America. Few conservatives of past decades (see **anticommunism**) dared dream that the communist state would "wither away," as Marx promised it would—although, he believed, after a *successful* reign—and that only China and Cuba would remain steadfastly communist at the end of the century. **Read:** E. Lyons, *The Red Decade* (1970); A. Solzhenitsyn, *The Gulag Archipelago* (1974); A. Ulam, *The Communists* (1992). **"And, on bended knee, we give thanks to Providence for the transfiguration of Russia, thanks from those of us who lived to see it, and thanks to those, departed, who helped us to understand why it was right to struggle to sustain the cause of Western civilization."** William F. Buckley, Jr., "We Won" in *National Review* (November 23, 1991)

community: A basic (perhaps *the* basic) concept of political theory, but one often undervalued or even ignored. Its most primary meaning is of *families* residing in villages, towns, or cities and sharing a common government, culture, and history. Only secondarily does the word suggest a union of shared interests, ideas, or activities as in the "gay community" or the "academic community." From the **conservative** point of view, a true community is necessarily organic, rooted; and the modern "problem" is very much that of the petrified community, the rootless individual. (See also **alienation**.) The breaking down of **family** unity—and by extension the larger unities of community (in this case meaning town or neighborhood) and commonwealth—is seen in the absurdities of multiculturalism, in which "community" is defined by ever narrower characteristics, some a matter of genetics, others matters of will. The conservative view denies this rationalist basis of community, and rather insists that true community is not a matter of choice. Accordingly, the conservative view of community negates the idea of the contractual basis of society. Without civil society (community), **Burke** (1790) argued, "man could not by any possibility arrive at the perfection of which his nature is capable, nor even make a remote or faint approach to it." We have duties towards community—simply by being born into it—that have nothing to do with consent. **Read:** R. Nisbet, *The Quest for Community* (1953). **"Society is indeed a contract. Subordinate contracts for objects of mere occasional interest may be dissolved at pleasure—but the state ought not to be considered as nothing better than a partnership agreement in trade of pepper and coffee, calico or tobacco . . . to be taken up for a little temporary interest, and to be dissolved by the fancy of the parties. It is to be looked on with other reverence; because it is not a partnership in things subservient only to the gross animal existence of a temporary and perishable nature. It is a partnership in all science; a partnership in all art; a partnership in every virtue, and in all perfection. As the ends of such a partnership cannot be obtained in many generations, it becomes a partnership not only between those who are living, but between those who are living, those who are dead, and those who are to be born. Each contract of each particular state is but a clause in the great primaeval contract of eternal society. . ."** Edmund Burke, *Reflections on the Revolution in France* (1790)

II

The Jewish Tradition

by

Jacob Neusner

Classical Judaism, as set forth in the Hebrew Scriptures and as interpreted in the light of oral tradition by the sages of the Mishnah and the Talmud, defines the social order in profoundly conservative terms. As Hillel, the principal first-century Pharisaic master, put it, "If I am not for myself, who is for me? And when I am for myself [alone], what am I? And if not now, when?" His words echo the Judaic recognition of the God-given rights to life, liberty, and property; they assert an individual's right to defend himself and to retain his possessions; and they affirm that a man bears an obligation to the public interest. Conservatism is the opposite of radical privatism, not to mention of naked selfishness, whether by the rich or the poor. And Hillel emphasizes that the time for action is the present. Those who deny the legitimacy of self-interest will hardly derive satisfaction from Hillel's statement, which scarcely endorses socialism in any form. The laws of the Hebrew Scriptures, with their heavy emphasis on ownership rights and community obligations, express the same principle, only in massive detail. Judaism's essential assertion about the social order is simple and powerful: we are responsible for what we do.

The same document in which Hillel's saying occurs presents sayings that exhibit profound suspicion of natural man: "Pray for the welfare of government," says Hananiah, Prefect of the Priests. "For if it were not for fear of it, one man would swallow his fellow alive." At the same time, the sages take a hard-headed view of government itself. Shemaiah says, "Love work. Hate holding authority, and don't get friendly with the government." And still more to the point, Rabban Gamaliel says, "Be wary of the government, for they get friendly with a person only for their own convenience. They look like friends when it is to their benefit, but they do not stand by a person when he is in need." The philosophy of limited government surely finds itself in accord with these views.

Judaism is sometimes alleged to favor socialism, to condone homosexuality, to encourage the "entitlements" version of welfare, and to champion the abolition of capital punishment. Such views may indeed represent the attitudes of many liberal Jews, but the authoritative canon of Judaism sees matters otherwise. Take for example the oft-cited prophetic critique of injustice, as for instance in Psalm 82: "Uphold the cause of the weak and fatherless, and see right done to the afflicted and destitute." Apologists for the Left take this to indicate that ancient Israelite sentiment supports radical causes—from anarchism to confiscatory socialism—then and therefore also now. But justice for the prophets hardly corresponds with maudlin sympathy for those who, though they bear heavy burdens, deny responsibility for their reclamation. In fact, in the law of Scripture and in the Talmud all parties, rich and poor, are accorded the same justice.

And homosexuality? Yes, some Jews treat marriage as relative, not absolute, but those who would dismantle the family will find no support in Scripture, which insists upon heterosexual union alone. And long-term public support of those who will not work? Here again Scripture offers no sanction. For while Mosaic law does provide for upkeep of the poor (through gleanings and the "leaving of the corner of the field"), it also assumes that the poor will take action on their own initiative to first get the support supplied to them, and then to overcome poverty if and when it is possible. For the Talmud, public policy requires provision not of fish but of a fishing rod. As the great Maimonides (1135–1204) wrote in his *The Laws of Philanthropy*:

There are eight degrees of philanthropy, each one superior to the next. The highest degree, than which there is none higher, is the one who upholds the hand of an Israelite reduced to poverty by handing that person a gift or loan or by entering into a partnership with him or by finding . . . [him] work, in order to strengthen his hand, so that he will have no need to beg from others.

Here is no conception of entitlement.

Indeed, the prophetic appeal is to tradition and to the restoration of the revealed law of Sinai. No one of the prophets or sages of traditional Judaism may serve as a patron of the radical destruction of the social order, although each of them has been so characterized by the Left.

More to the point, it is the *stable* society—governed by God through the law of Moses and in consultation with the sages of the day—that emerges as the divine prescription for Israel, the kingdom of priests and holy people. That society, so ordained and so established, provided courts of justice and administration in order to secure fundamental rights: the rights to personal security and private property. So it is that, far from commanding pacifism and condemning capital punishment, Scripture supports the right to bear arms and the justice of the death penalty. On these and many other of today's conflicted causes, conservatives, not liberals, find the blessing of Jewish tradition.

This view of Judaism as essentially conservative will surprise those whose impression of contemporary Jews—secular, Reform, and even Conservative—is of the religious version of liberalism. A final point will help to dispel the illusion that Judaism is whatever individual Jews favor at a given moment rather than the Biblical and Talmudic tradition. The issue: abortion.

The organized Jewish community—the national institutions of Reform Judaism, as well as many secular Jewish organizations—maintain that a woman's right "to choose" (or "to control her own body") fully accords with "Judaism." But the canonical and authoritative writings take a different view. First, they maintain that, from the fortieth day, the fetus receives his soul and is fully human. Second, they hold that the unborn child possesses the single trait indicative of humanity: the fetus has an intellect and, therefore, can study the Torah. The following passage from the Babylonian Talmud is as explicit as it is beautiful:

Simlai gave the following exposition: "To what may the fetus be likened in the mother's womb? To a writing tablet that is folded up. . . . When it comes forth to the world's breathing space, what is closed is opened, and what is open is closed, for otherwise it could not live for even a single hour.

"A light flickers above its head, and it gazes and perceives from one end of the world to the other, as it is said, '. . . his lamp shined above my head, and by his light I walked through darkness.' (Job 29:3)

"And you have no time in a person's life so full of well-being as those days: 'O that I were as the months of old, as in the days when God watched over me." (Job 29:2) Now what are 'the days' that make up 'months' but not years? They are, of course, the months of pregnancy.

"And the fetus is taught the entire Torah, as it is said, 'And he taught me and said to me, Let your heart hold fast my words, keep my commandments and live' (Prov. 4:4), and it is said, 'When the converse of God was upon my tent.' (Job 29:4)

"As soon as the fetus comes out into the world's air, an angel comes and slaps it on the mouth and makes it forget the entire Torah: 'Sin crouches at the door.'" (Gen. 4:7)

It must follow that, since the fetus possesses intelligence, feticide (abortion) is the killing of a being with the same nature that makes infanticide or homicide murder. How, in light of such an exposition, Judaism can be represented as permitting, let alone favoring, abortion on demand I cannot say.

On a broad variety of issues that separate conservatism from liberalism, Judaism in its authoritative writings adopts one position after another congruent with conservatism in principle, viewpoint, and practice. Representations to the contrary signal the hijacking of the religion by secularists bent on using the authority of faith to buttress their positions.

Jacob Neusner is Distinguished Research Professor of Religious Studies, University of South Florida and Visiting Professor of Religion, Bard College. He is the author of numerous books, including *The Price of Excellence: Universities in Conflict During the Cold-War Era* (with Noam M. M. Neusner, 1995).

---

conservatism: Attempts to define conservatism have been numerous and somewhat elusive. The difficulty lies partly in the history of the "movement" and partly in the word itself. Of the word it may be said that to be **conservative** can mean two things: first, that one opposes rapid **change**; second, that one professes certain "conservative" beliefs. The distinction is (again *partly*) between *inclination* and *principle*, and while most principled conservatives are also conservative by inclination this does not mean (as is frequently asserted) that they are ipso facto defenders of the status quo—or of a status quo ante (see **reactionary**). Conservatism does not champion regnant conditions in society per se, although it surely does resist the rapid redesign of society. As Ambrose Bierce put it in his *Devil's Dictionary* (1911): "Conservative, *n*. A statesman who is enamored of existing evils, as distinguished from the Liberal, who wishes to replace them with others." **Kendall**'s definition of conservatism was simply resistance to the "Liberal Revolution," which was similar to **Viereck**'s "the revolt against the revolt," although there the similarities end. In both cases the subject is *modern* conservatism. It has been remarked that it is impossible to discern conservatism in politics before the Reformation, "not because there was none, but because there was nothing else." However, that particular conservatism—which amounted to a defense of feudalism—is not what Americans intend the word to signify. And while it is true, as **Kirk** (1982) observed, that in different eras and nations conservatives have thrived under "monarchical, aristocratic, despotic, and democratic regimes, and in a considerable range of economic systems," it remains true that American conservatism is wedded to **capitalism** and republican **democracy** (see also **repub-licanism**); not because that system satisfies the complete range of conservative principles and inclinations, but because no other system so dependably ensures individual **liberty**. Conservatism is said to have begun with **Burke** and his *Reflections on the Revolution in France* (1790) on the excesses of the *philosophes'* **rationalism** (or, as he called it, "speculatism"). For Burke the status quo was inherently preferable to over-hasty, violent change, but, again, that was less an embrace of present circumstances than a rejection of uncertain consequences. In politics from Burke forward, conservatism's emphasis has not been simply on the maintenance of existing governmental and other structures as much as it has been on the effort to ensure that those structures are limited in their diversity and power, and that individuals (in families, communities, and associations) remain largely in control of their own lives. (See **individualism**, **family**, **community**.) Indeed, **limited government** may be said to be conservatism's first principle; in so far, that is, as conservatism is viewed as a political philosophy. A more extensive list of "conservative verities" is offered by **Nisbet** (1986): "a minimal state, a strong but unobtrusive government, **laissez-faire** in most matters, family, neighborhood, local community, church and other mediating groups to meet most crises, decentralization, localism, and a preference for tradition and experience over rationalist planning, and withal an unconquerable prejudice against redistributionist measures." In economics, conservatism is most often indistinguishable from **classical liberalism**. From the **Enlightenment** forward, there has been a split on the **Right** between those whose sense of **tradition** demands strong government (where appropriate) and those whose absolutist sense of liberty demands a minimalist, caretaker state (see **libertarianism**). **Read:** S. Francis, *Beautiful Losers* (1993); R. Kirk, *The Conservative Mind* (1953); R. A. Nisbet, *Conservatism*; P. Viereck, *Conservatism Revisited* (1949). **"(1) Belief in a transcendent order, or body of natural law, which rules society as well as conscience. . . . (2) Affection for the proliferating variety and mystery of human existence, as opposed to the narrowing uniformity, egalitarianism, and utilitarian aims of most radical systems . . . (3) Conviction that civilized society requires orders and classes, as against the notion of a 'classless society.' . . . (4) Persuasion that freedom and property are closely linked . . . (5) Faith in prescription and distrust of 'sophisters, calculators, and economists' who would reconstruct society upon abstract designs. . . . (6) Recognition that change may not be salutary reform: hasty innovation may be a devouring conflagration, rather than a torch of progress."** Russell Kirk, *The Conservative Mind* (1953)

conservative: The word has two primary meanings: the disposition to preservation (and/or resistance to **change**); and one who espouses the principles of **conservatism**. Tertiary meanings emphasize tendencies to caution, as in "conservative estimates of the cost . . . ," or to

tradition, as in "Roy's a conservative in manners and dress . . ." *Conservatism* at least suggests some intellectual substance and may even imply a philosophical unity, but *conservative* is a word so fluid as to be bereft of predictable meaning. Thus, as the Cold War died, the news media often reported that skepticism about Mikhail Gorbachev's reforms was equally strong among Soviet conservatives and American conservatives. One word was thus used to "define," at least in part, two groups whose intentions could not have been more dissimilar: the so-called conservative in Russia sought to resuscitate **communism**, whereas the American conservative aspired to kill it. Like so many words that deal with political concepts, *conservative* almost certainly comes to us from the French. In the 1820s the Vicomte de Chateaubriand (1768–1848) and F. R. de Lamennais (1782–1854) founded the journal *Le Conservateur* to oppose revolutionary forces, and Chateaubriand is generally credited with coining the term as a political adjective. During the 1830s England's Tory party began calling itself conservative, and in America the word began to have currency after 1850. In their erstwhile heyday, liberals made great sport of the word; a conservative was: "[a] sickly, weak, timid man [who] fears the people" (**Jefferson**); "a tame man" (Henry David Thoreau); "a man who just sits and thinks, mostly sits" (Woodrow Wilson); "a man with two perfectly good legs who has never learned to walk" (Franklin D. Roosevelt); "a paper tiger" (Mao Zedong). Frankly, conservatives probably should have—despite the enduring and distinguished history of the usage—long ago dumped the word in favor of "Burkean." **Read**: R. Kirk, *The Conservative Mind* (1953); F. A. Hayek, *The Constitution of Liberty* (1960). **"It is with infinite caution that any man ought to venture upon pulling down an edifice which has answered in any tolerable degree for ages the common purposes of society, or on building it up again without having models and patterns of approved utility before his eyes."** Edmund Burke, *Reflections on the Revolution in France* (1790)

Constant de Rebecque, **Benjamin** (1767–1830): Swiss-born French philosopher of **classical liberalism**, and the lover of Madame de Staël ("I am not the rose, but I have lived with her."). Constant's mature work was largely a sustained attack on Rousseau's notion of a General

Will. That doctrine led inevitably to dictatorship, and Constant—contrasting ancient and modern conceptions of <u>liberty</u>—argued instead the virtues of <u>republicanism</u>. In this he influenced <u>Tocqueville</u>. Read: *Adolphe*, a novel (1815); **About**: B. Fontana, *Benjamin Constant* (1991). **"Every time the government attempts to handle our affairs, it costs more and the results are worse than if we had handled them ourselves."** *Cours de Politique Constitutionnelle* (1818)

constitution: The written or unwritten rules that govern the political organization of a society. A constitution necessarily includes some definition of its component parts, and therefore implies (if it does not in fact specify) the independence of those parts. True constitutions are accordingly documents of <u>limited government</u> and reflect the assumptions of <u>natural law</u>. (False constitutions, such as the one that governed the USSR, are false precisely because the defined government's constituent parts are de facto *not* independent, despite what the de jure document proclaims.) Thus a constitution fulfills Aristotle's view of a government based upon laws not men, and refutes Rousseau's belief that the "general will" cannot be limited. As <u>Rossiter</u> put it (1955): "Every constitution is both a grant of power and a catalogue of limitations; the best constitutions lay stress on the second of these purposes." The great constitutional period came in the century between England's Glorious Revolution (1688) and the ratification of the American Constitution (1788). In each case, a principal concern of the constitution makers was the "rule of law"; that the use of power be neither absolute nor arbitrary; and that a state's powers be controlled through a separation of its functions. The British constitution is unwritten, and has developed through the force of <u>tradition</u>, both cultural and judicial, whereas in the United States the Constitution is written. Although they largely based their document on that British tradition, the American Framers believed—largely as a result of various arbitrary Acts of Parliament—that specific, written limitations upon state power had been proved to be necessary. They further believed that history demonstrates that <u>democracy</u> may also be an occasion for the exercise of absolute and arbitrary power (see <u>Madison</u>'s arguments in *The Federalist*, Nos. 10 and 19), and so they built in structural restraints not only on the state but on the people as well. Peculiar to the American Constitution is the Bill of Rights, which at the time of the Founding some "conservatives" opposed; **Hamilton** in particular thought them unnecessary. "Why," he asked, "declare that things shall not be done which there is no power to do? Why, for instance, should it be said that the liberty of the press shall not be restrained when no power is given by which restrictions may be imposed?" And since no list of "rights" could hope to be complete, Hamilton worried that those rights not listed would come to be considered unimportant. **Read:** W. Kendall and G. Carey, *The Basic Symbols of the American Political Tradition* (1970); R. Kirk, *The Conservative Constitution* (1990); Harvey C. Mansfield, *America's Constitutional Soul* (1991), where he writes, **"Constitutionalism . . . faces a dilemma that helps explain the condition of democratic souls today. On the one hand, limited, constitutional government requires that the people and society be independent and distrustful of the state. . . . They must be able to feel that they control government rather than the reverse. But on the other hand, if the people feel themselves independent and capable of ruling themselves, what prevents them from extending their sense of responsibility, not merely to the behavior, but to the souls of others? . . . [O]ne can infer that the desire to rule others derives from the desire to rule oneself, so that there is something dangerous to liberty in the responsible individual. It is better . . . that he should stick to his interest and forget about his soul. But then . . . your interest can make you the servant of whoever serves your interest, leaving you dependent and apathetic and suffering under the false consciousness that being a free rider is the same as being free. Constitutionalism demands a people that is independent, but not so much as to think itself capable of governing without a constitution; it needs a sense of responsibility that is aware of the limits to responsibility."**

Cooper, James Fenimore (1789–1851): American novelist of enduring popularity and arguable skill. He wrote no fiction before the age of thirty, at which point (after commenting to his wife about a book they'd just read together, "I believe I could write a better story than that"), he proceeded to produce a book a year until his death three decades later. Mark Twain famously titled one of his essays, "Why Mr. Fenimore Cooper Can't Write," claiming that Cooper had no idea how to create characters or write dialogue. Cooper was a critic of Jacksonian **democracy**, which he considered "mobocracy," and a defender of America's landed "aristocracy," which he considered essential to the nation's stability. (Still, he voted for Jackson.) He did not believe that this virtuous aristocracy was a matter of primogeniture, but would be a class of gentlemen, educated, independent, and public-spirited. He was an heir of the Founders' **conservatism**, and very much echoed **Madison** when he warned (1838) that "the true theater of a demagogue is a democracy"; and, "Perfect and absolute liberty is as incompatible with the existence of society, as equality of condition." According to Robert Penn Warren (in Kronenberger, 1965), Cooper was the literary/philosophical precursor of William Faulkner since both offer "rebuke to what Faulkner calls the world of 'manipulators of money and politics and land' and to those who, corrupted by the 'abstractions' of civilization, deny reverence before nature and compassion toward man." **Read:** *The American Democrat* (1838); **About:** R. Long, *James Fenimore Cooper* (1990); D. Ringe, *James Fenimore Cooper* (1988). **"The secret of all enterprise and energy exists in the principle of individuality. Wealth does not more infallibly beget wealth, than the right to the exercise of our faculties, begets the desire to use them. The slave is every where indolent, vicious and abject; the freeman, active, moral and bold. It would seem that is the best and safest, and consequently the wisest Government, which is content rather to protect than direct the National prosperity, since the latter system never fails to impede the efforts of that individuality which makes men industrious and enterprising. . . . Herein, as it appears to me, is to be traced the real motive of that glaring unwillingness, to allow the natural effects of the unprecedented liberty in America, which one must be blind not to see has taken root in the feelings of most of our Eastern politicians. The American, himself, . . . is derided because he cannot bring his wishes to the level of the snail paced and unnatural progress of European Society . . . [which is] so heavily cumbered . . . with artificial restrictions."** *Notions of the Americans* (1828)

Cram, Ralph Adams (1863–1942): American author/architect (exponent of the neo-Gothic style—in architecture if not also in politics) who designed New York City's Cathedral of St. John the Divine, and whose **conservative** philosophy was a major influence on **Nock**. Cram designed St. John the Divine to be huge—only St. Peter's in Rome is bigger—in order that it make a "great showing" and be a reminder "that religion is . . . the very essence of human life and that any community that disregards it will disintegrate . . ." In one famous essay, "Why We Do Not Behave Like Human Beings," Cram demolished the idea of human perfectibility. He was more than a little **reactionary**, believing the **Constitution** ought to be amended so that the president would be elected by state governors and anyone not owning real estate would be denied suffrage. A convert to Roman Catholicism, Cram was unashamedly nostalgic for the Middle Ages, and would happily have banished from American life **democracy**, the printing press, and the automobile. **Read:** *The End of Democracy* (1937); **About:** R. Muccigrosso, *American Gothic: The Mind and Art of Ralph Adams Cram* (1981). **"The first law in the Book of Man is inequality. Individuals vary in intelligence, character, capacity for doing one thing or another, and well or ill, far more than they do in their physical characteristics. . . . Any society that does not recognize this and attempts to liquidate this disparity can last but a short time and is bound to quick dissolution after a sad and unsavoury record. . . . Where status is eliminated, caste takes its place and democracy is no longer attainable."** *The End of Democracy* (1937)

Davidson, Donald (1893–1968): American writer and critic whose work influenced a generation of Southern conservatives, including **Weaver**, through his teaching at Vanderbilt University and through his contribution to *I'll Take My Stand* (Ransom et al. 1930). (See also **Southern conservatism.**) Like his teacher and friend **Ransom**, Davidson came to see agrarianism as perhaps too wedded to "moonlight and magnolias," yet still believed that, against the industrialism and statism that seemed to him to be taking hold of American life, the "cause of the South was and is the cause of Western civilization." In *The Attack on Leviathan: Regionalism and Nationalism in the*

United States (1938)—which was recently reprinted by publishers who perversely switched title and subtitle—Davidson attacked the notion of a "Great Society" (keep in mind that this was nearly thirty years before President Johnson used the term) as "motivated ultimately by men's desire for economic welfare of a specific kind rather than their desire for personal liberty." Davidson asserted (after Frederick Jackson Turner), with conviction but not always convincingly, that regionalism (or *sectionalism*) is a significant extra-constitutional factor in American life. He advocated the emergence of regional planning commissions and sectional artistic movements as weapons in an effort to uncover "what politicians and economists have ignored," namely that many Americans were worn out with "abstraction and novelty, plagued with divided counsels . . . [and] have said: I will believe the old folks at home, who have kept alive through many treacherous outmodings some good secret of life." **Read:** *Regionalism and Nationalism in the United States* (1991); **About:** T. D. Young, *Donald Davidson* (1971). **". . . [O]ver and above all . . . bonds of unity, it is necessary to understand that we are a diverse people, and that we cannot exist as a nation but as a sectionally diverse people. . . . No Leviathan state can ever abolish sectionalism, unless like Tamerlane it proposes to rule from a pyramid of skulls. . . . What a Leviathan state might do, by too strenuous generalizations and applications of power, would be to provoke a sectional reaction so severe as to bring civil conflict; or else, not being able to deliver on its own promises, it might fall into such weakness and loss of prestige that it could no longer govern . . ." *The Attack on Leviathan* (1938)**

Declaration of Independence: The document by which America's newly united states justified to the "candid world" their separation from the Great Britain of King George III (Parliament is not mentioned), announcing that henceforth America would be, "and of Right ought to be, FREE AND INDEPENDENT STATES" without allegiance to any external, earthly power. (The Declaration was only a justification; a more straightforward proclamation of independence was approved by the Continental Congress two days earlier.) Written principally by <u>Jefferson</u>, the Declaration is a monument to the <u>En-lightenment</u> version of <u>natural law</u> (especially as derived from <u>Locke</u>

and, for that matter, from Isaac Newton), i.e., **natural rights**: its truths are "self-evident"; the rights it asserts are "unalienable" (a scribe's miscopying of *inalienable*) because given by God and known through knowledge of human nature; the government it conjures (but does not define, except to imply that it is limited in power) is based upon consent (or *assent*). The Declaration also presents an original (and, for the future of America, essential) theory of **federalism**: that Great Britain was a *voluntary* union of independent polities. (In effect, the Declaration is an ordinance of nullification. See **Calhoun**.) The Declaration differs from other colonial appeals, most made in the name of English legal **tradition**, primarily in its universalism, which was important, both tactically and philosophically, as an appeal to the approbation of the French. The Declaration is primarily remembered (perhaps properly so) for the phrases "all men are created equal" and "the pursuit of happiness." How an American reads those words says much about his philosophy. In both cases, Jefferson was expounding not only Locke but his fellow Virginian, George Mason, whose Virginia Declaration of Rights had just a month before asserted the familiar triad plus "the Means of acquiring and possessing Property." Jefferson's original draft in fact included the modifier "and independent" (as in "equal and independent"), which went a long way towards making clear the document's distance from modern **egalitarianism**. The narrow, egalitarian view of the Declaration is what led **Santayana** to fear it had become a "salad of illusions." But Jefferson *was*, to a degree, a rationalist. In his equivalence of the "Laws of Nature" and "of Nature's God," in the words of Becker (1922), Jefferson "deified Nature" so he could "dismiss the Bible." Still Jefferson believed that Man needed to be "bound down," as he later said, by a **constitution**. He may have admired **rationalism**; he did not espouse **positivism**. **Read:** W. Kendall and G. Carey, *The Basic Symbols of the American Political Tradition* (1970). "The [American] Revolution, because it was conceived as essentially affirming the British constitution, did not create the kind of theoretical vacuum made by some other revolutions. . . . The colonial situation, it would seem, had provided a *ne plus ultra* beyond which political theorizing did not need to range. Even Jefferson, the greatest and most influential theorist of the Revolution, remained loath to trespass that boundary, except under pressure: the pressure of a need to create a new federal structure. Mainly in the realm of federalism were new expedients called for. And no part of our history is more familiar than the story of how the framers of the federal Constitution achieved a solution: by compromise on details rather than by agreement on a theory." Daniel Boorstin, *The Genius of American Politics* (1953)

Decter, Midge (1927–   ): See **Podhoretz, Norman**

democracy: That system of government in which the people at large—in shifting majorities—are at **liberty** to rule. Thus stated, the concept remains extremely fluid, and has been applied to systems as diverse as anarchy and autocracy. Conservatives have rarely been completely comfortable with the democratic process, fearing that waves of contemporary passion may lead to imprudent assaults upon **tradition**. (Do we really want a show of hands about the Ten Commandments?) Thus John **Adams** believed, "There never was a democracy that did not commit suicide." In ancient Greece, *demokratia* meant that all citizens (male property holders) participated directly in decision making, but such a scheme was (and is) feasible only in small states—if then. In the **Enlightenment**, Rousseau's notion of a democratic "general will" became the principal justification for later totalitarianism: "Each of us puts his person and all of his power under the supreme direction of the general will . . ." (*Social Contract*, 1762). Dictatorships calling themselves democracies construe their policies as necessarily representing "popular" intent. In the American experience, democracy has always been *representative* rather than plebiscitary; *limited* rather than absolute. (Exceptions are the almost mythical New England town meeting, and Separatist communities such as the Shakers, Quakers, and Amish.) The distinction is therefore made between a democracy and a republic (see **republicanism**). It was the view of **Madison** that the danger of democracy lay in the potential for majoritarian dominance: "Pure democracies have ever been spectacles of turbulence and contention." Accordingly he helped to craft a constitutional system that established representation, separation of powers, and checks and balances—together designed to prevent both autocracy *and* unrestrained democracy. At its best, democracy is a political statement about *participation*; it says that all adult citizens ought to have a say in the process of governing; is an assertion of **natural rights**. And it is, to a degree, the political analogue of the free market in economics; that process through which the "best," if not necessarily the true, emerges through competition, and in which minorities may succeed in capturing majority allegiance. On the other hand, the "worst" may be on an equal footing with the best, unless undemocratic restraints are imposed and accepted. **Read**: J. Burnham, *The Machiavellians* (1943); J. Schumpeter, *Capitalism, Socialism and Democracy* (1962). "**Democracy, though slowly attained and never by revolutionary jumps, is the best government on earth when it tries to make all its citizens aristocrats. But not when it guillotines whoever is individual, superior, or just different.**" Peter Viereck, *Conservatism Revisited* (1949)

Dickinson, John (1732–1808): American lawyer/patriot (educated at Britain's Middle Temple) whose *Letters from a Farmer in Pennsylvania* (1767–1768) made a case for American independence from Britain along lines that might have pleased **Burke**. In opposition to the Townshend Acts, which placed duties on various products sent to the colonies, Dickinson argued that such laws denied to Americans the traditional rights of Englishmen. Dickinson was a member of the Stamp Act Congress and the Continental Congress (although he refused to sign the **Declaration of Independence**), fought in the Revolution, drafted the Articles of Confederation, and was a delegate (from Delaware) to the Convention that drafted the **Constitution**. At that last gathering he warned the assembled: "Experience must be our only Guide. Reason may mislead us." It was Dickinson who proposed the character of America's bicameral legislature. **Read**: *Letters from a Farmer in Pennsylvania* (1769); **About**: M. E. Bradford, *A Better Guide Than Reason* (1979); M. Flower, *John Dickinson* (1983). "**It was Dickinson—a devotee of Montesquieu—who came up with an approach [to achieving republican restraint upon democracy] that was theoretically sound, practically sound, and tailored to American realities.... In thinking about devising structural substitutes for the English baronies, Dickinson alone had perceived that the United States already had institutional substitutes in the form of individual states—which, in a manner of speaking, were permanent**

and hereditary. He therefore proposed a mixed system, partly national and partly federal, in which one branch of Congress would 'be drawn immediately from the people' and the other would represent the states as states and be elected by the state legislatures for long terms, 'through such a refining process as will assimilate it as near as may be to the House of Lords in England.' This combination of state governments with a strong national government, he added, was 'as politic as it was unavoidable.'" Forrest McDonald, *Novus Ordo Seclorum* (1985)

Disraeli, Benjamin (1804–1881): English statesman and writer; prime minister of Great Britain briefly in 1868 and then from 1874 until 1880. Disraeli was a study in contrasts, both a **conservative** and a radical, a Christian and a Jew, an artist and a politician, an aspiring aristocrat (who became Lord Beaconsfield) and a champion of the working class. He had the anti-rationalist prejudices of **Burke**, whom he esteemed, and he despised the reformers who tried "to form political institutions on abstract principles of theoretic science, instead of permitting them to spring from the course of event." But like his mentor **Coleridge**, he also distrusted **capitalism**. His political life began as a Radical candidate for election to Parliament. Defeated, he switched to the Tory party, and was defeated three more times. When finally elected in 1837, be began to rise steadily through party ranks. He is often called the "founder of the modern Conservative Party in Britain." Paradoxically, the aristocratic, romantic, and traditionalist Disraeli was responsible for the passage of the democratic Reform Acts (of 1867 and 1874), which are sometimes misinterpreted as radical, but which in fact were no more than an effort to "trim his sails to the 'liberal wind'" (Blake, 1966). Thus it was that **Bagehot** largely despised him, but **Chambers** liked to espouse what he called the "Beaconsfield position," i.e., that **conservatism** must be politically pragmatic if it is to achieve any of its public agenda. **Read:** *Tancred* (a novel, 1847); **About:** Robert Blake, *Disraeli* (1966). Blake writes: "It is easy to underestimate Disraeli's innate conservatism. He believed passionately in the greatness of England—not in itself a Tory monopoly. But he also believed no less deeply that England's greatness depended upon the ascendancy of the landed class. All the rest was 'leather and prunella.' This does not mean that he wished to set class against class. On the contrary he proclaimed the doctrine of one nation and asserted that if the Conservative party was not a national party it was nothing. But he did sincerely think the nation would decline with the decline of the landed interest. Like Gladstone he was 'an out-and-out inequalitarian.' He believed in a hierarchical ladder which certainly should not be inaccessible to men of talent—after all he was himself a marvelous example of successful climbing—but which should on no account be laid flat or broken or removed. He thought that under such a dispensation people of all classes would enjoy greater freedom and happiness that they would get under the dead hand of a centralizing Benthamite bureaucracy, however 'democratic.' "

Eastman, Max (1883–1969): American intellectual and writer who, as editor of *The Masses* (1913–17) and *Liberator* (1918–23) was an eloquent proponent of *Marxism*, but who broke—and was among the first to break—with **communism**. (His scorching *Since Lenin Died* came out in 1925.) Eventually he spent time as an editor of both *National Review* and *Reader's Digest*. His more libertarian (even libertine) and anti-religious views led to a break with *National Review*, and finally to a kind of intellectual homelessness, since he had earlier voiced support for **McCarthyism**, and so moved beyond the pale among his former liberal comrades. As a biographer unsympathetic to Eastman's political development put it, "no one would take him seriously except conservatives, which did not help him, since American intellectual life is dominated by liberals" (O'Neill, 1978). Eastman was a literary critic of the highest order, and increasingly reacted against the trend in **modernism** to obscurantism, attacking among others **Eliot**, Ezra Pound, and **Ransom**. Read: *Reflections on the Failure of Socialism* (1955); About: His own *Love and Revolution* (1965). " 'Man,' [Marx] said, 'is a complex of social relations . . . The individual has no real existence outside the milieu in which he lives.' By which he meant: *Change the social relations, change the milieu, and man will change as much as you like.* 'All history,' he added, 'is nothing but a continual transformation of human nature.' . . . That is all Marx ever said on this primary, and in a scientific mind, preliminary, question. And Lenin . . . said nothing. That is why their dream turned into a nightmare. That is the rock-bottom reason. Their scheme was amateur—and worse than amateur, mystical—on the very subject most essential to its success." *Reflections on the Failure of Socialism* (1955)

egalitarianism: That doctrine—anathema to **conservatism**—that interprets American **tradition** (or simply human progress) as demanding the evolution of society towards both equality of opportunity *and* equality of outcome. In the doctrines of the New Age, egalitarianism can even assert an essential equality among Men and ideas, as in the sophomoric proposition: "My opinion is just as good as any other." It is very much a fundamental tenet of conservatism that equality does not exist in the real world; therefore, that it ought not to be an end sought by public policy; that, indeed, if it becomes such an end, the consequences of such policies will be disastrous. (See **affirmative action**.) The lesson of **empiricism** is clear: justice, which is the stated rationale of egalitarianism (although its deeper source is probably envy), actually presupposes inequality: some are simply smarter, more talented, harder working, and less guilty than others. True, all Men are equally members of a single species, and each is deserving of a presumptive equality before God and the law, but there it ends. Political and religious philosophy have always asserted an essentially pacific and egalitarian "state of nature," whether in Eden or in the moment before the Big Bang, and they have never ceased trying to comprehend the Fall (see **sin**). The most common response—the **conservative** one—has been the embrace of **order**, and with it of hierarchy, in the most basic sense of good over evil, of virtue over sin. Less persuasive, but more visibly popular in the last three centuries, has been the response of liberal **utopianism**, which, despite its secular language, is really the search for the way back to Eden. But if all actually were equal, we would have to enforce inequality, since otherwise no organization, institution, or diversification would be possible. **Read:** I. Kristol, *Two Cheers for Capitalism* (1978). "**The equality of the Declaration is the equality to which, say, Abraham Lincoln was born—an equality that conferred upon him merely an equal right to compete . . . Not so the egalitarianism of the Liberals. It must pick Lincoln up at dawn in a yellow bus**

with flashing lights . . . feed him a free lunch, educate him for democracy, protect him from so-called concentrations of social and economic power, eke out his income by soaking the rich, doctor him, hospitalize him, and, finally, social work him—if, as he probably will now, he turns into a juvenile delinquent. Equality . . . encourages him to become self-reliant; egalitarianism encourages him to learn to play the angles." Willmoore Kendall, *The Conservative Affirmation* (1985)

Eliot, T. S. (1888–1965): Anglo-American poet-playright-essayist, author of *The Waste Land* (1922), and winner of the 1948 Nobel Prize for literature. Eliot's poetical work, full of a sense of the hollowness of modernity, looked back three centuries for its antecedents to the metaphysical poetry of John Donne, George Herbert, Andrew Marvell, et al. In this, as in many other matters, he was much influenced by Ezra Pound. (The "Men of 1914"—Pound, Eliot, James Joyce, and Wyndham Lewis—were all paradoxically modernist *and* **conservative**. See **modernism**.) At least from *Ash-Wednesday* (1930) on, Eliot's writing was characterized by the embrace of both religious and political orthodoxies. He liked to call himself a classicist in art, a royalist (or a **reactionary**) in politics, and "Anglo-Roman Catholic" in **faith**. **Kirk** (1953) wrote that Eliot is this century's principal conservative thinker. "Eliot's whole endeavor was to point a way out of the Waste Land toward order in the soul and in society." **Read:** *Collected Poems: 1909–1962* (1963); *For Lancelot Andrewes* (1928); *Notes Towards a Definition of Culture* (1948); **About:** P. Ackroyd, *T. S. Eliot* (1984); H. Kenner, *The Invisible Poet* (1960); R. Kirk, *Eliot and His Age* (1988). "If the lost word is lost, if the spent word is spent/If the unheard, unspoken/Word is unspoken, unheard;/Still is the unspoken word, the Word unheard/The Word without a word, the Word within/The world and for the world;/And the light shone in the darkness and/Against the Word the unstilled world still whirled/About the centre of the silent Word." from *Ash-Wednesday* (1930)

empiricism: Traditionally the philosophical belief that all knowledge is based upon experience. As Thomas Aquinas wrote (after Aristotle): "There is nothing in the intellect which is not first in the senses." Empiricism is thus opposed to **rationalism**, which holds that knowledge is based upon reason. Although **conservatism** is essentially hostile to rationalism, a **conservative** embrace of empiricism may be limited to a *method* of political analysis; to the belief that the experiences embodied in **prescription** and **tradition** are better mediators of political decisions than rationalist intervention. Thus **Oakeshott** (1962) emphasized that "empiricism by itself is not a concrete manner of activity," and requires a tradition (he uses the word "ideology"). As **Hume**, empiricism's founder, put it, the rationalism he opposed is a "catechism which [in setting] out the purposes to be pursued merely abridges a concrete manner of behaviour in which those purposes are already hidden." And **Burke** always emphasized his preference for custom over history, and experience over theory. **Read:** Michael Oakeshott, *Rationalism in Politics* (1962). Oakeshott writes: **"The understanding of politics as the activity of attending to the arrangements of a society under the guidance of an independently premeditated ideology is ... no less a misunderstanding than the understanding of it as a purely empirical activity. And in an attempt to improve upon this understanding of politics, we have already observed in principle what needs to be recognized in order to have an intelligible concept. Just as scientific hypothesis cannot appear, and is impossible to operate, except within an already existing tradition of scientific investigation, so a scheme of ends for political activity appears within, and can be evaluated only when it is related to, an already existing tradition of how to attend to our arrangements. In politics, the only concrete manner of activity detectable is one in which empiricism and the ends to be pursued are recognized as dependent, alike for their existence and operation, upon a traditional manner of behaviour."**

Enlightenment: Also called the Age of Reason (in France, *Le Siècle des Lumières*) and comprising most of the 18th century. (It might be said to have begun with the death of Louis XIV in 1715—or even with the English Revolution of 1688—and to have ended with the publication of **Burke**'s *Reflections on the Revolution in France* in 1790.) *Reason* in this context meant human speculation unguided by experience or **prescription**; the a priori assumption toppling the a posteriori **tradition**; agnosticism defrocking **faith**. (See also **empiri-**

cism, humanism, natural law, and rationalism.) The Enlightenment's precursors were English (Thomas Hobbes, Locke, and Isaac Newton), but the Germans were the first to use the term (*Aufklärung*). Immanuel Kant (1724–1804) answered his own question, "What Is Enlightenment?" by describing the movement as "man's emergence from his nonage." Although Europe had hardly been immature prior to this time, Kant's sense—almost of an awakening—was shared by most of the *philosophes*. Denis Diderot (1713–1784), writing in his *Encyclopédie*, written over three decades from 1751, captured the spirit of the age: "Everything must be examined, everything must be shaken up, without exception and without circumspection." Above all the Enlightenment believed in progress—that every innovation was an improvement. Radical in many ways, the Enlightenment was nonetheless the period in which the idea of individual liberty came to dominate Western political thinking. A sequential dissolution of French Enlightenment thought is represented in the edifying balance of Montesquieu, the brilliant indifference of Voltaire, and finally the demented fanaticism of Rousseau. On the other hand, the Scottish Enlightenment produced Hume, Smith, and Walter Scott. For the alienated Rousseau, emphasis on the rights of individuals was not balanced by a parallel stress on personal responsibility. He was radically egalitarian, and thought that Man's "state of nature" implied an innate perfectibility. Whether or not he was himself a totalitarian (he did observe that Man must be "forced to be free"), Rousseau's work gave inspiration to the egalitarianism and despotism of the French and later revolutions. Rousseau's brand of modernism has provided conservatism with much of its reactionary content. As Hannah Arendt observed (1966), the Enlightenment "meant nothing more or less than that from then on Man, and not God's command or the customs of history, should be the source of Law." Read: P. Johnson, *Intellectuals* (1988). "Enlightenment rationalism was a remarkable, and remarkably intolerant, tradition of thought because it was a combination of classical and modern elements. It combined two famous conceptions of reason. The first was the classical reason which, after the manner of Plato, was a faculty deemed capable of discovering the only right and natural order of human life. The second was the modern conception of reason as a limited instrument for exploring an alien world, and in particular, for finding means for the attaining of whatever ends the passions might suggest. This was the type of reason described by Hobbes as a scout to spy out the land, and by Hume as a slave of the passions. From the first conception of reason, the revolutionaries of the Enlightenment derived a total certainty about their opinions; from the second, they derived the propensity to believe that technology (including the technologies of government and education) can solve all problems. The shock, as well as the excitement, generated by the French revolution corresponded to the unveiling of what this combination might achieve." Kenneth Minogue, *Alien Powers: The Pure Theory of Ideology* (1985)

extremism: A term that gained media currency during the presidential election of 1964 and that refers to the role in that year's campaign of ideas thought to be outside the American mainstream. In his acceptance speech at the Republican nominating convention, <u>Goldwater</u> threw a lob pass directly into the media's coverage when he said: "Extremism in the defense of liberty is no vice, moderation in pursuit of justice is no virtue." (The line is generally attributed to <u>Jaffa</u>.) According to Lipset and Raab (1970), American extremism is not only a "deviance" but is also "the more specific tendency to violate democratic procedures." In this sense, it could hardly have been Goldwater's views that were at issue—except in the calculating and feverish imaginings of Democratic ad men and liberal news hounds—but rather his "association" with the <u>Right</u>, a term and a concept with which the American public has never been comfortable. (The media went to great lengths to link Goldwater with the <u>John Birch Society</u>, even though he had, in fact, repudiated it.) Four years after the Goldwater defeat George Wallace (1919–   ) put a genuine note of extremism into a political campaign. Wallace's obstructionism with regard to race was taken to be the "resistance to change" that glibly passes for conservatism in the media, whereas he was actually more a man of the Left. Without question, however, extremism, whether of the Left or Right, upsets what Shils (1981) called "the politics of civility," and threatens America's "fragile consensus." That consensus itself, sustained by personal <u>liberty</u> and the two-party system, is probably not fragile, but the electorate clearly has no taste for wide swings of political temper. **Read**: Daniel Bell, ed., *The Radical Right* (1963), in which Richard Hofstadter wrote ("Pseudo Conservatism Revisited: A Postscript"): "[A]t times politics becomes an arena into which the wildest fancies are projected, the most paranoid suspicions, the most absurd superstitions, the most bizarre apocalyptic fantasies. From time to time, movements arise that are founded upon the political exploitation of such fancies and fears, and while these movements can hardly aspire to animate more than a small minority of the population, they do exercise, especially in a democratic and populistically oriented political culture like our own, a certain leverage upon practical politics. Thus, today, despite the presence of issues of the utmost gravity and urgency, the American press and public have been impelled to discuss in all seriousness a right-wing movement whose leaders believe that President Eisenhower was a member of the 'Communist conspiracy.' It seems hardly extravagant to say that the true believers in a movement of this sort project into the arena of politics utterly irrelevant fantasies and disorders of a purely personal kind. Followers of a movement like the John Birch Society are in our world but not exactly of it."

faith: A hard concept to define precisely in terms of belief, **conservative** faith is in some measure equivalent to its more familiar religious meaning, intending an acceptance of the transcendent sources of individual life and society. Of course, not all conservatives share religious faith. Still, few do not accept some a priori realities—e.g., **tradition**—"on faith," and some others maintain that—whatever the truth of theism may be—belief in the good can be sustained only by belief in the perfect (see **Strauss**). Although it is the religious sense that must dominate any definition of faith, it is possible to conceive of it in secular terms as "faith" in right effort or right principle reflecting the conservative beliefs in personal responsibility (and enterprise) and cultural experience (or **prescription**). Thus **Gilder**, wedding both senses, could write (1981) that faith works against the notion "that the human race can become self-sufficient, can separate itself from chance and fortune in a hubristic siege of rational resource management, income distribution, and futuristic planning. Our greatest and only resource is the miracle of human creativity in a relation of openness to the divine." As Gilder further suggests, the loss of faith is at least as dangerous as the presence of faith is beneficial. **Read:** R. Neuhaus, *The Naked Public Square* (1984). "**There has grown up . . . a . . . different sort of Christianity. Its adherents are sure that man is by nature good and that he will get sufficiently better if only education is made more generally available and environment improved. To them Jesus is not God come to save man from himself. They see no need for such redemption. To them Jesus is a moral teacher and a good man, no more. He is the son of God only as we are all God's children; He differs from us in degree of divinity but not in kind of divinity. To them prayer is a process of affirmation of the highest values that they know, but is not otherwise effective since there can be no possible intervention from that which is beyond or behind the sensible universe. . . . The ancient creeds may be said if one desires, but only as poetry. The sacraments are only dramatic devices by which we remind ourselves of the example of Jesus and of the love and kindness of God who is imminent but not transcendent. As for the Church, it is a voluntary association of earnest people who wish to help one another become more like Jesus the man. This is Liberal Christianity.**" Bernard Iddings Bell, *Crowd Culture* (1952)

family: The contemporary sense of family is of "parents and their children," but the traditional understanding runs deeper, and has (or had) great implications for the structure of society. A family was formerly a **community** of kinship ("of generations in time, the family of blood line, of **tradition** and history, of ancestors and planned-for posterity," **Nisbet**, 1982), and it involved grandparents, parents, children, grandchildren, and cousins bound together in support of their collective interests and in opposition to the individuals and other families who opposed those interests. As **Burke** understood, family is the medium through which tradition, morality, **private property**, love, and **faith** are imparted to individuals. The family stands, even more than community, as the primary wedge protecting individuals from the power of the state, which fact is seen nowhere more clearly than in those areas (America's inner cities, for example) where the institution of family is most in crisis. The basis of family, at least in the Christian view, is sacramental marriage in which mother, father, and children become a miniature society; that basic unit which itself encodes the proper structure of the larger world. Read: G. Becker, *A Treatise on the Family* (1981); G. Gilder, *Men and Marriage* (1986). "The current family in the United States, that nuclear household group of 2.78 members, is in no way the enemy of the state or indeed the whole modern temper. Its very feebleness, its anemic structure, and its institutional insignificance make it the perfect handmaiden of the mammoth, intrusive state, as well as a fit receptacle of the narcissisms and hedonistic egoisms of the day. The family will again become strong only if this pathetic end-result of the long decline of kinship authority in the West is replaced by family in the full longitudinal sense, the family of generations, of entail in some form or degree, of recognized authority over its members, and of mutual dignity, respect, and duty rather than mere indulgence of marital passion. Divorce rates do not mark the weakness of the nuclear kinship group, for divorce in considerable measure, not to mention marital hatred and desertion, have accompanied the strongest family systems. What best measures the sickness of the current family is the collapse of its intergenerational significance, its communal-corporate character, its close alliance with property (social democratic tax policy alone doing the family far more injury than can divorce), and its natural authority over members, especially the young." Robert Nisbet, *Prejudices* (1982)

federalism: That more-or-less uniquely American system of republican governance in which the people and the states delegate certain well-defined responsibilities to a national government, the powers of which are both separated and limited. Ironically, the word "federal" (from the Latin *foedus* or covenant), which originally meant the *partnership* of the national government with the states, has come exclusively to mean that national government itself. A proper definition must emphasize the way federalism unites separate polities within a single system but does not diminish the polities' individual integrity. (See **subsidiarity**.) Ours is, as Chief Justice Salmon P. Chase put it in

1869, "an indestructible Union, composed of indestructible states." Federalism is opposed to political *pluralism*, the system in which interests, not localities, confederate, and it depends for its proper functioning—if not for its very survival—upon a consensus politics. Only consensus can reconcile differences among the federated constituents. For **Hamilton**, **Madison**, and John Jay, authors of *The Federalist* (1787–88), the **Constitution** was an exercise in nation building, much like the ancient covenant of Israel, and a further development of the common Colonial view that America and Britain had constituted a federal entity that King George III and Parliament had undermined through the usurpation of American authorities (see **Declaration of Independence**). The federal system was seriously undermined by the Civil War, in which the Confederates fought the "Federals," and because of which the word took on its now distorted meaning: Washington, D.C. Indeed, much of the familiar conservative argument against the world-government pretensions of the United Nations is similar in tone and content to the constitutional criticisms of the Anti-Federalists. (See also **states' rights**.) **Read**: Hamilton, Jay, and Madison, *The Federalist* (1788); F. Morley, *Freedom and Federalism* (1959); V. Ostrom, *The Meaning of American Federalism* (1991). **"The essence of federalism is reservation of control over local affairs to the localities themselves, the argument for which becomes stronger if the federation embraces a large area, with strong climatic or cultural differences among the . . . states . . . One justifying assumption for such a loose-knit system is that citizens as a body are both interested in, and for the most part competent to handle, local problems. When that assumption is valid there is little doubt that federalism, despite its disadvantages, serves admirably to foster freedom without the sacrifice of order."** Felix Morley, *Freedom and Federalism* (1959)

FEE (Foundation for Economic Education): Free-market research organization (based in Irvington-on-Hudson, NY) founded in 1946 by Leonard E. Read. Read's main advisor in FEE's early years was **Mises**. FEE publishes *The Freeman*, a journal of "economics, history, and moral philosophy" founded by John Chamberlain in 1950, as well as books and pamphlets, including *The Law* (1850) by **Bastiat**.

(The name of the magazine was borrowed from that of an earlier journal published by Nock.) Among the early staff members were Hazlitt (whose library now resides at FEE) and Chodorov, as well as Suzanne LaFollette, Willi Schlamm, and Meyer, each of whom went on to *National Review*. William Rusher (1984), former publisher of *National Review*, calls *The Freeman* "a sort of journalistic John the Baptist," in that it paved the way for the coming of Buckley et al. (Buckley was offered a job at *The Freeman* in 1951, which he declined, and he published his first major magazine article there in May of that year—about McCarthyism.) A recent Internet description of FEE by its president, Hans F. Sennholz, reads in part: "Everyone carries a part of society on his shoulders; no one is relieved of his share of responsibility by others. . . . Whether he chooses or not, every man is drawn into the great historical struggle, the decisive battle into which our epoch has plunged us." The current issues of *The Freeman* deal largely with economics, but unlike most journals that do, it manages to be lively and readable—even if some of the books reviewed deal with arcana of what Thomas Carlyle called the "dismal science" that only an expert could appreciate. **Read:** G. Nash, *The Conservative Intellectual Movement in America* (1976). **". . . [N]o government can pay for the extravagances of welfarism solely with taxes, for the productive members of society will tolerate only so much taxation. The politicians in power inevitably turn to the expedient of monetary inflation . . . through manipulation of the Federal Reserve System . . . [But] one cannot inflate the money supply . . . without eventually causing higher prices. If government then tries to prevent prices from rising through price controls, it eliminates profits, slows production, and causes shortages. The lower supply of goods, combined with monetary expansion, tends to raise prices still further. What was intended to stop rising prices—price controls—cause prices to rise."** Nelson Hultberg, "Prelude to the Total State" in *The Freeman* (September 1992)

[*The Freeman* is published monthly and is provided to those who contribute $30.00 to the Foundation. Individual copies are $2.00 per issue. Student subscriptions (nine issues) are available for $10.00 ($5.00 per semester). For information write to: FEE, Irvington-on-

Hudson, NY 10533; phone: (914) 591-7230; FAX: (914) 591-8910. A book catalogue is also available at no charge.]

feminism: Although subject to many interpretations, feminism is fundamentally a *world view* with one or both of two aspects: equity and gender. The first is, in large measure, simply an appeal for the same rights as persons (in terms of positive law, not **natural law**, the sexes obviously sharing equally in the latter) that men possess. (See **autonomy** and **liberty**.) "Gender" feminism (sometimes called "second-stage feminism") asserts an essential feminine character to nature that is historically and currently oppressed by male dominance. "Gynocentric feminism," writes Iris Marion Young in *Throwing Like A Girl* (1990), "defines women's oppression as the devaluation and repression of women's experience by a masculine culture that exalts violence and individualism." Gender feminism is Marxist **ideology** at its most reductionist extreme (but with sex replacing class). As a *movement*, feminism has undergone numerous changes through several notable stages, from the late 18th-century publication of Mary Wollstonecraft's *Vindication of the Rights of Woman*, through the Emancipation movement in the 19th century, to the contemporary Women's Movement. Modern gender feminism has been, at least in the view of the **Christian Right**, hostile to the **family** and in favor of unrestricted **abortion**. Paradoxically, the feminist campaign for the Equal Rights Amendment (ERA) was unsuccessful largely through the efforts of women, especially one woman, Phyllis Schlafly (1924–). After writing *A Choice Not an Echo* (1964), which helped **Goldwater** win the 1964 Republican presidential nomination, Schlafly formed Eagle Forum, the main intention of which was to defeat the ERA . . . which it did. **Read:** M. Decter, *The New Chastity, and Other Arguments Against Women's Liberation* (1972); P. Schlafly, *The Power of the Positive Woman* (1977); Christina Hoff Sommers, *Who Stole Feminism?* (1994). Sommers writes: "Th[is] is the corrosive paradox of gender feminism's misandrist stance: no group of women can wage war on men without at the same time denigrating the women who respect those men. It is just not possible to incriminate men without implying that large numbers of women are fools or worse. Other groups have had their official enemies—workers against capitalists, whites against blacks, Hindus against Muslims—and for a while such enmities may be stable. But when women set themselves against men, they simultaneously set themselves against other women in a group antagonism that is untenable from the outset. In the end, the gender feminist is always forced to show her disappointment and annoyance with the women who are to be found in the camp of the enemy. Misandry moves on to misogyny."

First Things: See **Neuhaus, Richard John**

freedom: See **liberty**

The Freeman: See **FEE**

free market: See **capitalism** and **free trade**

free trade: The principle of **liberty** in international economics; as opposed to protectionism. Free trade keeps governments idle and individuals active—an almost ideal state. **Jefferson** said, "I am for free commerce with all nations," because he understood, as did **Smith**, that goods at low prices benefit the nation more than protected goods benefit a few producers (whether management or labor). Of all the many economic illusions none is more vapid than the "balance of trade" so strenuously advocated by Jefferson's latter-day followers. As **Hazlitt** and others have pointed out, "imports and exports must equal each other" in the long run, since the one pays for the other. Protectionism, the policies—especially tariffs—that enforce the belief that native producers should be protected from foreign competition, was the stimulus for Smith's attack upon *mercantilism* in *Wealth of Nations* (1776). A few nominal conservatives, putatively as *patriots*, argue that protection is justified by reasons ranging from national security to domestic hardship, but most conservatives accept that protection is simply another—prototypical—form of **welfare**, and that the free association of consumers and producers is the only sensible guarantor of low prices and high quality. As **Mises** (1949) put it: "Many people simply do not realize that the only effect of protection is to divert production from those places in which it could produce more per unit of capital and labor expended to places in which it produces less. It makes people poorer, not more prosperous." **Read**: R. and M. Friedman, *Free to Choose* (1979); G. Gilder, *Wealth and Poverty* (1981); H. Hazlitt, *Economics in One Lesson* (1946). **"In every country, it always is and must be the interest of the great body of the people to buy whatever they want of those who sell it cheapest. The proposition is so very manifest, that it seems ridiculous to take any pains to prove it; nor could it ever have been called in question, had not the interested sophistry of merchants and manufacturers confounded the common sense of mankind."** Adam Smith, *The Wealth of Nations* (1776)

Friedman, Milton (1912–   ): American economist and controversialist, winner of the 1976 Nobel Prize, called variously **conservative** and **libertarian** (he is opposed to a military draft, medical licensing, and drug laws), Friedman is arguably the leading economic thinker since John Maynard Keynes. More dedicated to **laissez-faire** than his **Chicago School** teacher Frank Knight, Friedman has championed an economic theory known as **monetarism**. Basically, monetarism holds that the main cause of inflation is excessive growth in the money supply, which growth is itself the result of a shortfall between government revenues and expenditures, and, further, that interest rates are tied directly to—and exchange rates inversely to—inflation. Monetarism challenges the short-term, interventionist assumptions of Keynesianism, asserting instead the value in government policy of *stable, long-term rules* (especially with regard to the money supply, i.e., that it should grow slowly). And, under such conditions, government will spend less (a horror to Keynesians), which is important since public expenditures of money diminish private investment. His monetarist theories were validated in one of the great empirical studies of the century, *A Monetary History of the United States* (1963), which he wrote with Anna J. Schwartz. Friedman recognizes that "positive economics" depends upon principles that work—that accurately predict how people will behave—more than it does upon ambiguous "scientific" calculations. He was an early champion of school vouchers and a flat-rate income tax. Indeed, much of Friedman's influence is due to his genius for making provocative yet workable proposals for reform, and to the fact that his intellectual efforts have not been focused just on the "dismal science" or aimed at just an academic audience. Most of his academic career was spent at the University of Chicago, where he taught an interdisciplinary seminar with George Stigler and Hayek. He is currently a fellow at the Hoover Institution. "No other thinker of our time has so brilliantly exposed and publicized the perversities that can be engendered by governmental intervention in the economic life of a nation." (Kristol) Read: *Capitalism and Freedom* (1962); *Free to Choose* (1979). About: R. Fryer, *Recent Conservative Political Thought* (1979); R. Gordon, ed., *Milton Friedman's Monetary Framework* (1974). "Some monetarists conclude that deliberate changes in the rate of monetary growth by the authorities can be useful to offset other forces making for instability . . . They favor fine tuning, using changes in the quantity of money as an instrument of policy. Other monetarists, including myself, conclude that our present understanding of the relation between money, prices and output is so meager, that there is so much leeway in these relations, that such discretionary changes do more harm than good. We believe that an automatic policy under which the quantity of money would grow at a steady rate—month in month out, year in year out—would provide a stable monetary framework for economic growth without itself being a source of instability and disturbance." "The Counter-Revolution in Monetary Theory" in *Monetarist Economics* (1991)

fusionism: See Meyer, Frank E.

Gilder, George (1939–): American writer and economist whose books *Sexual Suicide* (1975) and *Wealth and Poverty* (1981) helped to give contemporary conservatism its sharp edge. (Because it attacked feminism, the former book was despised in some intellectual circles, and needed to be re-titled when reissued, so infamous had it become. It is now called *Men and Marriage*.) With Charles Murray, Gilder was among the first to demonstrate how critical marriage is to the stability of society, and how detrimental, therefore, anti-family welfare policies are to the well being of individuals and communities. *Wealth and Poverty* was, in the author's words, a "theology for capitalism," and was the first widely read book to proclaim the virtues of supply-side theory. Attacked by liberals and some neo-conservatives (Kristol called the book "pseudo-anthropological analysis"), the book became the economic Bible of the <u>Reagan</u> White House. Gilder's early professional life—after a somewhat rocky educational career—was devoted to centrist politicians of the Republican Party, including stints as a speech writer for Nelson Rockefeller, Jacob Javits, and—during his successful presidential campaign in 1968— Richard Nixon. In recent years, Gilder has become an apostle of a <u>laissez-faire</u> approach to high technology. He is currently a senior fellow at Seattle's Discovery Institute. **Read:** *Microcosm* (1989); *Wealth and Poverty* (1981); **About:** his own *Visible Man* (1978). **"The ideology of the sexual liberationists sees society as a male-dominated construct that exploits women for the convenience of men. In evidence, they cite men's greater earning power, as if economic productivity were a measure of social control rather than of social service. But it is female power, organic and constitutional, that is real—holding sway over the deepest levels of consciousness, sources of happiness, and processes of social survival. Male dominance in the marketplace, on the other hand, is a social artifice maintained not for the dubious benefits it confers on men but for the indispensable benefits it offers the society: inducing men to support rather than disrupt it. Conventional male power, in fact, might be considered more the ideological myth. It is designed to induce the majority of men to accept a bondage to the machine and the marketplace, to a large extent in the service of women and in the interests of civilization."** *Men and Marriage* (1986)

Gingrich, Newt (1943–): American politician (House of Representatives from 1979; Speaker of the House since 1995), who probably deserves most of the credit for the post-<u>Reagan</u> political realignment of Congress. Gingrich first came to national prominence in his successful campaign to oust Representative Jim Wright, Democrat of Texas, from the House Speaker's post, and in his efforts to help timid Republican congressmen rediscover something like political courage. With a Ph.D. in history (Tulane, 1971), Gingrich has a style that is sometimes pedantic and almost always provocative. (He once called former Speaker "Tip" O'Neill a "thug," and famously called Senator Bob Dole the "tax collector for the welfare state.") People were astonished and amused when Gingrich began saying in the early 1980s that the Republican Party would win control of Congress by 1992. When it happened in 1994, Gingrich became the most powerful person in American government, with the possible—but not likely—exception of the president. His **conservative** philosophy is on display in his controversial, hastily written book, *To Renew America* (1995)—controversial not because of what it says but because of the amount paid for it by the publisher (most of which the Speaker returned). In the book, Gingrich proposes approaches to "six challenges" facing the nation: that young people don't know enough about our history and politics and need to be taught about American civilization (i.e., religion, responsibility, and entrepreneurship) "as a form of self-improvement"; that we need to heed Alvin Toffler and ride the wave—the Third Wave, that is—into the Information Age; that the American economy needs to be deregulated and de-taxed in order to be competitive in world markets *and* to grow out of our own budget deficit; that we need an "opportunity society" instead of a **welfare** state (which change depends primarily on volunteerism, jobs, and public safety); that the budget must be balanced by 2002 in order to avoid Weimar-style hyperinflation and/or the bankruptcy of Social Security and Medicare; and that power in America must be decentralized, thus freeing up the energies of the people to solve local problems locally. *Time* magazine named Gingrich "Man of the Year" in 1995, because "he did the work—crude, forceful, effective . . ." **Read:** *To Renew America* (1995); **About:** D. Williams, *Newt!* (1995). "**By blaming everything on 'society,' contemporary liberals are really trying to escape the personal responsibility that comes with being an American. If 'society' is responsible for everything, than no one is *personally* responsible for anything. We can all blame one another and that's the end of it. To be an American, however, is to be responsible— both for yourself and, as much as possible, for others. When confronted with a problem, a true American doesn't ask, 'Who can I blame this on?' A true American asks, 'What can I do about it *today?*'**" *To Renew America* (1995)

Glazer, Nathan (1923–): American scholar, whose liberal **anticommunism** gradually evolved to become **neoconservatism**. (As he put it, he was a "mild radical" and became a "mild conservative.") With Daniel Patrick Moynihan (now the senior U.S. senator from New York), he wrote the justly famous *Beyond the Melting Pot* (1970), which demonstrated the failures of liberal analysis, if not more specifically of liberal policy, and first headlined the "crisis of the black family." Glazer was also a co-author with David Riesman and Reuel Denney of *The Lonely Crowd* (1950), the epochal book that dissected a change in the American character from inner- to other-directed. With **Kristol**, he is co-editor of *The Public Interest*, one of America's leading intellectual journals. **Read:** *Affirmative Discrimination* (1975); **About:** G. Dorrien, *The Neoconservative Mind* (1993). "**The gravest political consequence [of affirmative action] is undoubtedly the increasing resentment and hostility between groups that is fueled by special benefits for some. The statistical basis for redress makes one great error: All 'whites' are consigned to the same category, deserving of no special consideration. That is not the way 'whites' see themselves, or indeed are, in social reality. Some may be 'whites,' pure and simple. But almost all have some specific ethnic or religious identification, which to the individual involved, may mean a distinctive history of past—and perhaps some present—discrimination . . . [for instance] the ethnic groups formed from the post-1880 immigrants from Europe. These groups were not particularly involved in the enslavement of the Negro or the creation of the Jim Crow pattern in the South, the conquest of part of Mexico, or the near-extermination of the American Indians. They came to a country which provided them with less benefits than it now provides the protected groups. There is little reason for them to feel they should bear the burden of redressing a past in which they had no or little part, or assisting those who presently receive more assistance than they did. We are a nation of minorities; to enshrine some minorities as deserving of special benefits means not to defend minority rights against a discriminating majority but to favor some of these minorities over others.**" *Affirmative Discrimination* (1975)

[*The Public Interest*, 1112 16th Street, NW, Suite 530, Washington, DC 20036; Irving Kristol and Nathan Glazer, editors. Subscriptions: $25/year, $42.50/2 years, $60/3 years from *The Public Interest*, Dept. PI, P.O. Box 3000, Denville, NJ 07834; (800) 783-4903.]

III

The Christian Tradition

by
James V. Schall, S.J.

Two dicta of conservative thought are: (1) Preserve what is worth saving; and (2) To preserve anything worthwhile, some change is necessary. Christianity came into the world as something new— new understandings about the inner life of the Deity (the Trinity) and about Man, each made manifest by the Incarnation of the Second Person of this Trinity. "The Word became flesh and dwelt among us" (John 1:13). If the Deity itself embraced the human condition, with all its ills and problems, Man could not be all bad. Indeed, this fact became the ultimate foundation of human dignity in Christian thought. All things remained, in their essence, "good," as Genesis had taught, even while we must account for the obvious presence of evil.

With regard to Israel, Christianity understood itself to be not a rejection of the Law and the Prophets, but their fulfillment. The "New" Law did not abrogate the Ten Commandments, the norms about how we should live. The spirit in which these Commandments were to be observed was deepened with the doctrines of mercy, forgiveness, love of enemies, and grace. These Commandments, when examined, covered the main moral disorders likely in most human lives—murder, adultery, lying, stealing, envying, coveting. The violation of the Commandments has filled the world with the various disorders that have appeared in every age. Men have sought in vain to replace this outline of correct living with other philosophies, ideologies, or faiths, but these justifications were really presented, on examination, as partial goods that sought to overturn the real good that was to be kept. As Edmund Burke put it:

> History consists, for the greater part, of the miseries brought upon the world by pride, ambition, avarice, revenge, lust, sedition, hypocrisy, ungoverned zeal, and all the train of disorderly appetites, which shake the public . . . These vices are the *causes* of these storms. Religion, morals, laws, prerogatives, privileges, liberties, rights of men, are the *pretexts*. The pretexts are always found in some specious appearance of a real good." (*Reflections on the Revolution in France*, 1790)

Christianity, moreover, though it generally accepted the state and property as reasonable, was not a teaching about politics or economics, but about man's ultimate purpose and destiny, on how to attain it and on an institution in which it was to be achieved—the Church, not the state. The teaching about politics and economics was to be learned primarily from experience and from the philosophers. Aristotle, Plato, Cicero (Athens and Rome generally), along with subsequent philosophers (and states), were worthy sources of practical wisdom, unless public life somehow interfered with a primary duty to God. When Peter and John were commanded to cease preaching, they responded with the ever-recurring counter question, "Do you think it better to obey God or man?" (Acts 4:19). This question alone always limits the state.

Peter and Paul were presumably executed under one of Rome's worst emperors, Nero. Both apostles, however, advised Christians to be obedient to the Emperor, for his power of the sword was given to chastise evildoers (Romans 13:4; 1 Peter 4:3). That is, Christians had to learn to distinguish between a tyrant and what a good ruler was supposed to do. If the tyrant demanded something outside his legitimate powers, they chose death rather than obey him.

Other New Testament brief comments on politics have, moreover, served to give guidance to conservative thinking. The most famous passage in the Gospels about politics has to do with tax collecting, that ever-present sign of political power: "Render unto Caesar the things that are Caesar's and unto God the things that are God's" (Matthew 22:22). This meant that religion did recognize that Caesar, the political power, was legitimate for its own purposes, even reasonable taxation. But it also meant that within the realm of politics itself, some things were not Caesar's. Caesar could not, for reasons of state, forbid the preaching of the Good News.

The subsequent history of Man has been marked with all sorts of Caesars who claim more than their due, and sometimes with religious leaders who claim more than theirs. Characteristic of conservative thought is the effort to preserve within its own structure both what belongs to Caesar and what belongs to God. From the point of view of religion, the most dangerous state is the one that is bound by no limits. From the point of view of conservatism, the most dangerous religion is the one that makes politics to be its most important interest.

The history of Christianity is surrounded by efforts to clarify and define in law what things do belong to God and what to Caesar. This duality of legitimacy, characteristic of conservative thought, sees a dynamism in the lack of power concentration. Christ's discussion with Pilate at His trial graphically shows what is at stake (John 19:10–11). Pilate, as Roman provincial governor, maintained that he had the power of life and death. Christ's response was that he (Pilate) would have no power unless it was given to him by Christ's Father. The manner in which political power was seen to be both natural and coming from God in its essence was one of the burdens of all Christian thought, particularly medieval thought, to demonstrate. Modern conservative thought preserves both of these aspects in its theoretical understanding of itself, both the authority of Pilate and its transcendent limits.

Generally, two Christian theories with regard to the legitimacy of the state are found, one from Saint Augustine and one from Aristotle via Saint Thomas Aquinas. The Augustinian tradition argues that government was necessary because of the Fall, because of original sin and actual sin. Therefore, we should not locate perfection in any form of government. The Thomist position held that there would have been government or rule even had Man not sinned, that government was, as Aristotle said, natural to Man. Saint Thomas held that both of these positions could be reconciled because both were true in different ways. Some governmental institution with coercive powers was needed because of the actual disorders manifested in public, stemming from Man's own personal disorders. The second position was that Man was a political animal and needed to rule even himself by reasonable argument and order. This background in conservative tradition has explained the presence of both a political realism about what to expect of Man, including his sins, and a kind of hesitant optimism about the importance of human ideals and the attraction of the good.

This Christian experience with government came generally to be argued under the heading of natural law. "Natural law" was a term arising from Plato, Aristotle, and the Stoics. Both Judaism and Islam were religions of "the Law." But Christianity used "law" in a rather different way. Law was conceived by Saint Thomas as an organizing principle, an "ordination of reason," by which all orders of reality could be distinguished with clarity. Thus, there was an eternal law, a natural law, a divine law, a civil law, and even a law of sin and disorder (*Summa Theologica*, I–II, 90–97). The careful elaboration of how these orders or laws related to one another was the way in which the principles of diversity and unity found in Christian tradition came to be intellectually understood.

All things had some proper mode of action or some law governing their normal functioning. What was characteristic of Christian thought was the enormous variety that was present within the same cosmic and human order. Hierarchy was not opposed to the ordinary, but both were necessary. Unity of doctrine was not opposed to a wide divergence in ways to live it. Eventually, this understanding gave rise to what came to be known with Pope Pius XI as the principle of subsidiarity. This principle simply means that all authority should remain at the lowest level possible. Not all things were well governed from the top downward. Thus, there might be an argument for the authority of a state or an empire, but there was also an argument for lesser units that had their own autonomy and tradition. The legitimate, even at times chaotic, variety within conservatism stems from this line of thought.

Thus, the main contributions of Christianity to conservatism are these: (1) incorporating change into abiding truths and principles; (2) distinguishing between God and Caesar as normal aspects of one civil society; (3) establishing the intrinsic worth of the individual who is at the same time a member of larger groups, including the Church, all of which are allowed a presence in society; (4) acknowledging that hierarchy and subsidiarity are normal elements of a healthy society; and (5) working out a theory of natural law that sought to understand the various orders in which men were to live and that would also explain why experience and diversity were normal parts of the social order.

Fr. Schall is a professor in the Department of Government at Georgetown University. Among his numerous books are *The Politics of Heaven and Hell; The Distinctiveness of Christianity;* and *Religion, Wealth, and Poverty.*

Goldwater, Barry M. (1909–   ): American **conservative** politician (five terms as U.S. senator from Arizona) who was the Republican presidential candidate in 1964. Although he lost (to Lyndon B. Johnson) in one of the largest landslides in American history, he still managed to accomplish two things: he put conservatism into the mainstream of American national politics, and he actually won the "solid South," thus initiating the transformation of what had been a Democratic party stronghold. The word "maverick" comes to mind when describing Barry Goldwater. Although he refused to censure Joseph McCarthy and voted No on the 1964 Civil Rights Act, there was little to justify the hysterical charges of **extremism** leveled against him during the 1964 campaign, except that in his nomination-acceptance speech he uttered the famous line (apparently written by **Jaffa**): "Extremism in the defense of liberty is no vice, moderation in pursuit of justice is no virtue." **Reagan** (1989) said it best: "He spoke from principle, and he offered vision. . . . When he ran for president, he won six states and he lost forty-four. But his candidacy worked as a precursor of things to come." **Read:** *The Conscience of a Conservative* (1960); *With No Apologies* (1979); **About:** L. Edwards, *Goldwater: The Man Who Made a Revolution* (1995). "Ronald Reagan is not the Republican Party any more than he is the conservative revolution. I always got angry with people who attributed such powers to me. In fact, I still get mad at people who say I was Reagan's political godfather or his prophet opening up the wilderness for him. . . . I don't believe that either Reagan or I started a conservative revolution because for most of our history the majority of Americans have considered themselves conservatives. They have often not voted that way because they were offered no clear choice. I began to tap, and Reagan reached to the bottom of, a deep reservoir that already existed. . . . Nor do I accept the idea that his presidency represents a permanent political realignment. Politics runs in cycles. The Democrats will come back strong about the year 2000 or shortly thereafter. But it will be a new Democratic Party largely because of Reagan. The nation's agenda has now been pulled to the right." *Goldwater* [his autobiography] (1988)

Hamilton, Alexander (1755–1804): American statesman (b. Nevis, West Indies), aide-de-camp to Gen. Washington, first treasury secretary, and—with John Jay and **Madison**—an author of *The Federalist* (1787–88), in which he paid homage to his philosophical heroes **Blackstone** and **Hume**. The *Federalist* essays were Hamilton's idea, and he wrote at least fifty-one of the eighty-five papers himself. Although he is properly considered a "conservative" figure in American political history, Hamilton was nonetheless a centralizer, one for whom a national government, although limited in its powers, was meant to be superior to the states, and was, by virtue of its *nationalism*, inclined to protective tariffs. (He admired **Smith**'s *Wealth of Nations* [1776] but ignored its call for **free trade**.) Still, he disparaged social innovations, and was content rather to "incur the negative inconveniences of delay than the positive mischiefs of injudicious expedients." Hamilton was perhaps the most visionary of the Founders, and his peculiar brand of conservatism, so far removed from the small-farm-and-business views of **Jefferson** and John **Adams**, anticipated the economic growth and cultural **change** that America would undergo. Thus he assumed and repaid the war debts of all the states, and created a single national currency. He reacted to the French Revolution with a horror equal to **Burke**'s, and the prospect of unbridled **liberty** (in the form of **democracy**) sickened him. ("Take mankind in general, they are vicious.") But he also knew that ordered liberty in America must inevitably lead to big cities and big industries, and he wanted to create a national government "energetic" enough to endure American expansion. Too much power in government, he acknowledged, leads to despotism, but too little leads to anarchy, "and both eventually to the ruin of the people." Ironically—and for him tragically—the government he admired most was the one he fought to be free of. So much did British tradition impress him that he wanted the Senate to be a House of Lords; the president to be a king. The **Constitution**, which he defended so vigorously in *The Federalist* and in the ratification debates in New York, was actually a "frail and worthless fabric." But because it created a federal government, it was preferable to the anarchy of competing states. But these views (especially the misinterpretation of them by his enemies) led to Hamilton's increasing marginalization. Although he disliked Jefferson, he threw Federalist Party support to the Virginian (1800) in order to thwart the presidential ambitions of Aaron Burr, whom he called, prophetically, an American Catiline (the ancient Roman who led an unsuccessful insurrection against the great Cicero). Four years later, Hamilton agreed to a duel with Burr, but at the moment of truth did not fire his weapon. Burr did. **Read:** *The Federalist* (1788); M. Frisch, ed., *Selected Writings & Speeches* (1985); **About:** F. McDonald, *Alexander Hamilton* (1979); C. Rossiter, *Alexander Hamilton and the Constitution* (1964). **"A government ought to contain in itself every power requisite to the accomplishment of the objects committed to its care, and to the complete execution of the trusts for which it is responsible, free from every other control but a regard to the public good and to the sense of the people."** *The Federalist*, No. 31

Hayek, Friedrich A. (1899–1992): **Austrian School** economist and champion of free markets and **libertarianism**. After service in World War I (and some Austrian government service under the direction of **Mises**), he taught at the Universities of Vienna (1929–31); London (1932–50, where he shared ideas with **Popper**, and came under the influence of—among others—**Locke**, **Hume**, **Burke**, **Tocqueville**, and **Acton**); and finally Chicago (1950–62), where he was closely associated with **Friedman** and others. (Hayek's early work had in some ways anticipated **monetarism**.) In all his academic appointments and in many articles and books, he nurtured a lifelong distaste for the interventionism of John Maynard Keynes. His *The Road to Serfdom* (1944) argued that central planning of the economy leads directly—albeit not inevitably—to totalitarianism. Government's proper role is to encourage **liberty**, not to plan progress. The book (first published in—and largely concerning—Britain) became an American sensation (the *New York Times*—well, **Hazlitt** writing there—called it "one of the most important books of our generation"), especially when it was widely distributed in condensed reprint by *Reader's Digest* in 1947. He summarized the book's central argument (and it was to a great extent the theme of his life's work) in an interview with the London *Spectator* (January 26, 1945): "In the piecemeal process of adaptation and change there has always been opportunity for the people to change institutions into something different from what they were intended to be, to create a society which was not the result of a single coherent plan but of innumerable decisions of free men and women."

Hayek later served as professor of economics at the University of Freiburg and visiting professor at the University of Salzburg. He was a founder (and for a dozen years president) of the **Mont Pélerin Society**, and in 1974 received the Nobel Prize in Economics (shared with Gunnar Myrdal) for "pioneering work in the theory of money and economic fluctuations and for . . . pioneering analysis of the interdependence of economic, social, and institutional phenomena." He famously refused to call himself **conservative** (see **classical liberalism**). His book, *The Constitution of Liberty* (1960), argues that modern intellectuals have abandoned the West's legacy of liberty: because they underestimate the complexity of life and the limits of "intellect"; because their impatience with "injustice" encourages intervention; and because they believe **democracy** justifies coercion. Among Hayek's more telling insights—very much an "Austrian" concept which he especially understood—is the idea of spontaneous **order**, in some ways the ultimate refutation of **rationalism**. Our most basic, successful, and pleasing social, political, and economic structures are never planned, but arise spontaneously from the course of history. Thus all notions of "social justice" (or "distributive justice") are false, since an unplanned (organic or natural) order can be neither just nor unjust. Hayek also made the link—extremely important to Eastern Europe as it shed its communist past—between free markets and political liberty. Significantly, his Nobel acceptance lecture was titled "The Pretense of Knowledge." **Read:** *The Road to Serfdom* (1944); *The Constitution of Liberty* (1960); **About:** R. Fryer, *Recent Conservative Political Thought* (1979); J. Gray, *Hayek on Liberty* (1984). **"If there were omniscient men, if we could know not only all that affects the attainment of our present wishes but also our future wants and desires, there would be little case for liberty. . . . [But i]t is because every individual knows so little and, in particular, because we rarely know which of us knows best that we trust the independent and competitive efforts of many to induce the emergence of what we shall want when we see it."** "The Creative Powers of a Free Civilization" in *The Constitution of Liberty* (1960)

Hazlitt, Henry (1894–1993): American journalist (*The New York Times, Fortune* magazine, and *The Freeman*), whose *Economics in One*

Lesson (1946) remains the best short statement of the conservative view of economics. Hazlitt's own short summary of that one lesson was this: "*The art of economics consists in looking not merely at the immediate but at the longer effects of any act or policy; it consists in tracing the consequences of that policy not merely for one group but for all groups.*" Hazlitt illustrated the point by use of **Bastiat**'s story of the broken window, in which the concentric circles of interrelated economic activity are demonstrated (the seen and the unseen), and the hoodlum who breaks the window is clearly seen to symbolize government in its taxing power. Hazlitt was an especially effective critic of Keynesian and other theories justifying government spending and deficits. (See also **FEE.**) **Read:** *Economics in One Lesson* (1946); **About:** J. Tucker, *Henry Hazlitt* (1994). "**Exceeded only by the pathological dread of imports that affects all nations is a pathological yearning for exports. Logically, it is true, nothing could be more inconsistent. In the long run imports and exports must equal each other (considering both in the broadest sense, which includes such 'invisible' items as tourist expenditures, ocean freight charges and all other items in the 'balance of payments'). It is exports that pay for imports, and vice versa. The greater the exports we have, the greater imports we must have, if ever we expect to get paid. The smaller imports we have, the smaller exports we can have. Without imports we can have no exports, for foreigners will have no funds with which to buy our goods. When we decide to cut down our imports, we are in effect deciding also to cut down our exports. When we decide to increase our exports, we are in effect deciding also to increase our imports.**" *Economics in One Lesson* (1946)

Heartland Institute: Midwestern think tank founded in 1984 to "apply market solutions to public policy issues." Its numerous publications (among them the magazine *Intellectual Ammunition*, a kind of *Reader's Digest* of free-market policy papers that reprints the work of the **Heritage Foundation**, the Cato Institute [see **Rothbard**], and other foundations) give special attention to privatization, health-care policy, school choice, and environmental issues. **Read:** *Intellectual Ammunition* (magazine). "**Environmental groups have their own reasons for hyping environmental hazards. . . . rely[ing] on a 'crisis**

of the month' strategy' . . . to keep the money coming in. . . . Thus we see our mailboxes filled with *urgent* appeals for *immediate* action to avert a new *crisis*. These fundraising pitches would not work nearly so well if they gave as much space to good news as to bad." Heartland president Joseph Bast in *Intellectual Ammunition*

[Heartland Institute, 800 East Northwest Highway #1080, Palatine, IL 60067; (708) 202-3060; fax (708) 202-9799. Joseph L. Bast, president. *Intellectual Ammunition*, subscriptions: $98.00/year (11 issues). PolicyFax information service telephone (510) 208-8000.]

Herberg, Will (1909–1977): American journalist who was religion editor of **National Review**. Like so many others of his generation, Herberg began his intellectual life on the Left. As David G. Dalin has observed, Herberg was a conservative very much according to **Burke**—whose work he read at the urging of Reinhold Niebuhr—in that he believed that religion is the "very basis of political culture, without which the maintenance of social **order** is an impossibility . . . Herberg argued for the necessity of religion as a 'civilizing force,' one that would enable the American body politic to survive as a moral entity in the postwar world." (Herberg, 1989) Herberg's fame during his life and his reputation today rest mainly on *Protestant, Catholic, Jew* (1955), which analyzed the paradox of America's alternately materialistic and religious character. What he saw was a nation in which religion was nearly inseparable from citizenship; a nation that was a "triple melting pot," in which in order to "be" an American, you had to "be" affiliated with one of the three great faiths. Herberg believed, incorrectly it now seems, that Protestant America was moving inexorably away from fundamentalism. On the other hand, he believed that working-class Americans, despite their pro-labor, liberal voting record, are fundamentally conservative. He was among the first to challenge **liberalism**'s assertions that religion must not play a role in public life. And he brilliantly attacked the notion that conscience (at least as expressed in civil disobedience) was morally superior to established order. **Read:** *From Marxism to Judaism* (1989); *Protestant, Catholic, Jew* (1955); **About:** H. Ausmus, *Will Herberg* (1987). "**It would be the crudest kind of misunderstanding to dismiss the American Way of Life as no more than a political for-**

mula or propagandist slogan, or to regard it as simply an expression of the 'materialistic' impulses of the American people. Americans are 'materialistic,' no doubt, but surely not more so than other people, than the French peasant or petty bourgeois, for example. All such labels are irrelevant, if not meaningless. The American Way of Life is, at bottom, a spiritual structure, a structure of ideas and ideals, of aspirations and values, of beliefs and standards; it synthesizes all that commends itself to the American as the right, the good, and the true in actual life. It embraces such seemingly incongruous elements as sanitary plumbing and freedom of opportunity, Coca-Cola and an intense faith in education—all felt as moral questions relating to the proper way of life. The expression 'way of life' points to its religious essence, for one's ultimate, over-all way of life is one's religion." *Protestant, Catholic, Jew* (1955)

Heritage Foundation: American think tank founded in 1973 by Paul Weyrich, Edwin J. Feulner, Jr., and Joseph Coors (Coors put up the seed money), with Weyrich as first president. (Feulner has held the top job since 1977.) One of the things that distinguishes Heritage from other research institutes is money, both in the amount of its income, and in the breadth of its sources: it took in more than $25 million in 1994, half of which was received from its more than 200,000 individual contributors. Like the **Hoover Institution**, the policy experts at Heritage are a distinguished group indeed, and—in part because of its location in Washington, D.C.—they regularly troop up to the Hill to offer expert testimony before every conceivable congressional panel. Beginning with its own vice-presidential "officer corps" those experts include chief operating officer Philip Truluck, who was an economist in the **Reagan** Administration; domestic policy chief Stuart Butler, who—with the possible exception of fellow Heritage analyst Robert Rector—is the **Right**'s leading **welfare** critic; writer-editor Adam Meyerson (of the Foundation's principal periodical, *Policy Review*); foreign policy expert Kim R. Holmes; and Washington-pulse-reader and *National Review* columnist Kate Walsh O'Beirne. Think tanks tend to be judged by the "fellows" they support, and among the more noted at Heritage are: Richard V. Allen, former national-security advisor to Reagan;

William J. Bennett, author of *The Book of Virtues* (1993), former Education Secretary, and former director of federal drug policy; Midge Decter, one of the nation's leading neoconservative critics (see **Podhoretz**); Jack Kemp, sometime presidential hopeful and former head of the Department of Housing and Urban Development; and Walter Williams, economist and author. The close association of Heritage with **Gingrich** and other **conservative** members of Congress was a major factor in the stunning success of the Republican Party in the 1994 midterm elections. Afterwards Gingrich called Heritage, "without question the most far-reaching conservative organization in the country." One little-noticed consequence of the impact of Heritage was the cancellation by Harvard's liberal Kennedy School of Government of its orientation program for new congressmen. Why? The freshmen members of the 104th Congress attended a Heritage orientation instead, just as they had earlier benefited from *Issues '94*, a Heritage briefing book for candidates, portions of which **Limbaugh** read to his national radio audience. Despite its political clout, Heritage is an educational and not a lobbying organization. **Read:** J. Smith, *The Idea Brokers* (1991). **"Just as government isn't the answer to most problems, it alone is not necessarily the culprit—especially in the area of culture and values. The government and the economy rest on society's underlying institutions. No amount of government spending or tinkering will alleviate social problems if our families, neighborhoods, and churches are in a state of decline. On the other hand, certain government policies in the area of taxes and welfare, for example, have undermined the family; and conservatives will argue that when two out of three black children are born to single mothers, advocates of the Great Society have a lot of explaining to do. . . . We've won the Cold War, and we've proved to everyone from Moscow to Buenos Aires to Beijing, if not at OMB and Harvard, that the market system works. Nonetheless, battles over national security and interferences with the market system will still have to be fought and refought. One thing I've learned from 26 years in Washington is that there's no such thing as a permanent political victory."** Edwin J. Feulner, "Building the New Establishment," interview with Adam Meyerson in *Policy Review* (Fall 1991)

[*Policy Review*, The Heritage Foundation, 214 Massachusetts Avenue, NE, Washington, DC 20002-4999. Subscriptions (quarterly): $22/year.]

Hillsdale College: American **liberal-arts** college in Michigan founded in 1844, when—the college likes to recall—there was no federal income tax and government spending totaled $3 million per annum. Established with a special charter to educate blacks and women, today Hillsdale may justly claim to be the nation's preeminent **conservative** school. The college refuses federal funds, equates **academic freedom** with financial independence, and accordingly does not accept any government supervision of its policies and procedures. (It privately provides the scholarship money its students cannot get from Washington.) In *Grove City v. Bell* (1984), a case in which Hillsdale acted in concert with Pennsylvania's Grove City College, the Supreme Court ruled that as long as one student received one dollar of federal assistance the college enrolling him must abide by all federal regulations. Hillsdale responded by notifying prospective and present students that they would not be accepted to the college if they accepted Uncle Sam's help. Much of the college's resolve stems from the outspoken leadership of its president since 1971, historian George Roche. From its inception, Roche has written (1990), "nondiscrimination and true academic freedom were principles carved in stone" at Hillsdale—this "a century before the federal government decided to get into the equal opportunity business." Fortunately for Hillsdale's 1100 students, the college has never in all its travails sacrificed solidity in its curriculum or quality in its pedagogy. The college recently established a chair in American Studies in honor of **Kirk**, who was a frequent visitor at Hillsdale. Among the college's notable extracurricular activities are: the Shavano Institute for National Leadership, which moves about the nation offering speakers and seminars on a wide range of issues; the Center for Constructive Alternatives (CCA), which boasts of being "the largest lecture series in American higher education," and has hosted, among other conservatives, **Reagan**, **Thatcher**, **Buckley**, **Sowell**, and **Muggeridge**, and such well-known liberals as George McGovern, Ralph Nader, and Michael Kinsley; the newsletter *Imprimis* (Latin for "in the first place"), which reprints lectures, offers book excerpts, and generally provides sound opinion. **Kristol** said of Hillsdale that the "small, traditional, and generally excellent liberal arts college, refused on principle to accept any government funds. Roche is therefore free to speak up, as most other college presidents are not—and he does." **Read:** G. Roche, *Fall of the Ivory Tower* (1994); B. Miner and C. Sykes, eds. *The National Review College Guide* (1993). "[After *Grove City v. Bell*, the government] promptly whipped up the Civil Rights Restoration Act, a bill to 'correct the defects' in the enforcement [of affirmative action rules]. The principal sponsor was Senator Ted Kennedy. What the bill provides is that the government may cut all funds to any institution that fails to comply fully with a regulation—in even one department. It applies to any direct or indirect recipient of federal funds. . . . This certainly 'corrects' the loophole. It is also, in my opinion, one of the most sweeping impositions of federal power over free Americans that has ever been seriously proposed. . . . With this, America's great experiment in self-government has lost its last battle. This kind of absolutism is cut from the cloth of the tyrannies of the Old World, whose peoples were not citizens but subjects with no basic rights. What is especially galling about this is that 'federal' money was forcibly extracted from us in the first place. When they 'give' some of it back, it comes not with strings attached but with chains." George Roche, *One by One* (1990)

[*Imprimis*, Hillsdale College, Hillsdale, MI 49242. Subscriptions: complimentary. Hillsdale College Admissions: (417) 437-7341.]

Himmelfarb, Gertrude (1922–   ): See **Kristol, Irving**

Hook, Sidney (1902–1989): American philosopher who was an early expositor of Marx (more from an ethical than an economic perspective), but became a leading **cold-war liberal** (meaning that he opposed **communism** but not "social democracy"), and a precursor of **neoconservatism**. As a student (and friend) of John Dewey, Hook was a pragmatist devoted to experiment and "reconstructive activity," but he was a fierce and feared opponent of Leftism and totalitarianism, especially in the contemporary university. He was also a relentless organizer. In 1939, he helped to found the international Committee for Cultural Freedom to combat both communism and fascism. This was followed in 1950 by the Congress for Cultural Freedom. He began teaching philosophy at New York University in 1927 and retired in 1972, having been departmental chairman for more than thirty years. He ended his long career as a fellow at the **Hoover Institution**. President **Reagan** honored Hook with the Medal of Freedom. Hook's many books (there are more than thirty) demonstrate one of the greatest intellects of the century—a mind capable of grasping the complexities of almost any field. He was a model intellectual, whose brain power never overwhelmed his courageous heart. "Having lived," William McGurn wrote of Hook in *The American Spectator* in 1987, "by his own account, a happy and fulfilled life, marked by what he confesses is not a small measure of luck, he's almost even moved to prayer—but for the realization that this is impossible because 'a world of chance rules out an author of nature.' Like Aquinas, who maintained a sense of humor was logically incompatible with a deity, Hook might be better off not always taking things all the way to their logical conclusions. But the cause of freedom in our time has been advanced largely because he has . . ." (See also **anticommunism**.) **Read**: *Heresy, Yes, Conspiracy, No* (1952); *Academic Freedom and Academic Anarchy* (1970); **About**: his own *Out of Step* (1987), where Hook writes: "**The most formidable criticism of intellectual support of the Cold War came from the growing uneasiness about the nuclear balance of terror. It was presaged in my debate with Bertrand Russell toward the end of the fifties. In an unfortunate interview with Joseph Alsop, Russell had proclaimed that, if the Kremlin could not be induced to agree to reasonable proposals for controlled nuclear disarmament, he would favor unilateral disarmament even if this meant universal Communist domination 'with all its horrors.' I contended that such a declaration was foolish, since it could only intensify Soviet obduracy in negotiations in the expectation that the West would capitulate. The only way to avoid the grim alternatives of war or capitulation was to adopt a defensive posture that would convince the Soviet regime that it could not be victorious in a nuclear conflict. In other words, the readiness to resist aggression by conventional or nuclear arms was the best insurance of peace. The inescapable consequence of unilateral disarmament by the West was surrender to totalitarian communism. It was simply foolishness to** accept this immediate and certain evil in order to escape the problematic evil of a possible nuclear holocaust. Out slogan should not be 'Red or Dead' but 'Neither Red nor Dead,' and more positively 'Better Free than Slave.'"

Hoover Institution: American public policy research center founded in 1919 by Herbert Hoover (1874–1964, president of the United States 1929–1933). Hailed by the *Economist* magazine as the world's top think tank, Hoover was originally established as an archive for protecting the century's historical documents, a function it still maintains. Today Hoover is, with the **Heritage Foundation**, the **American Enterprise Institute**, and the **Rockford Institute,** the leading center for American conservative and classical-liberal scholarship. The Institution is located on the campus of Stanford University and maintains an uneasy peace with that school's liberal faculty and administration. Hoover recently began cataloguing and copying mountains of formerly secret Soviet (specifically, Communist Party) documents under the guidance of fellow Robert Conquest. Among other notable Hoover fellows are: Martin Anderson, Gary Becker, Arnold Beichman, **Friedman**, **Lipset**, Paul Craig Roberts, and **Sowell**. The Institution maintains a 1.6-million-copy library (open to the public) devoted almost exclusively to the 20th century. (The library's holdings also include 50 million documents in the form of archives of historical information such as the above mentioned CPUSSR documents—utilized by **Solzhenitsyn**—and an astonishing variety of other materials, ranging from the papers of a former Polish Politburo member to campaign materials from the first all-race election in South Africa.) As is true of other think tanks, Hoover sponsors numerous seminars and conferences, and publishes books and essays by its scholars. Unfortunately, the Institution does not produce a magazine or journal as do Heritage and A.E.I. **Read:** J. Smith, *The Idea Brokers* (1991). "I am often asked to describe an ideal appointment to Hoover. No one approaches this ideal better than Milton Friedman, who has been a Hoover Fellow for more than fifteen years. What impresses me so deeply about Milton is that he is both a scholar of unsurpassed eminence and a master of rhetoric. I use rhetoric here in the traditional sense of the term—not empty words but high skill that permits Milton to write and speak in plain, persuasive English, making his views accessible not just to fellow academics but to policy makers and laypersons as well." John Raisian, Director, Hoover Institution, in *Hoover Institution Report 1994*

[Hoover Institution, Stanford University, Stanford, CA 94305-6010; (415) 723-1754. Hoover Institution Press, (415) 723-3373 for orders and catalogues.]

Hudson Institute: Indianapolis-based think tank founded by Herman Kahn (1922–1983) and others in 1961 with a self-described viewpoint that "embodies skepticism about the conventional wisdom, optimism about solving problems, a commitment to free institutions and individual responsibility, an appreciation of the crucial role of technology in achieving progress, and an abiding respect for the importance of values, culture, and religion in human affairs." Kahn had left the Rand Corporation (a think tank, not a manufacturer, by the way, whose name is simply an acronym for *research and development*), because he needed a place to conduct research free of the institutional pressures that attended the publication of *On Thermonuclear War* (1961), in which he "thought the unthinkable," namely that the United States could win a nuclear war. Among the first fellows of the Institute were **Aron**, **Bell**, and Henry Kissinger, reflecting its early concern with diplomatic and military issues—a concern which continues under the current leadership of retired general William E. Odom. Hudson's concerns have grown to include a range of foreign and domestic policy areas, and it has frequently published books that have sharply affected debate—if not changed it entirely: *Thinking About the Unthinkable* (1962) elaborated Kahn's views about nuclear war; *The Year 2000* (1967) predicted, among other things, the economic rise of Japan; *The Next 200 Years* (1976) was "Hudson's answer to limits-to-growth arguments"; and Kahn's *The Coming Boom* (1982) accurately forecast economic growth of the 1980s. Among Hudson's present group of notable fellows are: Alan Reynolds, director of economic research; Elliott Abrams, expert in international affairs (both Reynolds and Abrams are *National Review* contributors); Anna Kondratas, a specialist in urban affairs; and education experts Sally B. Kilgore and Carol D'Amico, who direct respectively Hudson's Modern Red Schoolhouse project and its Educational Excellence Network (EEN), co-chaired by Chester Finn and Diane Ravitch. Recent presidential contender Lamar Alexander is one of Hudson's senior research staff, and novelist Mark Helprin is a senior fellow. **Read:** W. Johnston and A. Packer, *Workforce 2000* (1987); J. Smith, *The Idea Brokers* (1991). **"Americans are going to be enormously wealthy, so they must learn how to spend their wealth without becoming satiated, disappointed or fashionably antimaterialistic. They have to learn to take certain everyday affairs seriously (without becoming obsessed with them) in order to avoid boredom, and to compensate for the fact that they no longer have life and death struggles to engage their emotions. . . . Americans must be like Athenians . . . If there was a war, they performed gymnastics to stay fit in order to fight. If there was peace, they had more time for gymnastics. Unfortunately, Americans tend to be more like the Spartans and Romans, who got into shape to fight anticipated wars, but tended toward sloth in peacetime and prosperity. We must learn the virtues of family life and conversation and social interaction with our friends. Epicurean (in both the Greek and the modern sense) values will be vital . . . if Americans are to spend their leisure time at home without killing everyone in sight because of overfamiliarity and boredom."** Herman Kahn, William Brown, and Leon Martel, *The Next 200 Years* (1976)

[Hudson Institute, Herman Kahn Center, P.O. Box 26-919, Indianapolis, IN 46226; (317) 545-1000. Leslie Lenkowsky, president.]

Human Events: See **Morley, Felix**

humanism: A noble word that is sometimes confused (and rejected) with *secular humanism*. True humanism—in its original sense—is simply the study of the great literature of antiquity, and is associated with the **liberal arts**. It was (and is) the study of the origins and greatness of Western civilization. Beginning in the Renaissance, the *studia humanitatis* have been the curricula of **tradition**. (Central to the rediscovery of ancient learning was the recovery of the Greek language, which prior to 1400 almost no one could read.) That tradition, then as now, is rooted in the religious view of Man. Secular humanism is then a view of Man torn from its roots; a view that Man, not God, is the center of existence. Until our own time, this was commonly called *pagan* humanism. The most notable modern statement of secular humanism appears in Thomas Mann's *The Magic Mountain* (1924): "[Man] is the measure of all things, and his welfare is the sole and single criterion of truth." A specifically Christian humanism has been proposed by such modern writers as Christopher Dawson and, especially, Jacques Maritain, whose "integral humanism" sought specifically to explicate the traditional ideas of the unity of Man and God. **Read**: J. Maritain, *Integral Humanism* (1968); T. Molnar, *Christian Humanism* (1978). **"To put matters very briefly, genuine humanism is the belief that man is a distinct being, governed by laws peculiar to his nature: there is a law for man, and there is a law for things. Man stands higher than the beasts that perish because he recognizes and obeys this law of his nature. The disciplinary arts of *humanitas* teach man to put checks upon his will and his appetite. These checks are provided by reason—not the private rationality of the Enlightenment, but the higher reason which grows out of a respect for the wisdom of our ancestors and out of the endeavor to apprehend order in the person and order of the republic. The sentimentalist, who would subject man to the forces of impulse and passion; the pragmatic materialist, who would treat man as a mere edified ape; the leveling enthusiast, who would reduce human personality to a collective mediocrity—these are the enemies of true human nature . . ."** Russell Kirk, in his Introduction to Irving Babbitt's *Democracy and Leadership* (1979)

human nature: No single, defining sentence may introduce so complex a topic, and a neutral statement (for example, "the essential psycho-social character of Man") begs the moral question. In the view of **conservatism**, ancient and modern, human nature is flawed (see **sin**), and in the view of contemporary **liberalism**, Man is perfectible. From this premise spring all differences between the two philosophies; the primary implications being the ends of politics and society. Liberalism is almost always, one way or another, enamored of **utopianism**, which conservatism rejects. And yet, the conservative still believes that Man longs for **liberty**; that—in the words of Dostoevsky (*Notes* *from the Underground*, 1864)—he longs to prove "to himself every minute that he is a man and not a piano key." Unfortunately, some of the ways some men *naturally* choose to demonstrate their power are deadly. The Holocaust was without question an extraordinary event, but it was accomplished by ordinary men. **Read:** L. Dawidowicz, *The War Against the Jews* (1975). **"I have a premonition which sounds like utter folly, and yet it will not leave me: the military state will become one single vast factory. Those hordes of men in the great industrial centers cannot be left indefinitely to their greed and want. What must logically come is a definite and supervised stint of misery, with promotions and uniforms, daily begun and ended to the sound of drums. . . . The big damage was done in the last century, especially by Rousseau with his preaching of the goodness of human nature. . . . As any child can see, this resulted in the complete dissolution of the concept of authority in the heads of mortals, whereupon they periodically had to be subjected to naked force instead . . ."** Jacob Burkhardt (1818–1897), quoted in Peter Viereck, *Conservatism Revisited* (1949)

Hume, David (1711–1776): Scottish philosopher-historian (he published an eight-volume history of England that was widely read by America's Founders) whose **empiricism** greatly influenced the work of his friend **Smith** (especially with regard to the moral basis of **free trade**). Hume proposed a simple apothegm, *Whatever is conceivable is possible*, as the starting point of a skeptical philosophy that was in part a critical elaboration of the work of René Descartes (1596–1650). (Hume was attacking the idea that causes may be known, or that extant conditions must be considered necessary.) Although a friend of Rousseau, Hume was perhaps (**Burke** excepted) the one thinker of the **Enlightenment** most opposed to its characteristic **rationalism**; especially of the notion that reason is capable of discovering what is morally good. (He was consistent, questioning equally the causal claims of science and theology. *Belief*, he asserted, is actually *habit*. See **Hayek** and also **Popper**.) Accordingly, he was at odds with much of the reasoning based on **natural law** and **natural rights** that dominated the 17th and 18th centuries, although he did believe that certain moral sentiments are innate. Among other implications, this meant he did not accept the contract theory of government (see **Locke**). As far as he was concerned (and in this he echoed **Montesquieu**) either a monarchy or a **democracy** could be appropriate if "established by custom and authority." Indeed, Hume was very much a supporter of established government, largely because of his skepticism; i.e., he mistrusted reasoned schemes for the betterment of mankind, because they inevitably (and falsely) claim to understand causes. "All plans of government which suppose great reformation in the manners of mankind are plainly imaginary," he wrote, and concluded that custom "is the great guide of human life." He was a Tory, but, according to Dr. Johnson, only "by accident." His influence on later philosophy, beginning with Immanuel Kant and Jeremy Bentham (and not least on **Hamilton**'s and **Madison**'s views about balanced power), has been great. So great is his stature that he is sometimes hailed as a precursor of **positivism**, which is an utter falsehood. **Read:** *Essays Moral, Political, and Literary* (1741–1777/ 1985); *A Treatise of Human Nature* (1740). **About:** J. Stewart, *The Moral and Political Philosophy of David Hume* (1963). "Were all men possessed of so inflexible a regard to justice, that, of themselves, they would totally abstain from the properties of others; they had for ever remained in a state of absolute liberty, without subjection to any magistrate or political society: But this is a state of perfection, of which human nature is justly deemed incapable. Again; were all men possessed of so perfect an understanding, as always to know their own interests, no form of government had ever been submitted to, but what was established on consent, and was fully canvassed by every member of society: But this state of perfection is likewise much superior to human nature. Reason, history, and experience shew us, that all political societies had an origin much less accurate and regular; and were one to choose a period of time, when the people's consent was the least regarded in public transactions, it would be precisely on the establishment of a new government. In a settled constitution, their inclinations are often consulted; but during the fury of revolutions, conquests, and public convulsions, military force or political craft usually decides the controversy." "Of the Original Contract" in *Essays Moral, Political, and Literary* (1777)

ideology: From its origins in France early in the 19th century, the word ideology has always suggested a comprehensive, scientific basis for its various forms of socio-political thought about the nature of the world. From Marx's attack on the "ideology" of religion, we derive our essentially negative sense of the word as representing a *false consciousness*, stridently held. That Marx himself spawned one of history's dominant ideologies is no minor irony. One commentator (Minogue, 1985) has defined ideology as "a form of social analysis which discovers that human beings are the victims of an oppressive system, and that the business of life is liberation." As such, **conservatism**, with its essential skepticism, cannot qualify as an ideology. (Neither can **classical liberalism**.) Of ideology, John **Adams** quipped that it was the "science of idiocy." **Read:** K. Minogue, *Alien Powers* (1985); K. Popper, *The Open Society and Its Enemies* (1962). "**The quest for a pure community begins with a revolution designed to destroy bourgeois oppression, where 'bourgeois' stands for a reasonably determinate set of people who inhabit the executive suites of industry and the offices of government. In some of the more gruesome cases, ranging from Adolf Hitler to Pol Pot, the project of purification amounted quite straightforwardly to killing off everyone identified as impure, but in all ideological revolutions, death and exile have become commonplace.**" Kenneth Minogue, *Alien Powers* (1985)

Imprimis: See **Hillsdale College**

individualism: The belief that we understand society only by understanding individuals, and that diverse individual actions create, usually without intending to, the traditions and institutions of society. Individualism is the social, political, and economic philosophy of **liberty**. But this is hardly the definition most commonly associated with the word. The term was coined by **Tocqueville** to describe the dominant ethos of democratic America, an ethos he saw as historically liberating, but also as potentially atomizing, and this latter sense has predominated among liberals and conservatives alike; not a complicated view of decentralized economic and political power but a facile misanthropy (in Tocqueville's estimation, the successor to simple *égoïsme*). **Nisbet** (1953) summed up that view of individualism as follows: "The philosophy of individualism . . . began with the Christian-Judaic stress upon the ethical primacy of the person; but . . . it became a rationalist psychology devoted to the view . . . that groups and institutions are at best mere reflections of the solid and ineffaceable fact of the individual." The definition given here, however, describes an individualism far from the selfishness epitomized by **objectivism**, although not necessarily divorced from **libertarianism**. **Socialism**, according to **Hayek** (1984), was a term "coined to express its opposition to individualism," and he and other "libertarians" (see also **Nock** and **Chodorov**) extol the word accordingly. A few go so far as to deny the very reality of what we call society, which is what makes many others suspicious of the term—**conservative** Catholics especially—although it is far from certain that **John Paul II** would condemn the social individualism of a Hayek as Pius XI condemned economic individualism in general (*Quadragesimo Anno*, 1931). A proper individualism rejects neither **authority** nor **community**, and is entirely compatible with **subsidiarity**. Without a sense of individuality, there would be no (could not have been any) commitment to liberty anywhere at any time, and, as **Popper** pointed out (1985), individualism is "the central doctrine of Christianity. ('Love your neighbor,' say the Scriptures, not 'love your tribe'. . .") **Read**: F. A. Hayek, *The Road to Serfdom* (1944). **"It is illusory to believe that it is possible to visualize collective wholes. They are never visible; their cognition is always the outcome of the understanding of the meaning which acting men attribute to their acts. We can see a crowd, i.e., a multitude of people. Whether this crowd is a mere gathering or a mass (in the sense in which this term is used in contemporary psychology) or an organized body or any other kind of social entity is a question which can only be answered by understanding the meaning which they themselves attach to their presence. And this meaning is always the meaning of individuals. Not our senses, but understanding, a mental process, makes us recognize social entities."** Ludwig von Mises, *Human Action* (1949)

inequality: See **egalitarianism**

ISI (Intercollegiate Studies Institute): American educational institution founded by **Chodorov** in 1953 as the Intercollegiate Society of

Individualists. **Buckley** was ISI's first president. The Institute's primary stated goal is "to educate for liberty." (The articulated "principles of a free society" include individual **liberty**, personal responsibility, the rule of law, **limited government**, a **free-market** economy, and "cultural norms," by which is meant the Judeo-Christian **tradition**, because without "such ordinances, society induces its decay by embracing a relativism that rejects an objective moral order.") ISI's educational activities are promoted through its sponsorship of conferences, lectures (310 in 1995), fellowships, and publications. A recent ISI-sponsored lecture series on multiculturalism (see **academic freedom**) featured Dinesh D'Souza, Christina Hoff Sommers, Hilton Kramer, and Walter Williams. What is most significant about ISI, however—especially in an age in which the campus is generally assumed to be a radical hotbed—is its recruitment and mobilization of conservative activists: on-campus reps at more than 1000 schools, and more than 50,000 student and faculty members. ISI publications, with total circulation in excess of half a million copies, include *Modern Age* (founded by **Kirk**), the *Intercollegiate Review, CAMPUS* (a kind of *USA Today* for youth on the **Right**), and *The Political Science Reviewer*, an annual survey of scholarship. *Modern Age*, currently edited by George Panichas, is now the preeminent journal—paradoxically, given its title—of the non-isolationist **Old Right**. *The Intercollegiate Review*, edited by Jeffrey O. Nelson, is a lively meeting place for exponents of both **tradition** and **libertarianism**. **Read**: G. Nash, *The Conservative Intellectual Movement in America* (1976). "We have to be reminded that we cannot climb out of the abyss of negation without reference to the spirit of affirmation. . . . We need . . . to revere the spirit of affirmation in its concrete forms—and with the concrete evidence—that subdues modern habits of doubt and denial, of rejection and renunciation. These forms contain the voice of affirmation which encourages us to secure higher life-meaning and life-purpose and to reach a higher moral ground. Especially in a time of trouble and confusion, when we increasingly glorify the tawdry, the trivial, the vulgar, even the diabolic, we have a pressing need to encounter values and to treasure experiences that dramatize the truth of Martin Buber's words: 'The spark that leaps from him who teaches to him who learns rekindles a spark of fire which lifted the mountain of revelation to the very heart of heaven.'" George A. Panichas in *Modern Age* (Summer 1995)

[ISI, 3901 Centerville Road, P. O. Box 4431, Wilmington, DE 19807-0431. T. Kenneth Cribb, Jr., president. *CAMPUS* and *Intercollegiate Review* are available free to students, graduates students, and faculty. Non-academic (i.e., paid) subscriptions: *Intercollegiate Review* ("2–4 times during the academic year"): $10/4 issues or $18/8 issues; *Modern Age* (quarterly): $15/year or $25/2 years.]

isolationism: The traditional American belief that the nation ought to avoid "entangling alliances" (**Jefferson**), which was once as common among "liberals" as among "conservatives," but which after 1940 became associated with the America First Committee, which opposed America's entry into World War II, and, because of the other affiliations and beliefs of the Committee's members, with **conservatism** itself. With the Japanese invasion of Pearl Harbor at the end of 1941, however, isolationism ceased to be a serious political issue, and effectively exited center stage with the rejection of **Taft** by the Republican party in 1952. Some sociological evidence has indicated that American isolationism is as much a reflection of ethnicity as of political philosophy: in the two world wars, German Americans opposed American involvement out of support for **family** and friends in the old country, and Irish Americans did so because they were against the provision of any aid to England. There is no doubt something to this, given that isolationism has been strongest in those areas, especially the Midwest (but also in neighborhoods of cities like New York), where many German-Americans and Irish-Americans live. But at least as important have been the agrarian and individualist impulses to self-sufficiency that like a raw nerve have been aggravated by the general growth of government intervention in all aspects of American life, and have cast increasing suspicion upon the national government's motives. In a questionable cause-and-effect association, the inevitable consequence of war and other aggressive foreign adventures—such as **free-trade** agreements—is seen as bigger and more intrusive government. Thus, isolationism and protectionism have been the two primary issues defining conflict on the **Right**

throughout most of this century, up to and including the Gulf War (1990) and the North Atlantic Free Trade Agreement (1994). **Read:** R. Radosh, *Prophets on the Right* (1975). **"From what I know of the American people, the conscience of the majority does not at the present time cry out for the type of neo-isolationism we see being promoted in the halls of Congress and the intellectual centers of our country. I believe the American people have become deeply disturbed and at least partially disenchanted with the whole idea of foreign adventures because of the war in Vietnam. But it must be remembered that there perhaps has never been a conflict so ideally suited to the task of heightening American frustration as this dirty little war in the jungles and rice paddies of Southeast Asia. There can be no doubt that the Americans are tired of the cost, both in lives and money . . . [and] of our inability or refusal to come out of it with a clear-cut victory over the forces of Communism. . . . But it would be a vast miscalculation to take this to mean that the conscience of America seriously desires a return to isolationism and a consequent heightening of the concept of the jungle law where only the fittest survive."** Barry Goldwater, *The Conscience of a Majority* (1970)

Jaffa, Harry V. (1918–   ): American political scientist and legal scholar closely associated, in both method and philosophy, with **Strauss**. Jaffa is currently an emeritus professor at Claremont McKenna College (where he has taught since 1964), and was previously a professor at Queens College, the University of Chicago, and Ohio State. With **Bloom** he wrote the delightful *Shakespeare's Politics* (1964), and Jaffa has also produced notable books on religious philosophy (reflecting his interest in **natural law**), the American Revolution, and early-American **conservatism**, but his most enduring work has dealt with the basic principles of the American **order**, especially as embodied in our understanding of the **Constitution**, the **Declaration of Independence**, and the role of **Lincoln**. These subjects were developed in his classic *The Crisis of the House Divided* (1959). The question he poses is this: is our system based upon legal **positivism**, or upon the principles of natural law? At the beginning of the book, he gives the answer: "Those who believe anything sanctioned by law is right commit one great error; those who believe the law should sanction only what is right commit another." In other words, we need standards of right and wrong that cannot be violated—even by majority rule; and those standards need to anchor but not shackle our legal creativity. To believe that all men are created equal is not Leftist pap; it is the soul of the American way—an embrace of a transcendent ideal derived from natural law. Equality is, of course, a *political* ideal and not a description of abilities or outcomes. Still, Jaffa's views have brought him into sometimes bitter conflict with, among others, **Kendall**, **Meyer**, **Kilpatrick**, and M. E. Bradford. Writing in *National Review* (January 22, 1990), he nicely summarized the brief for Lincoln's nationalist stand against the South's "peculiar institution": "Not one single moral commandment of the Judaeo-Christian tradition was not denied by slavery. Lincoln declared that if slavery was not wrong, nothing was wrong. Wherein did he err?" Professor Jaffa is also justly famous for being a devotee of bicycling. **Read:** *The Crisis of the House Divided* (1959); *Equality and Liberty* (1965); **About:** T. Silver and P. Schramm, eds., *Natural Right and Political Right* (1984); G. Nash, *The Conservative Intellectual Movement in America* (1976). "[T]he problem of understanding human nature, the especial concern of political scientists, can never be solved by the method of modern science, insofar as that method conceives of man as an epiphenomenon, as a by-product of a more fundamental subhuman reality. While plants and animals other than man may without self-contradiction be conceived as forms that are epiphenomena of some more fundamental subhuman reality, man cannot be so conceived. Intelligence cannot be regarded as a by-product of unintelligence. The 'what' of man, his self-consciousness, his awareness of himself as an 'other,' linked by the symbols of articulate speech to other selves, and linked not merely by these symbols but by an intelligible reality of which the symbols are symbols, cannot be conceived as the effect of an unintelligent cause. For in that case man's intelligence would, like the secondary qualities, be regarded as an illusion, corresponding as it would to nothing in a reality outside man's brains. But the doctrine of an unintelligent primary reality, being itself a product of man's brain, would also have to be regarded as an illusion. The doctrine that man, the intelligent being, is 'caused' by an unintelligent first principle cannot then escape self-contradiction. Intelligence is an irreducible reality." *Equality and Liberty* (1965)

Jefferson, Thomas (1743–1826): Third president of the United States and principal author of the **Declaration of Independence**. He was an anti-aristocratic aristocrat, whose vision of political America was agrarian **democracy**. However, Jeffersonian democracy—as opposed to the later Jacksonian variety—was set squarely against centralization of power in the national government, and he was accordingly an opponent of **Hamilton**. Without question, Jefferson was a "liberal," but a devotee of **classical liberalism** and the **liberal arts** who could say, "I am certainly not an advocate for frequent and untried changes in laws and institutions." And it was he who famously said (paraphrasing Cicero) that "that government is best which governs least." It is no small irony that the heirs of Hamilton now call for **laissez-faire**, and the heirs of Jefferson for centralization. "[F]or all his acquaintance with the *philosophes* and his affection for France, Jefferson had [Sir Edward] Coke, Locke, and [Lord Henry] Kames for his real political mentors; and, like them, he had half a mind to be conservative—and sometimes more than half a mind for it (**Kirk**, 1953)." **Read:** *Thomas Jefferson: Writings* (1984); **About:** A. Mapp, *Thomas Jefferson: A Strange Case of Mistaken Identity* (1987); A. J. Nock, *Mr. Jefferson* (1926). "[W]e may say with truth and meaning, that governments are more or less republican as they have more or less of the element of popular election and control in their composition; and believing, as I do, that the mass of the citizens is the safest depository of their own rights, and especially, that the evils flowing from the duperies of the people, are less injurious than those from the egoism of their agents, I am a friend to that composition of government which has in it the most of this ingredient. And I sincerely believe, with you, that banking establishments are more dangerous than standing armies; and that the principle of spending money to be paid by posterity, under the name of funding, is but swindling futurity on a large scale." Letter to John Taylor, May 28, 1816 in *Thomas Jefferson: Writings* (1984)

John Birch Society: Right-wing, patriotic, and anti-communist organization founded in 1958 by Robert Welch (1899–1985), and named for an American soldier/missionary (and intelligence analyst for Chennault's Flying Tigers) killed by the "Red Chinese" in 1945. Several of Welch's books, including *May God Forgive Us* (1952) and *The Politician* (1963), were best sellers, and put the terms "international communist conspiracy" and (in reaction to Welch) extremism into wide use. Welch believed that Secretary of State John Foster Dulles and even President Eisenhower were conscious agents of the conspiracy, and he mounted a billboard campaign to "Impeach [Chief Justice] Earl Warren." (At a meeting in 1962 Kirk encouraged Goldwater to renounce the Birch Society. "Eisenhower isn't a Communist," Kirk argued. "He's a golfer.") Many conservatives tolerated the Society—but not Welch—until 1965, when *National Review* condemned its "psychosis of conspiracy," and read the JBS out of the conservative movement, calling it "a grave liability to the conservative and anti-Communist cause." *American Opinion*, the society's magazine, has been re-named *The New American*. **Read:** D. Bell et al., *The Radical Right* (1963); Lipset and Raab, eds., *The Politics of Unreason* (1970); R. Welch, *The Politician* (1963); R. Oliver, *America's Decline* (1981). **"When that private letter [a draft of *The Politician*] became public in 1960, the Establishment, shaken to its foundation by the possibility of exposure, commenced its usual screams for blood. Always prepared to insist on 'freedom of expression' and the 'sacred rights' of a 'free speech' when such cant serves its own interests, the liberal media joined in a uniform howl of indignation . . . Mr. Welch was never, of course, given access to that [sic] same media to defend himself."** "Remembering Robert Welch," *The New American* (December 13, 1993)

[The John Birch Society, P.O. Box 8040, Appleton, WI 54913. G. Vance Smith, CEO. *The New American*, 770 Westhill Blvd., Appleton, WI 54914; (414) 749-3784. Subscriptions: (biweekly) $39/year.]

John Paul II (1920–): Polish-born pope of the Roman Catholic Church (since 1978), the first non-Italian to be chosen by a conclave of the College of Cardinals since 1523. Karol Jozef Wojtyla was a resistance fighter during World War II and then an active opponent of communism after 1946, the year of his ordination. After education in

Rome, he became a professor of ethics at Poland's Catholic University, and was consecrated Auxiliary Bishop of Krakow in 1958. At the Second Vatican Council, Bishop Wojtyla emerged as a champion of religious freedom, and Pope Paul VI made him a cardinal in 1967. Cardinal Wojtyla's relations with Poland's communist government were superficially cordial, but the future pope clearly did all he could to keep the Polish people's attention fixed on the failures of **Marxism**. The year after his ascension to the papacy, John Paul went home to Poland, officially atheist, and the effect of his trip was electrifying. Barely three months later, on September 30, 1979, he celebrated an outdoor Mass in Dublin, Ireland that was without doubt the largest in history—nearly one-and-one-half-million people attended. On journey after journey—from America to Africa—he has had a similar impact. Few popes have ever combined the philosophical depth and pastoral charm of the man often called the Pilgrim Pope. His encyclicals have helped to revivify the Church's traditional dogma, and his visits around the world have helped restore people's **faith** in both the accessibility and the majesty of religion. His role in hastening the fall of communism cannot be overstated. With **Reagan** and **Thatcher**, and with both forcefulness and subtlety, he has commanded the West's (and perhaps the world's) moral attention as no other figure in the last half of the century. **Read:** *Sign of Contradiction* (1979); **About:** P. Johnson, *John Paul II and the Catholic Restoration* (1981); R. Neuhaus, *Doing Well and Doing Good* (1992). "*This is truly the key for interpreting reality.* Original sin is not only the violation of a positive command of God but also, and above all, a violation of *the will of God as expressed in that command. Original sin attempts, then, to abolish fatherhood,* destroying its rays which permeate the created world, placing in doubt the truth about God who is Love and leaving man only with a sense of the master-slave relationship. As a result, the Lord appears jealous of His power over the world and over man; and consequently, man feels goaded to do battle against God. No differently than in an epoch of history, the enslaved man is driven to take sides against the master who kept him enslaved. . . . *In order to set contemporary man free from fear . . . it is necessary to pray fervently that he will bear and cultivate in his heart that true fear of God, which is the beginning of all wisdom.*" *Crossing the Threshold of Hope* (1994)

Jouvenel, Bertrand de (1903–1987): French political philosopher and journalist, whose classical-liberal views have been described as "pro-monarchical, aristocratic, and anti-democratic." From shortly after his graduation from the Sorbonne, Jouvenel's interest became focused on socio-economic realities in America. The Depression convinced him that free-market **capitalism** with its potential for growth is the only economic system capable of avoiding the destabilizing effects of economic stagnation. Among the more telling distinctions made by Jouvenel is that between *nomocracy* and *telocracy*. He was an inveterate coiner of words. Nomocracy is the society governed by the rule of law. In one way or another, it is the form of traditional culture, and it is necessarily as conscious of the past as of the future. In a telocracy, which is the trend in modern governments, the vision is primarily forward; it is the rule of ends, which, at its most telocratic, all means are bent to serve. He dated the start of telocracy in 1776, not with the two most famous events of that year, **Smith**'s *Wealth of Nations* and the American **Declaration of Independence**, but with James Watt's invention of the steam engine. (Never mind that Watt was not really its inventor.) The shift from agriculture to industry made Man ever more goal-oriented and, therefore, progress-obsessed. Jouvenel himself became rather obsessed with the future structure of the world, with what (in one of his least felicitous coinages) he called *futuribles*, which is both the process of looking ahead and those who do the looking. Although he became something of an environmentalist, Jouvenel never lost his abhorrence of **socialism**. In *The Ethics of Redistribution* (1952), he brilliantly exposed the fallacies of redistribution: by taking from the most productive it reduces productivity (by reducing investment), so that the effect is to reduce the total available resources to be redistributed (an early expression of **supply-side theory**); by raising expectations it cannot fulfill, redistribution leads to disorder. By the way, Jouvenel's stepmother was the novelist Colette. **Read:** *On Power* (1948); *Sovereignty* (1957); **About:** R. Fryer, *Recent Conservative Political Thought* (1979). **"It is untrue that the supremacy of law can be procured by Power working alone. By far the most of the work is done by beliefs and folkways, of which there must be no incessant calling into question; their relative stability is an essential condition to the**

welfare of society. The necessary cohesion of society cannot be procured by Power alone. There must exist, rooted in a common faith, a deep community of feeling, passing into an acknowledged ethic and maintaining an inviolable law. . . . Power can achieve nothing of all this. Once this community of feeling is in dissolution, and law is delivered over to the good pleasure of the legislature, then no doubt Power not only can but must extend. It must intervene, widely and continuously, to restore, if it can, the threatened cohesion." *On Power* (1948)

Kendall, Willmoore (1909–1967): American political scientist (born and raised in Oklahoma) who championed a uniquely American **conservatism**. Like many of his generation, he began adulthood on the Left but moved right as his understanding of **communism** grew. He received his undergraduate degree from the University of Oklahoma at the age of 18 (his precociousness due in part to time spent reading to his blind father, a Methodist minister), later became a Rhodes Scholar, flirted with the Spanish Civil War, and then, in 1940, earned a Ph.D. at the University of Illinois (under **conservative** Francis Wilson), his dissertation the justly famous *John Locke and Majority Rule* (1941). As a professor at Yale, Kendall taught **Buckley**, and later became a senior editor of *National Review*. Kendall was contemptuous of the "open society" (and, therefore, of **Mill** and **Popper**) and defended what he termed "American orthodoxy," often calling himself an "Appalachians-to-the-Rockies patriot." That orthodoxy, Kendall argued, is manifest in political majoritarianism, not in abstract and proliferating "rights." It seemed to some that this majoritarianism—Kendall's emphasis on the people's "deliberate sense" (or the "public orthodoxy")—came perilously close to a version of the "general will," and indeed Kendall never lost his admiration for Rousseau. However, his most deeply held beliefs about American government were not compatible with **Enlightenment** thinking. Those beliefs were: that our system is representative and *not* plebiscitary; that **egalitarianism** is *not* a fundamental American premise; and that our system *is* the system of *The Federalist* (1787). At the time of his conversion to Catholicism in 1956, and before his move to the University of Dallas in 1963, he came increasingly under the influence of **Voegelin** and **Strauss**. But Kendall was very much his own man, and his conservatism was unique, his personality combative. Dwight MacDonald quipped that Kendall could "get a discussion into the shouting stage faster than anybody I have ever known." **Read:** (with G. Carey) *The Basic Symbols of the American Political Tradition* (1970); *The Conservative Affirmation* (1985); *Willmoore Kendall Contra Mundum* (1971); **About:** J. East, *The American Conservative Movement* (1986); G. Nash, *The Conservative Intellectual Movement in America* (1976). "[I]f the future of individual initiative depends upon keeping alive the motivations of the entrepreneur, and if that is a matter of containing the advance of leveling for the sake of leveling, of principled egalitarianism, then the future of private initiative in America . . . is safe for the foreseeable future because . . . there exists in America a healthy public opinion which, when the chips are down, is against leveling. Healthy public opinion exists because the Conservatives among us have taken the steps, in the public forum, necessary for keeping it alive. American opinion perhaps nibbles at the cheese of leveling, but as far as I can see, its *heart* is never really in it." "The Future of Individual Initiative in America," a lecture (1966) reprinted in *Willmoore Kendall Contra Mundum* (1971)

Kilpatrick, James Jackson (1920–): American journalist (former editor, *Richmond Times-Dispatch*; contributing editor, *National Review*; syndicated columnist, "A Conservative View"; former commentator, *60 Minutes*), whose 1957 book, *The Sovereign States*, was a lucid defense of **states' rights** (and thus attracted the ire of the liberal press for its defense of segregation), and whose TV tangles with liberal journalist Shana Alexander were watched by millions. He advocated gradual integration, arguing (in *The Southern Case for School Desegregation*, 1962) that since Southern "racial separation begins in the cradle . . . [w]hat rational imagines this concept can be shattered overnight?" Kilpatrick's defense of Southern **tradition** has been both highly intellectual and deeply emotional, and he has written with equal grace about decisions of the Supreme Court and the garden in his own backyard. **Read:** *The Sovereign States* (1957); **About:** G. Nash, *The Conservative Intellectual Movement in America* (1976); M. Rozell and J. Pontuso, *American Conservative Opinion Leaders* (1990). "In this Republic, what the States choose to do in their reserved fields is their own business, *for good or ill*, until the Constitution itself be amended by the States themselves to establish a rule applicable to all alike. . . . The abiding prayer of many Southern conservatives is that this individuality and responsibility be preserved; their continuing apprehension is that local government will be reduced to impotence by gradual consolidation, and the States in essence will be destroyed by judicial erosion. This is seen as a perversion of law, but more than this: It is seen as a surrender to a remote statism, a submission to some massive Orwellian control too powerful ever to be restrained. There is a tyranny of the majority. Nothing was recognized more clearly than this when the Union was formed, and a dozen provisions were inserted in the Constitution to forestall it. Now these provisions are being circumvented or ignored; and this is being done, as Plato long ago imagined it would be done, in the name of liberty: 'Tyranny springs from democracy,' he said, when liberty magnified and intensified overmasters necessary restraints against license. 'The excess of liberty, whether in States or individuals, seems only to pass into excess of slavery.' Understanding this, conservatism pleads for a system of government kept close to the people governed, subject to their wishes, responsive to what they perceive to be their own needs. This is the sort of government envisioned by the wise men, genius-struck, who fashioned our Constitution, We will abandon it at our peril." "Conservatism and the South" in Louis D. Rubin, ed., *The Lasting South* (1960)

Kirk, Russell (1918–1994): American political theorist and author of the influential *The Conservative Mind* (1953). Kirk was the founding editor of *Modern Age* (see ISI), the long-time editor of *The University Bookman*, and for twenty years a columnist for *National Review*. Kirk is often credited with the 20th century's rediscovery of Burke, and, therefore, of conservatism's rediscovery of intellectual respectability. Kirk identified a half-dozen aspects of the conservative worldview: (1) belief in natural law, which "rules society as well as conscience"; (2) opposition to egalitarianism; (3) insistence upon order, which is the positive expression of point 2; (4) "Persuasion that freedom and property are closely linked"; (5) "Faith in prescription" and opposition to abstraction; and (6) the recognition that hasty <u>change</u> may not be prudent reform. Political problems, Kirk believed, are at heart religious problems. The actions of the "levellers," as he liked to call <u>welfare</u> liberals, lead to an achromatic world, and not to their promised "rainbow." Since Kirk's death, his work is carried on by The Russell Kirk Center for Cultural Renewal. **Read:** *The Conservative Mind* (1953); *The Portable Conservative Reader* (editor, 1982); **About:** his own *The Sword of Imagination* (1995); J. East, *The American Conservative Movement* (1986); G. Nash, *The Conservative Intellectual Movement in America* (1976). "Although the tree of American order has grown in height and breadth during the past hundred years, it could not have flourished so if those roots had been unhealthy. Those roots go deep, but they require watering from time to time. Whatever the failings of America in the eighth decade of the 20th century, the American order has been a conspicuous success in the perspective of human history. Under God, a large measure of justice has been achieved; the state is strong and energetic; personal freedom is protected by laws and customs; and a sense of community endures. . . . [T]he history of most societies is a record of painful striving, brief success (if success at all), and then decay and ruin. No man can know the future, but most Americans believe that their order will continue to 'bring out in this life the dialectic union of authority and liberty.' That will be true so long as the roots of order have proliferating life in them." *The Roots of American Order* (1974)

[<u>Russell Kirk Center</u>, P.O. Box 4, Mecosta, MI 49332; (616) 972-7655. *The University Bookman*, c/o ISI, 14 South Bryn Mawr Ave., Bryn Mawr, PA 19010-3275; (800) 526-7022. Subscriptions (quarterly): $10/year.]

Kristol, Irving (1920–   ): American writer and editor, and a founder of **neoconservatism**. Setting the neoconservative pattern, Kristol was an early proponent of <u>socialism</u>, then a <u>cold-war liberal</u>, and finally a <u>conservative</u>, although one who retains a "reforming spirit." Kristol has been associated with many leading opinion journals: *Commentary* (managing editor), *Encounter* (co-editor), *The*

Public Interest (co-editor, see **Glazer**), and *The National Interest* (publisher). He is a fellow of the **American Enterprise Institute**, and a member of the Board of Contributors of the *Wall Street Journal*. As he has frequently written, Kristol counts **Hook**, Lionel Trilling, and **Strauss** among the most important influences upon his intellectual development. He is married to historian Gertrude Himmelfarb, and is the father of William Kristol, founder of the Project for the Republican Future and publisher of *The Weekly Standard*. Ms. Himmelfarb (1922–   ) also admits an obligation to Trilling, but includes **Burke** and **Acton** along with numerous sociological, historical, and psychological authors as influential in the development of her unique view: the analysis of our period through the lens of the Victorian Age. The early years of her academic career were spent in part on the study of Acton, whom she called "one of our great contemporaries": her dissertation for the University of Chicago was on Acton's thought; she published a collection of his essays, *Essays on Freedom and Power*, several years later; and her first book was about him—*Lord Acton: A Study in Conscience and Politics* (1952). Her analyses of Acton and **Mill** are essential for the modern understanding of both great thinkers, and of the evolution of the distinctions between **conservatism** and **liberalism**. ("The ambiguities and ambivalences that are to be found in . . . [Mill] are those that have beset much of modern political thought and continue to plague us today." **Read**: [Kristol] *Neoconservatism* (1995); *Reflections of a Neoconservative* (1983); [Himmelfarb] *Lord Acton: A Study in Conscience and Politics* (1952); *On Liberty and Liberalism: The Case of John Stuart Mill* (1974); **About**: C. DeMuth, ed., *The Neoconservative Imagination* (1995); P. Steinfels, *The Neoconservatives* (1979). [Kristol:] **"It is in the nature of heresies to take a part for the whole. Thus, our version of the 'free society' is dedicated to the proposition that to be free is to be good. The New Left, though it echoes this proposition when it is convenient for its purposes, is actually dedicated to the counter belief—which is the pre-liberal position—that to be good is to be free. In the first case, the category of goodness is emptied of any specific meaning; in the second case, it is the category of freedom which is emptied of any specific meaning. In the war between these two heresies, the idea of a free society that is in some specific sense** virtuous (the older 'bourgeois' ideal) and the idea of a good community that is in some specific sense free (the older 'socialist' ideal . . .) are both emasculated; and the very possibility of a society that can be simultaneously virtuous and free, i.e., that organically weds order to liberty, becomes ever more remote." "Capitalism, Socialism, and Nihilism" from *Two Cheers for Capitalism* (1978). [Himmelfarb:] "By making truth so dependent upon error as to require not only the freest circulation of error but its deliberate cultivation, he reinforced the relativism of later generations. In the democratic marketplace of ideas, truth and error appear to be equal. Mill himself did not actually subscribe to this view. He did not mean to suggest that there was no such thing as truth or even that it was unknowable. He only meant to assert, as a practical proposition, that society could not presume to decide between truth and error. But it was the practical purport of his doctrine that has prevailed and that seems to lend credence to the current relativist temper." *On Liberty and Liberalism* (1974)

[*The National Interest*, 1112 16th Street, NW, Suite 540, Washington, DC 20036. Owen Harries, editor. Subscriptions (quarterly): $26/year; $44/2 years; $59/3 years; from Subscription Dept., *NI*, P.O. Box 622, Shrub Oaks, NY 10588-0622; (914) 962-6297.]

laissez-faire: The view in economics and government that advocates the **autonomy** of individual action, and opposes government intervention. It is practically synonymous with **libertarianism**, especially in the work of **Mill**. The term is, of course, French, and means "allow to do." It is a phrase imported into English by **Smith** and other advocates of **classical liberalism** from the slightly longer slogan of the French physiocrats: *laissez faire, laissez passer;* the sense of which is: *let people do what they want to do and go where they want to go.* Not all conservatives believe in laissez-faire, although it should be remembered that **Burke**, **Tocqueville**, and **Acton** did. Smith insisted that economic decision making must be decentralized—that neither king nor council were capable of directing an economy, and that nothing was more dangerous than that man or body be so overweening as to try. As **Mises** (1949) succinctly put it: "Laissez faire does not mean: Let soulless mechanical forces operate. It means: Let each individual choose how he wants to cooperate in the social division of labor; let the consumers determine what the entrepreneurs should produce." **Read**: W. Williams, *All It Takes Is Guts* (1987); T. Sowell, *Knowledge and Decisions* (1980). **"I cannot help thinking that what we need above all else in this age is a new philosophy of *laissez faire*. The old *laissez faire* failed because it was based on erroneous premises regarding human behavior . . . because it mistook for ineradicable characteristics of individuals characteristics that were in fact inseparable from social groups. . . . Far from proving a check upon the growth of the omnicompetent State, the old *laissez faire* actually accelerated its growth. Its indifference to every form of community and association left the State as the sole area of reform and security. . . . To create conditions within which autonomous individuals could prosper, could be emancipated from the binding ties of kinship, class, and community, was the objective of the older *laissez faire*. To create conditions within which autonomous groups may prosper must be, I believe, the prime objective of the new *laissez faire*."** Robert A. Nisbet, *The Quest for Community* (1953)

Lewis, C. S. (1898–1963): British novelist, critic, and Christian apologist. A professor of English literature, Lewis spent nearly his entire teaching career at Oxford University, although his last nine years were at Cambridge. Primarily a scholar (mediaeval and renaissance literature), and possessed by a bookworm's shyness, Lewis nonetheless became a celebrity with the publication of *The Screwtape Letters* (1942), which was instantly recognized as a classic by the public and critics alike, and made him the heir of **Chesterton**. His "science fiction" work (the *Perelandra* series) should really be termed *theological fiction*, since as a novelist—and this is equally true of his *Chronicles of Narnia* for children—Lewis is concerned above all with the battle between good and evil, and hardly at all with science. **Read**: *The Abolition of Man* (1947); *Mere Christianity* (1943); *The Screwtape Letters* (1942); **About**: J. Como, *C. S. Lewis at the Breakfast Table* (1979); R. Green and W. Hooper, *C. S. Lewis* (1974); T. Howard, *C. S. Lewis: Man of Letters* (1987). **"This conception [i.e., 'reality beyond all predicates, the abyss that was before the Creator Himself'] . . . I shall henceforth refer to . . . as 'the *Tao*' [or natural law]. . . . It is**

the doctrine of objective value, the belief that certain attitudes are really true, and others really false, to the kind of thing the universe is and the kind of things we are. Those who know the *Tao* can hold that to call children delightful or old men venerable is not simply to record a psychological fact about our own parental or filial emotions at the moment, but to recognize a quality which demands a certain response from us whether we make it or not. . . . And because our approvals and disapprovals are thus recognitions of objective value or responses to an objective order, therefore emotional states can be in harmony with reason (when we feel liking for what ought to be approved) or out of harmony with reason (when we perceive that liking is due but cannot feel it). No emotion is, in itself, a judgment: in that sense all emotions and sentiments are alogical. But they can be reasonable or unreasonable as they conform to Reason or fail to conform. The heart never takes the place of the head: but it can, and should, obey it." *The Abolition of Man* (1947)

liberal arts: The system of education begun in the Middle Ages that emphasizes seven areas of study in two divisions: the *trivium* (grammar, rhetoric, and logic—leading to a B.A. degree); and the *quadrivium* (arithmetic, geometry, astronomy, and music—leading to the M.A.). An education befitting a free (*liberalis*) man, the liberal arts system opposes narrow notions of relevance, and encourages, as Strauss (1968) put it, "a universal aristocracy." Kirk (1987) wrote that "it defends order against disorder." And in the most famous definition of all, Newman (1873) called it the "process of training, by which the intellect, instead of being formed or sacrificed to some particular or accidental purpose, some specific trade or profession or study or science, is disciplined for its own sake, for the perception of its own object, and for its own highest culture . . ." Thus the "liberal" in liberal education is not, again as Strauss wrote, "the opposite of conservative education, but of illiberal education." **Read:** L. Strauss, *Liberalism: Ancient and Modern* (1968); J. Barzun, *The Teacher in America* (1944). **"The method of liberal education is the liberal arts, and the result of liberal education is discipline in those arts. The liberal artist learns to read, write, speak, listen, understand, and think. He learns to reckon, measure, and manipulate matter,**

quantity, and motion in order to predict, produce, and exchange. As we live in the tradition, whether we know it or not, so we are all liberal artists, whether we know it or not. . . . The liberal arts are not merely indispensable; they are unavoidable." Robert M. Hutchins, *The Great Conversation* (1948)

liberalism: A term nearly as unsettled as **conservatism**, having different meanings in various contexts. Beginning from the word's Latin root, *liberalis*, its meanings converge upon freedom, but whereas that freedom formerly implied political **liberty**, i.e., universal individual rights (political and economic) and limited governmental power, it now tends to indicate *progressivism*, meaning rationalist goals pursued by an intrusive state. It is ironic, as **Bell** (1980) has pointed out, that traditional liberalism is "not only anti-State, it is antipolitical." A typical contemporary definition would be "favorable to progress or reform," and indeed *progressive* should now probably be preferred to *liberal*, this new liberalism being dedicated to the proposition that *everything* is politics. The term was first used derisively in England (1815) as "*liberales*," the Spanish form, to demean the allegedly alien character of the ideas. (Ironically, the word was used in Spain in the same period to denote the party favoring an English-style **constitution**.) In the modern American context, the word has become synonymous with its compound, *welfare liberalism*; and thus represents the second path of historic liberalism; the first being its "classical" cousin. (See **classical liberalism**.) "Welfare" liberalism derives philosophically from the **Enlightenment** version of participatory **republicanism** (a.k.a. **democracy**), and underwent rapid growth from the Depression until the final decades of the century. As Bell concluded: "What has happened, and it is a profound change in both terms and consequences, is a shift from *liberty* to *liberation*." The modern liberal creed runs something like this:

> Human nature, although not necessarily good, is plastic and, therefore, Man may be brought to goodness through progressive education and institutions. (Evil is really only ignorance.) The creation of progressive educational programs and progressive political and economic institutions is possible through the application to historic social problems of scientific thinking, which is the process of reason overcoming

prejudice. (Liberalism instinctively opposes **tradition**.) The great barrier to progressive education and institutions is the traditional belief in an objective **order**, whether derived from **faith** or experience, whereas progressive science has proved that truth is relative. (Like Man, society is plastic.) The idea of differences among people is rooted in the illusions of a traditional belief in order, and the primary goal of progressive education and institutions is, again, the eradication of these prejudices. (Liberalism is egalitarian both as to people and ideas.) The new ends of society are too important, by reason of their scientific basis and their egalitarian motive, to be left to the democratic process. (Modern liberalism is synonymous with **statism**.)

Because it assumes human malleability, liberalism accepts no barriers to human improvement, and impatience with the pace of **change** leads to frequent interventions designed to propel (or restore) humanity to a natural state of perfection. Partly as a defense against the appeal of **Marxism** (or in imitation of it), late 19th-century liberalism—finally pulling free of its classical attachment to liberty—began to advocate aggressive state actions on behalf of equity. (See **egalitarianism**.) In America, that process reached its climax, although not its peak, in the New Deal. The legacies of this new liberalism include progressive taxation, massive **bureaucracy**, stifling regulation, **welfare** dependency, reverse discrimination, and perhaps even crime in the streets. In America, "liberal" is sometimes synonymous with "socialist," whereas in Europe (although no longer in Britain) the words are antagonistic. At the heart of progressive liberalism is a *theoretical instrumentalism*, a calculus of transformation fundamentally incapable of grasping the social forces it intends to shape. A middle-of-the-road definition of liberalism might be "the belief that government can act to improve the lives of its citizens," which was offered by *Newsweek*'s Joe Klein in his report on the 1994 mid-term Republican landslide in which American voters seemed largely to have rejected the idea. [And not that it's exactly germane, but recently we learned from FBI intercepts—released at long last—that that the KGB code name for Julius Rosenberg was "Liberal."] **Read**: D. Bell, *The Winding Passage* (1980); J. Gray, *Liberalism* (1986); K. Minogue, *The Liberal Mind* (1963). **"Previous civilizations have been overthrown from without** by the incursion of barbarian hordes; ours has dreamed up its own dissolution in the minds of its own intellectual élite. It has carefully nurtured its own barbarians . . . Not Bolshevism, which Stalin liquidated along with all the old Bolsheviks; not Nazism, which perished with Hitler in his Berlin bunker; not Fascism, which was left hanging upside down, along with Mussolini and his mistress, from a lamp-post—none of these, history will record, was responsible for bringing down the darkness on our civilization, but liberalism. A solvent rather than a precipitate, a sedative rather than a stimulant, a slough rather than a precipice; blurring the edges of truth, the definition of virtue, the shape of beauty; a cracked bell, a mist, a death wish." Malcolm Muggeridge, *Things Past* (1979)

libertarianism: A philosophy of <u>limited government</u> and <u>individualism</u>. The term has become useful in distinguishing a contemporary interpretation of <u>classical liberalism</u> from the more familiar "welfare" <u>liberalism</u>. Its emphasis is on consent, that is, if two people agree to do a thing, and if that thing is not harmful to another, their agreement should not be prohibited by any <u>authority</u> other than their own wills. (Thus the familiar libertarian bumper sticker: "I'm pro-choice on everything.") Superficially attractive to conservatives, libertarianism might Hudibrastically be called <u>conservatism</u> without a soul. This is not simply because libertarianism fails to give to religious <u>faith</u> the centrality that conservatism does, but because there are a number of branches of libertarian thought, several of which verge on the atomistic. Some libertarians share a kinship with anarchists. Others are more properly termed "minarchist," as in the work of <u>Rothbard</u>, who has been called the "founder" of contemporary American libertarianism. Still others, specifically the followers of the philosophy of Ayn Rand (see <u>objectivism</u>), equate individualism and selfishness. Finally, there is a brand of "classical libertarianism" that balances individualist claims with the larger interests of <u>community</u> and <u>tradition</u>, and is explicated in the writings of <u>Hayek</u> and <u>Friedman</u>. Anarchism, by pronouncing government illegitimate, has no congruity whatsoever with conservatism. Minarchists see governmental functions as extremely limited—the most common analogies employed are the referee or the nightwatchman—usually to the settling of contractual disputes between individuals and the exercise of police powers, both for personal and national defense. (See **Nozick**.) The basic schism among libertarians is the disagreement over *consequentialism*, that is, over the utilitarian character of government action. The more utilitarian, the closer to the Left, the further from the **Right**. The Libertarian Party, founded in 1971 and today claiming to be America's "third largest" political party, arose as both an anti-big government and anti-Vietnam War organization. The best journal of libertarian opinion is *Reason* magazine (see below), published by the Reason Foundation, and the leading libertarian think tank is the Cato Institute (see **Rothbard**). Libertarian writers have a penchant for portentous tomes with two- or three-word titles. **Read:** G. Carey, *Freedom and Virtue: The Conservative/Libertarian Debate* (1984); T. Machan, *Capitalism and Individualism* (1990); R. Nozick, *Anarchy, State, and Utopia* (1974); M. Rothbard, *Man, Economy, and State* (1962). **"Libertarianism is the view that each man is the absolute owner of his life, to use and dispose of it as he sees fit; that all man's social actions should be voluntary; and that respect for every other man's similar and equal ownership of life and, by extension, the property and fruits of that life, is the ethical basis of a humane and open society. In this view, the only function of law or government is to provide the sort of self-defense against violence that an individual, if he were powerful enough, would provide for himself."** Karl Hess, quoted in J. Tuccille, *Radical Libertarianism* (1970)

[Reason Foundation, 3415 S. Sepulveda Blvd., Suite 400, Los Angeles, CA 90034; (310) 391-2245. Robert W. Poole, Jr., president. *Reason* magazine, P.O. Box 526, Mt. Morris, IL 61054; (815) 734-1102; subscriptions: $26.00 per year for 11 issues.]

liberty: The condition of *political* freedom. A distinction is made between the sometimes synonymous words "freedom" and "liberty." **Acton** made clear the political character of liberty. It is, he explained, the guarantee that each of us will "be protected in doing what he believes his duty against the influence of **authority** and majorities, custom and opinion." Liberty is not a "state of nature," but the result of political evolution. It necessarily involves the right and the ability to dissent, whether or not one happens to be a dissenter. Anyone is *free* to utter an unpopular opinion when no one else is around to hear, but we have *liberty* only when we may speak freely in the presence of others. Liberty is a negative, not a positive concept, and that is its primary difference from freedom. Liberty does not require a person to do anything; it entails no positive commands to action. But it does require that, as a rule, a person (or a government) not limit or negate another's freedom. As **Montesquieu** put it, "Liberty can consist only in the power of doing what we ought to will, and in not being constrained to do what we ought not to will." Liberty is endangered in any political system that fosters dependency, whether the dependent is a poor **welfare** recipient or a wealthy farmer. **Read:** F. A. Hayek, *The Constitution of Liberty* (1960). **"It is only when there are several different major social forces, not wholly subordinated to any one social force, that there can be any assurance of liberty, since only then is there the mutual check and balance that is able to chain power. There is no force, no group, and no class that is the preserver of liberty. Liberty is preserved by those who are against the existing chief power. Oppositions which do not express genuine social forces are as trivial, in relation to entrenched power, as the old court jesters."** James Burnham, *The Machiavellians* (1943)

IV

Reformation and Revolution

by
Peter J. Stanlis

In 1793, in answer to the radical political theory of Thomas Paine and utilitarian claims that no one really knew the meaning of natural law, John Quincy Adams stated his conservative defense of the American Revolution and defended the two-thousand-year-old tradition of moral natural law: "When the glorious congress of 1774 declared that the inhabitants of the English colonies in North America were entitled to certain rights by the immutable laws of nature . . . they knew very well what they meant, and were perfectly understood by all mankind." From the Protestant Reformation to the end of the 18th century the historical continuity of belief in moral natural law remained unbroken.

Natural law taught that the first principles of a good social order, of individual and corporate freedom, and of justice under constitutional law, required recognition, acceptance, and adherence to a God-given moral law by all men, rulers and subjects alike. This meant that the power of the state was not absolute and arbitrary, that political sovereignty was restrained by constitutional law. Except for Christianity, moral natural law was probably the most important single ethical, legal, political, and cultural force to maintain the conservative tradition in Western civilization.

On the secular level natural law sustained the orthodox Christian conception of the moral nature of man as a dual creature of spirit and matter, capable, despite its flawed nature, of perceiving through "right reason" the difference between good and evil in fundamental matters regarding life, liberty, and property. Natural law also extended into the modern era the Aristotelian doctrine that by his innate nature man is a social creature, united in corporate society. Thus it rejected all anarchical political theories of a social contract based upon a supposed pre-civil or primitive "state of nature." As Thomas Jefferson was to say, the moral natural law taught that it is "self-evident" that all men are created equal in the sight of God, and, therefore, their inherent right to life, liberty, and property was not a gift to be granted or withheld by the state, but was divinely ordained in their nature. Tyrannical rulers had the power but not the moral and legal right to deprive their subjects of their natural and civil rights. The precepts of normative ethics transcended the power and will of rulers.

Early in the 17th century, when Sir Edward Coke appealed to moral natural law against the claims of absolute royal power by James I, and insisted that the law is above the king, he was following the tradition of jurisprudence set forth by the medieval jurists Bracton, Fortescue, and More. Coke became the archetypal symbol of civil liberty among English constitutional-minded jurists and statesmen, such as Selden, who opposed monarchical absolutism based upon claims of divine right. The conservative lawyers who sanctioned the Glorious Revolution of 1688 refined upon Coke. Their system of natural law was embodied in Blackstone's *Commentaries on the Laws of England* (1765–1769), which became the basis for legal education in Britain and America. In 1775, Burke noted that the Americans had bought as many copies of Blackstone as the British, and warned that armed with their knowledge of English law the colonists were very formidable opponents of British abuses of power. In Blackstone's view, only adherence to the natural law gave legal sanction to political sovereignty.

A vital derivative from moral natural law was the development of the "law of nations" during the 16th, 17th, and 18th centuries. The seeds of modern international law were planted by, among others, Grotius, Pufendorf, and Vattel. International law was based upon moral natural law and the *jus gentium*, or universal law in the Justinian Code, because these transcended the common law and political sovereignty of individual nations. By humanizing warfare, distinguishing between a just or defensive war and an unjust war of aggression, by establishing rules for peace and diplomacy between nations, defining freedom of the seas, providing immunity from violence for embassies, and defending the natural rights of native populations in European colonies in America, international law aimed at bringing within the norms of natural law the barbarous practices of nations sanctioned in the might-makes-right nationalism of Machiavelli, Jean Bodin, and Hobbes.

In religion, the principles of moral natural law were defended by most branches of Christianity, but particularly by the Catholic and Anglican churches. In England the great fountainhead of post-Reformation canon law was set forth in Richard Hooker's Aristotelian *summa theologiae, Of the Laws of Ecclesiastical Polity*, parts of which appeared in 1594, 1597, and early in the 17th century. In 1954, John S. Marshall (in *Richard Hooker and the Origins of American Constitutionalism*) contended that in his natural-law legal philosophy of the national sovereign state, Hooker certainly opposed absolutism in both church and state, and was a true constitutionalist. He established a tradition in English political and religious thought that was carried forward by such Anglican divines as Bishop Bramhall in the 17th century and Bishop Butler to the ear of Burke; the conservative Whig Burke much admired Hooker's account of the proper roles of church and state in society.

The classical philosophy of education which flourished in Europe and America from the 16th century well into the modern era derived from the humanism of Erasmus, More, Colet, and others, and combined Christian and natural-law principles in the established culture of Western civilization. Through the liberal arts in education, the philosophy of Plato, Aristotle, Cicero, the Roman stoics, and remnants of medieval scholasticism provided a conservative basis for the ethical and aesthetic norms of Europe and America. In its cultural manifestations, moral natural law and Christianity opposed both the hedonist and materialist philosophies of life. The passion for a humane social order is very evident in the literary works of such English writers as Milton, Dryden, Swift, Pope, and Johnson, and in the political speeches and writings of Burke.

Professor Stanlis is Distinguished Professor of Humanities, Emeritus at Rockford College. He is the author of numerous books—including seven on Burke—and scores of articles on his specialty, 18th-century English thought.

Limbaugh, Rush (1951–): American entertainer and political commentator whose three-hour weekday broadcast is the most listened to nationwide, whose books have been best sellers, and whose late-night television show reached No. 3 in the ratings. All these have made him the most popular **conservative** voice in America, perhaps ever. Limbaugh, the son of Republican activists, began his radio career while still a teenager in Cape Girardeau, Missouri, landed his first big job as a news reader in Kansas City, and began to master "talk" radio in 1984 when he replaced "shock jock" Morton Downey, Jr. at KFBK in Sacramento, California. Four years later, Limbaugh's program began reaching a national audience in the millions through the ABC network's flagship station in New York City, and liberals began calling him (ruefully)—and he began calling himself (gleefully)—"the most dangerous man in America." Limbaugh's book *The Way Things Ought to Be* (1992) stayed atop [hardcover] best-seller lists for more than a year, and total sales of hardcover, paperback, and audio versions of the book have reached 5 million copies. **Read:** *The Way Things Ought to Be* (1992); **About:** P. Colford, *The Rush Limbaugh Story* (1993). "[I]t is Utopian to believe that we can eliminate suffering of all kinds. It is . . . simply not realistic to expect that every citizen will have what he considers enough good food and fine health care. It's not even possible to guarantee everyone an adequate supply of those things, because the definition of *adequate* always changes with rising affluence. The poor in America today are incredibly rich compared with the much higher percentage of poor people at the turn of the century. . . . [O]ver half those classified as poor own a dishwasher, most have a car, and nearly all have a television set. Most have enough to eat, but now we hear complaints about the quality of their food. We hear that too many fast-food joints operate in poor neighborhoods and therefore the poor aren't getting a nutritious enough diet. You can never wipe out the poor because the standard for being poor keeps rising. . . . Equalizing outcomes and ensuring everyone a mediocre minimum was what communism tried to accomplish. That's what the socialists tried to accomplish. . . . They failed because Utopia is impossible. Every human being has different abilities, talents, desires, and characteristics. There is no way those differences can be equalized, other than through the use of force. I don't mean military force, but laws backed up by force, if necessary, which redistribute wealth and penalize achievement." *The Way Things Ought to Be* (1992)

limited government: Perhaps the first principle of political **conservatism**, limited government is quite simply the omega of political theory. Its meaning derives from ideas based in **natural law**, principally **liberty** and **individualism**, i.e., that each person ought to be free, but will not be unless the state's power is restrained. The question becomes: How is a government's power to be limited? There are a number of ways, some organic and some artificial. There is in the first case custom or **tradition**, which may be manifest in the laws and practices of strong families, communities, or ethnic groups, and which is the most solid basis for limiting government. In the second case (the artificial) there may be specific checks and balances or other structural limitations as established in a **constitution**. Among the strongest power-dispersing customs is the free market, through which private institutions develop powers (primarily through satisfying the myriad needs of people) that rival government's. Another way of thinking about the ways a government's power is limited is that they may be either internal or external. An independent judiciary is an internal control; **capitalism** is an external check. **Read:** M. Stanton Evans, *The Theme Is Freedom* (1994). Evans writes: "Self-professed traditionalists that they were, the framers [of the U.S. Constitution] were more conservative than they knew. They were in a sense the last survivors of the feudal-medieval order, insisting that all earthly power must be subject to some limit. And, like their medieval forebears, they backed this up with pluralist, decentralized arrangements that gave practical content to the doctrine. . . . If this reading be accepted, a number of important conclusions are in order. One is that the chief political tradition of our culture *is*, above all, a tradition of limited government, in the interest of protecting personal freedom. Those who profess this view today accordingly defend a legacy passed down to us, at considerable hazard, through many generations. The oft-stated conflict between traditional values and libertarian practice in our politics is therefore an illusion—a misreading of the record, or an artifact of special pleading. In the Anglo-American context, 'big government conservative' is the oxymoron—whatever its vogue among paternalists in Europe. . . . Also, it is worth repeating that this tradition is rooted in religious faith, not secular abstraction. The very concepts of the limited state and personal liberty, and the institutions that gave these practical force, grew from the religious vision of the West."

Lincoln, Abraham (1809–1865): Sixteenth president of the United States, whose legendary career and character have been a major incitement to the **conservative** movement. Why an incitement? Because (some have asserted) Lincoln, whose greatness is beyond dispute, changed America. Only George Washington looms as large in the American consciousness, although there is nothing particularly controversial about Washington. Lincoln on the other hand has been honored by some conservatives and damned by others, and it mostly has to do with the role his presidency may have played in affecting the momentum of American political power. Beginning with **Kendall**, **Meyer**, **Morley**, and others, some conservatives have claimed that the Lincoln administrations sought to concentrate power in the executive even as they embraced unlimited majority rule, the effect being to sew the seeds of a despotic **democracy**—of the sort America would be swept up in during the New Deal and Great Society periods. Meyer was especially caustic, calling Lincoln an ideologue who ran roughshod over the **Constitution** in service to "the spurious slogan of Union" (**National Review**, August 24, 1965). However, Lincoln is not without his conservative defenders. **Jaffa**, in his closely reasoned *The Crisis of the House Divided* (1959), argued that Lincoln simply recognized a more "ancient faith," which is to say **natural law**, and sought to defend it against the Confederate attack. For Lincoln, pragmatic politician though he clearly was, the Civil War *was* about ending slavery and preserving union—about truly accepting the fundamental tenet of America's founding: the "all men are created equal" phrase of the **Declaration of Independence**, which history had now prepared the nation to fully accept. It is helpful, I believe, to compare the 19th-century debate over slavery to our current brooding about **abortion**. Everything depends upon premises: if you believe the fetus is a person, you are opposed to its killing. Lincoln believed (as, in one way or another, many Founders obviously had not) that the slave was a person, a *Man*. Thus African-Americans, as Men, were entitled to "life, liberty, and the pursuit of happiness," and it had become—notwithstanding tradition—un-American to defend slavery. Kirk (1991) wrote: "Out of the American democratic experience he came; and his life proved that a democracy of elevation can uphold resolutely the public order and the moral order." It was Lincoln who asked (in his speech at the Cooper Union—then Cooper Institute—in 1860): "What is conservatism? Is it not adherence to the old and tried, against the new and untried?" **Read**: *Speeches and Writings: 1859–1865* (1984); **About**: M. E. Bradford, *The Reactionary Imperative* (1990); H. Jaffa, *The Crisis of the House Divided* (1959); S. B. Oates, *With Malice Towards None* (1977). **"If slavery is right, all words, acts, laws, and constitutions against it, are themselves wrong, and should be silenced, and swept away. If it is right, we cannot justly object to its nationality—its universality; if it is wrong, they cannot justly insist upon its extension—its enlargement. All they ask, we could readily grant, if we thought slavery right; all we ask, they could as readily grant, if they thought it wrong. Their thinking it right, and our thinking it wrong, is the precise fact upon which depends the whole controversy."** Address at Cooper Institute (February 27, 1860)

Lippmann, Walter (1889–1974): American journalist (a founding editor of *The New Republic*), and author of *The Good Society* (1937), which Hayek called "a brilliant restatement of the fundamental ideals of classical liberalism." As a Harvard student, Lippmann worked as assistant to Santayana, and went from there to a succession of journalistic and government jobs that took him from progressive liberalism to a kind of conservatism. Classical liberalism, more than conservatism, was indeed the spirit behind Lippmann's attack on the New Deal's emphasis on central planning. The complexity of human nature, he believed, demands a laissez-faire state. But Lippmann's philosophy was never an ideologically singular view, and he insisted that "every truly civilized and enlightened man is conservative and liberal and progressive." His early work was decidedly based upon rationalism, but the spectacle of World War I upset his confidence in progressive ideals, including **democracy** itself. In *The Good Society*, he excoriated the New Deal as just another version of the "collectivist heresy," and asserted the importance of the free market and the rule of law. **Read**: C. Rossiter and J. Lane, eds., *The Essential Lippmann* (1982); *The Good Society* (1937); *The Public Philosophy* (1955). **About**: R. Steel, *Walter Lippmann and the American Century* (1980). "No a priori reasoning can anticipate the precise formulae which will reconcile the varied interests of men. . . . Thus in Plato's great scheme each man was assigned his station and his duties; any architectural plan is necessarily based on the same presumption. But Plato's scheme only worked in Plato's imagination; never in the real world. . . . For the scheme implies that men will remain content in the station which the visionary has assigned to them. To formulate such plans is not to design a society for real men. It is to re-create men to fit the design." *The Good Society* (1937)

Locke, John (1632–1704): English philosopher whose contract theory of government asserted a **natural-rights** basis of life, **liberty**, and property. His thought greatly influenced the revolutionary movements in America and France. In the first—and less influential—of his *First* and *Second Treatises of Civil Government* (1690), he argued against the divine right of kings and in favor of the view that all are equal before God (see **egalitarianism**) in an "appeal to Heaven." ("I myself can only be the judge in my own conscience, as I will answer it, at the great day, to the supreme judge of men.") This equality is the source of the second treatise's development of the idea of government by consent (see **community**), and was a direct refutation of the **absolutism** advocated by Thomas Hobbes and Robert Filmer. (Indeed, Locke considered monarchy a form of war.) Locke also asserted that economic right (**private property**) derives almost exclusively from the creative investment of each man's labor. Thus Locke embraced economic inequality, and provided a key premise for the early **capitalism** of **Smith**, and—in the reverse (or *perverse*)—of **Marxism**. Locke was also an advocate of religious tolerance, and of the separation of religious and civil authorities. His work is primarily seen as perhaps the single most important influence on the development of **liberalism**, but it may be fair to say that **classical liberalism** and **libertarianism**

follow the spirit of Locke more closely. When we think of **Madison**'s concern about the restraint of majority power, we encounter Locke; when we read the *Federalist*'s emphasis on delineated powers, we are reading Locke. However, Locke's notion that Man is born *tabula rasa* played an influential role in liberalism's assumption that reform can lead to Utopia, a place where Man recovers his "state of nature," a condition of perfect freedom and equality "within the bounds of the law of nature." And Locke, by seriously weakening the status of **natural law** in asserting the primacy of natural rights, elevated political will above political **tradition**. As Peter Stanlis has written (1986): "The natural rights introduced by Hobbes and popularized by Locke exalted man's private reason and will above any eternal and unchangeable divine law." **Read:** *Two Treatises on Government* (1690); *An Essay Concerning Human Understanding* (1690). **About:** F. McDonald, *Novus Ordo Seclorum* (1985). **"In the history of thought, especially of thought bearing on action, Locke is, not the greatest certainly, but the largest of all Englishmen, looming tremendously, and filling an immense space. . . . [H]e is the master of Voltaire and Condillac. As the—unscientific—inventor of the division of power, he is the master of Montesquieu. By his theory of Education and the Social Contract, he is the master of Rousseau, the most powerful political writer that ever lived. By his political economy he is the master of Adam Smith, and in a sense, of Turgot. He gave to Whiggism whatever general ideas it mixed with the specific national elements, and he is the theorist of government by the great families. Lastly, in the Catena of tradition on Toleration, he is very nearly the principal classic."** Lord Acton, *Essays in Religion, Politics, and Morality* (1988)

Macaulay, Thomas Babington (1800–1859): English historian, author, and political leader. Macaulay wrote regularly for the *Edinburgh Review* before being elected to Parliament in 1830, where he served on and off until a few years before his death. He served on the governing council of the East India Company and undertook the reform of India's educational and legal systems, although not on Indian terms, reflecting his admiration for the progressive philosophy of Francis Bacon. His most famous work was *The History of England* (five volumes, 1849–1861), a biased account of British life from the 15th century. Macaulay's political philosophy has been alternately described as a variant of **liberalism** or of **conservatism** (he described himself both ways); as being an heir of **Locke** or of **Burke**. He preferred to call himself a *trimmer*. The trimmer's primary concern is the organization of society in ways that unify **liberty** and **order**. Above all Macaulay despised fanatics and championed gradual **change**, and he was especially distrustful of pure **democracy**. Although in India he had behaved like a proper Benthamite reformer, he attacked utilitarianism (the doctrine that democratic government should seek the greatest happiness of the greatest number) as a formula for class war and economic redistribution. Aspects of his philosophy were influential on the development of **Disraeli**'s thinking, although the latter took a more pragmatic view. Curiously, for one so enamored of progress—of the role education might play in taming the herd—Macaulay was cool towards **capitalism**, which has been a major check on English and American **egalitarianism**. **Read:** H. Trevor-Roper, ed., *Critical and Historical Essays* (1965); **About:** O. D. Edwards, *Macaulay* (1988). "I seriously apprehend that . . . [America] will, in some season of adversity . . . do things which will prevent prosperity from returning; that you will act like people who should in a year of scarcity, devour all the seed corn, and thus make the next year a year, not of scarcity, but of absolute famine. There will be, I fear, spoilation . . . distress . . . [and the] distress will produce fresh spoilation. There is nothing to stop you. Your Constitution is all sail and no anchor. . . . [W]hen a society has entered on this downward progress, either civilization or liberty must perish. Either some Caesar or Napoleon will seize the reins of government with a strong hand; or your republic will be as fearfully plundered and laid waste by barbarians in the twentieth Century as the Roman Empire was in the fifth;—with this difference, that the Huns and Vandals . . . came from without, and that your Huns and Vandals will have been engendered within your own country by your own institutions." Letter (1857) to H. S. Randall (an American biographer of Thomas Jefferson) quoted in Russell Kirk, ed., *The Portable Conservative Reader* (1984)

Madison, James (1751–1836): American Founder, fourth United States president (1809–1817), author (with **Jay** and **Hamilton**) of

The Federalist (1787–1788), and (arguably) "the father" of the **Constitution**. An early champion of centralized power, Madison was later an advocate of **states' rights**, and with **Jefferson** a founder of the Republican Party. He came to consider his meticulous notes on the Constitutional Convention something of an embarrassment because they so showcased his arguments in favor of a strong national government, and he kept them under wraps for many years, fearing that ultranationalists would use them to attack state sovereignty. Nonetheless, he vigorously opposed **Calhoun**'s doctrine of nullification. Forrest McDonald (1985) says, after Sartre, that Madison had a "nostalgia for the absolute," but that did not deter him from belief in religious **liberty**. In any event, Madison held fast to the two founding principles he did so much to shape: **federalism** and **republicanism**. As was the case with so many of his fellow Founders, Madison was a skeptic, and like Hamilton, had deep reservations about **human nature**. As McDonald sums up Madison's brand of nationalism: "At bottom, Hamilton and other court party nationalists trusted themselves and therefore trusted power if was in their own hands. Madison and other men of his temperament did not trust themselves and therefore did not trust power in anyone's hands." **Read:** C. Rossiter, ed., *The Federalist* (1787–1788); **About:** J. Ketcham, *James Madison* (1990); R. Morris, *Witnesses at the Creation* (1985). **"If men were angels, no government would be necessary. If angels were to govern men, neither external nor internal controls on government would be necessary. In framing a government which is to be administered by men over men, the great difficulty lies in this: you must first enable the government to control the governed; and in the next place oblige it to control itself."** *The Federalist, No. 51* (1787–1788)

Maine, Henry Sumner (1822–1888): British legal scholar at both Oxford and Cambridge, whose "anthropological jurisprudence" had a more profound effect on the Anglo-American view of law than anyone since **Blackstone**. His *Ancient Law* (1861) contrasted communities dominated by status with those governed by contract. The status-contract variance is basically between ancient and modern (or primitive and developed) societies, and is exemplified by the former's emphasis on kinship and the latter's on individuality. Maine believed that the movement of history was away from status and towards contract, which to an extent was also from the sacred to the secular. **Read:** *Popular Government* (1886); **About:** R. Kirk, *The Conservative Mind* (1953). **"A . . . formidable conception bequeathed to us by Rousseau is that of the omnipotent democratic State rooted in natural right; the State which has at its absolute disposal everything which individual men value, their property, their persons, and their independence; the State which is bound to respect neither precedent nor prescription; the State which may make laws for its subjects ordaining what they shall drink or eat, and in what way they shall spend their earnings; the State which can confiscate all the land of the community, and which, if the effect on human motives is what may be expected to be may force us to labour on it when the older incentives to toil have disappeared. Nevertheless this political speculation, of which the remote and indirect consequences press us on all sides, is of all speculations the most baseless. The natural condition from which it starts is a simple figment of the imagination."** *Popular Government* (1886)

Maistre, Comte Joseph Marie de (1753–1821): French Catholic philosopher-diplomat who admired <u>authority</u>, despised the <u>Enlightenment</u>, and asserted papal infallibility long before it became Church dogma. A prototypical big-government, i.e., *royalist*, <u>conservative</u> (he hoped the pope would become head of a "universal civilization"; see <u>ultramontanism</u>), Maistre nonetheless believed in a slow-evolving, constitutional structure for society. He was a powerful influence on later French thinkers as diverse as the philosopher Auguste Comte (see <u>positivism</u>), the historian François Guizot, and the journalist Charles Maurras. At bottom Maistre believed that all civil law is derived from and subordinate to divine law; that law's purpose is to bridle human <u>sin</u>. <u>Burke</u>'s *Reflections on the Revolution in France* (1790) and Maistre's *Considérations sur la France* (1796) demonstrate the distinction between a conservative and a <u>reactionary</u> mind. Remembered today perhaps most for his memorable observation, "*Toute nation a le gouvernement qu'elle mérite*," which is to say: "Every nation has the government it deserves," Maistre also declaimed that the American project of building a capital, *de novo*, in a Maryland swamp would prove a failure (see Nisbet, 1986). He believed a capital ought to be in a city with its own history and tradition, and that Washington, D.C. would surely be consumed by the narrowly political focus of its founding. **Read:** and **About:** J. Lively, ed., *The Works of Joseph de Maistre* (1965). "**The more you examine the part human action plays in the formation of political constitutions, the clearer it becomes that it is effective only in an extremely subordinate role or as a simple instrument; and I do not believe that any doubt at all remains of the incontrovertible truth of the following propositions: 1. That the fundamentals of political constitutions exist before all written laws. 2. That a constitutional law is and can be only the development or the sanction of a preexistent and unwritten right. 3. That the most essential, the most intrinsically constitutional, and the really fundamental is not written and even should not be if the state is not to be imperiled. 4. That the weakness and fragility of a constitution is in direct relationship to the number of written constitutional articles.**" "Essay on the Generative Principle of Political Constitutions" in Jack Lively, ed., *The Works of Joseph de Maistre* (1965)

Mandeville, Bernard (1670–1733): Dutch-born English physician/writer and social satirist. His monumental *Fable of the Bees* (first published in 1714, and then in expanded versions through completion in 1730) expounded on his view of "private vices, public benefits," which influenced Hume and anticipated the work of Smith by a generation. (Mandeville coined the term "division of labor," and just as Smith had his illustrative pin factory, Mandeville used the example of a manufacturer of hoops and petticoats to show how many hands are involved in the production of even simple items.) The *Fable* was widely condemned but almost universally read, and became one of the most influential anti-rationalist books of the Enlightenment period. According to Hayek, Mandeville was the first to understand that order in society is spontaneously created. Mandeville argued that the heart of social and economic commerce is self-interest (his bees are successful when wicked; decimated when virtuous), and he has frequently been cited as a precursor of utilitarianism, but such an association overlooks his views of human nature and the role of government, which were hardly the positive, progressive views of a Jeremy Bentham. **Read:** *The Fable of the Bees* (1730); **About:** M. Goldsmith, *Private Vices, Public Benefits* (1985). **"So vice is beneficial found,/When it's by Justice lopt and bound;/Nay, where the People would be great,/As necessary to the State,/As Hunger is to make 'em eat."** From "The Moral" of *The Grumbling Hive, or Knaves Turned Honest* (1705)

Marxism: The <u>socialism</u> of Karl Marx (1818–1883) which greatly affected the content and temper of American <u>conservatism</u> in the 20th century (see <u>anticommunism</u>); objections to socialist theory and practice were detailed and passionate. "Marx's contributions, in whatever modified form, have entered the consciousness of our time, affected the idiom of our language and understanding, and left an ineradicable imprint on the world of scholarship" (<u>Hook</u>, 1987). But often as not these objections had more to do with the consequences of militant totalitarianism than with the implications of the Marxian view of labor and capital, especially the notion of "surplus value," upon which Marx based his argument against <u>private property</u>, or the bizarre but obviously compelling reductionism that "the mode of production produces the mode of consciousness" (*Communist Manifesto*, 1848). The crux of socialist theory is that economic *value* and, therefore, ownership are, or ought to be, determined not by free exchanges in capital markets but strictly according to the investment by workers of their labor. Marxist leveling stifles the very basis of human <u>liberty</u>—the freedoms to create and choose—and its demise was brought about less by its political failures than by its economic collapse. Marx was an optimist who wanted to force Man (through a dictatorship of the proletariat) into a classless, if not selfless, future; to make a heaven on earth. His legacy was hell on earth. "He could not see," wrote Stephen Tonsor (in <u>Meyer</u>, 1964), "that . . . the banishment of inequality would mean the extinction of liberty." **Read:** B. Crozier and A. Seldon, *Socialism* (1986); F. A. Hayek, *The Fatal Conceit* (1988). **"Things can always be found for idle hands to do in a controlled situation. In the extreme, an army can order its soldiers to dig trenches and then fill them in again. That is why armies never have unemployment; nor do Communist states. The**

crucial difference is between work whose benefits to the consumers exceed their costs to the producers and work whose value is less than its costs. The second kind of work cannot persist in a capitalist economy, where inherent waste is conveyed forcibly in falling profits (or mounting losses) and growing unemployment. To conceal this with the hidden subsidies made possible by 'planning' does not change the underlying reality—the human inability to continuously apply all resources to their most valued uses in an economy with changing tastes, output, and production innovations." Thomas Sowell, *Marxism* (1985)

McCarthyism: The sweeping **anticommunism** of United States senator Joseph R. McCarthy (1908–1957) and his supporters. Few "conservative" figures have been so controversial or, within the **conservative** movement, so divisive. Republican McCarthy (he had only recently changed parties) defeated the liberal/progressive incumbent in the 1946 Wisconsin Senate primary, trounced his Democratic opponent in the general election, and then hid out in Washington for the next three years, until on February 9, 1950, he made a speech in Wheeling, West Virginia that set the tone for the rapid rise and sharp decline in his public life. He told a Republican women's group that he held in his hand a list of communists (205 of them, more or less—depending upon when you asked him) who had infiltrated the American government, largely in the State Department. The term *McCarthyism* was largely the senator's own self-important coinage, as in his book, published later that year, *McCarthyism: The Fight for America*. Through his speeches, writings, and in televised hearings (his own investigations and investigations *of* him), McCarthy continued to make charges that he often would not or could not substantiate, until he was brought down by his attempt to secure special military treatment for an aide (David Schine), who was the special friend of his chief counsel, the extremely unpleasant Roy Cohn. Indeed, the very worst thing about McCarthyism, which has come to mean a kind of dogged judicial or journalistic libel, is that it threatened to discredit all accusations of subversion; to obscure the obvious fact that American **communism** *was* seditious. McCarthy's smoky rise and fall tended to obscure the evidence of guilt of figures such as

Alger Hiss, Owen Lattimore, and Harry Dexter White, and the extent to which their influence had led to weakness in American foreign policy, especially toward Eastern Europe and China. In *McCarthy and His Enemies* (1954), **Buckley** and Brent Bozell dissected the liberal reaction to the senator, carefully analyzed the senator's own charges, and offered a partial vindication of McCarthyism, although not of McCarthy himself. (Critic Dwight Macdonald called the book a legal brief "on behalf of a pickpocket caught in the men's room of the subway.") In that same year, **Burnham** published *The Web of Subversion* (excerpts in *Reader's Digest*), an even more thoroughly documented study of congressional investigations of communist activity that pre-dated McCarthy's own. **Read:** W. F. Buckley and B. Bozell, *McCarthy and His Enemies* (1954); J. Burnham, *The Web of Subversion* (1954); N. von Hoffman, *Citizen Cohn* (1988); H. Klehr, et al., *The Secret World of American Communism* (1995); A. Weinstein, *Perjury: The Hiss-Chambers Case* (1978). **"It is curious that what is widely thought of as a contemptible aspect of Senator McCarthy's method actually amounts to nothing more than his intimacy with people. McCarthy's continuous appeal to the people sorely aggravates the same Liberals whose certified faith in the people's judgment never extends to those situations in which the people disagree with the Liberals."** William F. Buckley, Jr. and Brent Bozell, *McCarthy and His Enemies* (1954)

Mencken, H. L. (1880–1956): American social critic, journalist, and wit, whose public career brought him to a fame unprecedented in the age before television. (**Lippmann** called him "the most powerful influence on this whole generation of educated people.") He was an editor of two Baltimore newspapers, the *Morning Herald* (1905–1906) and the *Sun* (he edited or wrote for the paper from 1906 until his death), and of two magazines, *Smart Set* (1914–1923) and *American Mercury* (1924–1933), the latter of which he called an organ of "civilized Toryism." (It was a civility, of course, that made no quarrel with Mencken's anti-Semitism.) As an editor, he championed the work of such naturalistic writers as Theodore Dreiser, Sinclair Lewis, and Sherwood Anderson. Mencken's **conservatism** was in fact a variant of **libertarianism**, and he is often counted among the leaders of **Old Right**. Certainly, he was a consistent advocate of **isolationism**, and an unrelenting critic of **democracy**. He famously referred to the American middle class as the "booboisie," and called the American South the "Sahara of the Bozart." (He was wrong: see **Southern conservatism**.) Such criticisms were often stimulated by his hatred of an earlier **Christian right** that he saw as pinheaded and puritanical. Although remembered mostly for his mordancy, Mencken also had a more serious, scholarly side, and his most valuable contribution to the nation's literature was *The American Language*, a tour-de-force study of our idioms and expressions. **Read**: *Prejudices* (1919/1955); **About**: F. Hobson, *H. L. Mencken: A Life* (1994). **"The United States, to my eye, is incomparably the greatest show on earth. It is a show which avoids diligently all the kinds of clowning which tire me most quickly—for example, royal ceremonials, the tedious hocus-pocus of *haut politique*, the taking of politics seriously—and lays chief stress upon the kinds which delight me unceasingly—for example, the ribald combats of demagogues, the exquisitely ingenious operations of master rogues, the pursuit of witches and heretics, the desperate struggles of inferior men who claw their way into Heaven. . . . Human enterprises which, in all other Christian countries, are resigned despairingly to incurable dullness—things that seem devoid of exhilarating amusement by their very nature—are here lifted to such vast heights of buffoonery that contemplating them strains the midriff almost to breaking. I cite an example: worship of God. Everywhere else on earth it is carried on in a solemn and dispiriting manner; in England, of course, the bishops are obscene, but the average man seldom gets a fair chance to laugh at them and enjoy them. Now come home. Here we not only have bishops who are enormously more obscene than even the most gifted English bishops; we have also a huge force of lesser specialists in ecclesiastical mountebankery—tin-horn Loyolas, Savanarolas and Xaviers of a hundred fantastic rites, each performing untiringly and each full of grotesque and illimitable whimsicality."** "On Being An American" in *Prejudices* (1919)

Meyer, Frank E. (1909–1972): American journalist, whose early covenant with **Marxism** gave way to a blend of **conservatism** (he was an early editor of *National Review*) and **libertarianism**. With some sarcasm Brent Bozell dubbed Meyer's philosophy *fusionism*. Meyer (1964) believed that two "streams of thought, although they are sometimes presented as mutually incompatible, can in reality be united," and he sought to do so in the pages of *National Review*'s books section, and in his column "Principles and Heresies." His main point simply put: Virtue (the **conservative** goal) ought to be the end of human endeavor, but there is no virtue that is not freely chosen (the libertarian structure), "otherwise, virtue could be no more than a conditioned tropism." As much as anyone save **Buckley**, Meyer set the tone of *National Review*'s early years, and more than anyone, he forged the intellectual alliance that allowed American conservatism to transcend its sectarian squabbling and achieve ascendancy in the nation's politics. Meyer was also the principal founder of the Philadelphia Society, a conservative discussion group dedicated—at least while Meyer lived—to fusionism. **Read:** *The Conservative Mainstream* (1969); *In Defense of Freedom* (1962); **About:** J. East, *The American Conservative Movement* (1986); G. Nash, *The Conservative Intellectual Movement in America* (1976). **"[A]lthough these contrary emphases in conservative thought can and do pull away from each other when the proponents of either forsake one side of their common heritage of belief in virtue as man's proper end *and* his freedom under God as the condition of the achievement of that end, their opposition is not irreconcilable, precisely because they do in fact jointly possess that very heritage. Extremists on one side may be undisturbed by the danger of the recrudescence of authoritarian status society if only it would enforce the doctrines in which they believe. Extremists on the other side may care little what becomes of ultimate values if only political and economic individualism prevails. But both extremes are self-defeating: truth withers when freedom dies, however righteous the authority that kills it; and free individualism uninformed by moral value rots at its core and soon brings about conditions that pave the way for surrender to tyranny."** "Freedom, Tradition, Conservatism" in *What Is Conservatism?* (1964)

Mill, John Stuart (1806–1873): English philosopher and economist, generally acknowledged to be the dominant intellectual force of the 19th century. Mill's legendary education (he could read Greek before he was five) was undertaken entirely by his father, James, and by his father's friends (such as Jeremy Bentham), whose intention was to raise John Stuart to leadership of the Utilitarians (who held that which is right or good to be that which produces the greatest happiness for the most people). Their efforts were not entirely successful. Attacking Bentham's unrestricted hedonism, Mill observed that it was "better to be a human being dissatisfied than a pig satisfied." Mill referred to conservatives as "the stupid party," but he has been an inspiration to later "Rightists," especially advocates of liber-tarianism. *On Liberty* (1859), his greatest work, put forward "one very simple principle," namely that the individual ought to be able to do or say anything as long as it does not harm *others*. Mill's apparently absolutist view of free speech has animated much of liberalism's passionate defense of pornography—a development that Mill himself would not have appreciated. At the heart of all Mill's work is rationalism, the belief that we can know why we want what we want and why we do what we do, which belief is unlikely at best. Contemporary reactions to *On Liberty* were strong. Among the books written to answer Mill were *Liberty, Equality, Fraternity* (1873) by Stephen, *Apologia Pro Vita Sua* (1864) by Newman, and *Culture and Anarchy* (1869) by Matthew Arnold. From 1830 onwards, Mill was pulled in several directions: by the utilitarianism of his upbringing, by the historicism of Auguste Comte (see positivism), and by the traditionalism of Coleridge. Mill was not so "liberal" (in the classical sense) about economics, and abandoned an early preference for laissez-faire in favor of socialism, justifying its limitations on freedom by virtue of what he believed would be its ability to maximize security. Read: *Essays on Politics and Culture* (G. Himmelfarb, ed., 1962); *On Liberty and Other Essays* (1859/1991); About: M. Cowling, *Mill and Liberalism* (1990); J. Gray, *Liberalisms: Essays on Political Philosophy* (1989); G. Himmelfarb, *On Liberty and Liberalism: The Case of John Stuart Mill* (1974). "The object of this Essay is to assert one very simple principle, as entitled to govern absolutely the dealings of society with the individual in the way of compulsion and control, whether the means used be physical force in the form of legal penalties, or the moral coercion of public opinion. That principle is, that the sole end for which mankind are warranted, individually or collectively, in interfering with the liberty of action of any of their number, is self-protection. That the only purpose for which power can be rightfully exercised over any member of a civilized community, against his will, is to prevent harm to others. His own good, either physical or moral, is not a sufficient warrant. He cannot rightfully be compelled to do or forbear because it will be better for him to do so, because it will make him happier, because, in the opinions of others, to do so would be wise, or even right. These are good reasons for remonstrating with him, or reasoning with him, or persuading him, or entreating him, but not for compelling him . . ." *On Liberty* (1859)

Mises, Ludwig von (1881–1973): Austrian-born libertarian economist, who was the first member of the **Austrian School**'s second generation, and its most ardent champion of **laissez-faire**. His *Theory of Money and Credit* (1912—in English, 1935) argued that the value of money was subject to the same supply-and-demand pressures (marginal utility) as are the prices of goods, since money is a commodity like any other. Mises attacked inflationary governmental monetary policies (including central banking), and advocated the gold standard. Mises taught at the University of Vienna from 1913 until 1934, spent six years in Switzerland after that, and then was a professor at New York University until the late 1960s. Although not so famous as his student **Hayek** or so prolific as his student **Rothbard**, Mises' theory of human action, *praxeology*, has been widely influential. Praxeology is economics as a deductive and empirical social science concerned with real people in the real world. **Read:** *Human Action* (1949/1966); **About:** J. East, *The American Conservative Movement* (1986); J. Herbener, *The Meaning of Ludwig von Mises* (1993). "The teachings of praxeology and economics are valid for every human action without regard to its underlying motives, causes, and goals. The ultimate judgments of value and the ultimate ends of human action are given for any kind of scientific inquiry; they are not open to any further analysis. Praxeology deals with the ways and means chosen for the attainment of such ultimate ends. Its object is means, not ends. . . . In this sense we speak of the subjectivism of the general science of human action. It takes the ultimate ends chosen by acting man as data, it is entirely neutral with regard to them, and it refrains from passing any value judgments." *Human Action* (1949)

[Ludwig von Mises Institute, Auburn, AL 36849-5301; (334) 844-2500. Llewellyn H. Rockwell, Jr., president. The Institute offers a yearly week-long conference ("Mises University") on the Austrian School and related topics at Auburn University, and publishes newsletters: *The Free Market*, (monthly), *The Mises Review* (periodically), *The Austrian Economics Newsletter* (periodically), and *The Review of Austrian Economics,* all issued semi-annually at $10.00 per issue.]

modernism: A term used to refer to various—and diverse and unrelated—movements away from **tradition**, whether in religion or art, philosophy or even automobile mechanics. Although not synonymous with the tenets of **classical liberalism**, modernism does share its embrace of **individualism**. Additionally, modernism is characterized by a general discounting of the content and influence of religion, and with it the unintended consequence of despair. As **Bell** has described it—at least in the political realm—modernism is the **change** from **liberty** to *liberation*. In art, however, modernism is not necessarily impious (although it often has been), but it is perforce inventive. No artist ever more perfectly embraced both inventiveness and piety than did **Eliot**. **Read**: S. Gablik, *Has Modernism Failed?* (1984); H. Kenner, *A Homemade World* (1975). "Because of the religious crisis in modern society, social 'homelessness' [estrangement from society] has become metaphysical—that is, it has become 'homelessness' in the cosmos. This is very difficult to bear. . . . In one way or another, [traditional] religion made meaningful even the most painful experiences . . . Modern society has threatened the plausibility of religious [explanations], but it has not removed the experiences that call for them. . . . It is important to understand the additional burden to modernity implicit in this. Modernity has accomplished many far-reaching transformations, but it has not fundamentally changed the finitude, fragility and mortality of the human condition. What it has accomplished is to seriously weaken

those definitions of reality that previously made that human condition easier to bear. This has produced an anguish all its own . . ."
Peter L. Berger, Brigitte Berger, and Hansfried Kellner, *The Homeless Mind* (1973)

Molnar, Thomas (1921–   ): Hungarian-born American historian and journalist, whose life has been a sustained struggle against political **absolutism** and **utopianism**. He has also been a critic of American **democracy**, when, that is, it has pretensions to **egalitarianism**. A member of Hungary's Catholic Resistance in World War II, Molnar was imprisoned by the Nazis (in Dachau), and then forced to flee the communists after the war. Molnar came to the United States, where he earned a Ph.D. (in modern languages) from Columbia University (1952). As Allitt (1995) has pointed out, Molnar prefers to call himself a man of the **Right**, rather than a **conservative**, because he believes American conservatives are too much in the thrall of popular culture. Indeed, Molnar has said that in a comparison between the oppressive Soviet culture and the immoral American culture, the former comes off rather better, given that in Russia no one believed that communism was good, whereas in the United States nearly everybody loves television. Somewhat in the manner of **Voegelin** and **Strauss**, Molnar saw the sources of the West's moral decline in the 13th-century conflict between Thomas Aquinas and the gnostic and nominalistic heresies. Despite the triumph of Thomism, the world outside the church has grown ever more secular, leading to the errors of **liberalism**: messianism in foreign policy; **utopianism** in domestic policy. Molnar was able in 1991 to return to Hungary, where he now teaches six months of the year. **Read:** *Authority and Its Enemies* (1976); **About:** P. Allitt, *Catholic Intellectuals and Conservative Politics in America* (1995). "There is today terror even in philosophy and literature, because these are no longer regarded, in good revolutionary logic, as disciplines and art forms, but as *means* of eradicating all hitherto existing images and concepts of man. The bomb and the bullet hit only human beings, they cannot abolish them as exemplars of existence; the *word*, when used deliberately not as logos but as antilogos, is able to shame them into self-denial, self-abolition. In this sense, many fashionable modern doctrines are revolutionary, they deny man as a *subject*: they isolate him in a meaningless world, so that he is forced to give up the axis of his being. Psychoanalysis, Marxism, existentialism, structuralism, either *reduce* man to elements in which he cannot recognize himself, toward which his sense of self, his consciousness, can build no bridges, or *diminish* man until he is dissolved in a structure, independent of him, overwhelming him." *The Counter-Revolution* (1969)

monetarism: The economic school which contends that the money supply is the engine of economic activity. <u>Friedman</u> is the foremost spokesman of monetarism, although its origins may be found in the work of Henry Simons, who held that monetary policy be "conducted according to rule rather than to discretionary manipulation" (Stigler, 1988). There is an equation that summarizes the theory, and as economic calculations go it is reasonably intelligible: $MV = PQ$; where M is the *money* in supply, V is the *velocity* of the money supply (specifically the number of times each year that one dollar is spent on one or another goods and services), P is the average *price* level, and Q is the *quantity* of goods and services produced. This money-times-velocity-equals-price-times-quantity view is said to be a "left-handed" equation, meaning that raising or lowering the amount of money in circulation affects the production side of the calculus. The most theoretically influential of Friedman's books, *A Monetary History of the United States, 1867–1960* (written with Anna J. Schwartz, 1963) demonstrated that government intervention in the economy—in whatever form—tends to have perverse effects. <u>Hayek</u> held (1991) that the chief defect of monetarism was that really there is "no such thing as *the* quantity of money," given our various media of exchange. **Read:** T. Buchholz, *New Ideas from Dead Economists* (1989); M. Friedman, *Monetarist Economics* (1991). **"Why would anyone be foolish enough to argue about the money supply? The more money the merrier, right? Wrong. . . . If the amount of money overwhelms the capacity to produce goods, consumers, with more money to spend, bid up prices. . . . [People are] no wealthier than before; more bills do not bring a higher standard of living any more than if everyone added two zeroes to his or her salary. Remember that wealth is measured by the goods and services it can buy, not by nu-**

merals. Since one U.S. dollar can buy thousands of pesos, a Mexican millionaire might be poor compared to a low-income American. Giving all the Mexicans suitcases packed with pesos would not help. Merriment does not necessarily follow more." Todd Buchholz, *New Ideas from Dead Economists* (1989)

Montesquieu, Charles-Louis de Secondat, **Baron de** (1689–1755): French jurist and philosopher, and a major influence on both the conservative and liberal doctrines that emerged from the Enlightenment. Inspired in part by Locke (with whom he often disagreed), Montesquieu was an amusing and effective critic of absolutism, whether in politics or religion. In *The Spirit of the Laws* (1748)—the most frequently cited work at America's Constitutional Convention forty years later—Montesquieu argued (and in this influenced Burke) that Man's need to resist his own destructiveness leads inevitably to the creation of law—a universal code of behavior. This "universality," however, is relativistic—applicable only within a single culture ("the general spirit of each nation," which in Montesquieu's view included everything from customs to climate). Still, three legal systems predominate, each with its own spirit: despotism's spirit is its subjects' fear; monarchy's is kingly honor; and the republic's is public virtue. Montesquieu preferred republican government, but he concluded that, historically, its virtue depended upon men not laws, which led him to praise Britain's structural union of constitutionalism and commerce. He was among the first to influentially assert that liberty is best safeguarded by a separation of executive, judicial, and legislative powers, and he clearly regarded laissez-faire as the best means of satisfying human ambitions across the full spectrum of talent and class. ("Peace is the natural effect of trade . . .") Because of his concern with the close study of culture, Montesquieu is sometimes called the "father of sociology." His influence upon America's founding generation (in such doctrines as balance of powers, religious tolerance, and separation of church and state) was considerable. **Read:** *The Spirit of the Laws* (1748); *Montesquieu: Selected Political Writings*, M. Richter, ed. (1990). **About:** R. Aron, *Main Currents of Sociological Thought*, vol. I (1965); T. Pangle, *Montesquieu's Philosophy of Liberalism* (1989); M. Richter, *The Political*

Theory of Montesquieu (1977). "It is true that in democracies the people seem to act as they please. But political liberty does not consist simply in doing whatever one wishes. In governments, that is, in societies directed by laws, liberty can consist only in the power of doing what we ought to do, without being constrained from doing what we ought not to do. We must distinguish freedom from liberty. Again, liberty is the right to do everything the laws permits. If a citizen does what the law prohibits, he sacrifices his liberty . . ." *The Spirit of the Laws* (1748)

Mont Pélerin Society: Free-market coffee-klatsch founded in 1947 by Hayek at the eponymous resort near Montreux, Switzerland. Its goal was to bring scholars together to discuss the state of classical liberalism in the wake of the twin experiences of totalitarianism and total war. "Members," according to the Society's brief mission statement, "have included high governmental officials, men of affairs, journalists, and scholars—all philosophically isolated in their own communities . . ." Among the thirty-six attendees at the first meeting were Friedman, Popper, and Morley. (Lippmann was invited but was unable to attend.) Its proceedings are generally off the record, yet its influence has been considerable, and its members are surely no longer "philosophically isolated." Hayek originally thought to call the organization the Acton-Tocqueville Society. **Read:** G. Nash, *The Conservative Intellectual Movement in America* (1976). "The group holds that these developments [the erosion of individual liberty and the expansion of state power] have been fostered by the growth of a view of history which denies all absolute moral standards and by the growth of theories which question the desirability of the rule of law. It holds further that they have been fostered by a decline of belief in private property and the competitive market; for without the diffused power and initiative associated with these institutions it is difficult to imagine a society in which freedom may be effectively preserved." From the Society's original "Statement of Aims," April 10, 1947

More, Paul Elmer (1864–1937): American classicist, critic, and editor (once of *The Nation*), who with Babbitt espoused the New Humanism. His multi-volume *Shelburne Essays* (11 vols., 1904–1921) and *New Shelburne Essays* (3 vols., 1928–36) celebrate humanism, classicism, and religion, which put him publicly at odds with Mencken. Like Babbitt, he read Sanskrit fluently, and undertook a lifelong attempt to harmonize Eastern and Western religious tradition. What emerges from these efforts is a Neoplatonic vision of a republic governed by just men (a "natural aristocracy"). The prospect of egalitarianism in America led him to assert that private property is a right *superior* to the right to life. But such dubious notions never formed the heart of his world view. For More what mattered most was Man's efforts to overcome the illusion that the world is made by Man. What we need most, he wrote, is "to get the fear of God back into society." **Read**: *Demon of the Absolute* (1928); B. Lambert, ed., *The Essential Paul Elmer More* (1972); *Selected Shelburne Essays* (1935); **About**: F. X. Duggan, *Paul Elmer More* (1966). **"Our most precious heritage of liberty depends on the safeguarding of that realm of the individual against the encroachments of a legal equalitarianism. For there is nothing surer than that liberty of the spirit, if I may use that dubious word, is bound up with the inequality of men in their natural relations; and every movement in history to deny the inequalities of nature has been attended, and by fatal necessity always will be attended, with an effort to crush the liberty of distinction in the ideal sphere."** *Shelburne Essays* (1935)

Morley, Felix (1894–1982): American journalist and educator: *Washington Post* editor (1933–40), Haverford College president (1940–45), and co-founding editor (1945–50) of *Human Events* with Henry Regnery, Frank Hanighen, and William Henry Chamberlain. (Buckley tried to buy the paper early in the 1950s; his failure forced him to start up his own periodical, National Review.) In *Freedom and Federalism* (1959), Morley argued that Man's needs for both order and liberty were uniquely wedded in American federalism. Morley was one of the original members of the Mont Pélerin Society. **Read**: *Freedom and Federalism*; **About**: his own *For the Record* (1979). **"The essence of the Constitution is, of course, the federal system which it established. Every provision of the organic law is based on the fundamental concept of *these* United *States*. They are not and cannot be merged into a single state as long as the Constitution stands. And so, for all who revere the Constitution, States'**

Rights is a vital issue, whereas political democracy decidedly is not. If, as and when democracy runs sharply counter to States' Rights, then many Americans will rally to oppose democracy. It should be obvious to all that an organic law which specifically safeguards minorities is for that very reason antagonistic to unqualified majority rule." *Freedom and Federalism* (1959)

[*Human Events*, 7811 Montrose Road, Potomac, MD 20897-5400; (800) 787-7557. Thomas S. Winter, editor. Subscriptions: $49.95/year (50 issues); $89.95 for two years.]

Muggeridge, Malcolm (1903–1991): English man of letters and one of the century's most celebrated converts—from **socialism** to **conservatism** and from atheism to Christianity. Raised in an ardently socialist home, and then married to the niece of the Fabian socialists Beatrice and Sidney Webb, Muggeridge began his journalistic career in earnest at the *Manchester Guardian*, where he hoped to expose the follies of a "dead culture." In 1932, he became the *Guardian's* Moscow correspondent. Disillusionment came quickly. His novel, *Winter in Moscow* (1934), tells the story in semi-autobiographical form. This was the origin of one of the great themes of his life: the futility of **utopianism**. A period during World War II in which he worked as an Allied spy led to a nearly suicidal depression, and then to the discovery of another great theme: the necessity of suffering. In 1953, he became editor of the British humor magazine *Punch*, and guided it through its brief Golden Age. (He left in 1958.) At the same time, he began to appear regularly on television, and became—both in Britain and in North America—one of that medium's most popular figures. In 1969 he shocked many of his viewers, listeners, and readers, who were used to his acerbic pessimism, by publishing *Jesus Rediscovered*, in which he professed an individualistic but fairly traditional English Protestantism. Then, largely under the influence of Mother Teresa of Calcutta, he converted to Catholicism in 1982. Although "orthodox" in his beliefs for more than a decade, his reason for crossing over to Rome was interesting: "It was the Catholic Church's firm stand against contraception and abortion which finally made me decide to become a Catholic." **Read**: *Confessions of a 20th Century Pilgrim* (1988); *Winter in Moscow* (1934); **About**: his own *Chronicles of*

Wasted Time (1989). "The absurdities of the kingdom of heaven, as conceived in the minds of simple believers, are obvious enough—pearly gates, angelic choirs, golden crowns, and shining raiment. But what are we to think of the sheer imbecility of the kingdom of heaven on earth, as envisaged and recommended by the most authoritative and powerful voices of our time? Wealth increasing forevermore, and its beneficiaries, rich in time-payment merchandise, stupefied with television and with sex, comprehensively educated, told by Professor Hoyle how the world began and by Bertrand Russell how it will end; venturing forth on broad highways, three lanes a side, with layhys to rest in and birth pills to keep them *intacta*, if not *virgo*, blood spattering the Tarmac as an extra thrill; heaven lying about them in the supermarket, the rainbow ending in the nearest bingo hall, leisure burgeoning out in multitudinous shining aerials rising like dreaming spires into the sky; happiness in as many colors as there are pills—green and yellow and blue and red and shining white; many mansions, mansions of light and chromium, climbing ever upwards. This kingdom, surely, can only be for posterity an unending source of wry derision—always assuming there is to be any posterity. The backdrop, after all, is the mushroom cloud; as the Gadarene herd frisk and frolic, they draw ever nearer to the edge of the precipice." *Jesus Rediscovered* (1969)

Murray, Charles (1943–   ): American social scientist and author of the epoch-changing *Losing Ground: American Social Policy, 1950–80* (1984), the book that transformed American attitudes about <u>welfare</u> policy. After graduation from Harvard (1965), Murray spent six years in Southeast Asia (with the Peace Corps and a research institute), before returning to MIT to earn his doctorate in political science (1974). Murray then spent seven years at the American Institutes for Research in Washington, where he had the opportunity to closely monitor the range of national-government social services. The evidence convinced him that, at best, poverty programs were no more effective than <u>laissez-faire</u>, although a whole lot more expensive. Murray published his observations in a **Heritage Foundation** paper, and then undertook the writing of *Losing Ground* for the Manhattan Institute. Murray quite simply devastated the Great Society's policy assumptions. He showed that: "It was wrong to take from the most industrious, most responsible poor—take safety, education, justice, status—so that we could cater to the least industrious, least responsible poor." He demonstrated that eligibility rules inevitably expand the number of "poor," that transfer payments increase the "value" of poverty, and that if people are not highly motivated to change their economic lives, "poverty" programs will actually—again through eligibility rules—wed them to poverty. The social-service apparatus is mostly positive reinforcement with little negative reinforcement. His solutions involved the repeal of all affirmative action programs, the adoption of a voucher system and honest testing in education, and, most dramatically, an end to welfare—forcing the young and the poor into the job market, like it or not. He wrote: "Cut the knot, for there is no way to untie it." Even liberal critics, who accused him of neo-Malthusian cruelty, were inclined to admit that Murray was both courageous and prescient. The controversy surrounding *Losing Ground*, however, tended to pale in comparison to the reception of *The Bell Curve: Intelligence and Class Structure in American Life* (1994), which Murray wrote with Richard J. Herrnstein. This time, Murray found he even had enemies on the **Right**. The idea that certain poor people are poor largely because they cannot compete with a "cognitive elite" seemed to some an embrace of the old eugenics of racism. Still, the book's vision of social **order** did not differ from the one offered in Murray's *In Pursuit: Of Happiness and Good Government* (1988) which the same critics had praised. **Read:** *The Bell Curve* (1994); *Losing Ground* (1984); **About:** *In Pursuit* (1988). **"The result [of the War on Poverty's rationale] was that the intelligentsia and the policymakers, coincident with the revolution in social policy, began treating the black poor in ways that they would never consider treating people they respected. Is the black crime rate skyrocketing? Look at the black criminal's many grievances against society. Are black illegitimate birth rates five times those of whites? We must remember that blacks have a much broader view of the family ... Did black labor force participation among the young plummet? We can hardly blame someone for having too much pride to work at a job sweeping floors. Are black high-school graduates illiterate? The educational system is insensitive. Are their test scores a hundred** points lower than others? The tests are biased. Do black youngsters lose jobs to white youngsters because their mannerisms and language make them incomprehensible to their prospective employers? The culture of the ghetto has its own validity. . . . Whites began to tolerate and make excuses for behavior among blacks that whites would disdain in themselves or their children." *Losing Ground* (1984)

Murray, John Courtney, S.J. (1904–1967): American political scientist and theologian. Murray was a student, teacher, and editor (of the quarterly *Theological Studies*) at Woodstock College, the Jesuit school of theology in Maryland. He edited *Theological Studies* for more than twenty-five years. Murray was an early ecumenist, anticipating by several decades the Second Vatican Council's embrace of pluralism. For him, it was a matter of embracing the American way, which he understood to be a world view that is religious, in the sense of believing in certain definable (and fixed) first principles, and yet pluralistic, in that it accepts that interpretations of those principles will differ. Indeed, Murray was convinced that American **tradition** was directly descended from medieval scholasticism. His was a uniquely visionary sense of the conflict between unity and pluralism. These issues and others were played out in *We Hold These Truths* (1960), Murray's first book, published when he was fifty-six. The book argues that consensus in American politics and society must be based upon **natural law**. He served on the board of the Center for the Study of Democratic Institutions with, among others, Reinhold Niebuhr, and he was the principal author of the Vatican Council's decree on religious freedom. **Read**: *We Hold These Truths* (1960); **About**: T. Ferguson, *Catholic and American* (1994); R. Hunt and K. Grasso, *John Courtney Murray* (1992). "The first truth to which the American Proposition makes appeal is stated in that landmark of Western political theory, the Declaration of Independence. It is a truth that lies beyond politics; it imparts to politics a fundamental human meaning. I mean the sovereignty of God over nations as well as over individual men. This is the principle that radically distinguishes the conservative Christian tradition of America from the Jacobin laicist tradition of Continental Europe. The Jacobin tradition proclaimed the autonomous reason of man to be the first and the sole principle of political organization. In contrast, the first article of the American political faith is that the political community, as a form of free and ordered human life, looks to the sovereignty of God as to the first principle of its organization. In the Jacobin tradition religion is at best a purely private concern ... This whole manner of thought is altogether alien to the authentic American tradition." *We Hold These Truths* (1960)

The National Interest: See **Kristol, Irving**

National Review: America's pre-eminent **conservative** magazine, founded (the incorporation documents were drawn up by future CIA director William Casey) in 1955 by **Buckley** with the help of Willi Schlamm (formerly of *Time* and *The Freeman*). Schlamm was the first of many ex-communists who formed the magazine's original staff. Initially intended to be titled *National Weekly, National Review* was published on November 19, and carried the famous Buckley editorial statement proclaiming that the new magazine "stands athwart history, yelling stop." Reviewing the premiere issue for *Commentary*, liberal critic Dwight Macdonald called it "as elegant as a poke in the nose, as cultivated as a camp meeting, and as witty as a prat-fall." Other founding editors included **Burnham**, **Kendall**, and, a few months later, **Meyer**. **Chambers** at first declined to sign on, then did, and **Kirk**, although he wrote an educational column for many years, preferred not to become an editor. William Rusher became publisher (a title Buckley had held, along with editor-in-chief, since the founding) in 1957. Such a group, a balance between Christians and Jews, libertarians and traditionalists, ensured that *National Review* would, from the start, tend to chart a course less in terms of **isolationism** (let alone of anti-Semitism) and protectionism than had earlier conservative magazines such as *The American Mercury* (see **Mencken**). What's more, that Buckley was the sole owner of the magazine (there were other stockholders, but none with voting rights) meant that disagreements would not lead to the divisive power struggles that had cannibalized previous conservative journals. *NR* is now edited by English journalist John O'Sullivan, a former advisor to **Thatcher**. **Read:** P. Buckley, *The Joys of National Review* (1994); J. Hart, *The American Dissent* (1966); G. Nash, *The Conservative Intellectual Movement in*

America (1976); W. Rusher, *The Rise of the Right* (1984). "It is simply the case that *National Review* is the most consequential journal of opinion ever. There is not, I think, a scintilla of hyperbole in that judgment. Think about it. For two generations it has been the beating heart of the movement that has transformed America. It has changed first the ideas and then the politics and ultimately the policies of the most important nation the world has ever known. And this change, this journey up from liberalism, was necessary to winning the most important war ever waged, the fifty-year war against the totalitarians. For that reason it is the most important magazine of opinion ever. Because history is the history of mind, and it will be impossible to write the history of the 20th century of the modern world without dwelling at length and respectfully on the history of *National Review*." George Will in remarks on *National Review's* thirty-fifth anniversary (*National Review*, November 5, 1990)

[*National Review*, 150 E. 35th St., New York, NY 10016. John O'Sullivan, editor. Sunscriptions: $57/year (25 issues), *National Review*, PO Box 667, Mount Morris, IL 61054-7529.]

natural law: Sometimes called natural *right* (as distinct from **natural rights**, plural) or *higher law*, it is the moral **order** of the world known to all men in all times in all places. This is the Ciceronian "right reason," that "summons men to performance of their duties; [and] . . . restrains them from doing wrong." It is what Augustine famously called "the law written in the hearts of men, which iniquity itself effaces not." Aquinas called the innate knowledge of this law *synderesis*, and defined the God-ordained natural law's first principle as, roughly: "Do good; avoid evil." Natural law is seen in relief against *positive law*—the codes derived from human experience and enacted by Man—and was the basis for the earliest notions of international law, as in the work of Hugo Grotius. For Plato, natural right logically led to a communitarian regime ruled by philosopher kings (dictators); the natural order of the world, as he saw it, was of sheep and shepherds. Aristotle thought natural law was "agnostic" as to the specifics of government, but that it did impose upon individuals the burden of civil responsibility. For the Greeks, and for the later Roman Stoics, the manifest principle of natural law was justice. For the Stoics, however, the justice of natural law was derived from its divine origin, and the concept thereafter has tended to be a problem for philosophy and theology rather than for politics and law. However, the Stoics' "divinity" was often materialistic; was absolute only as an embodiment of, for instance, Justice or Reason—concepts of objective but not necessarily theistic character. But from Aquinas forward, natural law—whatever its tenets and however it stands in relation to positive law—presupposes an *intentional nature*, i.e., God. However, a second view of natural law began to emerge at the start of the modern era (1500). A belief in natural law is necessary to refute the assertion of Thomas Hobbes that all positive law is just. What makes the concept of special interest to conservatives is its rejection of the instrumentalism of modern **liberalism**. The **empiricism** of **Burke**, for one, is often seen as an affront to the concept of natural law. However, it was not a natural law he denied but the severance of the concept (first by Hobbes and **Locke** and then by Rousseau) from its divine source. What it comes down to is this: natural law is that set of certainties (moral absolutes) without which we could not agree about right and wrong. Politically, as **Kirk** wrote (1987), natural law is "a loosely-knit body of rules of action, prescribed by an authority superior to the state." If, as Hobbes believed (and many liberals believe) there is no such **authority**, then the state must be all powerful. **Read:** J. Maritain, *The Rights of Man and Natural Law* (1943); C. Rice, *50 Questions on the Natural Law* (1993); P. Stanlis, *Edmund Burke and the Natural Law* (1986). "Democracy may become as oppressive as tyranny, when natural law is denied. The Athenian democracy that condemned Socrates to death for his opinions, the French democracy that invented the Terror under which half mankind now cowers, the Senate of the United States that in spite of all the written 'rights' of the Constitution degrades men's characters without due process of law, merely because they are suspected of unpopular ideas—all warn us that the People can be as dangerous as a Dictator if they fall into self-idolatry, forgetting that they are under a law not made by man. This is why we should never boast of our democracy to Russia or to Asian nations until we have made sure that the 'will of the people' is bound and limited by sanctions that no Assembly can repeal. Here we are close to the heart of our faith, which alone can impose such sanctions. If we fall into confusion on this point the outside world may reasonably wonder whether the soul of the West is corroded." Herbert Agar, *A Declaration of Faith* (1952)

natural rights: Although the concept of natural rights is derived from natural law, it is characteristic of this concept that it is not God (or truth) who is the ground of deduction but God's *works*. Nature (or an ancient civil society) replaces God. Jeremy Bentham famously called the doctrine of natural rights "nonsense upon stilts." He believed—and in this he voiced the opinion of later positivists (such as the contemporary critical legal studies movement)—that a right is "the child of law." Legislatures, not nature (let alone God), determine a people's rights. This view has been effectively refuted by Strauss and many of his disciples, most notably Jaffa. The terms *natural rights* and *natural law* are sometimes used synonymously and sometimes antithetically, and seem almost hopelessly confusing. But if the rights proposed are *individualistic*, in the sense that their actuality is based solely upon consent, then the animating philosophy is positivism. If, on the other hand, the rights in question are truly derived from "the Laws of Nature and of Nature's God," then they are asserted as standards no polity can refute. Read: L. Strauss, *Natural Right and History* (1953). "Equality in the sight of God, equality before the law, security in what is one's own, participation in the common activities and consolations of society—these are the true natural rights." Russell Kirk, *The Conservative Mind* (1953)

neoconservatism: Name given by socialist Michael Harrington (*The Other America*, 1962) to the belief system of that group of former leftists who by the 1970s were advocating a version of conservatism. ("A neoconservative," Kristol observed, "is a liberal who has been mugged by reality.") Indeed, a better term would probably have been *paleoliberal* (see classical liberalism), in that neoconservatives never embraced (and probably reject) conservatism's pre-Enlightenment cosmology, just as they accused paleoconservatism of not accepting the bourgeois revolution of the Enlightenment. Neoconservatives accept the necessity of a non-paternalistic welfare state. They accept the success of market economics, but also accept modest interventions (e.g., housing vouchers but not housing projects). They are vocal advocates of the West's cultural <u>tradition</u> and its institutions, and are among the most vocal critics of the academic counter-culture, liberation theology, and the various rights movements. They believe that absolute equality is the enemy of liberty. **Read:** M. Winchell, *Neoconservative Criticism* (1991). **"Unlike previous such currents of thought—for example, the Southern Agrarians or the Transcendentalists of the 19th century—neoconservatism is antiromantic in substance and temperament. Indeed, it regards political romanticism—and its twin, political utopianism—of any kind as one of the plagues of our age. This is but another way of saying it is a philosophical-political impulse rather than a literary-political impulse. Or, to put it still another way: Its approach to the world is more 'rabbinic' than 'prophetic.'"** Irving Kristol, *Reflections of a Neoconservative* (1983)

Neuhaus, Richard John (1936–   ): Canadian-born American religious leader and writer, whose *The Naked Public Square* (1984) was a warning call that when religion absents the state, the state's presence will be total—it will become a religion. His *The Catholic Moment* (1987) asserted the prominent saving role—*politically*—played by the contemporary Catholic Church's opposition to secularism in public life. It was a notion that was somewhat mystifying to his Lutheran colleagues, and which was predictive of his conversion to Catholicism just four years later. Neuhaus emigrated to the United States as a teenager—on his own—settled in Texas, where he ran a filling station-grocery store and managed to complete high school; he then enrolled at Concordia Theological Seminary in Missouri. Upon graduation he served as pastor of an inner-city church in the Bedford-Stuyvesant section of Brooklyn, New York, where he was the very model of the liberal activist, an intimate of Martin Luther King, Jr., and a co-founder, with Daniel Berrigan, of Clergy and Laity Concerned, an anti-Vietnam War group. The change in his views began to become visible during the early 1970s. He attacked the nascent ecology movement as neo-Malthusian, and the pro-choice movement as brutal. In 1975, Neuhaus signed the "Hartford Appeal," a document attacking many of liberal Christianity's (i.e., the National Council of Churches') most cherished beliefs as heretical. Still, Neuhaus supported Jimmy Carter in 1976. By the time **Reagan** won re-election in 1984, Pastor Neuhaus had embraced **neoconservatism**, **supply-side theory**, and **anticommunism**. He became director of the **Rockford Institute**'s Center on Religion and Public Affairs in 1984 (and editor of its journal, *This World*), the same year that saw publication of *The Naked Public Square*. Shortly thereafter, he became religion editor of *National Review*. A disagreement with Rockford led to the formation of the Institute on Religion and Public Life and its magazine *First Things: A Monthly Journal of Religion and Public Life*. Neuhaus and Peter L. Berger have jointly developed an important contemporary interpretation of **subsidiarity** that emphasizes the importance of employing "mediating institutions" in public policy. **Read:** *The Naked Public Square* (1984); **About:** I. Markham, *Plurality and Christian Ethics* (1995). "**The truly naked public square is at best a transitional phenomenon. It is a vacuum begging to be filled. When the democratically affirmed institutions that generate and transmit values are excluded, the vacuum will be filled by the agent left in control of the public square, the state. In this manner, a perverse notion of the disestablishment of religion leads to the establishment of the state as church. Not without reason, religion is viewed by some as a repressive imposition upon the public square. They would cast out the devil of particularist religion and thus put the public square in proper secular order. Having cast out the one devil, they unavoidably invite the entrance of seven devils worse than the first.**" *The Naked Public Square* (1984)

[*First Things*, P.O. Box 3000, Dept. FT, Denville, NJ 07834; (800) 783-4903. Subscriptions: $29.00 per year for 10 issues.]

New Conservatism: A term, first used by **Viereck** in 1940 (and little-used of late), for the more traditionalist form of American **conservatism** that emerged (or re-emerged) in the 1950s. It is not to be confused, although it often is, with **neoconservatism**. The New Conservatives differ from the neoconservatives primarily in the genesis of their philosophical development: the former are in a line of (more or less) direct transmission from **Burke** and John **Adams** to **Kirk**, and **Buckley**, whereas the neoconservatives came out of—and reacted against—the radical or liberal experience of the 1960s. The

New Conservatism found its roots in Europe, and—quite different from the present day—found its home in American universities. (See also **New Right**.) **Read**: P. Viereck, *Conservatism Revisited* (1949); R. Kirk, *The Conservative Mind* (1953). **"Not everyone accepted the label easily. Kirk in particular was distressed by its implied emphasis on novelty . . . Still, despite tendentious and partisan usage . . . it lingered on as a broad generic classification . . . One critic, in fact, writing in 1955, predicted that the entire decade would be remembered as 'the Era of the New Conservatism.'"** George H. Nash, *The Conservative Intellectual Movement in America* (1976)

The New Criterion: American magazine of cultural criticism edited by Hilton Kramer (1928–), and generally considered the pre-eminent culture-and-arts journal of **neoconservatism**, if not simply the best arts magazine in the world. Kramer had been art critic for several magazines (including the *Nation*) in the late 1950s and early 1960s before becoming first art news editor and then chief critic of the *New York Times* (1965–1982), and thus the most influential critic in America. With Samuel Lipman (1934–1994) he founded the *New Criterion* in 1982; its name coming from the earlier British magazine, *The Criterion*, edited by **Eliot**. The *New Criterion* has been a steadfast champion of artistic **modernism**, but a constant critic of post-modernism, which Kramer has characterized as "alternately nasty and boring." Managing editor Roger Kimball (1953–) is the author of one of the first (and perhaps the best) accounts of political correctness, *Tenured Radicals* (1990). As Paul Johnson put it in *The Wall Street Journal* (February 28, 1995), *The New Criterion* attacks the "culture of rebellion" that believes "it is not necessary to draw in order to paint, and a pop lyric has as much value as a poem by Keats . . ." **Read**: H. Kramer and R. Kimball, eds., *Against the Grain* (1995); H. Kramer, *The Age of the Avant Garde* (1973); S. Lipman, *Arguing for Music, Arguing for Culture* (1990). **"Many writers on the Left—and this includes a good many of our prominent critics, too—have never forgiven history for failing to conform to the fictions of radical prophecy. They have never forgiven American society for failing to live up to their critique of it. In some tender sanctum of the soul, socialism remains their moral and social** ideal—but a socialism so immune to historical contingency and moral reality that it is now indistinguishable from a religious dogma. It would therefore break their hearts and shatter every illusion they have inherited from the sacred traditions of radicalism to have to acknowledge that capitalism, for all its many flaws, has proved to be the greatest safeguard of democratic institutions and the best guarantee of intellectual and artistic freedom—including *their* intellectual and artistic freedom—that the modern world has given us. How profoundly they despise this elementary fact of their existence, and how energetically they work to disguise and distort its reality!" From "A Note on *The New Criterion*" in its first issue, September 1982

[*The New Criterion*, 850 Seventh Avenue, New York, NY 10019. Subscriptions: $36 for one year; $65 for two.]

Newman, John Henry (1801–1890): English Catholic clergyman and essayist. He was a leader of the Oxford Movement, which sought to *de-Protestantize* the Anglican Church, but which finally led him to convert to Catholicism in 1845. During the "Oxford" period—also known as the Tractarian Movement—Newman had advocated Anglicanism as the *via media* or middle way between the extremes of papal **authority** in Rome and the private judgment of Protestantism. The various tracts printed and sermons preached concerned themselves primarily with attacks upon freethinking and **liberalism**, which he called "an error overspreading, as a snare, the whole earth." Newman believed—and expounded the idea in his thinking and writing during the short period between leaving Anglicanism and turning to Catholicism—that religious truth is organic: it grows from Biblical seeds to become present dogma, which is not a corruption of original truth but its necessary growth. As rector of the new Catholic University of Dublin, Newman delivered his famous lectures on *The Idea of a University* (first published two decades later in 1873), in which he outlined a liberal education: "philosophical" and humanistic as opposed to "mechanical" and utilitarian. In 1864, Newman was attacked by a Protestant cleric (Charles Kingsley), who accused him of not believing in "truth for its own sake," but because it was embodied in Catholic dogma. Newman's response was his

Apologia Pro Vita Sua. In 1870, Newman (along with **Acton**) and some other English "liberals" (see **classical liberalism**), expressed misgivings (although not opposition) about the newly promulgated doctrine of papal infallibility, and in that same year published *Grammar of Assent*, a classic study of the experiential mechanisms of **faith**. He was made a cardinal in 1879. **Read:** *Apologia Pro Vita Sua* (1864); **About:** R. Pattison, *The Great Dissent* (1991) **"Many persons are very sensitive to the difficulties of religion; I am as sensitive as anyone; but I have never been able to see a connexion between apprehending those difficulties, however keenly, and multiplying them to any extent, and doubting the doctrines to which they are attached. Ten thousand difficulties do not make one doubt, as I understand the subject; difficulty and doubt are incommensurate."** *Apologia Pro Vita Sua* (1864)

New Right: That group of conservatives and libertarians whose **anticommunism** forced them after World War II to abandon the **isolationism** of the so-called **Old Right**. New Right (then synonymous with **New Conservatism**) was a term initially used to describe figures as diverse as **Viereck** and **Buckley**. This definition, however, is outdated. More recently, the term has been used to describe that group on the **Right** which after the defeat of **Goldwater** developed a more aggressive, less philosophical approach to politics: men such as William Rusher of *National Review*, Richard Viguerie of direct-mail fame, Howard Phillips of the Conservative Caucus, and the first politically active elements of the **Christian Right**. Indeed, Viguerie's self-congratulatory tome, *The New Right: We're Ready to Lead* (1980), was introduced by Moral Majority head Jerry Falwell. Perhaps the most telling distinction between Old and New is the *philosophical* versus the *social*; a variance best understood in the issues addressed and strategies employed. Although both groups oppose **abortion**, only the New Right would actively support Operation Rescue. **Neoconservatism** (if only because of etymology) is also often considered a component of the New Right, and, indeed, in recent years neocons have surprised even themselves by finding common cause with the Christian Right. According to Gottfried and Fleming (1988), however, there is a distinction: "For the neoconservatives, it was Democrats and young radicals who corrupted the great liberal tradition; for the New Right, the villains were moderate Republicans . . ." (Gottfried and Fleming, who are actually sympathetic, sum up Viguerie as a leader by observing that he is "distinguished neither by his learning nor by his literary style," and that compared to Buckley—with whom the authors are not always sympathetic—Viguerie "resembles a car salesman attending, uninvited, a formal dinner.") To further complicate the matter, in Britain "New Right" is a term used to describe the supporters of **Thatcher. Read:** R. W. Whitaker, ed., *The New Right Papers* (1982). **"I [have] said . . . that the Old Right tended to be intellectual and upper class. It is as accurate a generalization that the New Right tends to be middle class, blue-collar and ethnic in its origins. Eighteenth century British economic theory did not pertain very clearly to a German workingman's family in the 1950s. Though the upper classes had more intellectual expertise, they tended to become deficient in something that was strong in the working middle classes: values. In blue-collar areas, especially among first and second generation ethnics, be they Russian Jews or German Catholics, tradition was as real a part of life as paying taxes, and old world culture as close as home. Well-bred, well-heeled youth allowed right and wrong to become blurred, and tradition to become a romantic decoration. Respect among working people was a consciously instilled value, the cornerstone of everything else—respect for father and mother and grandparents, for priest or rabbi, for the institutions of society: teachers, police, law, government. Respect engenders discipline, and hard work was the means to achieve desired goals."** Paul M. Weyrich, "Blue Collar or Blue Blood? The New Right Compared with the Old Right," in Whitaker (1982)

Nisbet, Robert A. (1913–   ): American sociologist (educated at the University of California, Berkeley; taught in the University of California system and at Columbia University) whose *The Quest for Community* (1953) was a profound analysis of the seemingly inexorable assault by the state upon the **authority** of the "intermediate associations" of traditional life, namely the **family** and the church. The book set the tone for his life's work, which has been devoted to studying the sometimes conflicting, always shifting forces of **community** and authority. Indeed, the thesis of *The Quest for Community* is that the authority of the modern state—whether totalitarian or democratic—has supplanted the authority of the community—has *become* the community. Much of the reason for the state's growth, Nisbet believes, has been atomistic **individualism**, and he has sharply criticized **Popper**'s concept of the "open society" as subversive of **tradition**. As much as any contemporary writer, Nisbet has sought to define clearly the basic terms we use in discussing social and political realities. Thus his *Prejudices* (1982) is an invaluable "philosophical dictionary" establishing scholarly, sometimes provocative, definitions of seventy concepts ranging from **abortion** and **alienation** to war and wit. (On *victimology*: "There is no substitute for punishment in a social order, and that means holding human beings accountable, treating them as human, and therefore responsible. Concern for human rights is rampant these days, but a right is possible in the strict sense only for beings who can be rationally regarded as responsible." Nisbet has also written a fine, short survey called *Conservatism: Dream and Reality* (1986), in which he explicates the **conservative** vision through its American and European sources. He is currently a fellow of the **American Enterprise Institute. Read:** *The Quest for Community* (1953); *Conservatism* (1986). **About:** R. Fryer, *Recent Conservative Political Thought* (1979); G. Nash, *The Conservative Intellectual Movement in America* (1976). **"Neither personal freedom nor personal achievement can ever be separated from the community. These are the contexts not of mechanical restraint but of the incentives and values that men wish to express in enduring works and to defend against the wanton external aggression. This is not to deny the role of the individual, nor the reality of personal differences. It is assuredly not to accept the argument of crude social determinism—which asserts that creative works of individuals are but the reflection of group interests and group demands. It is merely to insist on the fundamental fact that the perspectives and incentives of the free creative mind arise out of communities of purpose. The artist may alter these, reshape them, give them an intensity and design that no one else has ever given them or ever will give them, but he is not thereby removed from the sources of his inspiration."** *The Quest for Community* (1953)

Nock, Albert Jay (1870–1945): American writer and champion of **libertarianism** and **individualism** whose distinction between society and state forms an important part of the modern attack on big government. (Nock effectively coined the word *statism*.) Like **Chodorov**, Nock was influenced by the writings of Henry George, especially George's idea of a single tax on land, and like Chodorov, Nock was an editor of *The Freeman* (1920–1924). Among his more famous ideas, taken from Isaiah, was the notion of the Remnant, which, to begin with, was more or less the opposite of the masses, the latter being that majority of people unable to understand "principle," let alone live by it. The Remnant is distinguished by its ability to see past mass culture to the "humane life," by which Nock meant a life lived in embrace of individualism. Nock had early been something of a radical, and changed when his view of human perfectibility changed (in part from reading **Cram**). The Remnant is that group— those few—actually capable of achieving true growth, if not actual perfectibility. During the New Deal he wrote a column ("The State of the Nation") for *American Mercury* that excoriated Roosevelt. Although born in Brooklyn, Nock grew up in Michigan on Lake Huron, which, in its isolation, he thought an ideal embodiment of "Mr. Jefferson's notion that the virtues which he regarded as distinctly American thrive best in the absence of government." **Read:** *Our Enemy the State* (1935); **About:** his own *Memoirs of a Superfluous Man* (1943); R. Crunden, *The Superfluous Men* (1977). **"Mr. Jefferson said that if a centralization of power were ever effected in Washington, the United States would have the most corrupt government on earth. Comparisons are difficult, but I believe it has one that is thoroughly corrupt, flagitious, tyrannical, oppressive. Yet if it were in my power to pull down its whole structure overnight and set up another of my own devising—to abolish the State out of hand, and replace it with an organization of the economic means—I would not do it . . ."** "On Doing the Right Thing" (1924) in *The State of the Union* (1991)

Novak, Michael (1933–   ): American philosopher and social scientist, who has been called a Catholic proponent of **neoconservatism** but who describes himself as *neoliberal*. Although trained for the priesthood, Novak chose a journalistic career instead. His early work was in support of the New Left, and his shift to the **Right** has been gradual and selective. This perhaps explains why underground translations of his work were influential in inspiring the Solidarity labor movement in Poland. **John Paul II**, whose encyclical *Centesimus Annus* (1991), which gave the strongest ever endorsement to **free-market** economics, is said to have been impressed by Novak's writings. His *The Spirit of Democratic Capitalism* (1982) has been called one of those few books "that actually changes the way things are." Basically, that book is a restatement of the "spiritual" content of **classical liberalism**. It argued—against the claims of liberation theology and other left-leaning interpretations of Christianity—that of all systems of political economy only "democratic capitalism" has changed the world for the better. Novak demonstrated that the link between the free market and **democracy** is both necessary and inevitable in a way that has proved highly appealing to leaders in those European nations emerging from **communism**. The "spirit" of his title (an elaboration of **Locke** and Max Weber) is simply that "Creation left to itself is incomplete, and humans are called to be co-creators with God, bringing forth the potentialities the Creator has hidden." God, he insists, made us free, and democratic **capitalism** is "an arena of liberty" in which *caritas*—caring—thrives. Novak is currently a fellow at the **American Enterprise Institute**. Read: *The Spirit of Democratic Capitalism* (1982); **About:** his own *Confessions of a Catholic* (1983): **"Some thinkers hold that the mistake of the West, especially since the Enlightenment, is to have generated a false ideal of the solitary individual. In fact, they say, the human being is always social; thus any genuine theory of the self must include an analysis of social institutions. Of course this is true. But this discovery of the social nature of human beings leads in two quite different directions. One direction is that of socialism, the inevitable (as it is said) collectivization of human life, one hopes on a democratic and cooperative basis. The other direction is that of democratic capitalism: a vision of cultural pluralism, economic pluralism, and political pluralism in which individuals are brought up to nourish a very wide range of social skills in tolerant, open, cooperative, and trusting behaviors. It is an analytical mistake to hold that** socialism respects the social nature of humans, while democratic capitalist societies are characterized by 'possessive individualism.' In actual history, exactly the reverse happens. One may test this proposition empirically. In which actual nations do voluntary associations and cooperative habits actually thrive, and in which do they wither? . . . Democratic capitalists argue that in order to produce cooperative citizens one must go by a different route: respect first their individuality, their liberty, and their own judgment about what is primary in their lives, and in actual practice you will produce a more socially cohesive, cooperative, and energetic society."

Nozick, Robert (1938–   ): American philosopher of **libertarianism** and **individualism**. Nozick was educated at Columbia and Princeton, and has been teaching at Harvard since 1969, where it is said he never teaches the same course two years running. He is the author of libertarianism's finest work of political theory, *Anarchy, State, and Utopia*. Published in 1974 (and winner of a National Book Award), Nozick's magnum opus details a compelling view (derived in part from **Locke**) of a government ("minimal state") limited to a few well-defined police powers and bereft of any power to redistribute income. Indeed, the book's most important section deals with Nozick's "entitlement theory," which holds that distributive justice is determined historically; i.e., if what is possessed has been acquired justly, no other redistributive claims may be made against the holdings. He agrees with **Hayek** (although only in part—Nozick's thinking is too original to find total agreement with anyone) that the pattern of just economic distribution must be random. "No overarching aim is needed, no distributional pattern is required." Or more simply: "liberty upsets patterns." Or, in Nozick's sly imitation of **Marxism**'s sloganeering: "*From each as they choose, to each as they are chosen.*" As has been widely noted, *Anarchy, State, and Utopia* is a direct refutation of the "justice as fairness" principle of **liberalism**, especially as elucidated by Nozick's Harvard colleague John Rawls (*A Theory of Justice*, 1971). Many of Nozick's arguments are made with hilarious freshness, as for example: his defense of unequal incomes in which earnings disparities are discussed in terms of what people will pay to watch Wilt Chamberlain play basketball as opposed to what they will pay to buy copies of *Dissent* magazine; or his analysis of the ownership of natural resources in which a man claims rights to an ocean by pouring into it a can of radioactive tomato juice. It may seem strange that he is a vegetarian and belongs to the ACLU, but it may also shed some light on his more recent "recantation" of libertarianism as lacking compassion. **Read**: *Anarchy, State, and Utopia* (1974); **About**: his own *The Examined Life* (1989). **"If the woman who later became my wife rejected another suitor (who she would otherwise have married) for me, partially because (I leave aside my lovable nature) of my keen intelligence and good looks, neither of which did I earn, would the rejected less intelligent and less handsome suitor have a legitimate complaint about unfairness? Would my thus impeding the other suitor's winning the hand of fair lady justify taking some resources from others to pay for cosmetic surgery for him and special intellectual training, or to pay to develop in him some sterling trait that I lack in order to equalize our chances of being chosen? (I take here for granted the impermissibility of worsening the situation of the person having better opportunities so as to equalize opportunity; in this sort of case by disfiguring him . . .).** *No such consequences follow.* **(Against whom would the rejected suitor have a legitimate complaint? Against what?) Nor are things different in the differential opportunities that arise from the accumulated effects of people's acting or transferring their entitlement as they choose."** *Anarchy, State, and Utopia* (1974)

Oakeshott, Michael (1901–1990): English political scientist and author of *Rationalism in Politics* (1962). A graduate of Cambridge, Oakeshott went on to teach at Oxford and the London School of Economics. His view of philosophy was, in a sense, modest: he believed that the philosopher's task is not to define whole systems but rather to clarify methodology. Oakeshott understood **rationalism** to be the dominant force of **modernism** as manifest both in **Marxism** and in deracinated **liberalism**. In this he was very Burkean, and echoes **Burke**'s attack on abstraction. Set against abstraction is the common sense of **tradition**, which Oakeshott understands to be that tangible reality we might improve if we choose to, but which we cannot even conceive of except in tradition. This is what he called the "politics of repair." Maurice Cranston has described Oakeshott as (among other things) a "traditionalist with few traditional beliefs, an 'idealist' who is more skeptical than many positivists, a lover of liberty who repudiates liberalism." He was not the descendant of Burke so much as of **Hume**, whose **empiricism** Oakeshott believed was the proper response to rationalism. He was not so much a champion of **conservative** policies as he was an opponent of liberal experiments. He favored **republicanism** ("parliamentary government" in his terminology) over "popular" **democracy**, because the former safeguards individual **liberty**. (See also **libertarianism**.) A fine summary of Oakeshott's view of government appeared in Jeffrey Hart's obituary of him in *National Review* (January 28, 1991). "Oakeshott rejected managerial government in favor of civil association. Government was not to be a teleocracy, imposing purposes and plans. Its function was to lay down neutral rules which citizens would observe while pursuing whatever ends they chose for themselves. . . . Oakeshott saw politics as a mode of protecting and adjusting customary forms of behavior, which rested upon experience. He loathed a politics which would impose new and unexperienced behavior." **Read:** *On Human Conduct* (1975); *Rationalism in Politics* (1962); **About:** P. Franco, *The Political Philosophy of Michael Oakeshott* (1990). **"To be conservative, then, is to prefer the familiar to the unknown, to prefer the tried to the untried, fact to mystery, the actual to the possible, the limited to the unbounded, the near to the distant, the sufficient to the superabundant, the convenient to the perfect, present laughter to utopian bliss."** "On Being Conservative" in *Rationalism in Politics* (1962)

objectivism: The libertarian-like philosophy propounded by the Russian novelist Ayn Rand (1905–1982) that makes human life the *summum bonum* of existence. The principles of objectivism are three: that reason is Man's only means of knowledge; that rational self-interest defines ethics; and that **capitalism** best orders society. (She qualified her own free-market philosophy by observing that she was "not primarily an advocate of capitalism, but of egoism.") A kind of rabid **Smith**, Rand envisaged a hyper-minimalist state with no taxation and no **tradition**. In morals, she advocated a sort of panting Aristotelianism in which freedom was made synonymous with orgasm. And in theology (so to speak) she believed that everything is real exactly as we see it, *unless* we see God. Objectivism was played out to a large extent in Rand's fiction, notably in *The Fountainhead* (1943) and the mega-hit *Atlas Shrugged* (1957). This latter work was the subject of one of the most famous book reviews ever written, "Big Sister is Watching You" by **Chambers** in *National Review* (December 28, 1957). The book ends, as Chambers points out, in a post-apocalyptic moment in which one of the novel's survivor-heroes blesses the "desolate earth" by tracing a dollar sign in the air. While acknowledging that "many of us dislike much that Miss Rand dislikes," Chambers renounced any association between **conservatism** and materialism, atheism, and immorality, all of which the author seemed to be promoting. "Randian Man," Chambers wrote, "like Marxian Man, is made the center of a godless world." And Rand thereafter called *National Review* "the worst and most dangerous magazine in America." Objectivism is in many ways the antithesis of conservatism: it champions **rationalism** and determinism, whereas conservatism embraces **empiricism** and free will. **Read**: L. Peikoff, *Objectivism* (1991); A. Rand, *The Virtue of Selfishness* (1965). "**The secret dread of modern intellectuals, liberals and conservatives alike, the unadmitted terror at the root of their anxiety, which all their current irrationalities are intended to slave off and to disguise, is the unstated knowledge that Soviet Russia is the full, actual, literal, consistent embodiment of the morality of altruism, that Stalin did *not* corrupt a noble ideal, that this is the only way altruism has to be or can ever be practiced. If service and self-sacrifice are a moral ideal, and if the 'selfishness' of human nature prevents men from leaping into sacrificial furnaces, there is no reason—no reason that a mystic moralist could name—why a dictator should not push them in at the point of bayonets—for their own good, or the good of humanity, or the good of posterity, or the good of the latest bureaucrat's latest five-year plan. There is no reason that they can name to oppose *any* atrocity. The value of a man's life? His right to exist? His right to pursue his own happiness? These are concepts that belong to individualism and capitalism—to the antithesis of the altruist morality.**" Ayn Rand, "Faith and Force: The Destroyers of the Modern World" (1960) in *Philosophy: Who Needs It* (1982)

Old Right: That group of conservatives and libertarians whose activism began with the New Deal and ended with the emergence of the **New Right** in the decade after World War II. Arguably, the Old Right has roots extending into the 19th century and earlier, but just as **conservatism** proper awaited the French Revolution to be born, so the Old Right became animated only in reaction to expanding state power and the threat of war in the 1930s. **Kristol** (1978) maintains that this group, which includes figures as diverse as **Chodorov**, John T. Flynn, **Mencken**, **Morley**, **Nock**, and **Taft**, "never did accept the liberal-bourgeois revolutions of the 18th and 19th centuries," and there may be some truth in this (although it would then be hard to count Nock or Chodorov as members of the Old Right), but the main difference between the Old and New Rights came in the clash between internationalism (or better, *interventionism*) and **isolationism.** Incidental to this conflict was the Old Right/Protestant-New Right/Catholic split on the degree to which **laissez-faire**, appropriate in economics, ought to spill over into the nation's cultural life. (See also **libertarianism** and **paleoconservatism**.) **Read:** P. Gottfried and T. Fleming, *The Conservative Movement* (1988); G. Nash, *The Conservative Intellectual Movement in America* (1976). "The Old Right may resent what neoconservatives have done with their cause, but for at least the foreseeable future will be in no position to do anything about it. The choices that are available to them are to wage an unpromising struggle or to do what some editors of *National Review* have already begun to do, to blur the distinction between paleo- and neoconservatives—or to pretend that none exists. A third more stoic alternative is also available to the Old Right. It is represented by George Panichas, the editor of *Modern Age*, a Christian Platonist, and a morally committed interpreter of modern literature. Troubled by the thoroughgoing politicization of the intellectual Right, Panichas has warned against the "contaminating" obsession with making it in Washington. He has stressed the distinction between Plato's attempt to spiritualize the political and the modern tendency to reduce spiritual questions to political ones. . . . Panichas laments the 'sad paradox that conservative leaders and thinkers often fail, in the present climate of their political victories, to recognize or implement their spiritual identity and responsibility. No authentic conservative metaphysic can be operable when the discipline of God and the discipline of the soul have been ceded to the *doxai*, the dialectical structures and superstructures of modern life.' This statement includes an admonition as well as a lament. Old conservatives may eventually come to heed both–out of despair as much as conviction." Paul Gottfried and Thomas Fleming, *The Conservative Movement* (1988)

Olin Foundation, John M.: Free-market philanthropy founded in 1953 by the successful manufacturer and conservationist for whom the foundation is named. Olin, who died in 1982, once said that his greatest ambition was "to see free enterprise re-established in this country . . ." The Olin Foundation has been a leading—probably *the* leading—funder of **conservative** causes and activities since former Treasury Secretary William E. Simon (1927–   ) took over as president in 1977. The Foundation gives money to organizations and institutions whose projects "reflect or are intended to strengthen the economic, political and cultural institutions upon which the American heritage of constitutional government and private enterprise is based." Olin has given sizable grants to universities for the support of professorships in a range of disciplines, has provided more considerable funding for national security educational programs at the military academies, and has earmarked specific funds for such distinguished scholars as (among others) **Kristol**, Robert Bork, **Novak**, Abigail Thernstrom, Christina Hoff Sommers, Walter E. Williams, **Berns**, William J. Bennett, Linda Chavez, Robert Conquest, and Charles J. Sykes. The Olin Foundation has supported magazines and television programs such as *The American Spectator, Commentary, Crisis,* and *The New Criterion,* "Firing Line" (with **Buckley**), "Think Tank" (with Ben Wattenberg) and "Peggy Noonan on Values." Finally, it has been a major sponsor of such organizations as the **Heartland Institute**, the **Heritage Foundation**, the **American Enterprise Institute**, and the Ethics and Public Policy Center. All in all, the 1993 annual report lists some 154 recipients of nearly $15 million. The activities of the Olin Foundation have made it indispensable to the **Right**, and have established Simon's reputation as one of **conservatism**'s greatest champions. And those activities have made the late Mr. Olin's greatest ambition come true. **Read:** William E. Simon, *A Time For Truth* (1978): **"During my tenure at Treasury, I watched with incredulity as businessmen ran to the government in every crisis, whining for handouts or protection from the very competition that has made this [capitalist] system so productive. I saw Texas ranchers, hit by drought, demanding government-guaranteed loans; giant milk cooperatives lobbying for higher price supports; major airlines fighting deregulation to preserve their monopoly status; huge companies like Lockheed seeking federal assistance to rescue them from sheer inefficiency; bankers like David Rockefeller demanding government bailouts to protect them from their ill-conceived investments; network executives like William Paley of CBS fighting to preserve regulatory restrictions and to block the emergence of competitive cable and pay TV. And always, such gentlemen proclaimed their devotion to free enterprise and their opposition to the arbitrary intervention into our economic life by the state."**

order: The arrangement of any reality in which the parts of that reality are in harmony. It can thus apply to the simple progression of numbers, 1-2-3-4, or to a complicated social system, the United States. (Obviously, the more *human* the reality, the less apparently harmonious the order.) **Hayek**, like **Mandeville** two centuries earlier, held that the structure of all aspects of human culture—politics, economics, *et alia*—is the result of the "spontaneous order" that emerges without "human design." This was the sense behind **Hume**'s claim that "the rules of morality are not the conclusions of our reason." Indeed, the order **conservatism** celebrates, no matter how it may be formalized, is not so much an act of human invention as it is a consequence of human cultural evolution. As **Kirk** pointed out (1974), we often—and properly—link the words "law and order," but they are not synonymous. "Laws arise out of a social order," not the other way around. Hayek and Kirk were not, however, in perfect agreement about the source of order, the former being agnostic and the latter Christian. Although true order is clearly not of human design, it may very well represent the design of the Creator. Not for nothing did Job

(10:22) imagine the "shadow of death" as a "land of loneliness . . . without any order . . ." Above all, the spontaneous order of <u>tradition</u> is to be distinguished from the imposed order of <u>rationalism</u>. **Read:** F. A. Hayek, *The Constitution of Liberty* (1960); Russell Kirk, *The Roots of American Order* (1991): **"Order is the first need of the soul. It is not possible to love what one ought to love, unless we recognize some principles of order by which to govern ourselves. . . . Order is the first need of the commonwealth. It is not possible for us to live in peace with one another, unless we recognize some principle of order by which to do justice. . . . The good society is marked by a high degree of order, justice, and freedom. Among these, order has primacy: for justice cannot be enforced until a tolerable civil social order is attained, nor can freedom be anything better than violence until order gives us laws."**

original sin: See <u>sin</u>

paleoconservatism: That "branch" of contemporary <u>conservatism</u> which rejects the internationalism of the <u>New Right</u> and of <u>neoconservatism</u> in favor of the <u>isolationism</u> of the <u>Old Right</u>; indeed, *paleoconservative* is simply a renaming of the earlier "discredited" term. This is not to say that paleocons may simply be described as isolationist. They are also more fundamentally opposed to <u>rationalism</u> than are neocons. Among other things, this means that paleocons do not accept the inevitability of the <u>welfare</u> state. Indeed, paleoconservatives insist that their main point of departure with neoconservatives is over the role of what <u>Nisbet</u> has called the "national community." Paleoconservatism represents the unification of the Old-Right conservatism of the Midwest with pugnacious and nostalgic <u>Southern Conservatism</u>, a marriage played out in the pages of *Chronicles* magazine (see <u>Rockford Institute</u>) and *Intercollegiate Review* (see <u>ISI</u>). Paleocons argue that the principles of <u>federalism</u> and localism demand that we be Ohioans, Texans, or Californians at least as surely as we are Americans. For what have the national government and the national identity and the national interests brought us except, serially: big war, big government, and big taxes? **Read:** P. Gottfried and T. Fleming, *The Conservative Movement in America* (1988). **" 'To make us love our country [Burke wrote], our country ought to**

be lovely.' Is it possible to love the gritty squalor of the Black Belt of Chicago, or Main Street in Los Angeles? Conceivably; but it is wiser not to put that strain upon loyalty. The better natures among us, surely, will be hard put . . . to love America if it becomes a nation wholly mannerless, an incivil society, in which generosity and charity are scorned as weakness, in which all great literature, and the whole stock of a moral imagination, is rejected out of a lust for the gratification of carnal appetites and a taste for second-hand narrations of violence and concupiscence. The conservative of reflection will not be afraid to defend the manners and the tastes of a gentle and generous nature . . . in this industrial age." Russell Kirk, *Prospects for Conservatives* (1989)

Podhoretz, Norman (1930–): American journalist (long-time editor of *Commentary*), who was among the first whose neoconservatism was more than simply a reaction against liberal sympathy with Soviet Marxism. His education included studies (at Columbia and at Cambridge) with such literary figures as Lionel Trilling, Mark Van Doren, and F. R. Leavis. After a short stint in the United States Army, Podhoretz joined the staff of *Commentary* (founded in 1940 by Elliot E. Cohen), became its editor several years later, and began steadily moving the magazine to the Right, or, as he might prefer, away from the Left. Together with his wife, Midge Decter, Podhoretz attacked the leftist drift in American domestic policies, but his main strength was in the analysis of foreign policy. After thirty-five years at the helm of *Commentary*, Podhoretz became editor-at-large in 1995. (He was succeeded by Neal Kozodoy.) "I learned many things from my years on the Left," he wrote in his valedictory, "not the least important of which was where and how and why it always seemed to go wrong . . ." Decter (1927–) was the executive director of the Committee for the Free World (which was founded in 1982 and disbanded with the fall of communism) and editor of its provocative publication *Contentions*. Decter's views on issues relating to sexuality and parenting put her at odds with feminism. She serves as a trustee of the Heritage Foundation, and as a member of the editorial board of *First Things* (see "Neuhaus"). **Read:** [Podhoretz] *The Present Danger* (1980); [Decter] *Liberal Parents, Radical Children* (1975); **About:** M. Winchell,

Neoconservative Criticism (1991); P. Steinfels, *The Neoconservatives* (1979). [Podhoretz]: "In part, the 'neoconservatives' became influential simply because they were able to best their opponents in argument. But they were certainly helped along by a series of events that eroded the foundations of the anti-American case. Thus the idea that the American role in Vietnam had been immoral or criminal became harder and harder to maintain in the face of the horrors the Communists began visiting upon the peoples of Indochina . . . Similarly, the idea that the United States was the cause of the nuclear arms race . . . became harder and harder to argue as the Soviet Union was permitted by the United States to achieve parity and then began pushing forward toward superiority. . . . As 'No More Vietnams' meant retrenchment and accommodation, 'No More Irans' will mean making sure that we never again have to submit helplessly to being 'pushed around'; and as the main 'Lesson of Vietnam' was taken to be that we must never again intervene into the Third World, the great 'Lesson of Afghanistan' is likely to be that unless we intervene under certain circumstances, we will find ourselves at the mercy of our enemies." *The Present Danger* (1980). [Decter]: "For women to claim that they are victims when they are so clearly not is merely an expression of their terror in the face of the harshness and burdens of a new and as yet not fully claimed freedom. Such a terror lies behind Women's Liberation's discussion of work; it is a response not to the experience of exclusion but to the discovery that the pursuit of career is but another form—in some ways more gratifying, in many ways far more bruising—of adult anguish. The equality demanded by the self-proclaimed victim is equality of attribution only: not to be, but to be *deemed*, equal—no matter what." *The New Chastity and Other Arguments Against Women's Liberation* (1972)

[*Commentary*, 165 East 56th Street, New York, NY 10022; (800) 829–6270. Subscriptions: $39.00 per year for 12 issues; $72.00 for 2 years; $105.00 for 3 years.]

political correctness: See **academic freedom**

Popper, Karl R. (1902–1994): Austrian-born English philosopher and champion of the "open society." His career was in some sense a

life-long refutation of the **positivism** which was a part of his education in Vienna. He was especially critical of **Marxism** and Freudian-
ism, which he considered pseudo-sciences. (His passion for precision
led him, after study at the University of Vienna, not directly into
academe, but into an apprenticeship with a cabinetmaker.) These
anti-rationalist insights were developed during meetings of the Vienna Circle, a group of distinguished positivist intellectuals who, in
Popper's estimation, "believed that everything is on the surface . . ."
At the heart of the analysis that grew from his study of scientific discovery is the *doctrine of falsifiability*. Falsifiability is the primary functional tool of **empiricism**. The Vienna Circle positivists measured the
development of doctrine by virtue of their ability to cite evidence in
support of their hypotheses. Popper turned this process on its head.
Truth in science—including social science—is determined by "error
elimination," or falsifiability. This means that mistakes are more important in establishing proof than are successes, and that unintended
consequences (especially in the "social" sciences) are not only probable but often preferable. (As **Hume** said of morality: "the rules . . . are
not the conclusions of our reason.") Along with **Hayek**, Popper also
effectively demolished the Marxian notion of historicism, the doctrine that we may learn the "principles" of cultural evolution and employ them in planning society. (Indeed, Popper was not shy about
asserting his success. "*I have shown*," he wrote [1957], "*that, for
strictly logical reasons, it is impossible for us to predict the future course of
history*.") In *The Open Society and Its Enemies* (1962/1971), Popper
attacked Plato, Hegel, and Marx as the most influential proponents
of collectivism and historicism, and showed how their **absolutism**
leads inevitably to tyranny. The **Hoover Institution**, of which he was
a senior fellow, has archived Popper's papers. When he was asked to
comment on the fall of **communism**, Popper refused. "I will not . . ."
he said, "except to say, 'I told you so.'" **Read:** *The Open Society and Its
Enemies* (1962/1971); *The Poverty of Historicism* (1957); **About:** his
own *Unended Quest* (1976). "**Individualism was part of the old intu-
itive idea of justice. That justice is not, as Plato would have it, the
health and harmony of the state, but rather a certain way of treating
individuals, is emphasized by Aristotle . . . when he says 'justice is
something that pertains to persons.' This individualistic element**

had been emphasized by the generation of Pericles. Pericles himself made it clear that the laws must guarantee equal justice 'to all alike in their private disputes'; but he went further. 'We do not feel called upon,' he said, 'to nag at our neighbour if he chooses to go his own way.' (Compare with Plato's remark that the state does not produce men 'for the purpose of letting them loose, each to go his own way . . .'.) Pericles insists that this individualism must be linked with altruism: 'We are taught . . . never to forget that we must protect the injured'; and his speech culminates in a description of the young Athenian who grows up 'to a happy versatility, and self-reliance. '. . . This individualism, united with altruism, has been the basis of our western civilization." "Individualism versus Collectivism" (1945) in D. Miller, ed., *Popper Selections* (1985)

positivism: The influential philosophical view (a version of **rationalism**) that only science provides real knowledge of the world, and that accordingly rejects all religious and metaphysical explanations of human experience. Beginning with Auguste Comte (1798–1857), positivism asserted that "positive" knowledge was real, utilitarian, unified, social, and—most significantly—*relative.* "All is relative—" Comte asserted without irony, "that is the only absolute." (See **relativism**.) As Man evolves, he—not God—determines the values under which he lives. Thus Man is free to act in "positive" ways to transform the world. Indeed, Comte believed in the divinity of humanity (and literally saw himself as its high priest), and believed that society would evolve through stages to a final "sociological" (his coinage) apotheosis not unlike the Platonic dream of the despotism of philosophers. He exerted a considerable influence on the development of **Marxism**. *Logical positivism* is the further application to positivism of the "verifiability principle": the meaning of a proposition is the same as the method of verifying it. (See **Popper**'s refutation.) This reductionist circularity (sometimes called "methodolatry" by its critics) has serious implications for political and moral philosophy since it replaces the "ought" with an "is," and is especially visible in *legal positivism*, which denies the existence of **natural law**. Read: L. Strauss, *Natural Right and History* (1950). "Why then did the South secede? The heart of the sectional conflict of the 1850s concerned the status of slavery in the territories. The South claimed, as a constitutional right, the right of citizens of the slave states to have the same access to the territories, with their human property, as citizens of the free states had with their non-human property. With it they claimed, also as a constitutional right, a federal guarantee of the security of that property. . . . These people believed that [their view] had received final confirmation in 1857 in the opinion of Chief Justice Taney in the case of *Dred Scott*. . . . Taney himself had recognized that Negroes did in fact belong to the 'human family,' not to be treated as property. But, he said, the Framers and ratifiers of the Constitution did not, and he was bound by their opinions. But why was he bound by their opinions if they were so wrong about what was a human being? Taney . . . was a legal positivist, who believed the judge was bound by the positive law, *whatever it was.*" Harry V. Jaffa, "Graglia's Quarrel with God" in *National Review*, August 14, 1995

prejudice: In the sense used by **Burke** (usually as "prejudice and prescription"), the judgments—especially those derived from the **authority** of **tradition**—by which one views the world. Although the word has come to be associated with negative and unreasoned opinion (as in "racial prejudice"), its more fundamental meaning is of prejudgment, as **Kirk** wrote (1953): "the answer with which intuition and ancestral consensus of opinion supply a man when he lacks either time or knowledge to arrive at a decision predicated upon pure reason." A judgment that certain things are true forms a necessary prejudice against that which is untrue. Prejudice is not antagonistic to reason; it does oppose gnosticism. (See also **Voegelin**.) **Read:** R. Nisbet, *Conservatism* (1986). "**Many of our men of speculation, instead of exploding general principles, employ their sagacity to discover the latent wisdom which prevails in them. If they find what they seek, and they seldom fail, they think it more wise to continue the prejudice, with reason involved, than to cast away the coat of prejudice, and to leave nothing but naked reason; because prejudice, with its reason, has a motive to give action to that reason, and an affection which will give it permanence.**" Edmund Burke, *Reflections on the Revolution in France* (1790)

prescription: The evolved directions of **tradition**. As noted above, **Burke** coupled the word with **prejudice**. Prescription is, in fact, *institutional prejudice*; the prejudice—the received wisdom—of socializing, governing, and enculturating tradition. In his *Thoughts on the Cause of the Present Discontents* (1770), Burke defined prescription as a "vestment which accommodates itself to the body," suggesting its evolutionary character, and—anticipating the great theme of **Hayek**'s work (which had antecedents also in **Mandeville**, Adam Ferguson [1723–1816], and **Smith**)—he notes that while individuals are foolish, the "species is wise, and, when time is given to it, as a species it almost always acts right." It is easy enough to assume that here Burke is following Pope's infamous epigram, "Whatever is, is right" (and there was a bit of this in his **antidisestablishmentarianism**), but more to the point is his conviction that society is complex and organic, and that people know the way of things almost as though by instinct. **Read:** R. Kirk, *The Conservative Mind* (1953). **"A sound political constitution must be the growth of generations; it must be worked into the whole fabric of society; it must give play for the harmonious action of all the private relations by which men are bound together; and if it requires the utmost watchfulness to prevent parts from becoming obsolete, it is the height of rashness to hack and hew such a system in obedience to some preconceived theory. Prescription, then, is but a legal phrase for that continuity of past and present, and that solidarity between all parts of the political order, the perception of which is the essential condition of sound political reasoning."** Leslie Stephen, *History of English Thought in the 18th Century* (1876)

private property: One of the few, certain **natural rights**. A person has a right to possess that which he justly acquires. "If historical experience could teach us anything," **Mises** wrote (1949): "it would be that private property is inextricably linked to civilization." True, but the question at the heart of *private* possession remains: What *right* (primary and nearly antediluvian) does any individual have to "own" a part of nature, of God's creation? The Bible does not mention property, let alone private property, although the idea of *owning* things and of things which are one's *own* is pervasive, especially in

Genesis. But as Mises points out, "Private property is a human device. It is not sacred." It is ancient, and was based upon survival. It is, therefore, justified and enfranchised by **tradition**, even though, theoretically, it "can be traced back to a point at which it originated out of acts which were certainly not legal." This history is fascinating speculation but irrelevant, except to identify a distinction between Man and nature; between the "discoverer" (see **Austrian School**) and the resources discovered. Private property is, according to **Locke**, a natural right with life and **liberty**, and the pessimistic **Weaver** famously termed it "the last metaphysical right." **Read:** F. A. Hayek, *The Road to Serfdom* (1944): "**What our generation has forgotten is that the system of private property is the most important guaranty of freedom, not only for those who own property, but scarcely less for those who do not. It is only because the control of the means of production is divided among many people acting independently that nobody has complete power over us, that we as individuals can decide what to do with ourselves. . . . Who can seriously doubt that a member of a . . . minority will be freer with no property so long as fellow-members of his community have property and are therefore able to employ him, than he would be if private property were abolished and he became owner of a nominal share in the communal property? Or that the power which a multiple millionaire, who may be my neighbor and perhaps my employer, has over me is very much less than that which the smallest *fonctionnaire* possesses who wields the coercive power of the state and on whose discretion it depends whether and how I am allowed to live or work?**"

public choice theory: The market-oriented view of economics and (or *especially*) politics (or the study of politics using the methodology of economics) that elevates self-interest over public interest. (Note: This is an acceptance of reality and *not* the advocacy of indifference in the manner of **objectivism**.) Because of its attention to behavior in the public, political "marketplace," public choice is also called *constitutional economics*. Its leading proponents are James Buchanan, who received the Nobel Prize in 1986, Gordon Tullock, and William Niskanen. Public choice theory goes a long way towards explaining, among other things, why voter apathy is common: since my vote can't possibly affect the outcome, I have little incentive to be informed and active. On the other hand, apathetic business people are less common, since competition provides constant compensations for their vigilance. Thus public choice theorists are skeptical about governments' motives in taxation—it's our money not theirs—and approving of government moves towards privatization. As in the **Austrian School**, the fundamental units of analysis in public choice theory are the decisions of individuals. Buchanan is fond of comparing politics to game playing, in which there are a set of rules (**constitution**) and strategies (economic and political behavior). Buchanan and Tullock, in their magisterial *The Calculus of Consent* (1962), analyzed the various kinds of decision making that individuals undertake in facing the rules of the game. Buchanan (1992) has said that the authors intended the book to be "an implicit defense of the Madisonian structure" of the American constitutional system: if we know the rules are fair, we will accept "unfair" outcomes. One sure insight of public choice (no news to most conservatives) is that legislators ostensibly acting in the "public interest" and spending other people's money without the people's consent in fact lack most of the incentives required for sound management. Thus the most important policy suggestion made by public choice is competition. Messrs. Buchanan and Niskanen are on the editorial board of *The Cato Journal*. **Read:** J. Buchanan, *Constitutional Economics* (1991); J. Buchanan and G. Tullock, *The Calculus of Consent* (1962); G. Tullock, *The Logic of the Law* (1971). **"To predict behavior, either in governmental bureaucracy or in privately organized non-proprietary institutions, it is necessary to examine carefully the constraints and opportunities faced by individual decision-makers. . . . Once we begin to look at bureaucracy in this way, we can, of course, predict that individual bureaucrats will seek to expand the size of their bureaus since, almost universally in modern Western societies, the salaries and perquisites of office are related directly to the sizes of the budgets administered and controlled. The built-in motive force for expansion, the dynamics of modern governmental bureaucracy in the small and large, was apparent to all who cared to think. This theory of bureaucratic growth was formalized by William Niskanen, who developed a model of separate budget-**

maximizing departments and sub-departments. In the limiting case, Niskanen's model suggested that bureaucracies could succeed in expanding budgets to twice the size necessary to meet taxpayers' genuine demands for public goods and services. In this limit, taxpayers end up by being no better off than they would be without any public goods; all of their net benefits are 'squeezed out' by the bureaucrats. The implication is that each and every public good or service, whether it be health services, education, transportation, or defense tends to be expanded well beyond any tolerable level of efficiency, as defined by the demands of the citizenry." James Buchanan, *Constitutional Economics* (1991)

[*The Cato Journal*, 1000 Massachusetts Ave., N.W., Washington, D.C. 20001-5403. James A. Dorn, editor. Subscriptions: (3 issues/year) $24/year; $48/2 years; $72/3 years.]

The Public Interest: See **Glazer, Nathan**

Randolph, John (1773–1833): American statesman (he took over the congressional seat of Patrick Henry, and then went on to the Senate), often called "Randolph of Roanoke," who was an ardent champion of **states' rights**, an admirer of **Burke**, and, although early a supporter, finally an implacable foe of the "liberal" **Jefferson**. (Randolph led the anti-Jeffersonian Republicans called Tertium Quids.) Indeed, he is often referred to as a *seething sectionalist*. "To ask any State to surrender part of her sovereignty," he said, "is like asking a lady to surrender part of her chastity." Randolph held above all other principles that the powers of the "federal" government ought to be severely limited, and that **democracy**, at least as understood as absolute majoritarianism, is anathema to **liberty**. Thus he famously condemned "King Numbers," and is said to have been fond of proclaiming: "I am an aristocrat; I love liberty, I hate equality." He was not, however, in favor of nullification, which he called "nonsense." This and his **isolationism** put him in conflict with his younger senate colleague **Calhoun**, for whom he coined the term "war hawk," and for whom he later became a mentor. Randolph disliked slavery, but kept possession of those slaves he had inherited. (He never bought or sold slaves.) Fifty years before the Civil War, he predicted it, and—despite his feelings about the "peculiar institution"—encouraged the South to resist the North's attempts to disrupt Southern life. It has been said of Randolph that he was "an ultra Anglomaniac," which affliction was just one of his many foibles. He claimed to be descended from Pocahontas. He fought a duel with Henry Clay. He drank to excess and was addicted to opium. **Kirk** wrote a sympathetic short study of Randolph (1951), and Henry **Adams** a not-so-sympathetic full-fledged biography (1882). Kirk wrote of Randolph (1953), whom he called "the most singular great man in American history," that the Virginian was an "implacable St. Michael who . . . denounced [John] Adams and Jefferson and Madison and Monroe and Clay and Webster and Calhoun with impartial detestation." **Read:** (and **About:**) R. Kirk, *John Randolph of Roanoke* (1951). **"Among the strange notions which have been broached since I have been in the political theatre, there is one which has lately seized the minds of men, that all things must be done for them by the Government, and that they are to do nothing for themselves: the Government is not only to attend to the great concerns which are its province, but it must step in and ease individuals of their natural and moral obligations. A more pernicious notion cannot prevail. Look at that ragged fellow staggering from the whiskey shop, and see that slattern who has gone there to reclaim him; where are their children? Running about, ragged, idle, ignorant, fit candidates for the penitentiary. Why is all this so? Ask the man and he will tell you. 'Oh, the Government has undertaken to educate our children for us.'"** *Proceedings and Debates of the Virginia State Convention* (1830)

Ransom, John Crowe (1888–1974): American poet, literary critic, and a member of the Fugitive Poets circle (a.k.a. *Agrarians*) that created *I'll Take My Stand* (1930). (See **Southern conservatism**.) Ransom was a leader of the New Criticism, which studied texts for their own sake—not as speculative biographies or psycho-social commentaries. (The view was best expounded by his students Cleanth Brooks and Robert Penn Warren in *Understanding Poetry*, 1938.) Ransom's poetry, elegant and reserved and often compared to that of Andrew Marvell, is invariably concerned with **order** and disorder; is an attempt to "realize" the world, not "idealize" it. His *God without Thunder* (also 1930), was a frankly **reactionary** call for the South to return to fundamentalist religion and agrarian economics as the only way of enduring against **modernism** in politics and scientism in culture. (He called it an "unorthodox defense of orthodoxy.") It was the stimulus for *I'll Take My Stand.* (Ransom wrote that book's "Statement of Principles," which he later considered something of an exercise in innocent idealism.) From 1937 until 1958, he taught at Kenyon College, where he founded the *Kenyon Review.* Ransom was not hostile to the literary **modernism** of **Eliot**, and was even considered something of a modernist himself by some of the more **conservative** Fugitives such as **Davidson** and **Tate**. **Read:** *Beating the Bushes* (1972); *The New Criticism* (1941); *The World's Body* (1938); **About:** L. Cowan, *The Fugitive Group* (1956); T. D. Young, *John Crowe Ransom* (1971). **"The concept of Progress is the concept of man's increasing command, and eventually perfect command, over the forces of nature; a concept which enhances too readily our conceit, and brutalizes our life. I believe there is possible no deep sense of beauty, no heroism of conduct, and no sublimity of religion, which is not informed by the humble sense of man's precarious position in the universe."** "Reconstructed but Unregenerate," from Ransom, ed., *I'll Take My Stand* (1930)

rationalism: That philosophical position which asserts that our knowledge of the world must be dominated by reason and which is opposed to **empiricism**, the claim that knowledge is based principally upon experience. At least since the **Enlightenment**, rationalism has often been set directly against religion; has been the handmaid of **positivism**—or vice versa. Its basic premise is that human intellect, independent of **tradition** and **prescription**, can, first, understand the world's "problems," and, second, discover the solutions to those problems. It is not reason, per se, that is denigrated in the critique of rationalism, but what **Burke**, its first and greatest critic, called "speculationism." Burke's and **conservatism**'s case against rationalism was nicely summed up in the observation of Blaise Pascal (1623–1662) that the last function of reason is "to recognize that there are an infinity of things which surpass it." Custom, tradition, and **natural law** do not depend for their validity upon our conscious acquiescence. **Read:** M. Oakeshott, *Rationalism in Politics* (1962); L. Strauss, *Natural Right and*

History (1950). "[The liberal] is not devoid of humility; he can imagine a problem which would remain impervious to the onslaught of his own reason. But what he cannot imagine is politics which do not consist in solving problems, or a political problem of which there is no 'rational' solution." Michael Oakeshott, *Rationalism in Politics* (1962)

reactionary: A term sometimes confused with **conservative**, but which is actually anti-conservative. A typical contemporary dictionary defines the word (in its secondary meaning—the primary being simply "action in reverse") as "one who moves in the direction of political conservatism or extreme Rightism." The implication of course is of a *return* to existential conditions more congenial to . . . well, to whatever the reactionary considers orderly and just. When this impulse is not patently utopian, it is demonstrably tenuous. More than many on the Left, conservatives may indeed be more conscious and respectful of the past as they assess the present or contemplate the future, but such awareness necessarily negates the nostalgia that is at the heart of reaction. "The conservative conserves discriminately," **Viereck** wrote (1949), "the reactionary indiscriminately." Conservative skepticism denies that there is, ever was, or ever will be a promised land of Man's making. On the other hand, American **conservatism**'s program legitimately seeks a "return" to a proper understanding and respect of the **Constitution**, given that the constitutional **tradition** defines normative America. Thus the "ordinary meaning" of *reactionary* proposed by Bradford (1990) is one who regards all **change** as dangerous, and the latest change as anathema. **Read:** M. E. Bradford, *The Reactionary Imperative* (1990): **"In order to complain of an outrage it is more productive to invoke a bygone felicity than it is to insist on counsels of perfection, even though such returns never get all the way back to 'the way things were,' and something better than that is the eventual objective of the exhortation. 'Reaction' is a necessary term in the intellectual context we inhabit late in the twentieth century because merely to conserve is sometimes to perpetuate what is outrageous."**

V

The American Centuries

by
Charles R. Kesler

A merican conservatism is in some respects as old as the United
States. The American Revolution was launched by an alliance
between tax rebels protesting the tyrannical impositions of a far-away
central government and religious believers who objected to the domination of the once great but now, they thought, morally decadent
British monarchy. A similar kind of alliance defines contemporary
American conservatism, although the 18th century was perhaps
clearer than the 20th on the moral and political principles that ought
to unite the conservative cause.

For the American revolutionaries, economic, political, and moral
issues were all related to the fundamental principles of the social contract affirmed in the Declaration of Independence: that "all men are
created equal," not in their talents or virtues but in their "unalienable," i.e., God-given or natural rights to "life, liberty, and the pursuit of happiness," which rights they attempted to secure through the
aid of government, preferably republican. As compared to most
strands of European conservatism, American conservatism is thus
friendlier to human equality, to natural rights, and to republican
government. And American conservatism takes its bearings from a

dramatic and quite public founding moment, whereas British and some Continental conservatism, deriving from the political thought of Edmund Burke, prefers to defend its constitutionalism as a kind of organic growth stemming from time out of mind.

In the democratic republic established by the Founders, American politics—and by extension American conservatism—has had more democratic and more republican sides, the one emphasizing popular sovereignty and the other the constitutional and habitual restraints on popular will. In the late 1780s, this tension was embodied in the debates between the so-called Anti-Federalists, the Constitution's opponents, and its supporters, whose reasoning was distilled and refined in the single classic of political science to emerge from the Founding period, *The Federalist Papers* (1788); and in the 1790s in the clashes between the Democratic Republican party, led by Thomas Jefferson and James Madison, and the Federalist party (later rechristened the Whigs), led by John Adams and Alexander Hamilton. In these debates, conservatives tended to take the side of the Federalists and Whigs, opposing the irreligious and leveling radicalism of the French Revolution, which enjoyed a vogue among many Democrats, and arguing for loose construction of the powers granted to the American national government in the interests of a firm Union and authoritative constitutional order.

By the early 19th century, these partisan issues had become inextricably linked with the question of slavery, the institution rightly called "peculiar" in a nation predicated on human liberty. The problem of slavery was in turn linked to the nature of the American Union. Southerners like John C. Calhoun and George Fitzhugh defended the justice of slavery as a positive good for whites and blacks alike, and held that secession in defense of slavery was constitutional on the grounds of states' rights or states' sovereignty. The opponents of slavery, assembled in the new Republican party formed out of the remnants of the Whig, Free Soil, and other parties, insisted on slavery's injustice and argued for confining it to the states in which it already existed—forbidding its spread to the Western territories. For the Republicans led by Abraham Lincoln, states' rights were not an ultimate principle but were themselves based on individual rights, and thus could not justify secession in defense of slavery.

These issues have proved controversial even for late 20th-century conservatives. Willmoore Kendall and M. E. Bradford, among others, have attempted to restate and vindicate parts of the Southern argument, and Harry V. Jaffa has mounted a spirited defense of Lincoln's statesmanship.

The Union's victory in the Civil War brought about the end of slavery in the United States and a reaffirmation of the Founders' natural-rights philosophy through the adoption of the 13th, 14th, and 15th amendments to the Constitution. But this reinvigorated constitutionalism proved short-lived. By the 1880s the Founders' notions of natural law, limited government, and constitutional restraints on popular will were under consistent and pointed attack by the vanguard of the Progressive movement. The Progressives argued instead for historically evolving notions of right and wrong, for positive government free to adapt and expand in order to manage society's endless modernization, and for the unshackling of the general will from what they regarded as the constraints of both corporate capitalism and an outmoded, 18th-century Constitution. In truth, the Progressive movement was the proximate intellectual and political origin of modern, 20th-century liberalism, even as the New Deal, the New Frontier, and the Great Society were but later installments of the reforming impulses of Woodrow Wilson's New Freedom.

Liberalism's long march through America's institutions was remarkably successful, transforming American politics and culture in ways that have proven difficult to undo; but resistance to its Napoleonic ambitions grew as the century progressed. In the Progressive era itself, shrewd critics such as Elihu Root opposed the radicals' efforts to dismantle representative democracy in favor of ever more direct democracy to be administered via initiative, referendum, recall, direct primary election of senators, and so forth. In the 1920s, Calvin Coolidge spoke eloquently on behalf of the truths and traditions of American constitutionalism, criticizing the facile relativism of the so-called reformers. Much conservative resistance was swept aside by the cataclysms of economic depression and war in the following decade, but even during those grim days, fugitive voices of dissent could be heard. Twelve Southern conservatives cast a cold eye upon the statism and scientism of the progressive world view in their famous manifesto of the Agrarian movement, *I'll Take My Stand* (1930). And H. L. Mencken, John T. Flynn, and other journalists denounced Franklin Roosevelt's interventionist foreign policy as well as his interventionist New Deal.

American conservatism did not coalesce into a self-conscious political movement, however, until after the New Deal and the Second World War. An amazing intellectual efflorescence led the way. Seven profound books that would largely define conservative political and social theory appeared within 15 years: Friedrich Hayek's *The Road to Serfdom* (1944), Richard Weaver's *Ideas Have Consequences* (1948), Leo Strauss's *Natural Right and History* (1950). Eric Voegelin's *The New Science of Politics* (1952), Russell Kirk's *The Conservative Mind* (1953), Robert Nisbet's *The Quest for Community* (1953), and Harry Jaffa's *Crisis of the House Divided* (1959). In 1955, these ideas found a public platform with the launching of *National Review* magazine (edited by William F. Buckley, Jr.), the first truly national conservative journal of opinion, which helped to form the principles, tastes, and agenda of the nascent conservative movement. A crucial part of this agenda was the purging of isolationism from the Right's foreign policy and the substitution of a vigorous anti-Communism, which would be a cardinal theme of conservative political figures from Barry Goldwater to Ronald Reagan.

Throughout its history the American conservative movement has been torn between its traditionalist and libertarian wings, and between populist and constitutionalist impulses. These are characteristic tensions in the form of government, really the way of life, established by the American Founders, healthy tensions so long as they do not obscure the genius of the Founding itself—the perpetuation of which remains American conservatism's highest reason for being.

Charles R. Kesler is a professor of government at Claremont McKenna College, and the co-editor with William F. Buckley, Jr. of *Keeping the Tablets: Modern American Conservative Thought* (1988)

Reagan, Ronald Wilson (1911–): Fortieth president of the United States, and the American politician who, more than any other, will be remembered for changing the terms of public debate from arguments based upon liberalism to principles derived from conservatism. Although his youthful experience of the Great Depression left him leaning towards liberalism and admiring Franklin D. Roosevelt, he moved gradually to the Right, and would call himself conservative by the 1950s, although he remained a registered Democrat until 1962. Reagan's public career began as a radio broadcaster, matured as a Hollywood actor, and took on its national political character between 1952 and 1962 when he toured the United States on behalf of General Electric giving speeches on conservative themes. Out of the Goldwater fiasco of 1964, Reagan emerged as America's pre-eminent conservative (with the possible exception of his friend Buckley), and was carried along to the governorship of California. His two terms as governor were notable for their fiscal restraint; although he initially raised taxes, he also cut spending, and when budget surpluses resulted, he was later able to offer rebates and reductions on a range of state taxes. Reagan made a tentative presidential bid in 1968, a more substantial one in 1976, and then was elected in 1980 in a stunning landslide defeat of incumbent Jimmy Carter. In his 1984 re-election, Reagan became the first (and still the only) president to receive more than fifty million votes, won the largest-ever number of electoral votes, and effectively completed America's electoral about-face, winning a popular vote margin against the liberal Walter Mondale that was as large as the one Lyndon Johnson had won over Goldwater two decades before. By 1981, Reagan had succeeded in achieving the largest tax cut in American history, and—perhaps more important—had begun to achieve the budget cuts necessary to support it. Supply-side theory, especially with regard to tax cuts, played an important role in shaping the policies of the first Reagan administration, and became known as Reaganomics. Internationally, his friendship with Thatcher and his implacable opposition to the Soviet "evil empire" were decisive factors in hastening the collapse of communism. Although his legacy is both uncertain and uneven (but then, so are those of Jefferson and John Adams), Reagan will be remembered as the man who inspired

America's recognition and embrace of the conservative aspects of its ethos, and who helped mobilize Americans at all levels of society in the cause of **limited government**. As Martin Anderson put it (1988): "What Reagan and his comrades have done is to shape America's policy agenda well into the twenty-first century." And he had a presence and a charm as president that was not just a veteran actor's technique. Everybody remembers his "Honey, I forgot to duck" quip to wife Nancy after a would-be assassin put a bullet within an inch of his heart in March of 1981, but there were a steady stream of such self-effacing gibes, as in his comments about the pressures surrounding the Iran-Contra affair: "With the Iran thing occupying everyone's attention, I was thinking: Do you remember the flap when I said, 'We begin bombing in five minutes'? Remember when I fell asleep during my audience with the Pope? Remember Bitburg? . . . Boy, those were the good old days." **Read**: *Ronald Reagan: An American Life* (1990); **About**: M. Anderson, *Revolution: The Reagan Legacy* (1988); G. Smith, *Reagan and Thatcher* (1991). ". . . [P]erhaps the greatest triumph of American conservatism has been to stop allowing the left to put the average American on the moral defensive. By average American I mean the good, decent, rambunctious, and creative people who raise the families, go to church, and help out when the local library holds a fund-raiser; people who have a stake in the community because they are the community. . . . These people had held true to certain beliefs and principles that for twenty years the intelligentsia were telling us were hopelessly out of date, utterly trite, and reactionary. You want prayer in schools? How primitive, they said. You oppose abortion? How oppressive, how antimodern. The normal was portrayed as eccentric, and only the abnormal was worthy of emulation. The irreverent was celebrated, but only irreverence about certain things: irreverence toward, say, organized religion, yes; irreverence toward establishment liberalism, not too much of that. They celebrated their courage in taking on safe targets and patted each other on the back for slinging stones at a confused Goliath, who was too demoralized and really too good to fight back. . . . But now one simply senses it. The American people are no longer on the defensive. I believe the conservative movement deserves some credit for this." "Remarks at the

Conservative Political Action Conference," March 1, 1985, in *Speaking My Mind* (1989)

relativism: The belief, ever more prevalent among this century's intellectuals, that "there are no absolutes," except of course the statement that "there are no absolutes." (See **positivism.**) Protagoras (c. 490–c. 420 B.C.) famously observed: "Man is the measure of all things; of things that are that they are, and of things that are not that they are not." Truth, in other words, depends upon the observer, although Protagoras applied the principle only to differently perceived experiences of identical phenomena (you say the glass is half full; I say it is half empty). The godfather of modern relativism was G. F. W. Hegel, although he seems practically a champion of orthodoxy compared to contemporary relativists. Hegel believed that no statement could be absolutely true, but got around the chaotic implications of that by positing an Infinite Mind of which all reality is simply a constantly changing *aspect*. Such ideas are rarely influential outside intellectual circles, and it took the exceptional figure of Albert Einstein to put relativism into the modern consciousness—much to his own despair. As Johnson has written (1992), relativism in our era has been greatly enhanced by a misinterpretation of the Special Theory of Relativity; by the improper application of a specific scientific observation to moral conditions. **Read:** R. Weaver, *Ideas Have Consequences* (1948). **"Aristotle was the first of the many philosophers who have pointed out that a wholly relativist theory of truth cuts the ground from under its own feet, is self-refuting. As a relativist, I say there is no way to be sure of the truth, and that therefore every man is entitled to his own opinion. But how do I know that it is true that there is no way to be sure of the truth? And how can I prove to you that every man is entitled to his own opinion if you deny this? By my own principle, may not your denial be just as true as my assertion? We are thus plunged into an unending series of mutual contradictions, with no way of reaching a conclusion. Suppose that you deny and reject the whole doctrine of liberalism. Then, by that doctrine itself, you are not only entitled to your opinion, but there is just as much chance that your opinion is true as that liberalism is true. . . . The fact is that all human discussion, all communication among**

human beings—and thus every form of human society—must assume that *not all* opinions are true, that some are false, that there is an objective difference between truth and falsity; and that if you and I hold contrary views, then at least one of us is wrong." James Burnham, *Suicide of the West* (1964)

republicanism: That form of government—fully emerging in Europe in the 18th century, but having its origins in the ancient world—which is free of hereditary rule and is characterized by limited powers and representation. (From *res publica*, the people's business.) Some republicans have emphasized the superiority of public over private life—even to the point of suppressing individual liberty. This was Rousseau's version of republicanism. More enduring has been the classical republican emphasis upon civic virtue. This was the American Founders' version. Because it rejects monarchy, republicans have always had to defend the theory's apparent weakness in establishing executive power, and the tendency to "factionalism" as well. **Read**: Hamilton, Madison, and Jay, *The Federalist* (1787), in which James Madison wrote (No. 39): **"If we resort for a criterion, to the different principles on which different forms of government are established, we may define a republic to be, or at least may bestow that name on, a government which derives all its powers directly or indirectly from the great body of the people, and is administered by persons holding their offices during pleasure for a limited period, or during good behaviour. It is essential to such a government that it be derived from the great body of the society, not from an inconsiderable proportion or a favored class of it."**

Right, the: With the Left (always capitalized), the terms used since the French Revolution to denote those on the political spectrum who, so the theory goes, either resist change (the Right) or embrace change (the Left). The terms are said to have arisen out of the habit of seating in meetings of the French Estates-General in the weeks just prior to the revolution of July 14, 1789: monarchists sat on the king's right; the revolutionists to his left. (Thus the even more specific right *wing*.) The words in French, *droite* for right and *gauche* for left, have interesting etymologies and uses. As in English, *droite* (or *droit*) stands for both position and privilege—for the side opposite the left, and for the legal claim to something. In the plural, *droits*, it is the "body of the law." *Gauche* is derived from an older verb form meaning *to veer*, and has the secondary meaning, especially when used by English speakers, of crudeness. In the 1850s the terms became further associated with economic notions, with the left wing (*not* capitalized) favoring state intervention, and the right wing favoring laissez-faire. This was actually an important development in the history of conservatism, since previously the Right would have been assumed to be in favor of oligarchic protection, not free trade, and also marked the point at which the Left parted ways with classical liberalism. Because of its more ancient association with absolutism—at least with monarchy—"the Right" has tended to be a term of derision in Europe, whereas in America it is "the Left" that has become a pejorative. If a single tradition can be said to unify the disparate individuals and groups on the Right it would be that of Western civilization. **Read:** R. Kirk, *The Conservative Mind* (1953). **"[The conservative] worldview is the worldview of Western civilization. Conservatism in a revolutionary age, like the one we are living through, cannot simply stand for a series of received opinions. Too much has been shattered for it to be possible ever simply to return to the forms and modes of the past. Conservatism must be something more than preservative; it must restore, and it must create new forms and modes to express the essential content of our civilization. That requires an activity far wider than the political, for the political is the sphere of struggle, struggle for a vision that is articulated. Conservatives today have the double task of simultaneously fighting for a position and articulating it. And this latter task is not secondary, but decisive. It is a task which is both moral (in the broad sense of living by high standards) and intellectual (in the broad sense of using reason to apply tradition to new circumstances)."** Frank Meyer, *The Conservative Mainstream* (1969)

Robertson, Marion G. "Pat" (1930–): American "televangelist" who more than anyone has brought the nation's Bible-centered Christians into political prominence and encouraged their secular allegiance to conservatism and the Republican Party. The son of a thirty-four-year veteran of Congress, Robertson grew up receiving equal doses of politics (from his father) and religion (from his mother), and so has a vision of America in which religion and politics are a unity. A graduate of Washington & Lee, Yale Law School, and the New York Theological Seminary, Robertson founded his Christian Broadcasting Network (CBN) in 1960. The most popular of CBN's programs, *The 700 Club*, arose from his early decision to raise the $7000-a-month operating capital needed to run his network by soliciting pledges of $10 per month from 700 benefactors. In its way, *The 700 Club* was the first of the interactive (call-in) television programs that now saturate the medium. In little more than a decade, CBN became the largest syndicator of satellite programming and the largest user of WATS telephone service in the United States. In 1988, Robertson moved to mobilize his nationwide television audience in a presidential campaign that saw some early successes, but faded as then Vice President Bush moved inexorably towards the Republican nomination. In Robertson's absence, CBN suffered, but even as he returned to deal with the network's mounting losses, he set in motion the formation of the Christian Coalition, a largely evangelical, grass-roots organization (but with strong cooperative ties to Catholic groups), the intention of which was to assert Christian viewpoints and sponsor Christian candidates in elections: local, state, and national. (See **Christian Right**.) **Read: About:** D. Harrell, *Pat Robertson* (1987). "A recent Gallup poll suggests that 70 million Americans consider themselves to be evangelical Christians. . . . These evangelical Christians may all look alike to the press, but in fact they are very different from each other. They attend great cathedrals and tiny storefront churches. Some shout and weep and lift their arms in praise. Others kneel in ordered, liturgical silence. Their biblical translations vary. They celebrate the Lord's Supper in dozens of different ways. They are scattered across the nation in great cities and tiny villages. They represent an amazing cross section of the total American culture and experience. And though these evangelicals love each other as their Lord commanded, they remain independent from each other in a thousand different ways. Evangelicals are not one uniform, homogeneous group as their critics fear. In fact, they are as wonderfully diverse from each other as they are from their unbelieving neighbors and as deeply committed to freedom, pluralism, and individuality as any people in the nation." *America's Dates with Destiny* (1986)

Rockford Institute: Illinois-based research and publishing organization that emphasizes the importance of personal responsibility in a free society. Founded in 1976 by Rockford College president John A. Howard—partly in reaction to campus unrest—the Institute has come to define the so-called **paleoconservative** wing of the **conservative** movement, with its emphases on **faith**, **family**, and **isolationism**, although the Institute would probably prefer *anti-imperialism* or *nationalism*. The one most common word of self-description in Rockford publications is **tradition**. And yet there is a strong element of **libertarianism**—at least sympathy to it—in the Institute's publications; demonstrating perhaps that it has no enemies in the cause of dismantling big government. Or that the **Old Right** lives. The Institute publishes several periodicals, most notably *Chronicles* magazine (formerly *Chronicles of Culture*). *Chronicles* is edited by classicist Thomas Fleming, who managed in a recent number of the magazine (April 1995)—while eulogizing **Rothbard**—to level his sights at "conservative turncoats and con-men" (principally the ones in Manhattan) who rule the journalistic "bases for the occupying army that has been imposed upon a once free people." In that same issue traditionalist Samuel Francis accused **Gingrich** of sophomoric gnosticism, and libertarian Llewellyn H. Rockwell, Jr. attacked **neoconservatism** for its dedication to "Reaganism, which meant a bigger welfare-warfare state in the name of limited government," and praised Warren G. Harding as "the best president of this century." Rockford president Allan C. Carlson has detailed the Institute's "traditionalist" vision as advocating: truth grounded in Scripture; **liberty** based upon **natural law**; loyalty to Western civilization in law and in education; marriage as the basis of social **order; free trade; limited government**; and realism in literature and tonality in music. How the apparent advocacy of free trade squares with *Chronicles'* support of Patrick Buchanan's nationalist presidential campaign is uncertain. Other Rockford publications reflect the Institute's think-tank activities. *The Family in America*, edited by Bryce Christensen, offers opinion and data on the state of this imperiled institution, often with a religious viewpoint, and *The Religion & Society Report*, edited by theologian Harold O. J. Brown, challenges "the cultural powers that be with the force of moral reason." Rockford also presents the Ingersoll Prizes, one (in creative writing) named for <u>Eliot</u> and another (in scholarly letters) named for <u>Weaver</u>. Recipients have included: Walker Percy, Mario Vargas Llosa, and Muriel Spark; <u>Burnham</u>, <u>Kirk</u>, and <u>Nisbet</u>. Read: P. Gottfried and T. Fleming, *The Conservative Movement* (1988). "Everywhere I go, I meet real Southerners who are not about to apologize for either their family or their flag. The other night I received a telephone call from a perfect stranger who wanted some historical ammunition. At a local high school named for General Lee, some students had been displaying the Confederate flag until the superintendent issued a decree prohibiting it, and my caller—an articulate but not educated Southerner—wanted to defend the students. When all is said and done, there is only one argument that counts in these flag controversies, and that is loyalty. One can argue all day about the comparative sins of Southern slave owners and Yankee capitalists, but for real men and women, all that matters is the love they bear for their people and their land. If Southerners are going to be asked to repudiate their flag and their history, do not imagine that it will make them good Americans. The most that can be hoped for is that they will turn into one more whining minority." T. Fleming, "Southern Men, American Persons" in *Chronicles*, May, 1994

[<u>Rockford Institute</u>, 934 North Main Street, Rockford, IL 61103-7061; (815) 964-5811. Allan C. Carlson, president. Subscriptions: *Chronicles* (published monthly) $39/year; (800) 877-5459; *The Family in America* (published monthly) $24/year; (800) 877-5603; *The Religion & Society Report* (published monthly) $24/year; (800) 877-5179.]

Rossiter, Clinton (1917–1970): American political scientist (Cornell) and author (*The American Presidency*, 1956), whose *Conservatism in America* (1955) was controversial, and—to some observers—flawed (if not downright heretical). His interpretation of <u>conservatism</u> has been compared to that of <u>Viereck</u> and <u>Lippmann</u>, and the introduction to the most recent edition of his book was written by <u>Will</u>. Rossiter went so far as to claim that <u>Kirk</u>'s assertion of <u>Burke</u>'s prominence in American conservatism was misguided (his word was "irrelevant"), and that Buckley was not as properly conservative of American tradition as was Adlai Stevenson! This was because Rossiter believed that conservatism, which he memorably termed "the thankless persuasion," is principally a defense of the status quo. Thus an assertion of Burke's influence on American conservatism rang false simply because he was English, and Buckley's principled stand "athwart [recent] history" was radical because history = the status quo = liberalism. (To be fair to Rossiter, we may say classical liberalism, and, indeed, he urged conservatives to become the philosophical voice of American capitalism.) Kendall called him the "false sage of Ithaca" (that being, of course, the home of Cornell). Rossiter's best book, reflecting his true expertise as a scholar of American constitutional development, was *Seedtime of the Republic* (1953), which analyzes the tradition of American liberty, and which won a Bancroft Prize. **Read:** *Conservatism in America* (1955); *Seedtime of the Republic* (1953); **About:** G. Nash, *The Conservative Intellectual Movement in America* (1976). "The last and highest kind [of conservatism] is philosophical ... The philosophical conservative subscribes consciously to principles designed to justify the established order and guard it against careless tinkering and determined reform. His conservatism is explained in intellectual as well as psychological, social, and economic terms. Nurture has joined with nature to make him the man he is. He is conscious of the history, structure, ideals, and traditions of his society, of the real tendencies and implications of proposals of reform, and the importance of conservatism in maintaining a stable social order. He is aware that he is conservative, and that he must therefore practice a conservative politics. This awareness of his nature and mission is to a substantial degree the result of hard thinking under radical pressure; he has examined his principles, candidly if not always enthusiastically, and found them good. His loyalty to country projects into the past, and his sense of history leads him to appreciate the long and painful process through which it developed into something worth defending." *Conservatism in America* (1955)

Rothbard, Murray N. (1926–1995): American economist and advocate of libertarianism, apologist for the Austrian School, and student-expositor of **Mises**. Rothbard has been described as an "anarcho-capitalist," and his views have a way of making **capitalism** sound like the soul of radicalism. In *Man, Economy, and State* (1962), Rothbard made the case for economic liberty through a massive work that was an exercise of "deductive science using verbal logic." As with all "Austrians," the emphasis is on *praxeology*; on human action rather than on mathematical calculation. Rothbard was an unceasing agitator against the "welfare-warfare state," and, while his anti-war **isolationism** sometimes seemed in tune with the New Left (he published in *Ramparts* magazine during the 1960s), he was always closer to the spirit of the **Old Right**. His point was simply this: big war makes for big government. As the institutions of the state grow, the vigor of voluntary associations declines. Few critics of taxation have been as voluble as Rothbard. The main problem with taxes is that they are not voluntary, a fact that has both moral and economic repercussions: taxes violate property rights and they diminish market efficiency. To Rothbard there was no difference between the IRS and a mugger. And although he was an advocate of **free trade**, Rothbard was an opponent of the North American Free Trade Agreement (NAFTA), since he believed it did not free North Americans to trade with one another so much as it unified government planning on the continent. Rothbard was among the founders of the Cato Institute, America's leading libertarian think tank. Originally established in San Francisco but now located in Washington, D.C., Cato was named not for the Roman statesman but for the eponymous *Letters* (1720—very influential in the development of **Southern conservatism**) of the English Whigs Thomas Gordon and John Trenchard, which marked the birth of libertarianism. ("Property is the best Support of the Independency so passionately desired by all Men.") Similar in structure and output to the **Heritage Foundation**, Cato, like Rothbard himself, has consistently taken contrarian positions on issues such as the Gulf War. Rothbard was also affiliated for many years with the Ludwig von Mises Institute. **Read:** *For a New Liberty* (1973); **About:** G. Nash, *The Conservative Intellectual Movement in America* (1976). **"To the libertarians, the arguments between conservatives and liberals over laws prohibiting pornography are distressingly beside the point. The conservative position tends to hold that pornography is debasing** and immoral and therefore should be outlawed. Liberals tend to counter that sex is good and healthy and that therefore pornography will only have good effects . . . Neither side deals with the crucial point: that the good, bad, or indifferent consequences of pornography, while perhaps an interesting problem in its own right, is completely irrelevant to the question of whether or not it should be outlawed. The libertarian holds that it is not the business of the law—the use of retaliatory violence—to enforce anyone's conception of morality. It is not the business of the law—even if this were practically possible, which is, of course, most unlikely—to make anyone good or reverent or moral or clean or upright. This is for each individual to decide for himself." *For a New Liberty* (1973)

Rusher, William (1923–   ): See *National Review*

Santayana, George (1863–1952): American philosopher, born in Spain. Taught at Harvard with William James and Josiah Royce (who had taught him), and was a teacher of **Eliot** and **Lippmann**. He saw religion as superstition but admired ritual, and saw **faith** (even if it was only "animal faith," i.e., the reaction of cornered beasts) as Man's ultimate creative, descriptive, and salvific achievement. What Santayana really admired was the past. "You are a modern 'intellectual,'" he wrote to a friend, "and I am an old fogey: that is probably the reason why I balk at your emphasis on 'newness.' Aren't you confusing newness with freshness or spontaneity? True religion, true philosophy, like true love, must be spontaneous, it must be fresh: but why should it be new?" His writing, both poetry, fiction, and philosophy, is oddly passionate and yet detached. His political **conservatism** was based upon a general philosophical skepticism that he dubbed "critical realism," and he was generally horrified by American **capitalism**, which he believed would lead to a bland uniformity. As he mused in *Soliloquies in England and Later Soliloquies* (1922): "If you refuse to move in the prescribed direction, you are not simply different, you are . . . perverse. The savage must not remain a savage, nor the nun a nun . . ." **Kirk**'s *Conservative Mind* (1953), in its most recent edition (the seventh), is subtitled "From Burke to Eliot," but in its first edition it was "From Burke to Santayana." **Read**: *Dominations and Powers* (1951); *The Last Puritan* (a novel, 1936). **About**: his own *Persons and Places* (1944). "In one respect . . . the ideal essence of chivalry never was obscured by either religious or worldly influences: the knight always preferred death to dishonour. Death he daily defied; at every turn of a corner, in every retort, in every love affair, his hand went to the hilt of his sword. When death is habitually defied, all the slavery, all the vileness of life is defied also. It belonged almost to the pride and joy of life to hold life cheap, and risk it, and be coolly indifferent to losing it, in defense of the least of one's life and liberties. A smiling and mystic neighbourliness with death, as with one's shadow, intensified life enormously in the dramatic direction; it kept religion awake; it gave a stiff lining to wit, to love, to fashionable swagger; and it concentrated the whole gamut of human passion and fancy within each hour. Shakespeare's theatre . . . is a living monument to the mentality of chivalry. In contrast with that freedom and richness we can see to what a shocking degradation modern society has condemned the spirit." *Dominations and Powers* (1951)

Schlafly, Phyllis (1924–   ): See **feminism**

secular humanism: See **humanism**

Simon, William E. (1927–   ): See **Olin Foundation**

sin: The willful violation of God's laws; this is the only proper meaning of the word. The assertion that, for instance, extreme wealth or poverty are sins is incorrect, since (at least within the canon of Judeo-Christian **tradition**) the *jus divinum* is not set against either. In a similar vein, alcohol or sexual intercourse—as *things*—are not sins, although their abuse may be. Sins are always actions (of the mind or in the world); always and only actions committed by thinking people. Thus, the only other beings capable of sin are angels. The dilemma of sin is that it is both *natural* and *unnatural*. We are all "natural-born sinners" (*fallen*, if one believes in original sin), and yet every sin is contrary to our nature—in the sense that Man is made in God's image. (But see **human nature.**) As Kreeft has pointed out (1990), the contradiction is shallow: "For we confuse the (ontologically) *natural* with the (statistically) *normal*, the qualitative with the quantitative." The modern tendency to assert the legal sanction of such "normative" sins as **abortion** or homosexuality reflects the dark side of **individualism**. But as Karl Rahner wrote (1978), Christianity at least "understands man as a being whose free, sinful acts are not his 'private affair' which he himself can absolve by his own power and strength." Contrast this with the secular view of (first among others) **Mill** that harm to oneself (what today would be called "victimless crime") is not a sufficient reason for an external, prohibitive "power" to be exercised. Of course, Mill was referring to the state or **community**, and not to religion, for which in any case he had no regard. But the blurring of the boundaries between the profane and the sacred has led to an increasingly diminished sense of sin in public life and law (see **modernism**). **Viereck** famously observed (1949) that **conservatism** "is the secularization of original sin." **Read**: G. Grisez, *Christian Moral Principles* (1983). **"The bottom line is that the Framers believed in original sin, believed that man has a nature that is unchanging and base. They understood that man is inherently flawed, imperfect, and imperfectible, driven by selfish desires, reasonable only in the sense of being able to contrive means of satisfying the appetites. They were utterly contemptuous of abstract political theories based upon the notion that man and society are perfectible, or that evil can be eradicated, or that man can be taught to be other than self-interested, or that man is or can become a creature governed by reason, or that there can be a durable and free social order based upon equality, brotherhood, and virtue."** Forrest McDonald, "I Have Seen the Past And It Works" in Edward B. McLean, ed., *Derailing the Constitution* (1995)

Smith, Adam (1723–1790): Scottish moral philosopher often called the "father of modern economics," or more accurately the founder of modern *political economy*. Smith's friendship with the French "Physiocrats" (Turgot, Du Pont de Nemours, Quesnay—the group that was the first to use the term **laissez-faire**) was influential in the development of his opposition to mercantilism (see **free trade**), but more directly affecting Smith's thought were the views of his teacher Francis Hutcheson (1694–1746) and of his friend **Hume**. In Smith's *Inquiry into the Nature and Cause of the Wealth of Nations* (1776)— which was equal parts economic history, industrial analysis, and

policy prescription—he laid the foundations of free-market economics: that individual ambition, effort, and choice are guided by an
"invisible hand"—a term employed in his earlier *Theory of Moral
Sentiments* (1759) and mentioned only once in *The Wealth of
Nations*—to create the highest social benefit; that in order to encourage individuals, government ought not to interfere in economic matters; that efficiency in production will be increased by division of
labor (his classic example was a pin factory in which worker special-
ization boosts output); that value and price are distinct aspects of economic transactions; that prices and wages are best determined
competitively; and that "balance-of-trade" justifications for tariffs and
other mercantilist protections are hogwash. Unlike many **Enlightenment**-era philosophers, Smith's influence was dramatic and immediate. William Pitt (the younger, who became Britain's prime minister
in 1783) embraced Smith's **free-trade** views, and launched Britain on
a two-centuries long expansion of wealth and power. Such enduringly
popular phrases as "supply and demand," "enlightened self-interest,"
and "invisible hand" testify to Smith's continuing impact. Smith's
friend **Burke** called *The Wealth of Nations* "probably the most important book ever written." If Smith's work has a serious flaw, it is his rationalistic insistence that man is an economic animal (seen especially
in his "labor theory of value"), an insistence that would influence the
economic determinism of Marx. **Read:** *The Wealth of Nations* (1776);
About: T. G. Buchholz, *New Ideas from Dead Economists* (1989).
**"Every individual is constantly exerting himself to find out the most
advantageous employment for whatever capital he can command. It
is his own advantage, indeed, and not that of the society, which he
has in view. But the study of his own advantage naturally, or rather
necessarily leads him to prefer that employment which is most advantageous to the society."** *The Wealth of Nations* (1776)

socialism: The opposite of **individualism**; the late 18th- and early
19th-century doctrine (developed in France, Germany, and Britain)
that treats society as a collectivity, and sees economic spoils (profits) as
accruing to the collective and not the individual owner/entrepreneur.
(Socialism may be said to have begun—or at least to have received
nascent support—in the collectivism of Plato.) The **conservative**

critique of socialism has two aspects: the ethical and the technical. On a technical level, socialism is theoretically and practically proven to be destructive of economic growth. It is ironic that socialists often describe themselves as progressive, since as an economic system socialism is unable to progress. One of socialism's fundamental charges against **capitalism** is the inefficiency of **free-market** production—the assertion that competition duplicates energies and improperly distributes rewards—whereas the fact is that only capitalism embraces the unintended consequences of human action, and is therefore capable of the adaptations necessary to innovate, create, and distribute products and resources with any sort of efficiency. As **Viereck** put it (1949): "If you base a society solely on the idea of economic gains, scrapping freedom and justice for the sake of the tyranny needed to organize total planning, then you lose not only the freedom but the economic gains." On the ethical level, **conservatism** objects to the socialist belief in Man's **alienation**, and to its assertion that **rationalism** can redesign people and society. It is the ultimate gnosticism of which **Voegelin** wrote. "So, priding itself on having built its world as if it had designed it, and blaming itself for not having designed it better, humankind is now set out to do just that (**Hayek**, 1988)." **Read**: F. A. Hayek, *The Fatal Conceit* (1988). "**Socialism presumes that we already know most of what we need to know to accomplish our national goals. Capitalism is based on the idea that we live in a world of unfathomable complexity, ignorance, and peril, and that we cannot possibly prevail over our difficulties without constant efforts of initiative, sympathy, discovery, and love. One system maintains that we can reliably predict and elicit the outcomes we demand. The other asserts that we must give long before we can know what the universe will return. One is based on empirically calculable human power; the other on optimism and faith. These are the essential visions that compete in the world and determine our fate.**" George Gilder, *Wealth and Poverty* (1981)

Solzhenitsyn, Aleksandr (1918–   ): Russian novelist (winner of the Nobel Prize in 1970) whose distinguished service in World War II (he was a decorated artillery captain) was followed almost immediately by his imprisonment for subversive writing—in this case not any one of his famous novels, but letters written home from the front. He spent the following decade in the prison camps he would later make famous in *The Gulag Archipelago* (1974). (*Gulag*—or GULag—is an acronym for "Main Administration of Corrective-Labor Camps.") After the death of Stalin (1953), Solzhenitsyn was able to publish *One Day in the Life of Ivan Denisovich* (1962), an early, masterful, harrowing account of the Gulag, although the author's good fortune was largely the result of the "de-Stalinization" then underway. His subsequent books were banned. In 1974, he was arrested (largely as a result of the embarrassment caused by publication in the West of smuggled copies of *The Gulag Archipelago*) and then deported to the West, coming to live in Vermont until his return to Russia in 1994 after the fall of **communism**. Solzhenitsyn's writing manages to elevate the "political" circumstances of his experience to the level of myth—in the great **tradition** of the classical literary works of a Homer and a Dante. During his time in America, Solzhenitsyn wrote and pronounced (in highly regarded speeches) some stinging condemnations of Western materialism and agnosticism based upon his Russian Orthodoxy and intense nationalism. **Read:** *One Day in the Life of Ivan Denisovich* (1963); *The Oak and the Calf* (1980); **About:** M. Scammell, *Solzhenitsyn* (1984). "**How does one get into this mysterious Archipelago? Not an hour goes by without airplanes taking off, ships putting out to sea, and trains rumbling away, all headed in that direction, yet not a single sign on any of them indicates their destination. Ticket agents or the employees of Soviet travel bureaus will be astonished if you ask them for a ticket there. They know nothing either of the Archipelago as a whole nor of any of its innumerable islands; they've never heard of it. . . . Those who are sent to run the Archipelago enter via the training schools of the Ministry of Internal Affairs. . . . Those who are sent to guard the Archipelago are inducted through the military conscription centers. . . . And those who are sent there to die—like you and me, dear reader—enter exclusively and necessarily through the procedure of arrest.**" *The Gulag Archipelago* (1974).

Southern conservatism: Although today there may be little to distinguish American conservatives from one region to the next, this was not true right up until the 1960s. In the South there was a very elegant philosophical and literary **tradition**, sometimes called *agrarianism*, which had its roots in the **states' rights** views of **Jefferson** and, later, **Randolph** and **Calhoun**, and was most notably summarized in *I'll Take My Stand: The South and the Agrarian Tradition* (1930), an anthology produced by a dozen writers: **Ransom**, **Davidson**, Frank Lawrence Owsley, John Gould Fletcher, Lyle Lanier, **Tate**, H. C. Nixon, Andrew Lytle, Robert Penn Warren, John Donald Wade, Henry Blue Kline, and Stark Young. Southern conservatism in this view was haunted by a tragic sense of history (what Ransom called a "fierce devotion to a lost cause"); by the neo-Aristotelian conviction that industrialism was swallowing up Southern identity and its good life, a life lived close to the soil. As Jefferson had written (*Notes on the State of Virginia*, 1785): "Those who labour in the earth are the chosen people of God . . ." This group, centered at Vanderbilt University, also published the earlier, short-lived magazine, *The Fugitive*, and is thus sometimes called the Fugitive Poets. Their **conservatism** was as nostalgic and aristocratic as it was agrarian. In the 1950s **Weaver** and **Kilpatrick** carried the torch, and Kilpatrick offered (1960) a succinct definition of the South's **conservative** philosophy: "An indwelling devotion to tradition and good manners, a resistance to industrialism, a coolness to the secular sirens who sing of material pleasures. . . . [And] the . . . abiding, unyielding opposition to centralism, and to the dead hand of the impassive state." **Read**: M. E. Bradford, *Remembering Who We Are* (1985); E. Genovese, *The Southern Tradition* (1994); J. J. Kilpatrick, *The Sovereign States* (1957); Ransom et al., *I'll Take My Stand* (1930); Weaver, *The Southern Tradition at Bay* (1968). **"What advantages does the southern writer have in dealing with what I [have called] the crisis in our culture? His first advantage is that the South is still the least 'modern' part of the country in its values, habits, and associations. It has been less riven by the severing of ends from means, techniques from values. Whatever the sins and deficiencies of the South, there has been less abstraction and intellectual confusion. There is still some personal connection with the past, some sense of history, and the stabilizing effect of traditional moralities. Whether or not religion can be said to flourish in the South, it still remains a force. The sense of community has not been** totally lost. There is still a folk culture in being. . . . Change has come—and of course is still coming—but the questioning of old attitudes and values is a powerful stimulant to observation, memory, and cogitation. If the loss of the old provokes in some no more than the irritation at being disturbed, it sends others back to an examination of their first principles. If the new constitutes a challenge to the old ways, in the philosopher and the poet the old may offer a counter challenge to the new." Cleanth Brooks, "The Crisis in Culture as Reflected in Southern Literature," in Louis D. Rubin, ed., *The American South* (1980)

Sowell, Thomas (1930–   ): American economist and one of **conservatism**'s most prolific authors and effective polemicists. Trained at Harvard, Columbia, and in the **Chicago School** by, among others, George Stigler and **Friedman**, Sowell is a senior fellow at the **Hoover Institution**. His teaching career has been extensive; he has taught at Rutgers, Howard, Cornell, Brandeis, and UCLA. (Like **Berns** and **Bloom**, he resigned in disgust from Cornell during its time of ideological crisis in the late 1960s.) He has written numerous books, many of them controversial. In such works as *Black Education: Myths and Realities* (1972), *Race and Economics* (1975), *Ethnic America: A History of Markets and Minorities* (1981), *Preferential Policies: An International Perspective* (1990), and *Race and Culture: A Worldview* (1994), Sowell has relentlessly debunked prevailing notions about **affirmative action**, **welfare**, racism, and big government, and brought down upon himself the wrath of black activists and white liberals alike. In fact, Sowell is a modern **Montesquieu**, an interdisciplinary genius ranging over many fields of inquiry and integrating each into a coherent worldview. In his most recent book, *The Vision of the Anointed: Self-Congratulation as a Basis for Social Policy* (1995), Sowell describes the "prevailing vision" of the liberal elite (a.k.a. the *anointed*) as the conviction that all social problems are the result of evil intentions; that these problems can be solved by the "rational" intervention of the elite; and that the rest of us (the *benighted*) are not enlightened enough to understand either the elite's analysis of the problems or their recommended solutions. The vision of pious **liberalism** is thus "cosmic" (or, if you will, *comic*): everything will turn out well in the end. But the stark **conservative** vision is tragic: "there are no solutions, only trade-offs." The former is justified by its rationalistic dreams; the latter by empirical reality. Or as he put it in an earlier work, it is the difference between *beliefs* and *facts*. **Read:** *Preferential Policies* (1990); *Race and Culture* (1994); **Read:** and **About:** "Those who emphasize the teaching of 'issues' rather than academic skills fail to understand that 'issues' are infinitely more complex and difficult to master than fundamental principles of analysis. The very reason why there is an issue in the first place is usually because no single principle can possibly resolve the differences to the mutual satisfaction of those concerned. Innumerable principles are often interacting in a changing environment, creating vast amounts of complex facts to be mastered and assessed—*if* one is serious about resolving issues responsibly, as distinguished from generating excitement. To teach issues instead of intellectual principles to school children is like teaching calculus to people who have not yet learned arithmetic, or surgery to people lacking the rudiments of anatomy or hygiene. Worse, it is teaching them to go ahead and perform surgery, without worrying about boring details." *Inside American Education* (1993)

sport: An irrelevancy to some conservatives; a sacrament to others. Called by **Novak** (1988), "a spiritual activity, a natural religion, a tribute to grace, beauty, and excellence." There is a tendency among intellectuals to admire those sports more related to **individualism**: golf, sailing, fly fishing. But team sports, baseball especially, can also satisfy the **conservative** taste for ritual. And the metaphor of the "level playing field" works as well—if not better—for conservatives as for liberals. **Read:** M. Novak, *The Joy of Sports* (1988); G. Will, *Men at Work* (1990); W. F. Buckley, *Racing Through Paradise* (1987). "Racial integration has worked better in baseball than in any other area of American life. The game has an unforced racial and ethnic balance. It succeeds because the rules are really impartial. Baseball is a refuge from 'social justice.' What it offers instead is simple fairness. There are no 'racist' balls and strikes, no 'affirmative action' balls and strikes, only balls and strikes. The umpires don't care who deserves to win on moral, progressive, or demographic grounds.

Their role is modest but crucial, and would be corrupted if they brought any supposed Higher Purpose to their work. They care only about the rules. The Supreme Court could learn from them." Joseph Sobran, "The Republic of Baseball" in *National Review*, June 11, 1990

states' rights: That **conservative** principle of the American constitutional republic that is in to a degree synonymous with **federalism**. The **Constitution** both implicitly and explicitly makes state sovereignty fundamental: implicit in the separation of powers, the establishment of the Senate and the Electoral College; explicit both in Article 4, Section 4—which guarantees republican state government (and which was a force for national unity)—and in the 10th Amendment. That Amendment, the coda of the Bill of Rights, is worth noting in its elegant entirety: "The powers not delegated to the United States by the Constitution, nor prohibited by it to the States, are reserved to the States respectively, or to the people." In other words, the national government ("United States") is the creation of the states, is given specific, limited powers by the states, and is therefore not superior to them except in its specified powers. All this being true, Patrick Henry still opposed ratification of the Constitution because he believed the initial words of the Preamble, "We the People . . ." should have read, "We, the States." Ironically, it was the "conservative" **Hamilton** who broadly interpreted the central government's power and the "liberal" **Jefferson** who was a "strict constructionist." Jefferson (for Kentucky) and **Madison** (for Virginia) even drafted nullification bills, and the spirit of nullification was everywhere, North and South, until after the Civil War. Again ironically, it was the Republican Party—until the presidency of Franklin Roosevelt—that was the centralizing party, and the Democrats the party of states' rights. The brief Dixiecrat episode, in which Strom Thurmond and other Democrats bolted the 1948 convention over civil-rights issues, gave a new character to the concept, seeming to equate the terms states' rights and racism. The media assumed that states' rights was a dead issue. Thus in the Johnson defeat of **Goldwater** (1964) the fact that the Republican carried Alabama, Georgia, Louisiana, Mississippi, and South Carolina, traditionally

Democratic states, was lost on the pundits, its significance for the future of conservative politics overlooked. The George Wallace candidacy in 1968 only reinforced the misperception. When the Western states became concerned about their rights (especially with regard to land and other resource use) vis-à-vis the national government's claims, the election of **Reagan** (1980) was assured. **Read:** J. J. Kilpatrick, *The Sovereign States* (1957). "**The various State resolutions promptly resulted in the Tenth Amendment. This amendment consists of a single sentence, only twenty-eight words long; it is in no way obscure.** *The powers* (not rights, as in the Ninth Amendment, but powers) *not delegated to the United States* (the verb is delegated, not 'surrendered,' or 'granted,' or 'vested in,' but merely delegated) *by the Constitution* (not by inference, or by any notions of inherent powers, but by the Constitution alone), *nor prohibited to it by the States* (prohibited by the Constitution, that is, by its specific limitations, and not by mandate of any court or Congress or executive, but only by the Constitution itself), *are reserved to the States respectively* (not to the States jointly, but to the States individually and respectively), *or to the people* (because there may be some powers the people will not wish to entrust even to their States)." James J. Kilpatrick, "Conservatism and the South" in Louis D. Rubin, ed., *The Lasting South* (1960)

Stephen, James Fitzjames (1829–1894): English Evangelical jurist and diplomat, a contemporary and friend of **Disraeli** and **Maine**, and the uncle of Virginia Woolf. His abolitionist father held the chair in history at Cambridge that was later taken up by **Acton**. Stephen wrote extensively about the history and character of English criminal law. However, his *Liberty, Equality, Fraternity* (1873) was a reply to *On Liberty* (1859) by **Mill**, and was one of the finest expositions of **conservative** thought in the 19th century. Although he was influenced by the utilitarianism of Mill (and Jeremy Bentham) and to some degree adopted its methodologies (see **empiricism**), he rejected its revolutionary prescriptions. From Thomas Hobbes, Stephen derived a view of the depravity of **human nature** and the necessity of mediating restraints upon it, especially law and religion. **Liberty**, in his view, is a value in the service of society, not the other way around. It is the absence of restraints upon the individual, but not the absence of all restraints. He uses the allusion of water (liberty) flowing through pipes (social restraints), and makes clear that without the conduit, the water is wasted. Paramount among the liberties he would not restrain (although, as a lawyer, he believed in deciding each case on its merits) were property and privacy. As to equality, he believed in only one kind: equality before the law. For the fraternity suggested by the phrase "the brotherhood of man," Stephen had a withering contempt. It was fanaticism pure and simple. **Read**: *Liberty, Equality, Fraternity* (1873); **About**: J. A. Colaiaco, *James Fitzjames Stephen and the Crisis of Victorian Thought* (1983). **"The substance of what I have to say to the disadvantage of the theory and practice of universal suffrage is that it tends to invert what I should have regarded as the true and natural relation between wisdom and folly. I think that wise and good men ought to rule those who are foolish and bad. To say that the sole function of the wise and good is to preach to their neighbors, and that everyone indiscriminately should be left to do what he likes, and should be provided with a ratable share of the sovereign power in the shape of a vote, and that the result of this will be the direction of power by wisdom, seems to me to be the wildest romance that ever got possession of any considerable number of minds."** *Liberty, Fraternity, Equality* (1873)

Strauss, Leo (1899–1973): German-born American political philosopher (*not* political scientist, a term he despised) whose influence as a teacher (New School for Social Research, University of Chicago, Claremont[-McKenna] College, St. John's College) was unprecedented. (He is the only contemporary teacher of politics whose students are referred to as *disciples*, as *Straussians*.) A refugee from the Nazis, Strauss was naturally concerned about how society makes judgments about political regimes, especially in terms of (he thought ill-defined) notions of progress that were clearly becoming with time "non-judgmental." For Strauss, judgment was everything, and <u>relativism</u> was anathema. This was the "fact-value distinction," a noteworthy aspect of his teaching. Political theory, he believed, in becoming "scientific" (in believing itself capable of analyzing facts only) had lost its philosophical senses—it was no longer able to assess the difference between right and wrong. Thus he went back to classical philosophy (the "Great Tradition") to demonstrate a political theory that was not value-free. Strauss was justly renowned for his close study ("careful reading") of an author's work. He thought it necessary, for instance, to know the influences upon, the sources of, Spinoza's conceptions of reason and revelation in order to adequately analyze those conceptions. This he did in an early (1930) book, and it would be a *leitmotif* throughout his writings: the ancient leading to the modern. Another major theme of his work was the conflict between the concepts of **natural law** and **natural rights**. He preferred the former, believing the law to be the manifestation of an "objective order," whereas natural rights are an assertion of a "subjective claim." This is not to say that Strauss believed in a divine hand behind the objective **order**. He sought a middle way between **positivism** and deism. As he summed up the distinction between natural law and natural right: "There is a universally valid hierarchy of ends, but there are no universally valid rules of action." Among his many notable students and disciples are: **Berns**, **Bloom**, **Jaffa**, **Kendall**, **Kristol**, and **Will**. Jaffa has written (1959) that Strauss developed "the only genuinely new political science of the past four hundred years." **Read**: *Natural Right and History* (1950); *Liberalism: Ancient and Modern* (1968); **About**: J. East, *The American Conservative Movement* (1986); S. Drury, *The Political Ideas of Leo Strauss* (1988). **"The difficulty of defining the difference between liberalism and conservatism with the necessary universality is particularly great in the United States, since this country came into being through a revolution, a violent change or break with the past. One of the most conservative groups here calls itself Daughters of the American Revolution. The opposition between conservatism and liberalism had a clear meaning at the time at which and in the places in which it arose in these terms. Then and there conservatives stood for 'throne and altar,' and the liberals stood for popular sovereignty and the strictly nonpublic (private) character of religion. Yet conservatism in this sense is no longer politically important. The conservatism of our age is identical with what originally was liberalism, more or less modified by changes in the direction of present-day liberalism. One could go further and say that much of what** goes now by the name of conservatism has in the last analysis a common root with present day liberalism and even Communism. That this is the case would appear most clearly if one were to go back to the origin of modernity, to the break with the premodern tradition that took place in the 17th century, or to the quarrel between the ancients and the moderns." *Liberalism: Ancient and Modern* (1968)

subsidiarity: A term (the Latin *subsidium* for aid, help) from Roman Catholic social philosophy which expresses the view that, wherever practicable, decisions ought to be made by those most affected by the decisions. Put another way: the national government ought only to do what the states cannot; the states only what communities cannot; communities only what families cannot; families only what individuals cannot. This is not to suggest that Catholic social theory (especially as read in papal encyclicals) is always in favor of the minimalist state. John XXIII in *Pacem in Terris* (1963), while reaffirming the doctrine of subsidiarity, called for publicly funded health and unemployment insurance, a minimum wage, and government support for the arts. Still, it is clear that "a planned economy . . . violates the principle of subsidiarity . . ." (*The Catholic Encyclopedia*, 1965). **Read:** R. J. Neuhaus, *Doing Well and Doing Good* (1992). **"Just as it is wrong to withdraw from the individual and commit to the community at large what private enterprise and endeavor can accomplish, so it is likewise unjust and a gravely harmful disturbance of right order to turn over to a greater society of higher rank functions and services which can be performed by lesser bodies on a lower plane."** Pius XI, *Quadragesimo Anno* (1930)

Sumner, William Graham (1840–1910): American social scientist and expositor of Social Darwinism, the creed that saw the force of evolution operating in contemporary society—especially the struggle for "survival of the fittest." In this, like Hayek after him, he was influenced by the English writer Herbert Spencer. A Yale graduate, Sumner entered the Episcopal ministry in 1867 but left three years later to return to Yale to teach political and social science. He remained at Yale until shortly before he died. It was Sumner as much as anyone who put the concept of laissez-faire into the American economic consciousness, and he extended it to politics as well. He believed that "folkways" developed gradually and powerfully, and that attempts by government to change them were pointless. He was an important influence on the development of American **libertarianism**, especially, but also of **conservatism**. He was opposed to **socialism** and **egalitarianism** and in favor of a laissez-faire economics and politics. Above all, he wanted government to be free of moralizing. He coined the term *ethnocentricity*. **Read**: *Folkways* (1907); *On Liberty, Society, and Politics* (1992); **About**: R. Hofstadter, *Social Darwinism in American Thought* (1955). **"During Jackson's second term the growth of the nation in wealth and prosperity was very great. It is plain ... that, in spite of all the pettiness and provincialism which marked political controversies, the civil life of the nation was growing wider and richer. It was just because there was an immeasurable source of national life in the physical circumstances, and in the energy of the people, that the political follies and abuses could be endured. If the politicians and statesmen would only let the nation alone it would go on, not only prosperously, but smoothly; that is why the non-interference dogma of the democrats, which the Whigs denounced as non-government, was in fact the highest political wisdom."** *Andrew Jackson* (1899)

supply-side theory: The view in economics propounded by, among others, Arthur Laffer, Paul Craig Roberts, and, to an extent, the editors of the *Wall Street Journal*, that is a modern-day version of Say's Law (c. 1803), which holds that *supply creates demand*. The term (popularized by Jude Wanniski in the *Wall Street Journal*, but coined by Herbert Stein) refers to the theories of Laffer and Robert Mundell that favor maximum stability in the economy: through low tax rates, a gold standard, and other production (supply) incentives. Supply-siders argue that **monetarism**, which would stabilize the economy by stabilizing the money supply (and thereby controlling inflation), is promoting only *half* the solution; that "since inflation, in the last analysis, is too much money chasing too few goods, it is at least as important to increase the output of goods supply as it is to reduce the flow of money demand" (Brookes, 1982). Like proponents of the **Austrian School**, supply-siders are not necessarily anti-monopoly. Famous among supply-side insights is the tax "curve" of Professor

Laffer, which graph demonstrates that lower tax rates may actually, over time, generate more revenue, since they will encourage businesses and individuals to invest more money in taxable activities; i.e., to shelter less. As to the gold standard, the supply-siders' interest is in its apparent stability. "As a 'standard of value,'" Jude Wanniski has written (1978), "the dollar is the same kind of measuring device as a yardstick. The Bureau of Weights and Measures maintains the precise length of one yardstick . . . and is unconcerned about the quantity in use in the world. . . . The problem is that it is easier to measure distance than . . . value. The supply-side argument for a gold standard rests on the empirical observation that for 2,500 years the global electorate has identified gold as the most reliable standard of value . . ." Supply-side economics was the much touted—and maligned—basis of what became known as Reaganomics (see **Reagan**), and was famously referred to as "voodoo economics" by George Bush. **Read:** B. Bartlett, *Reaganomics* (1981); G. Gilder, *Wealth and Poverty* (1981); P. C. Roberts, The *Supply-Side Revolution* (1984); J. Wanniski, *The Way the World Works* (1978). "**. . . Reagan's 1976 call** [in an op-ed article, "Tax Cuts and Increased Revenue"] **to examine the record of the tax rate cuts under presidents Harding and Kennedy is as close as anyone associated with Reagan ever came to claiming that a tax rate cut would instantly yield more government revenue. Yet the myth persisted—the myth that Reagan and his key economic advisers believed that large tax cuts would produce more revenue. . . . What Reagan and his advisers did believe . . . was that given the high level of taxation, a tax rate cut would** *not lose as much revenue as one might expect.* **People would work harder, and their incomes would rise over time to offset a substantial part of the revenue loss due to the tax rate cut. In fact, this is what happened—in spades. Reagan's very cautious 1980 campaign estimate of the effects of the supply-side tax cut on government revenue—that 17 percent of the lost revenue would be recouped by increased economic growth—proved far too conservative.**" Martin Anderson, *Revolution* (1988)

Taft, Robert A. (1889–1953): American politician (United States senator from Ohio, 1939 until his death) called by **Rossiter** "the very model of the American conservative," who ranked with Dwight

Eisenhower as a leader among the "middling conservatives." Compared with a **Goldwater** or a **Reagan**, Taft's views probably were less **laissez-faire** and more "moderate," much in the spirit of a **Churchill** or a **Disraeli**. He believed that **order** depended upon "affirmative Government action to preserve liberty," and he had no quarrel with, for instance, farm subsidies or minimum wage laws. He was very much a man of the **Old Right**, especially in his **isolationism** (he opposed entry into World War II before Pearl Harbor and into NATO after the armistice). Taft was co-author of the Taft-Hartley Act (1947) which, among many other provisions, provided protection to workers against coercive unions and gave the president power to declare a "cooling-off" period in any strike deemed a threat to national security. Taft, and his opposition to the Nuremberg trials of Nazi war criminals, was one of the subjects of John F. Kennedy's *Profiles in Courage* (1956). Taft believed that the Allied prosecutions were done *ex post facto*; that since there were no international statutes prohibiting "crimes against humanity," it was sheer legal **positivism** to use that pretext to try the Nazis. Taft's principled stand revealed much about his political courage, but it is far from certain that the **natural-law** basis of the trials was an exercise in positivism. It was Taft who coined the term "creeping socialism." His best statement concerning **limited government**: "If liberty prevails unimpaired, everyone who deserves security will have security." **Read:** and **About:** Russell Kirk and James McClellan, *The Political Principles of Robert A. Taft* (1967): **"In an humane economy, Taft repeatedly argued, equality of opportunity—though not equality of final reward—is a matter of public concern, at every level of government. . . . Through grants-in-aid to the several states, hedged about by precautionary clauses which would reserve the administration of such programs to state and local authorities, he hoped to improve the lot of that one-fifth of the nation which was not adequately providing for itself. . . . Such measures would guard the free economy and the free society against socialism by diminishing the afflictions for which the socialists pretended to offer radical remedy."**

Tate, Allen (1899–1979): American poet and critic, editor of the *Sewanee Review*, leader of the Southern Agrarians, a founder of the

New Criticism, and with his Vanderbilt University colleagues—
Ransom, Robert Penn Warren, and **Davidson** among others—a
"Fugitive" contributor to *I'll Take My Stand* (1930). Tate was, like
Eliot, a traditionalist at home with both the 17th-century Metaphysical poets and **modernism**. His most famous poem, "Ode to the
Confederate Dead" (which he began in 1927 and worked on until
1936), is an elegy to the South's lost chivalric past, which can also be
read as a memo on the decline of the West. Like the other Agrarians,
he was stung by the national reaction to the South—amounting to
ridicule (and led by **Mencken**)—as a consequence of the Scopes
"monkey" Trial in 1925, and came to believe that the "chief defect
the Old South had was that it produced . . . the New South," which
was a version of the North, faithless and egalitarian. He converted to
Roman Catholicism in 1950, the same year in which, with his first
wife, the novelist Caroline Gordon, Tate produced the best teaching
anthology in American literature, *The House of Fiction.* Tate was a
president of the National Institute of Arts and Letters, a winner of
the Bollingen Prize, and a recipient of the National Medal for Literature (1976). (See also **Southern conservatism**.) **Read:** *Collected
Poems: 1919–1976* (1977); *Essays of Four Decades* (1968); *The Fathers*
(a novel, 1938); **About:** R. Crunden, *The Superfluous Men* (1977).
**"Religion's respect for the power of nature lies in her contempt for
knowledge of it; to quantify nature is ultimately to quantify ourselves. Religion is satisfied with the dogma that nature is evil, and
that our recovery from it is mysterious ('grace'). For the abstraction
of nature ends . . . with the destruction of the reality of time, and
immediate experience being impossible, so do all ideas of tradition
and inherited order become timeless and incoherent. It is the indispensable office of the religious imagination that it checks the ab-
stracting tendency of the intellect in the presence of nature."**
Memoirs and Opinions (1975)

Thatcher, Margaret Hilda Roberts (1925–   ): British prime minister
(1979–1990) and, with her countryman **Churchill** and her friend
Reagan, one of the outstanding **conservative** leaders of the century.
During her tenure as prime minister, which was the longest in this century, Lady Thatcher often spoke of herself as a "conviction politician,"

and not a "consensus politician," and with stunning effectiveness she set about to implement her convictions. At Oxford University (where, notably, she became the first woman president of the Conservative Association) she trained in chemistry and the law (in order to become a patent attorney). She was first elected to the House of Commons in 1959, rose inexorably through the ranks of the Conservative Party in the 1960s, served as a cabinet minister in the 1970s, took over leadership of her party in 1975, and dominated British and European, if not *world*, politics throughout the 1980s. Her policies as prime minister set the stage for the international conservative renaissance: she attacked the power of labor unions (which had crippled the government of her predecessor); she promoted privatization; she cut income-tax rates; she eliminated trade barriers; she began doing away with wage-and-price controls and subsidies; and she asserted British military power (as in the Falkland Islands), often in league with Reagan. "Great Britain," she proclaimed on the eve of her first re-election, "is great again." She resigned from office having achieved her twin goals of affluence and security, although she went sooner than she had hoped. The very peace and prosperity she had helped to achieve meant that her stand against European monetary union left her vulnerable to a new, reckless spirit even within her own party. Of her, Reagan wrote (in *National Review*, May 19, 1989) that she "demonstrated two great qualities. The first was that she had thought seriously about how to revive the British economy and entered office with a clear set of policies to do so. . . . Her second great quality was the true grit of a true Brit . . . She never wavered. And she was proved right by events." In 1992 she was named to the House of Lords as the Baroness Thatcher of Kesteven. **Read:** *The Downing Street Years* (1993); **About:** G. Smith, *Reagan and Thatcher* (1991). **"Some Conservatives were always tempted to appease the Left's social arguments—just as before I became leader they had appeased their economic arguments—on the grounds that we ourselves were very nearly as socialist in practice. These were the people who thought that the answer to every criticism was for the state to spend and intervene more. I could not accept this. . . . [T]he root cause of our contemporary social problems—to the extent that these did not reflect the timeless influence and bottomless resources of old-fashioned human wickedness—was that the state had been doing too** much . . . Society was made up of individuals and communities. If individuals were discouraged and communities disorientated by the state stepping in to take decisions which should properly be made by people, families and neighborhoods then society's problems would grow not diminish." *The Downing Street Years* (1993)

Tocqueville, Alexis de (1805–1859): French author and statesman, whose *Democracy in America* (1835–1840) remains one of the most read and most quoted studies of the American experiment in self-government. Tocqueville spent less than a year traveling in the United States (on a commission to study prisons), but he quickly grasped, as **Aron** has written (1965), that a "democratic government . . . must not be such that the people can abandon themselves to all the impulses of their passions and determine the decisions of the government." In this he was influenced by his countryman **Montesquieu**. Tocqueville's most telling observations concerned the American sense of equality, which he both respected and feared, since he saw in America the impulses both to equality of opportunity and equality of result. He disliked **democracy**, but was resigned to it, and indeed felt malice toward the **reactionary** dream of subverting it. Still he was prescient in predicting the negative effects **egalitarianism** would have upon **family**, **community**, and even morality. And far from empowering individuals, Tocqueville knew, egalitarian democracy would inexorably empower the state: egalitarianism demands centralization. What is too often ignored is Tocqueville's insight that the principle works both ways; not only did he see centralization in democratic America's future, he also believed (and so argued in his *The Old Regime and the French Revolution*, 1856) that centralization in monarchic France's past had led to the egalitarian eruption of the French Revolution. He felt strongly that widely distributed property, "voluntary associations" (both civic and professional), a general localism, and perhaps especially religion were the keys to the survival of democracy. On his trip to America, Tocqueville was accompanied by his friend Gustave Beaumont (1802–1866), and the two men later collaborated on the writing of the Second Republic's **constitution** (1849). And it was Beaumont who edited Tocqueville's collected works (1860–1866). So influential have been Tocqueville's analyses that *Democracy in America* has practically become the "text" of 20th-century social criticism. His understanding of the of American "character" has special relevance for conservatives, who still combine those two elements Tocqueville thought essential: "the *spirit of religion* and the *spirit of liberty*." **Read:** *Democracy in America* (1840); **About:** R. Aron, *Main Currents in Sociological Thought*, vol. I (1965); B. Frohnen, *Virtue and the Promise of Conservatism* (1993); A. Jardin, *Tocqueville* (1988). **"When the religion of a people is destroyed, doubt gets hold of the higher powers of the intellect, and half paralyzes all the others. Every man accustoms himself to have only confused and changing notions on the subjects most interesting to his fellow-creatures and himself. His opinions are ill-defined and easily abandoned; and, in despair of ever resolving by himself the hard problems respecting the destiny of man, he ignobly submits to think no more about them. Such a condition cannot but enervate the soul, relax the springs of the will, and prepare the people for servitude. Not only does it happen, in such a case, that they allow their freedom to be taken from them; they themselves frequently surrender it."** *Democracy in America* (1840)

tradition: From the Latin *traditio*, meaning an unbroken transmission of knowledge from generation to generation. (As Nestor, the wisest of the Greeks in the *Iliad*, maintains, "The gods do not give people all things at the same time.") The word *tradition* can be applied loosely to modify nearly any idea or activity that endures over time, whether marriage or wife beating. But paramount in the minds of conservatives is the concept of the *customary* beliefs, practices, and institutions from which men and women derive a sense of <u>order</u>. Tradition potentially conflicts with <u>change</u>, and among the surer characteristics of modern life is that fewer and fewer customary beliefs and practices maintain their original orthodoxy; the experience of living is therefore more disorderly. As <u>Kirk</u> put it (1953): "The modern spectacle of vanished forests and eroded lands, wasted petroleum and ruthless mining, national debts recklessly increased until they are repudiated, and continual revision of positive law, is evidence of what an age without veneration does to itself and its successors." The psycho-spiritual component of tradition is what <u>Burke</u>

called **prejudice**; its socio-political component he called **prescription**. Perhaps the most often-quoted pronouncement about tradition is **Chesterton**'s paraphrase (1908) of Burke's "partnership": in *Reflections on the Revolution in France* (1790) Burke spoke of the bond "between those who are living, those who are dead, and those who are to be born." Tradition, Chesterton wrote: "is only democracy extended through time. . . . It is the democracy of the dead. Tradition refuses to submit to the small and arrogant oligarchy of those who merely happen to be walking about." It may be noted that without tradition education ceases, perhaps to be replaced by chaotic propaganda. **Read**: Edward Shils, *Tradition* (1981), in which Shils writes: ". . . [H]uman beings, at least most of them, much of the time do not fare well in a disordered world. They need to live within the framework of a world of which they possess a chart. They cannot construct these for themselves. This is one of the limits to the ideal of total emancipation and total self-regulation. Authorities in family, church, community, educational institutions, army, and factory cannot construct all of this chart, and those rudiments of the chart which they can present are limited in their range and their acceptance depends on the legitimacy of their promulgators. Human beings need the help of their ancestors; they need the help which is provided by their own biological ancestors and they need the help of the ancestors of their communities and institutions, of the ancestors of their societies and their institutions. . . . The destruction or the discrediting of these cognitive, moral, metaphysical, and technical charts is a step into chaos."**

Tyrrell, R. Emmett, Jr. (1944–): See **American Spectator**

ultramontanism: From the Latin *ultra montes*, meaning "beyond the mountains" (the perspective being the rest of Europe looking south—across the Alps—towards Rome), and meaning either the view that papal **authority** supersedes both the episcopal and secular authorities or the more limited position that in religious affairs the pope is supreme. To begin with (in 17th-century France), ultramontanists were opposed by Gallicans, those who wanted strictly national churches governed by local episcopal authority. Today the term is often applied to Catholic conservatives, such as the members of

Opus Dei, who not only consider papal authority supreme, but offer service to the pope in a way formerly assigned to the Jesuits. Few today believe the pope ought to have secular power. Historically—perhaps inevitably—ultramontanism conflicts with **classical liberalism**'s view of church-state relations as reflected in the American **constitution**. The great era of ultramontanism occurred in the two decades between 1850, when the Church began to harden its view of **modernism**, and 1870, when the first Vatican Council declared the doctrine of papal infallibility. **Acton**, who was of two minds, made clear that papal supremacy extended only to matters of **faith**: "The Catholic is subject to the correction of the Church when he is in contradiction with her truth, not when he stands in the way of her interests." It is often said that ultramontanism is a dead issue, given that all communicant Catholics recognize the authority of the pope. (See also **Maistre**.) **Read**: Lord Acton, "Ultramontanism" in *Essays in Religion, Politics and Morality* (1988): "**When a man has . . . worked out the problem of science or politics, on purely scientific and political principles, and then controlled this process by the doctrine of the Church, and found its results to coincide with that doctrine, then he is an Ultramontane in the real meaning of the term—a Catholic in the highest sense of Catholicism. The Ultramontane is therefore one who makes no parade of his religion; who meets his adversaries on grounds which they understand and acknowledge; who appeals to no extrinsic considerations—benevolence, or force, or interest, or artifice—in order to establish his point; who discusses each topic on its intrinsic merits—answering the critic by a severer criticism, the metaphysician by closer reasoning, the historian by deeper learning, the politician by sounder politics and indifference itself by a purer impartiality. In all these subjects the Ultramontane discovers a point pre-eminently Catholic, but also pre-eminently intellectual and true. He finds that there is a system of metaphysics, and of ethics, singularly agreeable to Catholicism, but entirely independent of it.**"

utopianism: Also *millenarianism*, the belief in the possibility of a perfect society. The term Utopia was coined by Thomas More (1478–1535) from the Greek words for "nowhere" (or "good place").

Literary utopias have ranged from the hierarchical (Plato's *Republic*) to the egalitarian (as in the socialistic and hedonistic "phalansteries" of Charles Fourier). Although it is the sure province of **socialism** and **communism** (at least in their visions of the end stages of societal development), and although it is superficially anathema to **conservatism**, some conservatives maintain a kind of utopianism, since visions of the "good society" are necessarily prescriptive of a desired **order**. More often than not though, the **conservative** view is anti-utopian or dystopian, meaning that the utopian dream is assumed to lead to hell, not heaven. Utopianism depends for its apotheosis upon the malleability and perfectibility of Man, and about this conservatives have no illusions. You can't get there from here. However, **libertarianism** at least skirts the notion of utopia in that it has a highly conceptual view of the state. But the minimalist, non-coercive state is as practically unattainable as it is theoretically attractive, even in the brilliant conception of **Nozick**, for whom the "utopian *process* [italics added] is substituted for the utopian end state of other static theories of utopia" (1974). We can't get there from here, so we must make the rules of travel our end. By backing away from prescribed ends, Nozick's process utopia at least avoids the inevitable consequence of all end-state dreamlands: the brutal repression required to achieve perfect equality. **Read:** A. Daniels, *Utopias Elsewhere* (1991); T. Molnar, *Utopia: The Perennial Heresy* (1990); R. Nozick, *Anarchy, State, and Utopia* (1974). "**Logically, there are two fundamental kinds of conservatism or negations of millenarianism. One argues that the contradictions within regimes are insurmountable; the other, that there is an eternal order to life in general that survives all revolutions. The theory of insurmountable contradictions and the theory of eternal order both rest on a certain view of human nature. Millennarianism always implies, in one way or another, that man, by his own creative effort or by grace from on high, is capable of eliminating his imperfections. Conservatism, on the other hand, recognizes a basic human nature that determines the characteristics of man in society.**" Raymond Aron, *Politics and History* (1978)

Viereck, Peter (1916–   ): American poet-philosopher and author of *Conservatism Revisited: The Revolt Against the Revolt, 1815–1949* (1949), the book that heralded the **New Conservatism**. His poetry (his first collection won a Pulitzer Prize) was in the tradition of classical **humanism**, and its influence on his political writings is clear, both in content and in style. Viereck believed that the American republic evolved from the Athens-Jerusalem axis, that what we call **conservatism** was the defense of that **tradition**, and that conservatism is, given its diverse sources and long history, *pluralistic*. During World War II, Viereck made clear the need for **classical liberalism** and conservatism to unite in opposition to the "communazis," which sometimes led to accusations that he was "soft on liberalism." Still, at war's end he called for a military invasion to overthrow Stalin. Notwithstanding that position, Viereck was vehemently opposed to **McCarthyism**. What galled some on the **Right** was Viereck's insistence on a non-ideological conservatism. "Totalitarianism is forced to retreat and recede," he wrote in *The New Republic* (September 24, 1962), ". . . not by counter-fanatics (who only egg it on) but by the pluralist quality of life itself. In the end Proteus conquers Procrustes." His sense of the necessary, practical need for a synthesis between **liberalism** and conservatism in America led him to praise Adlai Stevenson, whom he saw as the embodiment of a "Periclean-democratic aristocracy." Viereck is the author of the *Encyclopaedia Britannica*'s entry on conservatism, and famously observed that anti-Catholicism is "the anti-Semitism of the intellectuals." **Read**: *Archer in the Marrow* (poems, 1987); *Conservative Revisited* (1949); **About**: R. Fryer, *Recent Conservative Political Thought* (1979). **"Conservatism, which is for politics what classicism is for literature, is in turn the political secularization of the doctrine of original sin. In contrast, radicalism is Rousseau's 'natural goodness of man' collectivized into a touching political faith in the 'masses.' Nazi radicalism equates Rousseau's Noble Savage with the radical mass (the *Volk*); Marxist radicalism equates him with the economic mass (the proletariat). But he is not worshipped like this by the churches. The churches, Protestant, Catholic, or . . . Jewish, draw the fangs on the Noble Savage and clip his ignoble claws."** *Conservatism Revisited* (1949)

Voegelin, Eric (1901–1985): German-born American philosopher and historian who, like **Strauss** (with whose influence his is often compared), escaped Nazism. Voegelin taught at Louisiana State University from 1943 (after brief stops at Harvard and Bennington) until 1958 when he returned to Germany. In 1969 he began an affiliation with the **Hoover Institution**. Voegelin tended to reject the usual political labeling ("positionism" he called it), in large measure because such locutions improperly reduce the utter complexity (and mystery) of political history. And a priori judgments were a detriment to his thoroughgoing **empiricism**. (His was, of course, an empiricism bereft of historicism.) He sought nothing less than a full understanding of how parts of the West had fallen so completely into totalitarianism. In part, Man's problem is that he lives in, as Voegelin put it, "the between": we experience the world as the tension between poles of (and these were not Voegelin's terms) the animal and the angel. Much modern **ideology** creates dreamy "second realities" (**Marxism**, fascism) that deform our experience of "the between." The heart of Voegelin's extraordinary scholarly output (LSU's ongoing collection of his works is projected at 34 volumes) is the identification of **modernism** with *gnosticism*, the ancient heresy that claimed secret, immanent, and—above all—*personal* knowledge of God and human destiny. Modern gnostics (Marx in politics, Freud in religion) saw history as a path of progressive improvement, even salvation. Thus they (the latter-day Gnostics, beginning with Joachim of Flora, d. 1202, and climaxing in Thomas Hobbes, d. 1679, and Marx, Freud) conceive that heaven can be made on earth. Voegelin's work can be rough reading, requiring no less a dictionary than the unabridged *Oxford*, as for example in these famous sentences from *The New Science of Politics* (1952): "The problem of an eidos in history, hence, arises only when Christian transcendental fulfillment becomes immanentized. Such an immanentist hypostasis of the eschaton, however, is a theoretical fallacy." But the benefits of reading Voegelin far outweigh the difficulties. **Read:** *The New Science of Politics* (1952); the five-volume *Order and History* (1956–1987); **About:** J. East, *The American Conservative Movement* (1986); E. Webb, *Eric Voegelin: Philosopher of History* (1981). **"A civilization can, indeed, advance and decline at the same time—but not forever. There is a limit toward which this ambiguous process moves; the limit reached when an activist sect which represents the Gnostic truth organizes the civilization into an empire under its rule. Totalitarianism, defined as the** existential rule of Gnostic activists, is the end form of progressive civilization." *The New Science of Politics* (1952)

The Wall Street Journal: America's pre-eminent national daily, with a circulation in the millions. Although its news-reporting staff tends to reflect the usual news-media biases, i.e., <u>liberalism</u>, the *Journal's* editorial pages, especially under editor Vermont Royster and his successor (and pupil) Robert Bartley, who won a Pulitzer Prize for editorial writing in 1980, are decidedly <u>conservative</u>. Specifically, the *Journal's* "new classical economics" has advocated: tax cuts and incentives; privatization and deregulation; decentralization and <u>federalism</u>. Bartley is among those credited with convincing <u>Reagan</u> to follow <u>supply-side theory</u>. Read: R. Bartley, *The Seven Fat Years* (1992); E. Scharff, *Worldly Power* (1986). "... [C]onventional wisdom blames the deficits caused by the Reagan tax cuts for the recession that started before they were ever passed. ... The 1982 recession was caused by monetary policy, for better or worse. Or, to view it more instructively, it was caused by a timing mismatch. The tight money part of the policy mix was put in place as early as October 1979, and especially in the fall of 1980. The [Reagan] tax cuts didn't start until October 1981, and were not effective on a net basis until January 1983. In between there was a recession. ... As early as November 1981, we wrote in the *Journal* that the premise of supply-side economics was 'You fight inflation with a tight monetary policy. And you offset the possible recessionary impact of tight monetary policy with the incentive effects of reductions in marginal tax rates. Since we are now having a recession, you could claim the formula has failed, except for one detail: We've had tight money all right, but dear friends, we haven't had any tax cut.'" Robert Bartley, *The Seven Fat Years* (1992)

[*The Wall Street Journal*, Dow Jones & Company, Inc., 200 Liberty Street, New York, NY 10281. Robert L. Bartley, editor. Subscriptions: $284/2 years; $164/1 year; $86/6 months; $48/3 months, The Wall Street Journal, 200 Burnett Road, Chicopee, MA 01020.]

Waugh, Evelyn (1903–1966): English novelist and author of, among other fiction, *Decline and Fall* (1928), *A Handful of Dust*

(1937), *Brideshead Revisited* (1945 and revised in 1960), and *The Loved One* (1948). He began and ended his career as the best comic satirist since Swift, but his novels (and travel writings) also established him as one of the few writers whose work addressed the issues of **modernism** while maintaining classical literary form. His World War II trilogy, *Sword of Honor* (1952–1961), has been called "the most distinguished work of fiction about the war by an English writer." *Brideshead Revisited*, which became something of a fad when presented as a mini-series on American television, was a bold assertion of **tradition** and **faith** in the midst of post-war calls for **egalitarianism**. In eulogizing him, **Buckley** noted that Waugh "knew people, knew his century, and having come to know it, he had faith only in the Will of God and in individual man's latent capacity to strive toward it." **Read:** *A Handful of Dust* (1938); *Unconditional Surrender* (1961); **About:** M. Stannard, *Evelyn Waugh* (2 vols., 1989 and 1992); and Waugh's own autobiographical novel, *The Ordeal of Gilbert Pinfold* (1957). **"I believe that man is, by nature, an exile and will never be self-sufficient or complete on this earth; that his chances of happiness and virtue, here, remain more or less constant through the centuries and, generally speaking, are not much affected by the political and economic conditions in which he lives; that the balance of good and ill tends to revert to a norm; that sudden changes of physical condition are usually ill, and are advocated by the wrong people for the wrong reasons . . . I believe in government; that men cannot live together without rules but that these should be kept to the bare minimum of safety; . . . that the anarchic elements in society are so strong that it is a whole-time task to keep the peace. I believe that inequalities of wealth and position are inevitable and that it is therefore meaningless to discuss the advantages of their elimination; that men naturally arrange themselves in a system of classes; that such a system is necessary for any form of co-operative work, more particularly the work of keeping a nation together. I believe in nationality; not simply in terms of race or of divine commissions for world conquest, but simply thus: mankind inevitably organizes itself in communities according to its geographical distribution; these communities by sharing a common history develop common characteristics and inspire a local loyalty;**

the individual family develops most happily and fully when it accepts these natural limits." *Mexico: An Object Lesson* (1939)

Weaver, Richard M. (1910–1963): American writer and University of Chicago professor who believed that Southern **tradition** was the only **conservative** redoubt in the United States. (See also **Southern conservatism**.) Sometimes called the "St. Paul of the Agrarians" (i.e., a later contemporary who became their most successful apologist), Weaver was a socialist when he began graduate study at Vanderbilt University in 1933, but quickly moved **Right** under the influence of, among others, **Ransom**. Weaver shared the Agrarians' tragic sense, and mourned the loss of the region's erstwhile sense of chivalry. In *The Southern Tradition at Bay* (published in 1968 but written in the early 1940s as his dissertation), Weaver claimed that the South was the only remaining "non-materialist civilization" in the West. **Davidson** compared Weaver to Henry **Adams** in that the work of both "leads away from 'easy constructions' and toward faith" by dwelling on civilization's lost vitality. Weaver is best known for *Ideas Have Consequences* (1948), which begins: "This is another book about the dissolution of the West." He states clearly his premises: that the world is real; that Man is free; and that the decline of civilization is a result "not of biological or other necessity but of unintelligent choice." Weaver expressed the fear that every person had become "not only his own priest but his own professor of ethics," with the result that the consensus necessary to hold society together was lost in a fog of moral anarchy: above all loomed the specter of **relativism**. When Man measures all things by himself, the empowerment of the state inevitably follows. A native Carolinian (who grew up in Kentucky bluegrass country), Weaver described his move north to Chicago as "a strategic withdrawal" from which he could study America and discover ways to effectively assert conservative principle. Weaver was an early contributor to *National Review*. He famously defined **conservatism** as "that paradigm of essences towards which the phenomenology of the world is in continuing approximation." **Read:** *Ideas Have Consequences* (1948); *Visions of Order* (1964); **About:** J. East, *The American Conservative Movement* (1986); J. Scotchie, *The Vision of Richard Weaver* (1995). **"To say that the**

South had a *rationale* of society is not to say that it favored what has come to be known as 'rational planning.' On the contrary, it has held that society, though of intelligible structure, is a product of organic growth, and that a tested *modus vivendi* is to be preferred to the most attractive experiment. George Fitzhugh expressed the belief in an epigram when he wrote, 'Philosophy will blow up any government that is founded on it.' And today, when the South pleads to be allowed 'to work out its own problems in its own way,' it more often than not has no plans for working them out. Its 'way' is not to work them out, but to let some mechanism of adjustment achieve a balance. It is this which has clashed with the North's impulse to toil, 'to help the world go around,' to have a rational accounting of everything. Undoubtedly it has relation to the attitude of piety, which would respect the course of things and frowns on a busy human interference with what nature seems to have planned or providence ordained." *The Southern Tradition at Bay* (1968).

welfare: Primarily the provision of *public* assistance to those identified as needy, although in previous eras such help was given by private individuals and organizations—and with greater effectiveness. (For example, the Victorians spent more than a tenth of personal income on charity, and the monetary grant was accompanied by spiritual assistance as well.) The "federal" government currently operates more than five dozen major welfare programs (e.g., Aid to Families with Dependent Children, or AFDC) which cost taxpayers nearly $400 billion each year (more than is spent on defense), and which is three times the amount necessary to raise all poor families above the "poverty line" were the money simply proffered as direct cash payments. Since the Johnson Administration's "War on Poverty" was declared, the poverty rate has not changed, even though it had been declining through most of the previous decades. A conservative welfare policy would implement decentralization of services, encourage personal responsibility and independence among recipients, and demand flexibility in its programs, not hesitating to eliminate ineffective procedures. Burke believed that welfare (which he defined as the provision of help to those who can "claim nothing according to the rules of commerce," and therefore "come . . . within the jurisdiction of mercy") is a "direct obligation of all Christians"—second only to the payment of debts—but, as **Nisbet** (1986) concludes, Burke saw welfare as an "obligation of church, as it is of family and village or neighborhood, but never of the government." When government takes on the role of income redistribution, it acts—however good its intentions—in a fundamentally unjust manner. As **Hayek** put it (1960), "General altruism . . . is a meaningless conception. Nobody can effectively care for other people as such; the responsibilities we can assume must always be particular . . ." Hayek believed, in fact, that economic status (being poor, deserving or not, or being middle- or upper-income) can assert no compensatory claim to "economic justice" through redistribution. Perhaps the best term applicable to "conservative welfare" is *mutual-aid*, a system whereby individuals look to the needs of individuals, and not bureaucracies to the needs of groups. **Read:** S. Butler and A. Kondratas, *Out of the Poverty Trap* (1987); C. Murray, *Losing Ground* (1984); M. Olasky, *The Tragedy of American Compassion* (1992). **"The secret to making real progress against poverty and distress is to realize that it will come from a 'bottom up' and not a 'top down' process. America possesses a vast array of both private and public institutions and organizations that can move into action if they are allowed to. What the federal government has to do is create a climate hospitable to those institutions, enable them to learn from each other's successes and failures, and ensure that sufficient resources reach needy individuals and institutions for them to make reasonable progress. We have become trapped in a social welfare philosophy that assumes that diversity is a mark of chaos and inadequacy—a mistake that few of us would make when talking about the economy. Rather than try to stamp out diversity in an effort to find the unitary solution to welfare and social problems, we should be nurturing diversity, recognizing that it is the key to success and progress in all fields."** Stuart Butler and Anna Kondratas, *Out of the Poverty Trap* (1987)

Will, George F. (1941–   ): American writer (one of the most widely syndicated columnists in the country) and television commentator (*This Week with David Brinkley*), whose brand of **conservatism** is a very personal version of **neoconservatism**, one without the usual conversion from **Marxism**. Will, as often as any neocon, has been labeled a "big-government conservative." *Neo-Burkean activist* would probably be a better term. With a view to **Burke**, he has written (1983) that our main **conservative** concern must be to prevent a moral revolution in America. "It will be said, instantly and energetically and broadly, that [Burke's] 'sentiments, manners and moral opinions' are none of the government's business. Are they not 'private' and properly beyond the legitimate concern of public agencies? No, they are not." Will believes that law, whether common or constitutional, always presupposes an activist end: regulated **liberty** protecting and encouraging virtuous behavior. To believe otherwise is to invite the decline of both civic legitimacy and personal rectitude. Will believes we must stand with **Lincoln** against the belief that "there is no right principle of action but self-interest." Will believes that the state has legitimate altruistic motives that "express the community's acceptance of an ethic of common provision." This is not, as it sounds, **socialism**, but neither is it **laissez-faire**. His view of economics expresses skepticism concerning the tendency of **capitalism** to unsettle **tradition**. His view of the state is reminiscent of **Churchill** (if not, in fact, directly derived from him—or **Disraeli**), in that both see "conservative" **welfare** policies as necessary to "reconcile the masses to the vicissitudes and hazards of a dynamic and hierarchical industrial community." He has recently (1992) opted for term limits as a means of recovering "deliberative democracy." Educated at Trinity College (in Connecticut, where he was a "Kennedy liberal"), Oxford (where he came under the sway of **Hayek**'s free-market theories), and Princeton (where he received a Ph.D. in political science), Will is an admirer of **Strauss** and accordingly makes frequent reference to classical authors and concepts, and accepts the Straussian view of politics—"properly understood"—as ennobling. He worked for three years in the early 1970s for *National Review*, and helped **Reagan** prepare for debates against Jimmy Carter in 1980. He won a Pulitzer Prize for journalistic commentary in 1977. **Read:** *Restoration* (1992); *Statecraft as Soulcraft* (1983); **About:** M. Rozell and J. Pontuso, *American Conservative Opinion Leaders* (1990). **"Conservatism, properly understood, begins from premises about man and the natural that are diametrically opposed to the**

THE CONCISE CONSERVATIVE ENCYCLOPEDIA · 249

premises of totalitarianisms of the left and the right. To say that statecraft is soulcraft is not to say that the state should be the primary, direct instrument for soulcraft. An aim of prudent statecraft is to limit the state by delegating many of its chores to intermediary institutions. Government can become, to a dangerous degree, an interest group, as self-interested as any other, and more abusive than most. But government can apply to itself a kind of antitrust policy. With all its dimensions, from law through rhetoric, government can encourage strength in private institutions just as surely as totalitarian regimes work to enfeeble such institutions. . . . Conservative soulcraft has as its aim the perpetuation of free government by nurturing people so they can be comfortable and competent in society." *Statecraft as Soulcraft* (1983)

Wilson, James Q. (1931–   ): American political theorist, writer, teacher (at Harvard—for twenty-six years—and UCLA—since 1985), and fellow of the **American Enterprise Institute**. Wilson's reputation rests upon a number of distinguished books that analyze topics ranging from crime and punishment to character and morality. Wilson's views on police procedures have been especially influential, and led to his appointment as chairman of the Los Angeles Police Department's Advisory Committee on Community-Based Policing. In *Crime and Human Nature* (1985), written with Richard J. Herrnstein (which grew out of a course the authors team-taught at Harvard), lawlessness is analyzed in all its complexity, but the emphasis is primarily on the behavior of young urban males, since they commit crimes "to a much greater degree than would be expected by chance," and not only in America. The conclusion is that criminals are present-centered and non-criminals are future-centered, and these states are then discussed in terms of the moral, social, and physical factors that encourage their development. Of all those factors—notwithstanding the impact of certain "constitutional" (i.e., genetic) causes—none seems so influential as **family** life, especially in early childhood. This description of *Crime and Human Nature* oversimplifies arguments that ought to be read in their entirety, but, as in much of Wilson's work, there is a neo-Aristotelian conclusion: "men and women are law-abiding and faithful in part because they have learned it is the right way to behave and in part because the larger political **community** reinforces that belief." Victorian morality turns out to be a better civilizing influence than permissiveness. In *The Moral Sense* (1993), he wonders not so much why rampant moral **relativism** has contributed to contemporary lawlessness, but rather how it is that most people still do not commit crimes. It must be because we have a moral sense. Of course, if we look at the social sciences, we might conclude that the "box score has been something like this: Relativists 10, Universalists 1." Although he makes just two references to him, Wilson's perspective is very similar to Aquinas. (He does, of course, refer frequently to Aristotle, however.) **Read:** *The Moral Sense* (1993); **About:** R. Fryer, *Recent Conservative Political Thought* (1979). **"We are . . . convulsed in a debate over whether our schools should teach morality. Much of that debate is as misguided as the debate over families, because it is based on a misunderstanding of the sources of morality. Some conservatives argue that the schools should impress upon their pupils moral maxims; some liberals argue that, at most, the schools should clarify the 'value' choices the pupils might want to make. But if . . . [my] argument . . . is correct, children do not learn morality by learning maxims or clarifying values. They enhance their natural sentiments by being regularly induced by families, friends, and institutions to behave in accord with the most obvious standards of right conduct—fair dealing, reasonable self-control, and personal honesty. A moral life is perfected by practice more than by precept; children are not taught so much as habituated. In this sense the schools inevitably teach morality whether they intend to or not, by such behavior as they reward or punish. A school reinforces the better moral nature of a pupil to the extent it insists on the habitual performance of duties, including the duty to deal fairly with others, to discharge one's own responsibilities, and to defer the satisfaction of immediate and base motives in favor of more distant and nobler ones."** *The Moral Sense* (1993)

Zeitgeist (Ger., "the spirit of the time"): See **conservatism**

Afterword

On Reformation

As indicated elsewhere in this book (see **conservatism** and **conservative**), there are two primary facets of the conservative worldview: there is, first, a resistance to **change**; and there is, second, an acceptance of specific principles. With some trepidation (for I know that, as **Buckley** once put it, conservatives "eschew the recital of our credenda"), I discuss those principles below—and in dialectical form no less. But I begin here with the old bugbear of standpattism, of stick-in-the-muddishness, of reaction, of resistance. It is a matter to be considered both in the personal realm, where we experience it as an *inclination*, and in the political realm, where we understand it as part of a *philosophy*. My hope is to make clear that this, the most apparently vulnerable aspect of the conservative worldview (certainly the one most commonly belittled), is in fact not a weakness of character—not a fear of change or of life—but an indispensable accompaniment of personal and cultural sanity.

I. RESISTANCE TO CHANGE

The first of the soul's needs, the one which most nearly
touches its eternal destiny, is order . . .
   —Simone Weil, *The Need for Roots* (1952)

Think simply of little things. For instance: Each morning at six I arise, fetch the papers from the front walk, sit with my wife at the breakfast table—she with tea, I with coffee—and, before our children stumble down the stairs, we read ourselves awake. No matter how I might think about the way the world works—or ought to work—surely I would have such a morning routine. This is habit. Habit may seem a trivial matter, but habits reflect our most fundamental orientation to living. The things we do again and again, with so little variation in how we do them, mental things and physical things, are the keys to comfort, contentment, and character. If every morning we awakened unable to follow a routine, we can only imagine how disconcerted and downcast we would be. We'd hardly be human. But because we are human, we are *conservative* about the things we love. We want them near us always; we want them as they are, although we acknowledge that part of the reality of things—people especially—is their *becoming*.

Habits Good and Bad

The creation of a habit is an organic process. Habits emerge from practice, and largely from successful practice, although that success is usually unintended. And, true, success alone is not a sufficient measure of a habit's *goodness*. There are bad habits, whether personal or cultural—nail biting or racism. Evil can succeed and become habitual, but more frequently it is the constancy of goodness (of virtue and, to a lesser extent, pleasure) that arises slowly from experience to give spontaneous validity to our actions. Good or bad, big or small, it is a fact about habits that we live with them (with pride or regret), and to a very great extent they define us.

Habits may not be contrived. We may plan a daily routine, but it becomes habit—if it does—only when the affectation becomes unaffected; when the abstraction becomes organic. This is why bad habits are so difficult to break. Cigarette smoking is hard to stop only partly because of nicotine addiction; at least as powerful is the *concreteness* of the habit: "smoking" is an actuality the force of which dwarfs the abstraction, "Don't smoke." Nature, which is conservative, abhors the cold-turkey cure, whether or not it promises to be the most efficient, healthiest course of action.

Change constantly affects habits. The good gets better, although it can also get worse. The bad can become deadly, but it can be transformed into righteousness as well. In fact, change is constant, although mostly subtle and slow. My hair thins, my waist thickens, and although I am the same man, I don't look the same at forty as I did at twenty. I have some regrets about this. But, thank God, such organic transformation is gradual, indeed imperceptible, except at class reunions. Every age has its graces, and we slowly adjust. But if we went to bed one night at forty and awakened the next morning at eighty we would be deprived of the gradual reformation of body and mind that with time allows us to age gracefully. Grace (not the theological kind) in change is continuity in knowledge and action.

What is true of individuals is true of communities—of towns, states, and the nation. We cannot change our habits overnight, nor should we wish to. Just as we must accept ourselves as we are before we can begin to contemplate a personal reformation, so must we accept the **community** before we attempt to change it. As **Eliot** observed: "Only by acceptance of the past will you alter its meaning." And great cultural changes, as Jacques Barzun has written (1959), "begin in affectation and end in routine." Among other things, it would seem then that even the most radical innovator must, by his own definition of success, look forward in his triumph to a conservative retirement.

The Blue World

There are, of course, disordered individuals and provinces for whom or which the above simply cannot apply. Self-acceptance, let alone love, is a specious prerequisite for either a murderous psychopath or a poisonous tyranny. But for the rest us, abstract principles—however noble (abstinence from cigarettes, for instance, or "racial" color-blindness)—must be assimilated gradually. Instant transformation does a person little good; that which is easily changed is easily changed again. The process of turning change into habit is necessarily protracted. True, a person may, in the best sense, be "born again," and if a change is thus providential, it hardly matters how fast it comes. However, if one looks closely at such religious transformations, one sees that the instant change is narrow, however deep it may be. A truth is suddenly understood, but the implications of that truth may take a lifetime to grasp (we are so complicated, and as broad as we are deep), and without an equally rigorous commitment to seeking those implications (and making them habitual), the new truth will simply be swallowed up—gnawed on anyway—by old habits. The revelation may endure, but we and others will be only too painfully aware of a wearing hypocrisy, which, as La Rochefoucauld observed, "is the homage which vice pays to virtue."

Rarely are individuals or nations so dysfunctional that rapid and substantial changes are required. And even when such changes are needed, psychology and history demand skepticism concerning the probability of *successful* revolutionary change. Conservatism's scruples are not simply a reluctance to relinquish the comfortable past; they are rather a refusal to embrace an uncertain future. Since 1789, every single one of history's brutal despotisms has been a bold leap into chaos and away from **tradition**. Whereas, to use the famous observation of Thomas Carlyle, all *great* peoples are conservative: "slow to believe in novelties; patient of much error in actualities; deeply and forever certain of the greatness that is in law, in custom once solidly established, and now recognized as just and final." Of course, having recently re-read Charles Dickens' *A Tale of Two Cities* and Simon Schama's *Citizens*, I am not nostalgic for the pre-**Enlightenment** structure of social life. "Class," in the sense of a fixed caste, (and like "race" or sex) is an absurd structural discipline in society. But . . .

But, as **Chesterton** so elegantly put it in his parable of the man determined to make the whole world better by coloring it blue, we—all of us, the azure activist included—need *fixed ideals* from which to work. If our reformer "altered his favorite colour every day," his world would be nothing but chaos. Granted that Chesterton's point here does not address the specifics of public policy; still his insight ought to temper every impulse to change the world. It does not matter, he wrote in *Orthodoxy* (1908), "how often humanity fails to imitate its ideal; for then all its old failures are fruitful. But it does frightfully matter how often humanity changes its ideal; for then all its old failures are fruitless." This is the sense behind **Churchill**'s most conservative remark that the "maxim of the British people"— and this applies equally to Americans—"is business as usual." We need our usual business and our fixed ideals—our traditions. And what are they if not society's habits?

II. REFORMATION AND PRINCIPLE

Make the Revolution a parent of settlement, and not a
nursery of future revolutions.

  —**Burke**, *Reflections on the Revolution in France* (1790)

And speaking of history's violent upheavals, we've lately heard a lot of
glib buzzing about a "conservative revolution" in America. The
phrase is virtually oxymoronic, although I don't know which of the
two words is the more abused.

Neither the process nor the results of the recent transfer of power
in Congress (consequences of the 1994 mid-term election) was violent, fundamental, or total. The institutions of government were not
toppled, and not a single Democrat was beheaded. Not one. This
was in no sense a revolution (the long existence of a two-party system
in America should make this clear enough), and yet if it had been, it
could hardly have been *conservative* too.

Trouble is, conservatism seems unable to escape assertions about
its affinity with the political status quo, as for instance in this typical
encyclopedia entry: ". . . in politics, the desire to maintain, or conserve, the existing order," which, if we accept the characterization,
suggests that a conservative might be **reactionary** but never revolutionary. But is a political conservative, as the word's root certainly indicates, simply one who conserves? William Safire seems to think so.
In his *New Political Dictionary* (1993), he defines conservative as "a
defender of the status quo." Yet if that is so, how do we explain that it
is precisely the status quo that has fired up the Republicans and is the
target of their reform proposals?

The Tyranny of the Status Quo

The simple answer is: *Conservatism, the political philosophy as opposed
to the personal inclination, has nothing whatsoever to do with maintaining the status quo (or a status quo ante), and it never really has.* The familiar definitions simply have it wrong, although the misconception
is understandable. While conservatism *does not* champion regnant
conditions in society, it *does* resist rapid, rationalist redesign of society. It's not change conservatives oppose but social experimentation,

particularly of the sort that imposes simplistic bureaucratic solutions upon complex social problems (one thinks of the Clinton health-care proposals). What conservatism resists, in the words of **Aron** (1978), is "the possibility of a final regime that would overcome the contradictions of previous regimes and be immune to the constituent laws of human societies as such."

A more developed definition of political conservatism must emphasize the balance between orthodoxy and **liberty**. Complex and occasionally contradictory, *political* conservatism is the counterpoise of the prescriptive inheritance of tradition and the disruptive innovations of freedom; between, for instance, the ageless stability of the Ten Commandments and the instantaneous innovations of the Internet.

The new congressional majority (to the extent that it actually is conservative) is neither *arrière-garde* nor avant-garde. A political conservative ought not to be a standpatter, and he must not be a revolutionary. He can, however, be a reformer because, in Chesterton's formulation (again in *Orthodoxy*), "reform implies form."

> It implies that we are trying to shape the world in a particular image; to make it something that we see already in our minds. Evolution [by which Chesterton meant the mechanistic, Darwinian view applied to society] is a metaphor from mere automatic unrolling. Progress is a metaphor from merely walking along a road—very likely the wrong road. But reform is a metaphor for reasonable and determined men: it means that we see a certain thing out of shape and we mean to put it into shape. And we know what shape.

The Contract with America proposed by **Gingrich** is in this sense a conservative *reform* proposal. It represents a break with the status quo, but it is neither reactionary—not an exercise in nostalgia—nor revolutionary—not a severance from tradition. And the realignment we are witnessing is not a Conservative Revolution but the fulfillment (or, in any case, the continuance) of what might better be called the **Reagan** Reformation.

There's no Lenin in Speaker Gingrich, but there is a lot of Luther. Maybe too much, but that's not for this essay to consider.

III. THE DIALECTICS OF PRUDENCE

No dictum in traditional Christian doctrine strikes such
a note of strangeness to the ears of contemporaries, even
contemporary Christians, as this one: that the virtue of
prudence is the mold and "mother" of all the other
cardinal virtues, of justice, fortitude, and temperance. In
other words, none but the prudent man can be just,
brave, and temperate, and the good man is good in so far
as he is prudent.

    —Joseph Pieper, *The Four Cardinal Virtues* (1954)

An earlier entry in this book presented several versions of the characteristic tenets of the right-wing *Weltanschauung*. The lists of a **Kirk** or
a **Nisbet** are as good as any others. Well, better in fact. And I offer my
own ordering of conservatism's principles here, not because I have
anything new to propose, but simply because I believe a tidy and *comparative* enumeration may be helpful to some readers, and is anyway
appropriate in this book. The following is dialectical, because I believe
that every conservative principle casts its "liberal" shadow. Actually, it
goes deeper than that. In my preface I noted that "the conservative
mind—and the principles that lead to and derive from it—did not
(indeed could not) exist until the West found itself squinting into the
bright promises and glaring illusions of the Enlightenment." I might,
therefore, be accused of construing conservatism's content to be
largely, if not wholly, reactionary. Not so. I may be a bit Manichaean,
but I'm not the least reactionary, and neither is this list. My main mo-
tivation in constructing a comparative inventory is simply to make
clear both what we are for and what we are against.

I apologize in advance for the literary awkwardness of some of the
"isms" discussed. I should also note that there is some overlap among
the categories. This is, I believe, inevitable when discussing what are
after all organic realities.

Six Theses

The question of where to begin is easily answered: We begin at the beginning, at the most basic orientation of the human mind to existence

and experience. Conservatism is realistic; its opposite is relativistic. And so the first position on the list of dichotomies is:

1. Realism v. **relativism**. Conservatism insists there is an objective **order** in reality that is independent of our subjective conceptions of it. The *real*, understood in any category of experience, is set apart from both the *ideal* and the *relative*. Hegel and Marx were both idealists *and* relativists. No thing, Hegel insisted, can be completely real, nor can any idea be absolutely true. The implication of this (so famously incorporated in the dialectical materialism of Marx) is that "truth" (*not* just our understanding of it) changes progressively in the clash of opposing historical forces. Latter-day theorists in fields as wide-ranging as religious philosophy and literary analysis have personalized the historical context and used relativism to deny the possibility of objective, universal agreement on any subject. As Jeffrey Burton Russell writes (1986), in his analysis of the modern conceptions of evil, a void has been created in this century by the decline of the religious version of realism:

> This vacuum has to some extent been filled by Marxism (itself a variety of religion) and liberal progressivism, both of which profess a faith that humanity will advance . . . This Faustian trust in humanity's ability to solve its own problems, along with a baseless faith in the goodness of human nature, has reduced intuitions of good and evil to psychological phenomena unrooted in any transcendent reality and explained in physical, mechanistic terms. The result is a vague but pervasive moral relativism. Popular relativism assumes that we know nothing absolutely except the proposition that we know nothing absolutely. No values are transcendent; all are wholly relative according to individual or societal preference. Truth also depends upon preference: endless intellectual fads grip Western intellectual circles one after another, because the criterion for the validity of an idea has become its novelty rather than its approximation to truth.

Conservative realism, in opposition to relativism, is the modern embodiment of traditional natural-law theory. Without belief in **natural law**, there can be no agreement about right and wrong (or true and false, reality or fantasy), or rather such concord as might be reached will have neither immutability nor stability. As Dostoevsky has Ivan Karamazov state it: "Without God, anything is permissible." And Jean-Jacques Rousseau, who was not engaged in parody, proclaimed that in his relativistic, Man-centered social contract "it can no longer be asked whether the law can be unjust," because justice is whatever the majority (the "general will") says it is. There are in this reckoning no transcendent standards. (No wonder that Voltaire, upon reading Rousseau's *Discourse on Inequality* (1754), proclaimed: "I have received your new book against the human race and thank you for it. Never was such cleverness used in making us all stupid! One longs, in reading the book, to walk on all fours.")

In fact, if we cannot agree about premises—let alone if we deny that there may be premises—society must degenerate into disorder . . . or have order imposed through force and terror.

Besides, all philosophizing aside, as **Popper** wrote (1985): "Common sense is clearly on the side of realism . . ."

2. <u>Skepticism v. progressivism</u>. Conservatism differs from much of contemporary welfare **liberalism** in an especially fundamental matter: their respective views of **human nature**. Although, admittedly, it is an oversimplification, we may say, tentatively at least, that conservatives believe Man is fallen, and liberals believe he may become an angel. Of course, a conservative may actually be more likely to believe in the possibility of sainthood (and many liberals know that an angel is a created being which no human can "become"), but liberals are definitely more likely to believe that Man's innate goodness may, through "education," lead eventually, progressively to heaven on earth. Put in the simplest terms: conservatives believe that Man must be bound; liberals that he must be liberated. As our friend Rousseau put the liberal case in *Social Contract* (1762), in the new society Man "must be forced to be free." The implication of this in terms of policy prescription is huge. Conservatives must struggle to keep in play the traditional restraints of **family**, community, and religion, while liberals will frequently see those institutions as constituting "oppressions" which must be overthrown. (See **feminism**.) Trouble is, once those "oppressions" are gone, only tyranny will reign. No conservative may be a utopian, although that does not mean that conservatives are

unable to imagine a "better world" (see "evolutionism v. constructivism" and "theism v. secularism" below). What conservatives cannot believe is that human nature has changed one iota since God had Noah build a boat, or that human beings are evolving towards perfection. Most conservatives believe that Man's salvation, individually and collectively, depends upon the recognition of the capacity for <u>sin</u>.

Indeed, what conservatism is most skeptical about is Man's nature, and herein lies the chasm separating many contemporary conservatives from liberals. In 1751, Rousseau won an essay contest the point of which was to address the question of the salutary impact of science upon manners in 18th-century France. In *Discourse on the Sciences and Arts*, Rousseau began developing the theme that was to be the great "insight" of his literary career and would become, in one form or another, a motif of later liberalism. It came to him, Rousseau said, in a dream: "Man is naturally good, but our social institutions have rendered him evil." No wonder that he saw salvation in terms of dictatorship, of individuals submitting completely to the "general will."

It is more prudent to accept that Man's nature is divided, and prudence, as Burke wrote in *Appeal from the New to the Old Whigs* (1791), "is not only first in the rank of the virtues political and moral, she is the director, the regulator, the standard of them all." It has been suggested that Burke was neither pessimistic nor progressive but realistic. That seems right. Skepticism about human nature may be seen by many as pessimistic, but it seems to me simply unromantic, objective, *realistic* . . . true.

3. <u>Evolutionism v. constructivism</u>. Conservatism maintains that the evolved order is preferable to the constructed order. *Constructivism* is the term favored by **Hayek**, but "interventionism" or "rationalism" or even "liberalism" (at least as we have come to know it in the last fifty years) are essentially synonymous; their meanings converging upon that impulse to shape institutions according to the passions of political theory and/or present conflict. There are many people who frequently assert that America has always been and ought always to be a liberal polity. But the character of the Founding and the spirit of our history tell another story. As Daniel Boorstin writes (1953):

Our [American] geography and history have led us to an unspoken assumption, an axiom, so basic to our thinking that we have hardly been aware of it at all. This is the axiom that institutions are not and should not be the grand creations of men toward large ends and outspoken values; rather they are organisms which grow out of the soil in which they are rooted and out of the tradition from which they have sprung. Our history has fitted us, even against our will, to understand the meaning of conservatism. We have become exemplars of the continuity of history and of the fruits which come from cultivating institutions suited to a time and place, in continuity with the past.

In a similar vein, Francis G. Wilson said (1951) that conservatism is "a philosophy of social evolution," which has been the consistent view—the "stance"—of conservative opinion from Burke to Hayek. But it must be emphasized that the evolution spoken of here is not a *teleological* evolution. This is to say that conservatism is *not* synonymous with social Darwinism, although the Englishman Herbert Spencer and the American **Sumner**—early influences on the development of modern conservative thought—certainly did champion a distinctly survival-of-the-fittest social theory. However, the evolutionary process conservatism *properly* champions does not confuse (as both Spencer and Sumner probably did confuse) the process with the results; does not see society as a single organism that is growing or evolving through stages leading to ever-increased perfection—that is responding to the laws of history or science to become, inevitably, more highly developed—but rather sees society as an entity that naturally adapts in terms of its present shape; a shape determined by the individual choices of millions of men and women over the course of the generations. It is an evolution that may be, to a very limited degree, observed but which cannot be favorably affected by the application to it of radical measures derived from abstract theories. Even *effective* constructivism ultimately fails. As I put it elsewhere (1995), the nature of evolved society tames the power of all governments: "Before the collapse of state socialism it was less possible to assert this with confidence, but it is now clear that even the apparatus of terror, mastered in this century by Nazis and communists, is unable to shape to its ends the complex aspirations of a people."

The best illustration of this dichotomy is language. A handful of liberals—pretty screwy ones at that—have for years been beating the drums for Esperanto. What we need, they claim, is a *lingua franca* that can not only help speakers of different languages to communicate, but can also represent the aspiration for international unity. Trouble is, Esperanto (like Basic English and other such experiments) has none of the evolved richness of English, French, or Russian. Not only has there never been an Esperantan Hemingway, Flaubert, or Dostoevsky, there never could be. You can't invent or construct a language any more than you can invent a literary heritage, a social structure, or a constitutional tradition. Praxis makes perfect.

4. **Federalism** v. statism. Conservatism views the proper structure of government as limited, divided, and therefore balanced. Above all, government must not be above all. This is against Hegel's notion of the state as the "ultimate end which has the highest right against the individual."

Federalism is not exactly synonymous with **limited government**, but the spirit behind its American application is the recognition that individuals, families, communities, and even the states largely stand above the national government, given that the national government has within its orbit certain areas of sovereignty in which its power is (and ought to be) superior to the rest. (Two examples of those areas might be the waging of war and the building of interstate highways.) There is a single, simple principle that explains why this "upside-down pyramid" should be so. Call it: the Responsibility Principle.

The Responsibility Principle leads inevitably towards limited government and away from statism, because it places the individual— and those affinities closest to him—at the source of both happiness (virtue) and misery (evil). The more responsibility is assigned to and accepted by individuals, the stronger the communities, local and national. The more a person does for himself, the more fulfillment he takes from his life. The more people do for themselves, the less Big Brother needs to do for them.

Charles **Murray** (1988) uses the upside-down pyramid image to illustrate the way in which individuals derive satisfaction (happiness) from life:

> ... [T]he most privileged people are those with the largest number of options for finding satisfying ways of filling up the hours of their lives. The more privileged you are, the more options you have for pursuing happiness. ... I begin from the assumption that in a good society, *everyone* may pursue happiness, not just the smart or the rich or the gifted. But the pyramid of options for achieving happiness narrows rapidly as gifts narrow, and the people at the bottom of the socioeconomic ladder are often not only the poorest people and the least educated, but also those with the fewest *options* for achieving happiness. Whence the upside-down pyramid.

Rich, well-educated people, Murray goes on to say, may have *more* options but not necessarily *better* ones, and what matters most to rich man and poor man alike is the approbation of the "little platoon" (Burke's phrase) to which he belongs. Dr. Henry Kissinger's platoon may be more widely visible than the neighbors, co-workers, and friends of Mr. Henry Klutz, but both Henrys find fulfillment in the quite small world of their peers. "Affiliations" is the sociologist's word. We need, Murray says, "*rich* affiliations, imbued with responsibility and effort, used as a way of living according to one's beliefs . . ."

This view of personal life is mirrored in the conservative view of public life. We need to take responsibility for ourselves—each for his own individual education, employment, and entertainment—and government must be structured to reflect the primacy of individual responsibility. This means the national government must assume as little responsibility as possible where individuals, families, communities, and the states are able do what ought to be done. By this interpretation, the pyramid of *political organization* ought to be set right—at the wide base, where most people live, most power ought to be most widely diffused. As we go higher on the pyramid, there ought to be less power more narrowly concentrated. Thus the right-side-up pyramid is simply a graphical expression of **subsidiarity**.

[Although it is not directly applicable to the subject of federalism, I must add here that America's two-party system is among our more conservative institutions, and a key to the preservation of the American Way. Although it has no constitutional basis, this *de facto* limitation of political access has served to keep Americans united in aims, and, in spite of the nation's growth over two hundred twenty years, has allowed us to operate as though the United States were still young, small, and unified. Two parties dedicated to essentially similar platforms have helped to maintain a consensus that ought to be the envy of the world, and it's a consensus—structurally guaranteed by the two-party system—that accepts change reluctantly and rejects radical change entirely. Thus, after twenty years of lurching slowly leftward, the movement of the Democratic Party is towards the center, which is to say, towards the **Right**.]

Murray sums up his argument for subsidiarity (my interpretation, not his word) with a statement that I consider as perspicacious as any ever made by a social scientist:

> [H]appiness depends crucially on taking trouble over things that matter. *There must be a stopping point, some rule by which governments limit what they do for people*—not just because of budget constraints, not just because of infringements on freedom (though either of these might be sufficient reason in itself), but because happiness is impossible unless people are left alone to take trouble over important things.

This does not even take into account the proven inefficiency of government, because it need not. Were the public sector actually better at doing things than the private sector it would make no difference. The state cannot invent; it cannot create; it cannot teach; it cannot love.

5. **Capitalism** v. collectivism. Conservatism insists that individual economic decisions and individual ownership are the required accompaniment of political **liberty**. **Private property** is one of our few, true **natural rights**. According to **Weaver**, it has become our "last metaphysical right." In this, we do well to look to the "Austrians," and to the observations of Israel Kirzner concerning the "finders-keepers" character of economic reality. People are fundamentally entitled to *keep* the benefits of their insight, labor, and prudence—their "findings." The implications of this for public policy are quite simply staggering, because it implies that every revenue-enhancing act of government is a theft. Of course . . .

Some conservative critics of capitalism, **Will** for instance, worry that the marketplace may not necessarily reward truth and virtue, and they are right. The free market at century's end is as often the tawdry trade in vulgarity as it is the elegant engine of creativity. How can it be otherwise, Man being Man? But conservatives embrace the market because, with all its wretched excess, it is, in union with religion, our best guarantor of liberty; in this case, because mobile money puts real power in many hands. Thus the power of capitalism, as much as federalism, checks the power of the state.

And finally,

6. Theism v. secularism. One might think that this pair ought to have come first. After all, God *is* first. But the fact is religious **faith** is not an essential of conservatism. Realism and its attendant belief in natural law (or at least in objective truth) are required of the conservative, but theism, belief in a personal, omnipotent God, is not. I believe that the divorce of natural law from the assumption of its divine ordination is definitely peculiar and probably fallacious, but realism, skepticism, federalism, evolutionism, and capitalism may be embraced without an accompanying religious faith. They certainly are in practice. I know plenty of agnostic and even a few atheistic conservatives.

Why then include "theism v. secularism" at all? Because few conservatives, from Burke to Buckley, have not acknowledged the essential role of faith in the prescriptive character of right order. As Peter Kreeft has written (1990):

> There cannot really be moral absolutes without God; there cannot be an absolute moral law without an absolute moral lawgiver. But we can know the effect without knowing the cause: we can know the moral law without knowing the moral lawgiver, just as we can know God's natural effects in science without knowing God as the Creator-cause of these effects. There can't be the effect without the cause, but you can know the effect without knowing the cause.

Conservatism is never very far from its roots in religion.

And religion presents conservatism with a curious challenge, even an "existential contradiction" if you will. **Acton** proclaimed, "Christ is risen on the world and fails not." Man is fallen, yet God calls Man. Religious men and women live in hope—of heaven, certainly, but also of earth changed by love. As Stephen Tonsor writes (<u>Meyer</u>, 1964), ". . . Acton and Tocqueville understood both the necessity of faith and hope and the necessity of immediate political action." Both men were, Tonsor insists, pessimists on the subject of human nature and yet optimists about "overriding Providence." And so he quotes <u>Tocqueville</u>:

> I cannot believe that the Creator made man to leave him in an endless struggle with the intellectual wretchedness that surrounds us. God destines a calmer and a more certain future . . . I am ignorant of his designs, but I shall not cease to believe in them because I cannot fathom them, and I had rather mistrust my own capacity than his justice.

This is conservatism with teleology in its proper place.

Religious faith is thus important for two reasons: (1) it is true, and its truth gives meaning quite simply to everything (and the meaning of nothing may truly be known without reference to God); and (2) it is (some will find this ironic) the only sure protection against <u>absolutism</u>—whether of the Left or the Right. The point here may be simply stated: In order to be free, we must be obedient. "Freedom," <u>Chambers</u> wrote (1952), "is a need of the soul, and nothing else." Political freedom, he went on, is simply the West's reading of the Bible. "Religion and freedom are indivisible."

It remains only to mention that religious orthodoxy must never attempt to overmaster individual liberty. Because God made us free, obedience must never be compelled.

The Answer to All Our Problems

In what policy directions, one may justifiably wonder, do these principles point us? Above all, I believe, conservatism ought to aspire to the gradual strengthening of local communities—which I would define as entities no larger than small towns or the neighborhoods within large cities—so that much of the present apparatus of city, county, state and, especially, national government may be dismantled and passed down to localities. It is not, please note, so much that the *functions* of government need to be abandoned as that those functions need to be devolved. There is, for instance, nothing intrinsically wrong with <u>welfare</u> that a local-community approach could not easily reform. Frankly, if one community decides to leave its poor and homeless cold and alone on the streets in winter and another to provide cradle-to-grave support, conservatives—ones anyway who live elsewhere—can have no essential complaint, even though neither approach is properly conservative.

What ought to sicken the conservative is the incessant palaver about "national" solutions; the kind of talk that derives from the worst version of natural rights—the notion that *all Men are* ... whatever they are supposed to be or become, desire or deserve. Too many Americans have become enamored of a constitutionally inappropriate *policy nationalism*; of that brittle view that Congress, whether dominated by liberals or conservatives, ought to be charged with addressing—let alone with solving—"our" problems.

There are two errors that derive from policy nationalism. The first is the belief that the political process ought to be an ideological struggle to gain control of the mechanisms of concentrated power. This is transparently foolish. As a conservative, I'm apparently supposed to be thrilled (and I hear this all the time from my liberal friends) that "we" have managed to put our hands on the controls. But I am not thrilled, and I will not be until most of the "controls" in Washington have been crated up and shipped back to the states, and to the communities, and to the people, which is where such tools belong. I can imagine having not only a conservative Congress, and a conservative Court, but once again a conservative White House too, but on that fine day the conservatives who will roll up their sleeves to pursue right-wing policies at, for instance, the Department of Education will be engaged in acts of self-deception. For unless they abolish that **bureaucracy** (and so many, many others) the time will come—and soon—when liberal Democrats will take their places.

This first error of policy nationalism is tactical, and it affects conservatives and liberals alike. Instrumentalist policies can, given the swings of public opinion, be as easily undone as done. But the second error is a much more serious matter. It is, of course, the effect that the locus of power has upon the citizenry's sense of civic (and *personal*) responsibility.

I read the recent headline from Moscow and shivered. To learn that "COMMUNISTS LEAD THE RULING PARTY BY 2 TO 1

IN RUSSIA" is to be reminded that dependency is the main consequence of centralized power. After nearly three generations of Communist rule, many Russians are incapable of accepting the personal
responsibility that is the singular requirement of self-rule. Americans
have traditionally, almost instinctively, understood this. Once—and
here is my only venture into nostalgia—we knew we had to rely
upon ourselves; that as a whole people we had to be as each individual: as we grew (as *persons* and as *a people*), we grew in independence.
The very nature of what we used to call "upbringing" was coopera-
tion based upon self-reliance. You were a lousy parent if your children turned out to be incapable of getting on in the world when they
reached maturity. And this overarching value imbued the lives of
everyone at every level, from bootblack to bank president. And the
poor man and the rich man affirmed their lives in exactly the same
way: by helping first themselves, then their children, families, businesses, communities, and finally their nation to stand, as we used to
say, "on their own two feet."

Can we be this way again? The answer is yes. Most Americans are
still self-reliant and civic-minded, and those who are not may learn
from the example of those who are, if—and only if—dependence-
creating government bureaucracy stops standing between its citizens,
frustrating their God-given ability to care for one another when difficulties arise, and to inspire one another to achieve the good life.

And if this were not reason enough to devolve, there remains the
problem that blights all policy nationalism: the *Complexity Principle*.
Simply stated, the Complexity Principle holds that American society
is protean, and that it is utterly erroneous to suppose we can understand it. But, especially since the New Deal (and the war that followed it), we have become ever more convinced that we may
understand society by the artful employment of generalizations:
poor, middle-class, and rich; black, white, Hispanic, and Asian;
young, middle-aged, and old. We generalize, because there is no
other way to "comprehend" the complexity. Without ubiquity we
would be forced to face particularity; we would be forced to *discrimi-
nate*, which of course has the primary meaning of recognizing distinctiveness. We have grown blind to the fact that every one of our

treasured categories is a phantasm. There are no groups; there are only individuals.

And the answer to all our problems is nothing more or less than the embrace of the self-evident truth that "all men are created equal." If we honored that truth through policy, government would quickly shrink to its proper size.

We must not forget that we are *created*—made by God—and that in this fundamental creative act equality is identical with liberty. This great truth is finally what true conservatives want to conserve, and it explains why there is no real contradiction between libertarian economics and moral order.

A Conservative Reading List

A Dozen Volumes (and More) for a Basic Library

I am a little uneasy about suggesting a direction to another's reading, and yet because I am often asked, "What books ought I to read in order to understand conservatism?", I offer this short annotated list.

1. Russell Kirk's *The Conservative Mind: From Burke to Eliot* (1953/1985) is probably the first book most Rightish pundits would recommend, and it is an indispensable book. There is none other like it; no other book that so thoroughly covers the intellectual development of Anglo-American **conservatism** from the end of the 18th century until the middle of the 20th. Among the book's virtues is its forceful and thoughtful presentation of the great **Burke**'s thought. Read through once, *The Conservative Mind* provides a solid grounding in conservatism; kept at hand, it is a dependable reference; an essential accompaniment to further reading. A much shorter (about 100 pages long versus **Kirk**'s 500) is Robert Nisbet's *Conservatism: Dream and Reality* (1986). Although appallingly copy edited by the University of Minnesota Press, **Nisbet**'s little book is lively and remarkably comprehensive. And it gives attention to European conservatives such as **Bonald** and **Maistre**. And even though it is not about conservatism, per se, Forrest McDonald's *Novus Ordo Seclorum: The Intellectual Origins of the Constitution* (1985) is a must read for conservatives. Much of the contemporary debate about the direction of America's future makes reference—whether explicit or implicit—to the nation's *character*. Who are we really? Who are we supposed to be? If we know who we are, we will know where we are headed. Inevitably such references must address the *character* of the **Constitution**, and no book has ever done that with the grace and authority of *Novus Ordo Seclorum*. To be an American **conservative** is in large measure to be a constitutionalist, and I have often wished I could, like a character out of Ray Bradbury's *Fahrenheit 451*, simply

memorize McDonald's book, at which point my American conservatism would be . . . graceful and authoritative.

2. Russell Kirk's *The Portable Conservative Reader* (1982) is in some ways preferable to Kirk's more famous tome above. This anthology is arranged chronologically in seventeen sections from "The Tension of Order and Freedom" to "Resistance and Hope." All the important thinkers are included: Burke, of course; the American Founders: John **Adams**, **Ames**, and **Hamilton**; English writers, some known, others forgotten (at least by most of us): **Coleridge** and Southey, Lecky and Mallock; on through more than fifty selections, ending with contemporary American voices: **Kristol**, Nisbet, and Kirk himself. Few anthologies have ever offered the motivated reader so much satisfaction. And if you are wondering why on earth Edmund Burke's *Reflections on the Revolution in France* (1790) is not on this recommended list, it's because Kirk excerpts so much of the book in this anthology (and discusses it at length in *The Conservative Mind*). A more up-to-date collection is *Keeping the Tablets: Modern American Conservative Thought*, edited by William F. Buckley, Jr. and Charles R. Kesler (1988). This volume is an updated version of **Buckley**'s 1970 selection, which was entitled *American Conservative Thought in the 20th Century* (or in its trade paperback edition, *Did You Ever See A Dream Walking?*) This is a first-rate selection of essays representing the range of conservative thinking, from Kirk to **Meyer**, **Podhoretz** to **Nock**. Finally, is it all right for me to mention my own anthology *Good Order* (1994)? These collected essays (from thirteen writers including Neuhaus, **Gilder**, Charles **Murray**, and **Sowell**) address conservatism's five "orders": spiritual, social, economic, political, and cultural.

The reader of both of the books of Russell Kirk recommended above will sense a wistful quality to conservatism as he presented it. Although the edition of *The Conservative Mind* most widely available today is the seventh, revised by Dr. Kirk in 1985, and although *The Portable Conservative Reader* was published just a year before that, there is none of the now familiar triumphalism of the Reagan Reformation and the Newt Deal. Conservatives are by faith skeptics, but the generation which came of age in the shadow of ascendant **communism** abroad and insidious secularism at home was often downright pessimistic. Perhaps this is best. After all, optimists are inevitably meddlers, and ascendant conservatism will implode as soon as it becomes utopian.

3. George H. Nash's *The Conservative Intellectual Movement in America*

Since 1945 (1976) is without the slightest doubt the definitive history of contemporary American conservatism, up to the Reagan era. (With *The Conservative Mind*, it is the most frequently cited work in this book.) The great virtue of Nash's scholarship is its marriage of history and philosophy; he tells you who did what and, more important, *why*. And as a sobering update to Nash's scholarly survey, read David Frum's *Dead Right* (1994), a provocative critique of the failures of conservatism written from the standpoint of its greatest successes. Frum's book sent a chill through newly expansive conservatism, with its sobering reminder that the point of capturing power was not just to exploit its many channels but also to dam and drain some of them.

4. G. K. Chesterton's *Orthodoxy: The Romance of Faith* (1908) is my favorite book, one I've read half a dozen times. There is no political prescription in this book, no policy, and **Chesterton** was certainly not a thoroughgoing conservative (think of his curious views about economics), but withal *Orthodoxy* is one of the most deeply conservative books ever written—about Man's spiritual crisis; about the reality he faces and the creeds that sustain him. The consequences of civic life without those creeds is the subject of Richard John Neuhaus's *The Naked Public Square* (1984). Not "uplifting" in the way *Orthodoxy* is, *The Naked Public Square*—with its emphasis upon the "turmoil over the connections between laws and the law, between law and life"—is inspiring in its sobering reminder that "history was not created for nothing," and that **community** life lived without reference to the Author of history invites tyranny.

5. Whittaker Chambers' *Witness* (1952/1980) does present a profoundly conservative spirit, but it goes on my list only secondarily as any sort of primer of conservative thought. It is here primarily because I fear that young people, especially, will soon be utterly blasé about communism, and **Chambers** offers the cure. It's not that I believe Marx and Lenin are likely to make a comeback (although this morning's paper brought news of Reds on the march again in Moscow), but that I very definitely believe that—sooner than we'd like to think—some as yet undreamed-of **ideology** will begin herding bright young people into its fold. No one has ever made the reasons for resistance more clear than did Chambers. Alternatively, Richard Crossman's *The God That Failed* (1949), while not a "conservative" book—in that its contents reflect few of the principles of conservatism besides anti-statism—offers eloquent testimonies by its distinguished literary contributors that thoroughly dispel the romance of ideology. There are six essays: two by Americans (Richard Wright and Louis Fisher); two by Britons (Stephen

Spender and Arthur Koestler, who was originally Hungarian); and two by Europeans (the Frenchman André Gide, and the Italian Ignazio Silone). This book's publication was an important moment in the Cold War.

6. Leo Strauss' *Natural Right and History* (1950) may turn out to be—of all the books discussed in this section (if not of all the books listed in the bibliography that follows)—the most important. I say "may turn out to be," knowing full well that it is already considered a seminal classic, because nothing is more important in the preservation of civilization than the belief that the past matters, and because no one ever defended the West (or refuted its attackers) with more conviction and refinement than did **Strauss**. This book is the last word in the argument over **relativism**. James Burnham's *Suicide of the West: An Essay of the Meaning and Destiny of Liberalism* (1964) has lost none of its power in the more than thirty years since it was first published. The West had been contracting. Why? Not because of any external pressures—although there were plenty (communism again)—but because liberal intellectuals were engaged in a protracted felo-de-se. No one ever detailed the destructive aspects of **liberalism** as thoroughly and thoughtfully as **Burnham**. I like William F. Buckley, Jr.'s *Up From Liberalism* (1959) as much as any of the great man's books. The *Harvard Crimson* called it "Pernicious, toxic, and disastrous," which ought to be enough to recommend it to any conservative. According to John Dos Passos, who wrote the book's foreword, the liberalism Buckley assails is "the ideological camouflage of the will to power" of the intellectual class. Buckley doesn't just excoriate liberals; he also teaches conservatives how to "agonize more meticulously."

7. F. A. Hayek's *The Fatal Conceit: The Errors of Socialism* (1988) is just one of **Hayek**'s many books that one might recommend. *The Constitution of Liberty* (1960), or the three-volume *Law, Legislation, and Liberty* (1976–1982), or the epoch-making *The Road to Serfdom* (1944) are just as valuable, but *The Fatal Conceit* has the virtue of being Hayek's most accessible book. Don't let the subtitle fool you into supposing that this is yet another pedantic blow struck against the old dead horse. It is the final summa of the **Right**'s most eloquent, libertarian champion of **individualism**. What is the "fatal conceit"? Simply this: "that man is able to shape the world around him according to his wishes." Although it is a vastly different book than Hayek's, I must make mention of Robert Nozick's *Anarchy, State, and Utopia* (1974), because it is also "libertarian," but more importantly because it is so astonishingly well written. Few philosophical books have the twin qualities this one does: clarity and hilarity.

8. Milton and Rose Friedman's *Free to Choose: A Personal Statement* (1979) is, as the blurb on my paperback copy puts it, a "classic about economics, freedom, and the relationship between the two ..." It is that, and—in part because it was based upon a television series of the same name—it is an eminently *readable* classic. Basically, the Friedmans have written a primer on the unity of political **liberty** and economic freedom. They combine historical theory and policy prescription in a way that convinces the reader that careful thought and purposeful action need not be divorced. The only other book purely on the "dismal science" I can bear to suggest is Henry Hazlitt's *Economics in One Lesson* (1946). (See Paragraph 11 below where I contradict myself.) Like **Friedman**, Hayek, **Mises**, and **Smith, Hazlitt** demonstrates that our economic lives depend upon our acceptance of limited knowledge in a world of unlimited decisions.

9. Michael Oakeshott's *Rationalism in Politics and Other Essays* (1962) is, for us conservatives anyway, the magnum opus of the man the *London Times* called "one of the few outstanding philosophers of the 20th century." It is a challenge to read, in part because **Oakeshott**'s work reflects his unparalleled scholarship—it is as complex and layered as the messy human realities it analyzes. The book is a wholly convincing lesson in the axiom that politics ought not to be the end of life, and is notable especially for the inclusion of his famous essay "On Being Conservative." A book that shares with Oakeshott's an intellectual acuity rare in analytic philosophy is Kenneth Minogue's *Alien Powers: The Pure Theory of Ideology* (1985). No other work has ever so coolly dissected the illusions of our contemporary ideologues: Marxists, feminists, and others, all of whom share the "great discovery . . . that modern European civilization, beneath its cleverly contrived appearances, is the most systematically oppressive despotism the world has ever known." How *do* they manage to think so? Read Minogue.

10. Richard M. Weaver's *Ideas Have Consequences* (1948) is often listed with Hayek's *The Road to Serfdom*, Kirk's *The Conservative Mind*, and Robert Nisbet's *The Quest for Community* (1953) as one of the seminal works of modern conservatism. No less an authority on *Kultur Krankheit* than Reinhold Niebuhr called **Weaver**'s book "a profound diagnosis of the sickness of our culture." Here is the Southern agrarian analysis in summary (if not final) form. But the book is more than simply a regionalist's testament; it is a reaffirmation of the West's animating ideal: belief in transcendent **order**.

11. George Gilder's *Wealth and Poverty* (1981) was, with the possible exception of Charles Murray's *Losing Ground* (1984) and Allan Bloom's *The*

Closing of the American Mind (1987), the Book of the 1980s. To say that *Wealth and Poverty* was simply the textbook of **supply-side** theory is to miss the qualities in it that make Gilder's the prophetic voice it is. He makes the case, yes, but he stirs the soul as he does. To me, this is not really a book about economics at all, but rather an affirmation of, as the book's final chapter puts it, "The Necessity of Faith."

12. Paul Johnson's *Modern Times: The World from the Twenties to the Eighties* (1983, updated in 1991) presents the history of our peculiar century with elegance and authority, and its message is clear: the earth is turning gradually, fitfully away from "A Relativistic World" towards "Palimpsests of Freedom"; the lesson to be learned was simple: "Throughout these years, the power of the State to do evil expanded with awesome speed. Its power to do good grew slowly and ambiguously." A work of history which deals more specifically with the conservative origins of the United States is Russell Kirk's *The Roots of American Order* (1974). This is an ambitious work, tracing the "American" ideals of liberty and order from their geneses in ancient Israel through to their exposition in the work of Orestes Bownson.

13. Irving Kristol's *Neoconservatism: The Autobiography of an Idea* (1995) is not exactly what its subtitle might suggest (i.e., a history and an explication of neoconservatism), and is in fact (as a second subtitle informs) "Selected Essays, 1949–1995." Many of these essays have appeared previously in other collections of Kristol's work; indeed, in publishing, the work of an essayist often follows a path similar to that of a poet, in that the most recent collection largely duplicates earlier ones but is obviously more comprehensive and current than those that went before. In this case, two-thirds of the essays in *Neoconservatism* appeared in earlier books—principally *Two Cheers for Capitalism* (1978) and *Reflections of a Neoconservative* (1983). Notably missing from the new collection is Kristol's incisive commentary on foreign policy, but present are many of the essays that have made him renowned as the conservative movement's finest intellect.

Finally, a subscription to *National Review* seems to me an indispensable adjunct to the books listed above. There are other superb periodicals, but no other that can be depended upon for the consistent provision of both first-rate education and entertainment.

All the main books herein presented (plus a year's worth of *National Review*) may be purchased for around $200.00; to my mind, a bargain at ten times the price.

Bibliography

Including Books Consulted for or Cited in
The Concise Conservative Encyclopedia

[N]ote: In listing these books, I have occasionally indicated two dates, which are separated by a slash. The first date is the year of original publication;/the second is the year of either a reissue or a revision. And I have omitted the word "Press" from the names of publishers associated with universities.]

Ackroyd, Peter. *T. S. Eliot: A Life*. Simon & Schuster, New York, 1984.

Acton, Lord (John Emerich Dalberg, 1st Baron). *Essays in Religion, Politics, and Morality*, J. Rufus Fears, ed. Liberty Classics, Indianapolis, IN, 1988.

———. *The History of Freedom and Other Essays*. Macmillan, London, 1922.

Adams, Brooks. *The Law of Civilization and Decay*. Vintage, New York, 1895/1955.

———. *The Theory of Social Revolutions*. Macmillan, New York, 1913.

Adams, Henry. *Democracy: An American Novel*. Meridian Classics, New York, 1880/1983.

———. *The Education of Henry Adams*. Vintage Books/Library of America, New York, 1918/1990.

———. *John Randolph*. Robert McColley, ed. M. E. Sharpe, Armonk, NY, 1882/1996.

———. *Mont Saint-Michel and Chartres*. Penguin, New York, 1913/1986.

Adams, James T. *The Adams Family*. Greenwood, Westport, CT, (1930/1974)

Adams, John. *Defense of the Constitutions of Government of the United States*. Da Capo, New York, 1787/1971.

———. *Thoughts on Government*. Da Capo, New York, 1776/1971.

Agar, Herbert. *A Declaration of Faith*. Houghton Mifflin, Boston, 1952.

Allitt, Patrick. *Catholic Intellectuals and Conservative Politics in America: 1950–1985*. Cornell University, Ithaca, NY, 1995.

Anderson, Martin. *Revolution: The Reagan Legacy*. Hoover Press, Stanford, CA, 1988/1990.

Arnold, Matthew. *Culture and Anarchy*. Samuel Lippmann, ed. Yale University, New Haven, 1994.

Aron, Raymond. *Democracy and Totalitarianism: A Theory of Political Regimes*. Praeger, New York, 1969.

———. *Main Currents in Sociological Thought*. 2 vols. Basic Books, New York, 1965.

———. *Memoirs: Fifty Years of Political Reflections*. Holmes & Meier, New York, 1983.

———. *The Opium of the Intellectuals*. Doubleday, Garden City, NY, 1957.

———. *Politics and History: Selected Essays by Raymond Aron*. Miriam Bernheim Conant, ed. Free Press, New York, 1978.

Ashford, Nigel, and Stephen Davies, eds. *A Dictionary of Conservative and Libertarian Thought*. Routledge, New York, 1991.

Ausmus, Harry J. *Will Herberg: From Right to Right*. University of North Carolina, Chapel Hill, 1987.

Babbitt, Irving. *Democracy and Leadership*. Liberty Press, Indianapolis, IN, 1924/1979.

———. *Rousseau and Romanticism*. Transaction Publishers, New Brunswick, NJ, 1919/1991.

Bagehot, Walter. *Bagehot's Historical Essays*. Norman St. John-Stevas, ed. Doubleday, Garden City, NY, 1965.

———. *The English Constitution*. Cornell University, Ithaca, NY, 1867/1966.

———. *Physics and Politics*. Knopf, New York, 1872/1948.

Banfield, Edward C. *Here the People Rule: Selected Essays*. American Enterprise Institute Press, Washington, DC, 1991.

———. *Political Influence*. Free Press, New York, 1961.

———. *The Unheavenly City Revisited: The Nature and the Future of Our Urban Crisis*. Little, Brown, Boston, 1968/1974.

Bartlett, Bruce R. *Reaganomics: Supply-Side Economics in Action*. Morrow, New York, 1981.

Bartley, Robert L. *The Seven Fat Years: And How to Do It Again*. Free Press, New York, 1992.

Barzun, Jacques. *The House of Intellect*. Harper & Row, New York, 1959.

———. *The Culture We Deserve* Wesleyan University, Middletown, CT, 1989.

———. *The Teacher in America*. Little, Brown, Boston, 1944/54.

Bastiat, Frédéric, *The Law*. FEE, Irvington-on-Hudson, NY, 1850/1961.

———. *Economic Harmonies*. Van Nostrand, Princeton, NJ, 1964.

———. *Selected Essays on Political Economy*, Russell Dean, ed. Foundation for Economic Education, Irvington-on-Hudson, NY, 1995.

Becker, Carl. *The Declaration of Independence: A Study in the History of Political Ideas*. Knopf, New York, 1922/1972.

Becker, Gary. *A Treatise on the Family*. Harvard University, Cambridge, MA, 1981.

Bell, Bernard Iddings. *Crowd Culture*. Ayer, North Stratford, NH, 1952/1977.

Bell, Daniel. *The Cultural Contradictions of Capitalism*. Basic Books, New York, 1975.

———. *The End of Ideology*. Harvard University, Cambridge, MA, 1960/1988.

———. *The Winding Passage: Essays and Sociological Journeys, 1960–1980*. Basic Books, New York, 1980.

———, et al. *The Radical Right*. Doubleday, Garden City, NY, 1963.

Bendix, Reinhard, ed. *Embattled Reason: Essays on Social Knowledge*. Oxford University, New York, 1970.

Bennett, William J. *The Book of Virtues*. Simon & Schuster, New York, 1993.

———, and Terry Eastland. *Counting by Race: Equality from the Founding Fathers to Bakke and Weber*. Basic Books, New York, 1979.

Berger, Brigitte, and Peter L. Berger. *The War Over the Family*. Doubleday, New York, 1983.

Berger, Peter L., Brigitte Berger, and Hansfried Kellner. *The Homeless Mind: Modernization and Consciousness*. Random House, New York, 1973.

Bernard, Winfred, *Fisher Ames: Federalist and Statesman*. University of North Carolina, Chapel Hill, 1965.

Berns, Walter, *The First Amendment and the Future of American Democracy*. Basic Books, New York, 1976.

———. *In Defense of Liberal Democracy*. Regnery, Chicago, 1984.

———. *Taking the Constitution Seriously*. Simon & Schuster, New York, 1987.

Bierce, Ambrose. *The Enlarged Devil's Dictionary*. E. J. Hopkins, ed. Doubleday, Garden City, NY, 1967.

Blackstone, William. *Commentaries on the Laws of England*. 4 vols. University of Chicago, Chicago, 1765–69/1979.

Blake, Robert. *Disraeli*. St. Martin's, New York, 1966.

Bloom, Allan. *The Closing of the American Mind: How Higher Education Has Failed Democracy and Impoverished the Souls of Today's Students*. Simon & Schuster, New York, 1987.

———. *Giants and Dwarfs*. Simon & Schuster, New York, 1990.

———. *Love & Friendship*. Simon & Schuster, New York, 1993.

Boorstin, Daniel J. *The Americans: The Democratic Experience*. Random House, New York, 1973.

———. *The Decline of American Radicalism: Reflections on America Today*. Random House, New York, 1963.

———. *The Genius of American Politics*. University of Chicago, Chicago, 1953.

———. *The Mysterious Science of the Law: An Essay on Blackstone's Commentaries*. Harvard University, Cambridge, MA, 1941.

Bork, Robert H. *The Tempting of America: The Political Seduction of the Law*. Free Press, New York, 1990.

Bradford, M. E. *A Better Guide Than Reason*. Sherwood Sugden, Peru, IL, 1979.

———. *The Reactionary Imperative: Essays Literary and Political*. Sherwood Sugden, Peru, IL, 1990.

———. *Remembering Who We Are: Observations of a Southern Conservative*. University of Georgia, Athens, GA, 1985.

Brick, Howard. *Daniel Bell and the Decline of Intellectual Radicalism*. University of Wisconsin, Madison, WI, 1986.

Brinton, Crane. *The Anatomy of Revolution*. Prentice-Hall, Englewood Cliffs, NJ, 1938/65.

Brock, David. *The Real Anita Hill*. Free Press, New York, 1993.

Brookes, Warren T. *The Economy in Mind*. Universe Books, New York, 1982.

Brooks, Cleanth, and Robert Penn Warren. *Understanding Poetry*. Holt, Rinehart and Winston, New York, 1960.

Brownson, Orestes. *The American Republic: Its Constitution, Tendencies, and Destiny*. Americo D. Lopati, ed. College & University, New Haven, CT, 1972.

———. *Orestes Brownson: Selected Political Essays*. Russell Kirk, ed. Transaction, New Brunswick, NJ, 1990.

Buchan, Alastair. *The Spare Chancellor.* Chatto and Windus, London, 1959.

Buchanan, James M. *Better Than Plowing and Other Personal Essays.* University of Chicago, Chicago, 1992.

————. *Constitutional Economics.* Oxford University, New York, 1991.

————. *The Limits of Liberty: Between Anarchy and Leviathan.* University of Chicago, Chicago, 1975.

————, and Gordon Tullock. *The Calculus of Consent.* University of Michigan, Ann Arbor, 1962.

Buchholz, Todd G. *New Ideas from Dead Economists.* New American Library, New York, 1989.

Buckley, Priscilla, ed. *The Joys of National Review: 1955–1980.* National Review, New York, 1994.

Buckley, William F., Jr. *God and Man at Yale: The Superstitions of "Academic Freedom."* Regnery Gateway, Washington, DC, 1951/1977.

————. *Up from Liberalism.* Stein & Day, New York, 1959/1984.

————, and Charles Kesler. *Keeping the Tablets: Modern American Conservative Thought.* Harper & Row, New York, 1970/88.

————. *Racing through Paradise.* Random House, New York, 1987.

————, and Brent Bozell. *McCarthy and His Enemies: The Record and Its Meaning.* Regnery, Chicago, 1954.

Burke, Edmund. *Reflections on the Revolution in France.* Edited with an introduction by Conor Cruise O'Brien. Penguin Books, New York, 1790/1968.

————. *Selected Writings and Speeches.* Peter J. Stanlis, ed. Regnery, Washington, DC, 1963.

Burnham, James, *The Machiavellians: Defenders of Freedom.* Regnery, Washington, DC, 1943/1987.

————. *Suicide of the West: An Essay on the Meaning and Destiny of Liberalism.* Regnery Gateway, Washington, DC, 1964/1985.

————. *The Managerial Revolution, or What Is Happening in the World Now.* Penguin, New York, 1945.

————. *The Web of Subversion.* John Day, New York, 1954.

Burtchaell, James T. *Rachel Weeping: The Case Against Abortion.* Harper & Row, New York, 1982.

Butler, Lord, ed. *The Conservatives: A History from their Origins to 1965.* Allen & Unwin, London, 1977.

Butler, Stuart, and Anna Kondratas. *Out of the Poverty Trap: A Conservative Strategy for Welfare Reform.* Free Press, New York, 1987.

Calhoun, John C. *Union and Liberty: The Political Philosophy of John C. Calhoun.* Ross M. Lence, ed. Liberty Classics, Indianapolis, IN, 1992.

Canavan, Francis. *The Political Economy of Edmund Burke: The Role of Property in His Thought*. Fordham University, Bronx, NY, 1995.

Cappon, Lester J. *The Adams-Jefferson Letters*. University of North Carolina, Chapel Hill, NC, 1959.

Carey, George W. *Freedom and Virtue: The Conservative/Libertarian Debate*. University Press of America, Lanham, MD, 1984.

———. *In Defense of the Constitution*. Liberty Fund, Indianapolis, IN, 1989/1995.

Chambers, Whittaker. *Ghosts on the Roof: Selected Journalism of Whittaker Chambers, 1931–1959*. Terry Teachout, ed. Regnery Gateway, Washington, DC, 1989.

———. *Witness*. Regnery Gateway, Washington, DC, 1952/1980.

Charmley, John. *Churchill, The End of Glory: A Political Biography*. Harcourt Brace, New York, 1993.

Chesterton, G. K. *The Everlasting Man* in *The Collected Works of G. K. Chesterton*, vol. II. Ignatius Press, San Francisco, 1986.

———. *The Man Who Was Thursday*. Dodd, Mead, New York, 1908.

———. *Orthodoxy*. Image/Doubleday, New York, 1908/1990.

———. *The Victorian Age in Literature*. Holt, New York, 1913.

Chodorov, Frank. *Fugitive Essays: Selected Writing of Frank Chodorov*. C. H. Hamilton, ed. Liberty Press, Indianapolis, IN, 1980.

———. *One Is a Crowd*. Devin-Adair, New York, 1952.

———. *Out of Step*. Devin-Adair, New York, 1962.

Churchill, Winston S. *Blood, Sweat, and Tears*. Putnam, New York, 1941.

———. *The Second World War*. Introduction by John Keegan. Houghton Mifflin, Boston, 1995.

Cohen, Norman J., ed. *The Fundamentalist Phenomenon*. Eerdmans, Grand Rapids, MI, 1990.

Colaiaco, J. A. *James Fitzjames Stephen and the Crisis of Victorian Thought*. St. Martin's, New York, 1983.

Coleridge, Samuel Taylor. *Coleridge's Writings. Volume 1: Politics and Society*. John Morrow, ed. Princeton University, Princeton, NJ, 1991.

———. *Select Poetry and Prose*. Stephen Potter, ed. Noneshuch Press, London, 1971.

Colford, Paul *The Rush Limbaugh Story: A Talent on Loan from God*. St. Martin's, New York, 1993.

Como, James T. *C. S. Lewis at the Breakfast Table*. Harcourt, Brace, Jovanovich, New York, 1979.

Constant, Benjamin. *Adolphe*. Cambridge University, New York, 1815/1987.

Cooper, James Fenimore. *The American Democrat*. Liberty Press, Indianapolis, IN, 1838/1981.

———. *Notions of the Americans: Picked Up by a Travelling Bachelor*. State University of New York, Albany, NY, 1828/1991.

Coren, Michael. *Gilbert: The Man Who Was G. K. Chesterton*. Paragon, New York, 1990.

Cowan, Louise. *The Fugitive Group*. Louisiana State University, Baton Rouge, LA, 1956.

Cowling, Maurice. *Mill and Liberalism*. Cambridge University, New York, 1990.

Cram, Ralph Adams. *The End of Democracy*. Marshall Jones, Boston, 1937.

Crespigny, Anthony de, and Kenneth Minogue, eds. *Contemporary Political Philosophers*. Dodd, Mead, New York, 1975.

Cromartie, Michael. *No Longer Exiles: The New Religious Right in American Politics*. Ethics & Public Policy Center, Washington, DC, 1993.

Crossman, Richard, ed. *The God That Failed*. Harper & Brothers, New York, 1949.

Crozier, Brian, and Arthur Seldon. *Socialism: The Grand Delusion*. Universe, New York, 1986.

Crunden, Robert M. *The Superfluous Men: Conservative Critics of American Culture, 1900–1945*. University of Texas, Austin, TX, 1977.

Dale, Alzina Stone. *The Outline of Sanity: A Life of G. K. Chesterton*. Eerdmans, Grand Rapids, MI, 1982.

Davidson, Donald. *Regionalism and Nationalism in the United States [The Attack on Leviathan]*. Transaction, New Brunswick, NJ, 1938/1991.

Dawidowicz, Lucy S. *The War Against the Jews: 1933–1945*. Holt, Rinehart, and Winston, New York, 1975.

Decter, Midge, *Liberal Parents, Radical Children*. Coward, McCann, New York, 1975.

———. *The Liberated Woman and Other Americans*. Coward, McCann, New York, 1971.

———. *The New Chastity, and Other Arguments Against Women's Liberation*. Coward, McCann, New York, 1972.

DeMuth, Christopher, ed. *The Neoconservative Imagination: Essays in Honor of Irving Kristol*. American Enterprise Institute, Washington, DC, 1995.

Derrick, Christopher. *Church Authority and Intellectual Freedom*. Ignatius Press, San Francisco, 1981.

Dickinson, John. *Letters from a Farmer in Pennsylvania*. microfilm of 1769 edition by Wm. & Thos. Bradford, Philadelphia.

Disraeli, Benjamin. *Tancred, or the New Crusade.* Knopf, New York, 1847/1934.

Dolan, Edward, ed. *The Foundation of Modern Austrian Economics.* Sheed, Andrews & McMeel, Kansas City, 1976.

Donahue, John D. *The Privatization Decision: Public Ends, Private Means.* Basic Books, New York, 1989.

Dorrien, Gary. *The Neoconservative Mind: Politics, Culture, and the War of Ideology.* Temple University, Philadelphia, 1993.

Drucker, Peter F. *Men, Ideas, and Politics.* Harper & Row, New York, 1971.

Drury, Shadia B. *The Political Ideas of Leo Strauss.* St. Martin's, New York, 1988.

D'Souza, Dinesh. *Illiberal Education: The Politics of Race and Sex on Campus.* Free Press, New York, 1991.

Duggan, Francis X. *Paul Elmer More.* Twayne, New York, 1966.

East, John P. *The American Conservative Movement: The Philosophical Founders.* Regnery, Washington, DC, 1986.

Eastman, Max. *Love and Revolution.* Harper & Row, New York, 1965.

————. *Reflections on the Failure of Socialism.* Greenwood, Westport, CT, 1955.

Edwards, Lee. *Goldwater: The Man Who Made a Revolution.* Regnery, Washington, DC, 1995.

Edwards, Owen Dudley. *Macaulay.* St. Martin's, New York, 1988.

Eliot, T. S. *Christianity and Culture.* Harcourt, Brace, New York, 1939/1977.

————. *Collected Poems, 1909–1962.* Harcourt, Brace, New York, 1963.

————. *For Lancelot Andrewes: Essays on Style and Order.* Doubleday Doran, New York, 1929.

————. *Notes Towards a Definition of Culture.* Faber & Faber, London, 1948.

Evans, M. Stanton. *The Theme Is Freedom: Religion, Politics, and the American Tradition.* Regnery, Washington, DC, 1994.

Ferguson, Thomas P. *Catholic and American: The Political Theology of John Courtney Murray.* Sheed and Ward, Kansas City, MO, 1994.

Flower, Milton E. *John Dickinson: Conservative Revolutionary.* University of Virginia, Charlottesville, VA, 1983.

Foner, Eric, and John A. Garraty, eds. *The Reader's Companion to American History.* Houghton Mifflin, Boston, 1991.

Fontana, Biancamaria. *Benjamin Constant and the Post-Revolutionary Mind.* Yale University, New Haven, CT, 1991.

Francis, Samuel T. *Beautiful Losers: Essays on the Failure of Conservatism.* University of Missouri, Columbia, MO, 1993.

————. *Power and History: The Political Thought of James Burnham.* University Press of America, Lanham, MD, 1984.

Franco, Paul. *The Political Philosophy of Michael Oakeshott.* Yale University, New Haven, CT, 1990.

Friedman, Milton. *Capitalism and Freedom.* University of Chicago Press, Chicago, 1962.

————. *Monetarist Economics.* Basil Blackwell, Cambridge, MA, 1991.

————, and Rose Friedman. *Free to Choose: A Personal Statement.* Harcourt, Brace, Jovanovich, New York, 1980.

————, and Anna J. Schwartz. *A Monetary History of the United States, 1867–1960.* Princeton University Press, Princeton, NJ, 1963.

Frohnen, Bruce. *Virtue and the Promise of Conservatism: The Legacy of Burke and Tocqueville.* University of Kansas, Lawrence, KS, 1993.

Fryer, Russell G. *Recent Conservative Political Thought: American Perspectives.* University Press of America, Washington, DC, 1979.

Gablik, Suzi. *Has Modernism Failed?* Thames and Hudson, New York, 1984.

Genovese, Eugene D. *The Southern Tradition: The Achievements and Limits of an American Conservatism.* Harvard University, Cambridge, MA, 1994.

Germino, Dante. *Beyond Ideology: The Revival of Political Theory.* Harper & Row, New York, 1967.

Gilder, George. *Men and Marriage.* Pelican, Gretna, LA, 1986.

————. *Microcosm: The Quantum Revolution in Economics and Technology.* Simon & Schuster, New York, 1989.

————. *Visible Man: A True Story of Post-Racist America.* Basic Books, New York, 1978.

————. *Wealth and Poverty.* Basic Books, New York, 1981.

Gingrich, Newt. *To Renew America.* HarperCollins, New York, 1995.

Glazer, Nathan. *Affirmative Discrimination: Ethnic Inequality and Public Policy.* Basic Books, New York, 1975/1978.

Goldsmith, M. M. *Private Vices, Public Benefits.* Cambridge University, New York, 1985.

Goldwater, Barry M. *The Conscience of a Conservative.* Regnery, Chicago, 1960/1990.

————. *The Conscience of a Majority.* Prentice-Hall, Englewood Cliffs, NJ, 1970.

————. *With No Apologies: The Personal and Political Memoirs of United States Senator Barry M. Goldwater*. Morrow, New York, 1979.

————, with Jack Casserly. *Goldwater*. Doubleday, New York, 1988.

Gordon, Caroline, and Allen Tate. *The House of Fiction: An Anthology of the Short Story with Commentary*. Scribner's, New York, 1950.

Gordon, Robert J., ed. *Milton Friedman's Monetary Framework: A Debate with His Critics*. University of Chicago, Chicago, 1974.

Gottfried, Paul, and Thomas Fleming. *The Conservative Movement*. Twayne, Boston, 1988.

Gray, John. *Hayek on Liberty*. Basil Blackwell, New York, 1984.

————. *Liberalism*. University of Minnesota, Minneapolis, 1986.

————. *Liberalisms: Essays on Political Philosophy*. Routledge, New York, 1989.

Green, Roger L., and Walter Hooper. *C. S. Lewis: A Biography*. Harcourt, Brace, New York, 1974.

Grisez, Germain. *Christian Moral Principles*. Franciscan Herald, Chicago, 1983.

Guttman, Allen. *The Conservative Tradition in America*. Oxford University, New York, 1967.

Hamilton, Alexander, James Madison, and John Jay. *The Federalist Papers*. Clinton Rossiter, ed. Mentor, New York, 1788/1961.

————. *Selected Writings and Speeches*. Morton J. Frisch, ed. American Enterprise Institute, Washington, DC, 1985.

Hampsher-Monk, Iain. *A History of Political Thought*. Blackwell, Cambridge, MA, 1992.

Harbour, William R. *The Foundations of Conservative Thought: An Anglo-American Tradition in Perspective*. University of Notre Dame, Notre Dame, IN, 1982.

Harrell, David Edwin, Jr. *Pat Robertson*. Harper & Row, San Francisco, 1987.

Harrison, Gordon. *Road to the Right: The Tradition and Hope of American Conservatism*. Morrow, New York, 1954.

Hart, Jeffrey, *The American Dissent: A Decade of Modern Conservatism* (Doubleday, New York, 1966)

Hayek, F.A., *The Constitution of Liberty*. University of Chicago, Chicago, 1960.

————. *Economic Freedom*. Basil Blackwell, Oxford/Cambridge, MA, 1991.

————. *The Fatal Conceit: The Errors of Socialism*. University of Chicago, Chicago, 1988.

———. *Individualism and Economic Order*. University of Chicago, Chicago, 1948.

———. *Law Legislation and Liberty*. Volume I: *Rules and Order*. Volume II: *The Mirage of Social Justice*. Volume III. *The Political Order of a Free People*. University of Chicago, Chicago, 1976–1982.

———. *The Road to Serfdom*. With a new introduction by Milton Friedman. University of Chicago Press, Chicago, 1944/1994.

———. *The Essence of Hayek*. Chiaki Nishiyama and Kurt R. Leube, eds. Hoover Institution, Stanford, CA, 1984.

———, ed. *Capitalism and the Historians* (University of Chicago, Chicago, 1967)

Hazlitt, Henry. *Economics in One Lesson*. Crown, New York, 1946/1979.

Henderson, David R., ed. *The Fortune Encyclopedia of Economics*. Warner Books, New York, 1993.

Herbener, Jeffrey. *The Meaning of Ludwig von Mises*. Mises Institute, Auburn, AL, 1993.

Herberg, Will. *Four Existentialist Theologians*. Doubleday, New York, 1958.

———. *From Marxism to Judaism: Collected Essays of Will Herberg*. David G. Dalin, ed. Markus Weiner, New York, 1989.

———. *Protestant, Catholic, Jew: An Essay in American Religious Sociology*. Doubleday, New York, 1955/1960.

Himmelfarb, Gertrude. *Lord Acton: A Study in Conscience and Politics*. Knopf, New York, 1952.

———. *On Liberty and Liberalism: The Case of John Stuart Mill*. Knopf, New York, 1974.

Hobson, Fred. *H. L. Mencken: A Life*. Random House, New York, 1994.

Hoeveler, J. David. *The New Humanism: A Critique of Modern America, 1900–1940*. University of Virginia, Charlottesville, VA, 1977.

Hoffman, Nicholas von. *Citizen Cohn*. Doubleday, New York, 1988.

Hofstadter, Richard. *Social Darwinism in American Thought*. Beacon, Boston, 1955/1992.

Hook, Sidney. *Academic Freedom and Academic Anarchy*. Cowles, New York, 1970

———. *Heresy, Yes, Conspiracy, No*. John Day, New York, 1952.

———. *Out of Step: An Unquiet Life in the 20th Century*. Harper & Row, New York, 1987.

Howard, Thomas. *C. S. Lewis: Man of Letters*. Ignatius, San Francisco, 1987.

Hume, David. *Essays Moral, Political, and Literary*. Eugene F. Miller, ed. Liberty Press, Indianapolis, IN, c.1741–1777/1985.

————. *A Treatise of Human Nature*. Clarendon, Oxford, 1740/1958.

Hunt, Robert P., and Kenneth L. Grasso. *John Courtney Murray and the American Civil Conversation*. Eerdmans, Grand Rapids, MI, 1992.

Hutchins, Robert M. *Freedom, Education, and the Fund: Essays and Addresses: 1946–1956*. Meridian Books, New York, 1956.

————. *The Great Conversation*. University of Chicago, Chicago, 1948.

Hyneman, Charles S., and Donald S. Lutz, eds. *American Political Writing in the Founding Era: 1760–1805*, 2 vols. Liberty Press, Indianapolis, IN, 1983.

Jaffa, Harry V. *The Condition of Freedom: Essays in Political Philosophy*. Johns Hopkins University, Baltimore, MD, 1975.

————. *The Condition of Freedom: Essays in Political Philosophy*. Johns Hopkins University, Baltimore, MD, 1975.

————. *The Crisis of the House Divided*. University of Chicago, Chicago, 1959.

————. *Equality and Liberty: Theory and Practice in American Politics*. Oxford, New York, 1965.

————, ed. *Statesmanship: Essays in Honor of Sir Winston Churchill*. Carolina Academic, Durham, NC, 1981.

————, and Allan Bloom. *Shakespeare's Politics*. Basic Books, New York, 1964.

Jardin, André. *Tocqueville: A Biography*. Farrar, Straus and Giroux, New York, 1988.

Jefferson, Thomas. *Thomas Jefferson: Writings*. Merrill D. Peterson, ed. Library of America, New York, 1984.

John Paul II, Pope. *Crossing the Threshold of Hope*. Knopf, New York, 1994.

————. *Sign of Contradiction*. Crossroad, New York, 1979.

Johnson, Paul. *Intellectuals*. Harper & Row, New York, 1988.

————. *John Paul II and the Catholic Restoration*. St. Martin's, New York, 1981.

————. *Modern Times: The History of the World from the 20s to the 90s*. HarperCollins, New York, 1992.

Johnston, William B., and Arnold H. Packer. *Workforce 2000: Work and Workers for the 21st Century*. Hudson Institute, Indianapolis, IN, 1987.

Jouvenel, Bertrand de. *The Ethics of Redistribution*. Liberty Press, Indianapolis, IN, 1952/1990.

————. *On Power*. Liberty Press, Indianapolis, IN, 1948/1993.

————. *Sovereignty: An Inquiry into the Political Good*. University of Chicago, Chicago, 1957.

Judis, John B., *William F. Buckley, Jr.: Patron Saint of the Conservatives.* Simon & Schuster, New York, 1988.

Kahn, Herman. *The Coming Boom.* Morrow, New York, 1982.

———. *On Thermonuclear War.* Greenwood, Westport, CT, 1961/1978.

———. *Thinking About the Unthinkable.* Horizon Press, New York, 1962.

———, et al. *The Next 200 Years.* Morrow, New York, 1976.

———, et al. *The Year 2000.* Macmillan, New York, 1967.

Kelly, Alfred H., Winfred A. Harbison, and Herman Belz. *The American Constitution: Its Origins and Development,* 6th ed. W. W. Norton, New York, 1983.

Kendall, Willmoore. *The Conservative Affirmation in America.* Regnery, Chicago, 1963/85.

———. *John Locke and Majority Rule.* University of Illinois, Urbana, IL, 1941.

———. *Willmore Kendall Contra Mundum.* Nellie D. Kendall, ed. Arlington House, New Rochelle, NY, 1971.

———, and George W. Carey. *The Basic Symbols of the American Political Tradition.* Lousiana State University Press, Baton Rouge, LA, 1970.

Kennedy, John F. *Profiles in Courage.* Harper & Row, New York, 1956.

Kenner, Hugh. *A Homemade World: The American Modernist Writers.* Knopf, New York, 1975.

———. *The Invisible Poet.* McDowell, Obolensky, New York, 1960.

———, ed. *T. S. Eliot: A Collection of Critical Essays.* Prentice Hall, Englewood Cliffs, NJ, 1962.

Ketcham, James. *James Madison: A Biography.* University of Virginia, Charlottesville, 1990.

Kilpatrick, James Jackson. *The Southern Case for School Segregation.* Crowell-Collier, New York, 1962.

———. *The Sovereign States.* Regnery, Chicago, 1957.

Kimball, Roger. *Tenured Radicals: How Politics Has Corrupted Our Higher Education.* Harper & Row, New York, 1990.

Kirk, Russell. *Academic Freedom: An Essay in Definition.* Regnery, Chicago, 1955.

———. *The Conservative Constitution.* Regnery Gateway, Washington, DC, 1990.

———. *The Conservative Mind: From Burke to Eliot.* Regnery Gateway, Inc., Washington, DC, 1953/1985.

———. *Eliot and His Age: T. S. Eliot's Moral Imagination in the 20th Century,* 3rd ed. Open Court, Peru, IL, 1988.

————. *John Randolph of Roanoke: A Study in American Politics*. Liberty Press, Indianapolis, 1951/1978.

————. *Prospects for Conservatives*. Regnery Gateway, Washington, DC, 1989.

————. *The Roots of American Order*. Regnery Gateway, Washington, DC, 1974/1991.

————. *The Sword of Imagination: Memoirs of a Half-Century of Literary Conflict*. Eerdmans, Grand Rapids, MI, 1995.

————. *Wise Men Know What Wicked Things Are Written in the Sky*. Regnery Gateway, Washington, DC, 1987.

————, ed. *The Portable Conservative Reader*. Viking Penguin, New York, 1984.

————, and James McClellan. *The Political Principles of Robert A. Taft*. Fleet Press, New York, 1967.

Kirzner, Israel. *Discovery, Capitalism, and Distributive Justice*. Basil Blackwell, New York, 1990.

Klehr, Harvey, John Earl Haynes, and Fridrikh Igorevich Firsov. *The Secret World of American Communism*. Yale University, New Haven, CT, 1995.

Knight, Frank. *The Ethics of Competition*. Ayer, North Stratford, NH, 1935.

Kramer, Hilton, and Roger Kimball, eds. *Against the Grain: The New Criterion on Art and Intellect at the End of the 20th Century*. Ivan R. Dee, Chicago, 1995.

Kreeft, Peter. *Making Choices: Practical Wisdom for Everyday Moral Decisions*. Servant Books, Ann Arbor, MI, 1990.

————, ed. *Summa of the Summa*. Ignatius Press, San Francisco, 1990.

Kristol, Irving. *Neo-Conservatism: The Autobiography of an Idea*. Free Press, New York, 1995.

————. *On the Democratic Idea in America*. Harper & Row, New York, 1972.

————. *Reflections of a Neoconservative: Looking Back, Looking Ahead*. Basic Books, New York, 1983.

————. *Two Cheers for Capitalism*. Basic Books, New York, 1978).

Kronenberger, Louis, ed. *Atlantic Brief Lives: A Biographical Companion to the Arts*. Atlantic–Little, Brown, Boston, 1965.

Labaree, Leonard W. *Conservatism in Early American History*. New York University, New York, 1948.

Lewis, C. S. *The Abolition of Man*. Macmillan, New York, 1947.

————. *The Essential C. S. Lewis*. Lyle W. Dorsett, ed. Macmillan, New York, 1988.

————. *Mere Christianity*. Macmillan, New York, 1943.

————. *The Screwtape Letters*. Macmillan, New York, 1959.

Limbaugh, Rush. *The Way Things Ought to Be*. Pocket Books, New York, 1992.

Lincoln, Abraham. *Speeches and Writings: 1859–1865*. Library of America, New York, 1984.

Lipman, Samuel. *Arguing for Music, Arguing for Culture*. Godine, Boston, 1990.

Lippmann, Walter. *An Inquiry into the Principles of the Good Society*. Little, Brown, Boston, 1937.

————. *The Public Philosophy*. Little, Brown, Boston, 1955.

Lipset, Seymour Martin. *The First New Nation: The United States in Historical and Comparative Perspective*. Basic Books, New York, 1963.

————, and Earl Raab. *The Politics of Unreason: Right-Wing Extremism in America, 1790–1970*. Harper & Row, New York, 1970.

Locke, John. *An Essay Concerning Human Understanding*. Clarendon, Oxford, 1690/1975.

————. *Second Treatise on Government*. C. B. Macpherson, ed. Hackett, Indianapolis, IN, 1690/1980.

Lomasky, Loren, *Persons, Rights, and the Moral Community*. University of Chicago, Chicago, 1987.

Long, Robert E. *James Fenimore Cooper*. Continuum, New York, 1990.

Lynch, Frederick R. *Invisible Victims: White Males and the Crisis of Affirmative Action*. Praeger, New York, 1991.

Lyons, Eugene. *The Red Decade: Stalinist Penetration of America*. Arlington House, New Rochelle, NY, 1970.

Macaulay, Thomas Babington. *Critical and Historical Essays*. Hugh Trevor-Roper, ed. McGraw Hill, New York, 1965.

————. *The History of England, 1485–1685*. Folio Society, London, 1985.

Machan, Tibor. *Capitalism and Individualism: Reframing the Argument for the Free Society*. St. Martin's, New York, 1990.

MacIntyre, Alasdair. *After Virtue*. University of Notre Dame, Notre Dame, IN, 1981.

Magnet, Myron. *The Dream and the Nightmare*. Morrow, New York, 1993.

Maine, Henry Sumner. *Popular Government*. Liberty Classics, Indianapolis, IN, 1886/1976.

Maistre, Joseph de. *The Works of Joseph de Maistre*. Jack Lively, ed. Macmillan, New York, 1965.

Mandeville, Bernard. *The Fable of the Bees*. 2 vols. Liberty Press, Indianapolis, IN, 1714–30/1988.

Mansfield, Harvey C., Jr. *America's Constitutional Soul*. Johns Hopkins University, Baltimore, 1991.

———. *The Spirit of Liberalism.* Harvard University, Cambridge, MA, 1978.

———. *Taming the Prince: The Ambivalence of Modern Executive Power.* Johns Hopkins University, Baltimore, 1989.

Mapp, Alf J., Jr. *Thomas Jefferson: A Strange Case of Mistaken Identity.* Madison Books, Lanham, MD, 1987.

Maritain, Jacques. *Integral Humanism: Temporal and Spiritual Problems of a New Christendom.* Scribner's, New York, 1968.

———. *Man and the State.* University of Chicago, Chicago, 1951.

———. *The Rights of Man and Natural Law.* Scribner's, New York, 1943.

Markham, Ian. *Plurality and Christian Ethics.* Cambridge University, New York, 1995.

Marris, Peter. *Loss and Change.* Routledge, London, 1974.

McCarthy, Joseph R. *McCarthyism: The Fight for America.* Devin-Adair, New York, 1950.

McDonald, Forrest, *Alexander Hamilton: A Biography.* W. W. Norton, New York, 1979.

———. *Novus Ordo Seclorum: The Intellectual Origins of the Constitution.* University of Kansas, Lawrence, KS, 1985.

———. *We the People: The Economic Origins of the Constitution.* Transaction, New Brunswick, NJ, 1958/1992.

McLean, Edward B., ed. *Derailing the Constitution: The Undermining of American Federalism.* ISI, Bryn Mawr, PA, 1995.

Mencken, H. L. *Prejudices: A Selection.* James T. Farrell, ed. Knopf/Vintage, New York, 1919/1955.

Meyer, Frank. *The Conservative Mainstream.* Arlington House, New Rochelle, NY, 1969.

———. *In Defense of Freedom.* Regnery, Chicago, 1962.

———; ed. *What Is Conservatism?* Holt, Rinehart and Winston, New York, 1964.

Mill, John Stuart, *Essays on Politics and Culture.* Gertrude Himmelfarb, ed. Doubleday, Garden City, NY, 1962.

———. *On Liberty and Other Essays.* John Gray, ed. Oxford University, New York, 1859/1991.

Miller, David, et al., eds. *The Blackwell Encyclopaedia of Political Thought.* Blackwell, London, 1987/91.

Miner, Brad, ed. *Good Order.* Simon & Schuster, New York, 1995.

———, and Charles J. Sykes, eds. *The National Review College Guide.* Simon & Schuster, New York, 1991/1993.

Minogue, Kenneth. *Alien Powers: The Pure Theory of Ideology*. St. Martin's, New York, 1985.

————. *The Liberal Mind*. Random House, New York, 1963.

————. *Politics: A Very Short Introduction*. Oxford, New York, 1995.

————, and Michael Biddiss, eds. *Thatcherism: Personality and Politics*. St. Martin's, New York, 1987.

Mises, Ludwig von, *Bureaucracy*. Yale University, New Haven, 1944.

————. *Human Action*. Contemporary, Chicago, 1949/1966.

————. *Socialism*. Liberty Fund, Indianapolis, IN, 1981.

————. *Theory of Money and Credit*. Harcourt, Brace, New York, 1935.

Molnar, Thomas. *Authority and Its Enemies*. Arlington House, New Rochelle, NY, 1976.

————. *Christian Humanism: A Critique of the Secular City and Its Ideology*. Franciscan Herald, Chicago, 1978.

————. *The Counter-Revolution*. Funk & Wagnalls, New York, 1969.

————. *Utopia: The Perennial Heresy*. University Press of America, Lanham, MD, 1990.

Montesquieu, Baron de. *Selected Political Writings*. Melvin Richter, ed. Hackett, Indianapolis, IN, 1990.

————. *The Spirit of the Laws*. Cambridge University, New York, 1748/1989.

More, Paul Elmer. *Demon of the Absolute*. Princeton University, Princeton, NJ, 1928.

————. *The Essential Paul Elmer More*. Byron C. Lambert, ed. Arlington House, New Rochelle, NY, 1972.

————. *Selected Shelburne Essays*. Oxford University, New York, 1935.

Morley, Felix. *For the Record*. Regnery, South Bend, IN, 1979.

————. *Freedom and Federalism*. Liberty Press, Indianapolis, 1959/1981.

Morris, Richard B. *Witnesses at the Creation: Hamilton, Madison, Jay, and the American Constitution*. Holt, Rinehart and Winston, New York, 1985.

Muccigrosso, R. *American Gothic: The Mind and Art of Ralph Adams Cram*. University Press of America, Washington, DC, 1981.

Muggeridge, Malcolm. *Chronicles of Wasted Time*. Regnery, Washington, DC, 1989.

————. *Confessions of a 20th-Century Pilgrim*. Harper & Row, San Francisco, 1988.

————. *Jesus Rediscovered*. Doubleday, Garden City, NY, 1969.

————. *Things Past*. Collins, London, 1979.

———. *Winter in Moscow*. Eerdmans, Grand Rapids, MI, 1934/1987.

Murray, Charles. *In Pursuit: Of Happiness and Good Government*. Simon & Schuster, New York, 1988.

———. *Losing Ground: American Social Policy, 1950–1980*. Basic Books, New York, 1984.

———, and Richard J. Herrnstein. *The Bell Curve*. Free Press, New York, 1994.

Murray, John Courtney. *We Hold These Truths: Catholic Reflections on the American Proposition*. Sheed and Ward, New York, 1960.

Nash, George H. *The Conservative Intellectual Movement in America Since 1945*. Basic Books, New York, 1976.

Neuhaus, Richard John. *The Catholic Moment: The Paradox of the Church in the Postmodern World*. Harper & Row, San Francisco, 1987.

———. *Doing Well and Doing Good*. Doubleday, New York, 1992.

———. *The Naked Public Square*. Eerdmans, Grand Rapids, 1984.

Newman, John Henry Cardinal. *Apologia Pro Vita Sua*. Image, New York, 1864/1956.

———. *The Idea of a University*. University of Notre Dame, Notre Dame, IN, 1873/1989.

Nisbet, Robert A. *Conservatism: Dream and Reality*. University of Minnesota, Minneapolis, 1986.

———. *History of the Idea of Progress*. Basic Books, New York, 1980.

———. *Prejudices: A Philosophical Dictionary*. Harvard University, Cambridge, MA, 1982.

———. *The Quest for Community: A Study in the Ethics of Order and Freedom*. ICS Press, San Francisco, 1953/1990.

———. *Twilight of Authority*. Oxford University, New York, 1975.

Nock, Albert Jay. *Memoirs of a Superfluous Man*. Regnery, Chicago, 1943/1964.

———. *Mr. Jefferson*. Harcourt Brace, New York, 1926.

———. *Our Enemy the State*. Morrow, New York, 1935.

———. *The State of the Union*. Charles H. Hamilton, ed. Liberty Press, Indianapolis, 1991.

Novak, Michael. *Confessions of a Catholic*. University Press of America, Lanham, MD, 1983.

———. *Freedom with Justice*. Harper & Row, San Francisco, 1984.

———. *The Joy of Sports: End Zones, Bases, Baskets, Balls, and the Consecration of the American Spirit*. University Press of America, Lanham, MD, 1988.

———. *The Spirit of Democratic Capitalism*. Madison Books, Lanham, MD, 1982/91.

Nozick, Robert. *Anarchy, State, and Utopia*. Basic Books, New York, 1974.

———. *The Examined Life: Philosophical Meditations*. Simon & Schuster, New York, 1989.

Oakeshott, Michael. *On Human Conduct*. Clarendon Press, Oxford, 1975.

———. *Rationalism in Politics*. Liberty Press, Indianapolis, 1962/1991.

———. *The Voice of Liberal Learning: Michael Oakeshott on Education*. Timothy Fuller, ed. Yale, New Haven, CT, 1989.

Oates, Stephen B., *With Malice Toward None: A Life of Abraham Lincoln*. Harper & Row, New York, 1977.

O'Brien, Conor Cruise. *The Great Melody: A Thematic Biography of Edmund Burke*. University of Chicago Press, Chicago, 1992.

Olasky, Marvin. *The Tragedy of American Compassion*. Crossway, Elgin, IL, 1992.

Oliver, Revilo P. *America's Decline: The Education of a Conservative*. Londinium, London, 1981.

O'Neill, William L. *The Last Romantic: A Life of Max Eastman*. Oxford University, New York, 1978.

Ostrom, Vincent. *The Meaning of American Federalism*. ICS Press, San Francisco, 1991.

Paine, Thomas. *Common Sense, The Rights of Man, and Other Essential Writings of Thomas Paine*. Sidney Hook, ed. Meridian, New York, 1969.

Palmer, R. R., and Joel Colton. *A History of the Modern World*. Knopf, New York, 1950/92.

Pangle, Thomas. *The Ennobling of America: The Challenge of the Postmodern Age*. Johns Hopkins University, Baltimore, 1991.

———. *Montesquieu's Philosophy of Liberalism: A Commentary on* The Spirit of the Laws. University of Chicago, Chicago, 1989.

Pattison, Robert. *The Great Dissent: John Henry Newman and the Liberal Heresy*. Oxford University, New York, 1991.

Peikoff, Leonard. *Objectivism: The Philosophy of Ayn Rand*. Meridian, New York, 1991.

Perkins, Mary Ann. *Coleridge's Philosophy: The Logos as Unifying Principle*. Oxford University, New York, 1994.

Pocock, J. G. A. *The Ancient Constitution and the Feudal Law*. Norton, New York, 1967.

Podhoretz, Norman. *Breaking Ranks*. Harper & Row, New York, 1979.

———. *Making It*. Harper & Row, New York, 1967.

——. *The Present Danger*. Simon & Schuster, New York, 1980.

Popper, Karl R. *Conjectures and Refutations: The Growth of Scientific Knowledge*. Harper & Row, New York, 1963.

——. *The Logic of Scientific Discovery*. Harper & Row, New York, 1959.

——. *The Open Society and Its Enemies*. 2 vols. Princeton University, Princeton, NJ, 1962/1971.

——. *The Poverty of Historicism*. Harper & Row, New York, 1957.

——. *Popper Selections*. David Miller, ed., Princeton University, Princeton, NJ, 1985.

——. *Unended Quest*. Harper & Row, New York, 1976.

Quinlan, Mary Hall. *The Historical Thought of the Vicomte de Bonald*. Catholic University, Washington, DC, 1953.

Radosh, Ronald. *Prophets on the Right: Profiles of Conservative Critics of American Globalism*. Simon & Schuster, New York, 1975.

Rahner, Karl. *Foundations of Christian Faith: An Introduction to the Idea of Christianity*. Crossroad, New York, 1978.

Rand, Ayn. *Atlas Shrugged*. Dutton, New York, 1957/1992.

——. *The Fountainhead*. New American Library, New York, 1943.

——. *Philosophy: Who Needs It*. Bobbs-Merrill, New York, 1982.

——. *The Virtue of Selfishness*. New American Library, New York, 1965.

Ransom, John Crowe. *Beating the Bushes*. New Directions, New York, 1972.

——. *The New Criticism*. Greenwood, Westport, CT, 1941.

——. *The World's Body*. Louisiana State University, Baton Rouge, LA, 1938.

——, et al. *I'll Take My Stand: The South and the Agrarian Tradition*. Louisiana State University, Baton Rouge, LA, 1930/1980.

Reagan, Ronald. *Ronald Reagan: An American Life*. Simon & Schuster, New York, 1990.

——. *Speaking My Mind: Selected Speeches*. Simon & Schuster, New York, 1989.

Reed, Ralph. *Politically Incorrect: The Emerging Faith Factor in American Politics*. Word Books, Dallas, TX, 1994.

Regnery, Henry. *Memoirs of a Dissident Publisher*. Harcourt, Brace, Jovanovich, New York, 1979.

Revel, Jean-François. *How Democracies Perish*. Doubleday, New York, 1984.

——. *The Totalitarian Temptation*. Doubleday, New York, 1977.

Rice, Charles. *50 Questions on the Natural Law*. Ignatius, San Francisco, 1993.

Richter, Melvin. *The Political Theory of Montesquieu.* Cambridge University, New York, 1977.

Riesman, David, with Nathan Glazer and Reuel Denney. *The Lonely Crowd: A Study of the Changing American Character.* Yale University, New Haven, 1950.

Ringe, Donald A. *James Fenimore Cooper.* Twayne, Boston, 1988.

Roberts, Paul Craig. *The Supply-Side Revolution.* Harvard University, Cambridge, MA, 1984.

Robertson, Pat. *America's Dates with Destiny.* Thomas Nelson, Nashville, TN, 1986.

Roche, George. *Fall of the Ivory Tower: Government Funding, Corruption, and the Bankruptcy of Higher Education.* Regnery, Washington, DC, 1994.

―――. *Free Markets, Free Men: Frédéric Bastiat.* Hillsdale College, Hillsdale, MI, 1993.

―――. *One By One.* Regnery, Washington, DC, 1990.

Rossiter, Clinton. *1787: The Grand Convention.* Macmillan, New York, 1966.

―――. *Alexander Hamilton and the Constitution.* Harcourt, Brace, New York, 1964.

―――. *Conservatism in America.* Harvard University, Cambridge, MA, 1955/1982.

―――. *Seedtime of the Republic.* Harcourt, Brace, New York, 1953.

―――, and James Lane. *The Essential Walter Lippmann: A Political Philosophy for Liberal Democracy.* Harvard University, Cambridge, MA, 1982.

Rothbard, Murray. *For a New Liberty.* Fox & Wilkes, San Francisco, 1973/1985.

―――. *Man, Economy, and State.* Mises Institute, Auburn, AL, 1962/1993.

Rozell, Mark J., and James F. Pontuso, eds. *American Conservative Opinion Leaders.* Westview Press, Boulder, CO, 1990.

Rubin, Louis D., ed. *The American South: Portrait of a Culture.* Lousiana State University, Baton Rouge, LA, 1980.

―――, and James Jackson Kilpatrick, eds. *The Lasting South.* Regnery, Chicago, 1960.

Rusher, William. *The Coming Battle for the Media.* Morrow, New York, 1988.

―――. *The Rise of the Right.* Morrow, New York, 1984.

Russell, Dean. *Frédéric Bastiat: Ideas and Influence.* Foundation for Economic Education, Irvington-on-Hudson, NY, 1969.

Russell, Jeffrey Burton. *Mephistopheles: The Devil in the Modern World.* Cornell University, Ithaca, NY, 1986.

Safire, William. *Safire's New Political Dictionary*. Random House, 1968/93.

Santayana, George. *Dominations and Powers: Reflections on Liberty, Society, and Government*. Scribner's, New York, 1951.

———. *The Last Puritan*. Scribner's, New York, 1936.

———. *Persons and Places*. Simon & Schuster, New York, 1944/1981.

———. *Soliloquies in England and Later Soliloquies*. University of Michigan, Ann Arbor, MI, 1922/1967.

Scammell, Michael. *Solzhenitsyn: A Biography*. Norton, New York, 1984.

Schall, James V., and George W. Carey, eds. *Essays on Christianity and Political Philosophy*. University Press of America, Lanham, MD, 1984.

Scharff, Edward E. *Worldly Power: The Making of the* Wall Street Journal. Beaufort, New York, 1986.

Schlafly, Phyllis. *A Choice Not an Echo*. Pere Marquette, Acton, IL, 1964.

———. *The Power of the Positive Woman*. Arlington House, New Rochelle, 1977.

Schumpeter, Joseph A. *Capitalism, Socialism, and Democracy*. Harper & Row, New York, 1962.

Scotchie, Joseph, ed. *The Vision of Richard Weaver*. Transaction, New Brunswick, NJ, 1995.

Shand, Alexander H. *Free Market Morality: The Political Economy of the Austrian School*. Routledge, New York, 1990.

Shaw, Peter. *The Character of John Adams*. University of North Carolina, Chapel Hill, NC, 1976.

Shils, Edward. *Tradition*. University of Chicago, Chicago, 1981.

Silver, Thomas B., and Peter W. Schramm. *Natural Right and Political Right: Essays in Honor of Harry V. Jaffa*. Carolina Academic, Durham, NC, 1984.

Simon, William E. *A Time For Truth*. Reader's Digest, New York, 1978.

Smant, Kevin J. *How Great the Triumph: James Burnham, Anticommunism, and the Conservative Movement*. University Press of America, Lanham, MD, 1992.

Smith, Adam. *The Wealth of Nations*. Liberty Press, Indianapolis, IN, 1976.

Smith, Geoffrey. *Reagan and Thatcher*. Norton, New York, 1991.

Smith, James Allen. *The Idea Brokers: Think Tanks and the Rise of the New Policy Elite*. Free Press, New York, 1991.

Sobran, Joseph. *Pensées: Notes for the Reactionary of Tomorrow*. Human Life Review, New York, 1985.

Solzhenitsyn, Aleksandr, *The Gulag Archipelago*. Harper & Row, New York, 1974.

————. *The Oak and the Calf.* Harper & Row, New York, 1980.

————. *One Day in the Life of Ivan Denisovich.* Farrar, Straus & Giroux, 1963.

Sommers, Christina Hoff. *Who Stole Feminism? How Women Have Betrayed Women.* Simon & Schuster, New York, 1994.

Sowell, Thomas. *Black Education: Myths and Realities.* McKay, New York, 1972.

————. *Civil Rights: Rhetoric or Reality?* Morrow, New York, 1984.

————. *Ethnic America.* Basic Books, New York, 1981.

————. *Inside American Education: The Decline, the Deception, the Dogmas.* Free Press, New York, 1993.

————. *Knowledge and Decisions.* Basic Books, New York, 1980.

————. *Marxism: Philosophy and Economics.* Morrow, New York, 1985.

————. *Preferential Policies: An International Perspective.* Morrow, New York, 1990.

————. *Race and Culture: A Worldview.* Basic Books, New York, 1994.

————. *The Vision of the Anointed: Self-Congratulation as a Basis for Social Policy.* Basic Books, New York, 1995.

Sproul, R. C. *Abortion: A Rational Look at an Emotional Issue.* NavPress, Colorado Springs, 1990.

Stanlis, Peter J. *Edmund Burke and the Natural Law.* Huntington House, Lafayette, LA, 1986.

————, ed. *Edmund Burke: Selected Writings and Speeches.* Regnery, Washington, DC, 1963.

Stannard, Martin. *Evelyn Waugh.* Vol. I: *The Early Years, 1903–1939.* Vol. II: *No Abiding City, 1939–1966.* J. M. Dent, London, 1986 and 1992.

Steel, Ronald. *Walter Lippmann and the American Century.* Little, Brown, Boston, 1980.

Steele, Shelby. *The Content of Our Character: A New Vision of Race in America.* St. Martin's, New York, 1990.

Steinfels, Peter. *The Neoconservatives: The Men Who Are Changing America's Politics.* Simon & Schuster, New York, 1979.

Stephen, James Fitzjames. *Liberty, Equality, Fraternity.* Stuart Warner, ed. Liberty Classics, Indianapolis, IN, 1873/1993.

Stephen, Leslie. *History of English Thought in the 18th Century.* 2 vols. Harcourt, Brace, New York, 1876/1962.

Stewart, John B. *The Moral and Political Philosophy of David Hume.* Columbia University, New York, 1963.

Stigler, George J. *Chicago Studies in Political Economy*. University of Chicago, Chicago, 1988.

———. *Memoirs of an Unregulated Economist*. Basic Books, New York, 1988.

St. John-Stevas, Norman. *Walter Bagehot: A Study of His Life and Thought*. Indiana University, Bloomington, IN, 1959.

Strauss, Leo. *City and the Man*. Rand McNally, Chicago, 1964.

———. *Liberalism: Ancient and Modern*. Basic Books, New York, 1968.

———. *Natural Right and History*. University of Chicago, Chicago, 1950.

———, and Joseph Cropsey, eds. *History of Political Philosophy*, 3rd ed. University of Chicago, Chicago, 1987.

Sumner, William Graham. *Andrew Jackson*. Chelsea House, New York, 1899/1980.

———. *Folkways*. Ayer, North Stratford, NH, 1907.

———. *On Liberty, Society, and Politics: The Essential Essays of William Graham Sumner*. Robert C. Bannister, ed. Liberty, Indianapolis, IN, 1992.

Tate, Allen. *Collected Poems: 1919–1976*. Farrar, Straus & Giroux, New York, 1977.

———. *Essays of Four Decades*. Swallow Press, Chicago, 1968.

———. *The Fathers*. Putnam, New York, 1938.

———. *Memoirs and Opinions: 1926–1974*. Swallow Press, Chicago, 1975.

———. *Reactionary Essays on Poetry and Ideas*. Ayer, North Stratford, NH, 1977.

Thatcher, Margaret, *The Downing Street Years*. HarperCollins, New York, 1993.

Tocqueville, Alexis de. *Democracy in America*. Richard D. Heffner, ed. Mentor, New York, 1835/1956.

Toffler, Alvin. *Future Shock*. Bantam Books, New York, 1971.

Tuccille, Jerome. *Radical Libertarianism: A Right-Wing Alternative*. Bobbs-Merrill, New York, 1970.

Tucker, Jeffrey. *Henry Hazlitt: A Giant of Liberty*. Mises Institute, Auburn, AL, 1994.

Tullock, Gordon. *The Logic of the Law*. Basic Books, New York, 1971.

Tyrrell, R. Emmett, Jr. *The Conservative Crack-Up*. Simon & Schuster, New York, 1992.

———, ed. *Orthodoxy: The* American Spectator *Anniversary Anthology*. Harper & Row, New York, 1987.

Ulam, Adam. *The Communists: The Story of Power and Lost Illusions*. Scribner's, New York, 1992.

Viereck, Peter. *Archer in the Marrow: The Applewood Cycles of 1968–86*. Norton, New York, 1987.

———. *Conservatism: From John Adams to Churchill*. D. Van Nostrand, New York, 1956.

———. *Conservatism Revisited: The Revolt Against the Revolt, 1815–1949*. Scribner's, New York, 1949.

———. *Shame and Glory of the Intellectuals*. Beacon, Boston, 1953.

Viguerie, Richard A. *The New Right: We're Ready to Lead*. Free Congress Foundation, Falls Church, VA, 1980.

Vivas, Eliseo. *Creation and Discovery*. Regnery Gateway, Chicago, 1955.

Voegelin, Eric. *The New Science of Politics*. University of Chicago, Chicago, 1952.

———. *Order and History*. 5 vols. Louisiana State University, Baton Rouge, LA, 1956–1987.

———. *Science, Politics, and Gnosticism*. Regnery, Chicago, 1968.

Wanniski, Jude. *The Way the World Works*. Polyconomics, Morristown, NJ, 1978/89.

Ward, Benjamin. *The Conservative Economic Worldview*. Basic Books, New York, 1979.

Waugh, Evelyn. *Brideshead Revisited: The Sacred and Profane Memoirs of Captain Charles Ryder*. Little, Brown, Boston, 1945.

———. *Handful of Dust*. Little, Brown, Boston, 1938.

———. *Mexico: An Object Lesson*. Little, Brown, Boston, 1939.

———. *The Ordeal of Gilbert Pinfold*. Little, Brown, Boston, 1957.

———. *Sword of Honor* Trilogy: *Men at Arms* (1952); *Officers and Gentlemen* (1955); *Unconditional Surrender* (1961). Everyman's Library, New York, 1994.

Weaver, Richard M. *Ideas Have Consequences*. University of Chicago, Chicago, 1948.

———. *The Southern Tradition at Bay: A History of Postbellum Thought*. Regnery, Washington, DC, 1968/1989.

———. *Visions of Order*. ISI, Bryn Mawr, PA, 1964/1995.

Webb, E. *Eric Voegelin: Philosopher of History*. Louisiana State University, Baton Rouge, LA, 1981.

Weinstein, Allen. *Perjury: The Hiss-Chambers Case*. Knopf, New York, 1978.

Welch, Robert. *The Politician*. Belmont Publishers, Belmont, MA, 1964.

Whitaker, Robert W. *The New Right Papers*. St. Martin's, New York, 1982.

Will, George F. *Men at Work: The Craft of Baseball*. Free Press, New York, 1990.

———. *Restoration: Congress, Term Limits, and the Recovery of Deliberative Democracy*. Free Press, New York, 1992.

———. *Statecraft as Soulcraft: What Government Does*. Simon & Schuster, New York, 1983.

Williams, Dick. *Newt! Leader of the Second American Revolution*. Longstreet Press, Marietta, GA, 1995.

Williams, Walter. *All It Takes Is Guts: A Minority View*. Regnery, Washington, DC, 1987.

Wilson, Francis G. *The Case for Conservatism*. Transaction, New Brunswick, NJ, 1951/1990.

Wilson, James Q. *Bureaucracy: What Government Agencies Do and Why They Do It*. Basic Books, New York, 1989.

———. *The Moral Sense*. Free Press, New York, 1993.

———. *On Character*. American Enterprise Institute Press. Washington, DC, 1991.

———, and Richard J. Herrnstein. *Crime and Human Nature*. Simon & Schuster, New York, 1985.

Wiltse, C. M. *A Life of John C. Calhoun*. 3 vols. Bobbs-Merrill, Indianapolis, IN, 1944–51.

Winchell, Mark Royden. *Neoconservative Criticism: Norman Podhoretz, Kenneth S. Lynn, and Joseph Epstein*. Twayne, Boston, 1991.

Young, T. D. *Donald Davidson*. Twayne, Irvington, NY, 1971.

———. *John Crowe Ransom*. Steck-Vaughn, Austin, TX, 1971.

Acknowledgments

The Concise Conservative Encyclopedia was suggested to me by Mitch Horowitz, and I'm grateful to him for his confidence in my ability to write such a book. I leave it to him to judge how close to his original conception the finished book comes.

Penny Kaganoff has been the book's editor, and in my experience she sets the standard for enthusiasm and thoroughness.

My research was aided by the helpful staff of the Westchester County library system, and by Michael Rod of Quantum Computers, who has guided me expertly through the labyrinths of cyberspace.

I'm grateful too for the generous welcome I received at the fascinating library of the Foundation for Economic Education. My thanks go out especially to Bettina Bien Greaves, FEE's Resident Scholar.

Although I thanked them in the Preface, I want again to express my gratitude to Carnes Lord, Jacob Neusner, James V. Schall, S.J., Peter J. Stanlis, and Charles R. Kesler for their fine essays on "The Origins of Conservative Thought."

Finally, I want to thank my best friends, Roy Doliner and Sydny Miner, for their encouragement and patience. Nobody ought to have to hear so much about a book before it's published.

Index